PUBLIC
POLICY

POLITICS
AND PUBLIC
POLICY

CARL E. VAN HORN
Rutgers University
DONALD C. BAUMER
Smith College
WILLIAM T. GORMLEY, JR.
University of Wisconsin—Madison

A Division of Congressional Quarterly Inc.
1414 22nd Street N.W., Washington, D.C. 20037

Library of Congress Cataloging-in-Publication Data

Van Horn, Carl E.
    Politics and public policy / Carl E. Van Horn, Donald C. Baumer, William T. Gormley, Jr.
        p.   cm.
    Includes index.
    ISBN 0-87187-481-4
    1. United States--Politics and government. 2. Political culture-- United States. 3. Pressure groups--United States. 4. Policy sciences. I. Baumer, Donald C., 1950-   II. Gormley, William T., 1950- . III. Title.
JK274.V33 1989
320.973--dc 19   88-21543
                                                                              CIP

TO

Evan and Ross Van Horn
Ben and Maggie Baumer
B.J. and Ken Gormley

Contents

Tables and Figures

TABLES

FIGURES

Preface

This book on American politics and public policy is designed to make clear who in American society gets what from political and government institutions, when they get it, and how they get it. We will describe how a large, diverse, complex political system selects some problems for attention but ignores others, how various policy makers design and implement policies, and how those policies ultimately affect society.

Digging into these matters requires some diligence and patience; the practice of politics and policy making is messy and complicated and involves thousands of players in the public and private sectors. In *Politics and Public Policy* we examine the policy making of political institutions at various levels of government. Public policies are made not only by the most visible political actors—legislators and chief executives—but also by judges and bureaucrats. Moreover, the United States is a federal system in which states and local governments are taking increasing responsibility for the design and conduct of public policies.

The book goes beyond conventional policy making to investigate the roles of corporate officials, the media, and public opinion. We assess the public consequences of private decisions and the influence of ordinary citizens on the course of public affairs. The book integrates discussions about the policy process with a look at real policies and their results. *How* policies are chosen and implemented is important, but so is *what* is decided and what it means for citizens and society.

Politics and Public Policy describes and explains the new landscape of American politics. Policy makers are facing many difficult, unpleasant choices. Contemporary problems, such as budget deficits, tax reform, abortion, toxic waste cleanups, and immigration policy, do not yield to traditional solutions. We also show how changes in the conduct of American politics affect the way policies are made. The growing importance of the media, the role of money in political campaigns, the proliferation of interest groups, the disintegration of political parties, and the increasing fragmentation of political institutions all influence policy choices and outcomes.

In attempting to weave these ideas into a coherent whole, we have formulated a unique organization that uses six images of the policy process:

—Board-rooom politics: decisions by business elites and professionals, but with important public consequences

—Bureaucratic politics: rule making and adjudication by bureaucrats, with input from clients and professionals

—Cloakroom politics: policy making by legislators, constrained by various constituencies

—Chief executive politics: a process dominated by governors, presidents, mayors, and their advisers

—Courtroom politics: court orders, in response to interest groups and aggrieved parties

—Living room politics: the galvanization of public opinion, usually through the mass media

Each image suggests a different locus of power, a different arena for combat, a different set of participants, and different policy outcomes.

What we offer here is a road map for negotiating the twists and turns of this diverse and at times bewildering landscape. Aside from learning how policy making and implementation are accomplished, who is powerful and who is not, and how public policies affect individuals and society, readers should be equipped to arrive at their own assessments of how effectively contemporary political institutions and leaders deal with issues.

We appreciate the support and encouragement we have received from many people. Outstanding secretarial and research support was made available by the Eagleton Institute of Politics at Rutgers University. Joanne Pfeiffer turned our rough-hewn computer disks into finished products and remained cheerful through several revisions. Splendid research assistance was provided by Rob Horowitz, Caryn Paul, and Kristin Phillips. Ken Dautrich and Chris Lenart saved us from some near disasters by recovering text that nearly disappeared into computer space.

Several colleagues read and commented on the book at various stages of development. We especially thank Bob Beauregard, Bob Buchele, Leon Epstein, Gary Freeman, Steve Goldstein, Joel Grossman, Randall Ripley, Alan Rosenthal, and Cliff Zukin. Michael Kraft and Tony Rosenbaum reviewed the entire manuscript and provided helpful, detailed suggestions for revisions.

Joanne Daniels of CQ Press deserves our thanks for "inventing" this project. She challenged us to think about a public policy book and offered helpful encouragement and advice during its evolution. Carolyn Goldinger edited the manuscript and improved our prose where it needed help. Kerry Kern handled the production with her usual efficiency.

Finally, we are most grateful to our families for their support, encouragement, and occasional curiosity. We have dedicated this book to six family members who may improve public policy in the future.

THEMES
PERSPECTIVES
AND THE POLICY
ENVIRONMENT

PART I

Before exploring the finer points of politics and public policy, readers need to be reminded of the background against which policies are made and implemented. Part I provides a brief overview of American political institutions and the policy process. Some of the material will be familiar to those who have studied American government, but the emphasis here is not on the structure of political institutions, but on how they perform their functions. Part I also introduces readers to the themes and perspectives that shaped the authors' approach to *Politics and Public Policy*.

Chapter 1 identifies those who influence public policy. Chief executives, legislators, bureaucrats, and judges all shape policy; but corporate executives, journalists, lobbyists, and citizens also participate in significant ways. Chapter 1 also examines the role played by state and local governments in the conduct of public affairs and shows that the very nature of politics and policy outcomes differ according to which political actors and institutions are involved.

Chapter 2 examines the particular economic, social, and political forces that structure U.S. politics and public policy. Historical and contemporary political and economic conditions that influence public policies are identified. This chapter begins to make the connection between phenomena such as resource scarcity, increasing international economic competition, changing social mores, and the influence of the media and the policy responses of American political institutions.

1 American Politics and Public Policy

In November 1986 the American people learned for the first time that the United States had sold arms to Iran in an effort to win the release of several hostages and that the proceeds from the sale had been used to aid Nicaraguan rebels, known as contras, who were fighting to overthrow their country's Marxist regime. Promptly dubbed the Iran-contra affair, this episode triggered a series of congressional hearings, culminating in testimony by Rear Admiral John Poindexter, who had resigned as President Ronald Reagan's national security adviser following the disclosure. Congressional investigators listened spellbound to Poindexter's explanation of why he never informed the president about the diversion of funds. According to Poindexter, the diversion constituted "an implementation of very clear policy." [1] Poindexter's critics, including President Richard Nixon's national security adviser, Henry Kissinger, were shocked by the contention that a decision so grave and so unprecedented could be characterized as mere implementation of settled policy. In Kissinger's words, "I was a far more assertive security adviser than Poindexter, and I would never have dreamed of making a decision like that." [2]

Poindexter's testimony illustrates the need for clear thinking about public policy, which can be defined as the authoritative distribution of benefits and costs in society. As national security adviser, Poindexter was expected to participate in the policy-making process by offering advice and information and by implementing presidential decisions. He was not authorized to make public policy himself. Yet, when pressed by congressional investigators, Poindexter could not—or would not—cite a specific presidential decision to divert funds from the Iranian arms sale to the contras. Rather, he expressed confidence that the president would have approved the diversion had he been asked. If his testimony is to be believed, Poindexter confused the making of public policy with its implementation. He also seems to have forgotten that under the Constitution federal funds may be spent only if appropriations have been authorized by both houses of Congress and the president.

The same constitutional presumption in favor of joint action by the legislature and the president was ignored by Reagan when he authorized the sale of arms to Iran without consulting Congress. Historically, Congress has tolerated a certain amount of unilateral action by the president in foreign policy. However, Congress has stipulated that the president should inform certain of its members before engaging in "covert" operations. In disregarding this law, Reagan sacrificed his long-term credibility for a short-term goal. When the president's actions came to light, his popularity with the American people declined, and with it, his power on Capitol Hill.

If Reagan's policy of trading arms for hostages shocked and dismayed many observers, his policy-making style was equally horrifying. According to numerous accounts, the president exercised very loose control over White House aides such as Poindexter and his assistant, Lieutenant Colonel Oliver North. The president failed to read important memos, asked few questions at critical meetings, and seemed distracted by details. He often left meetings without announcing decisions. Eventually, unconfirmed reports of presidential decisions or near decisions would percolate through the executive branch. After one meeting, Secretary of State George Shultz and Secretary of Defense Caspar Weinberger thought they had effectively scotched the Iranian arms sale, only to discover later that the president was again favoring it. A presumptuous White House staff was able to substitute its judgment for the views of the president's top policy makers. In effect, policy was being made by the National Security Council.

This book is organized so that the connection between politics and public policy remains in view. It is important to be able to see the forest *and* the trees. Toward that end, this chapter introduces several important themes and perspectives, beginning with a discussion of the public officials authorized by the national and state constitutions to make policy. Next, the discussion turns to how governments interact with other governments in a federal system. Then the contributions of lobbyists and journalists to public policy are examined. The next section illustrates the remarkable elasticity of policy making in the United States by illuminating two ends of the policy-making spectrum: private decision making and public decision making. Last, the six "images" of the policy process are introduced, making apparent how complex and interdependent the process is. The six images will be explored in depth in Part II.

Policy Makers

Throughout American government, power over public policy is shared by different institutions—legislatures, executives, and courts. The U.S. Constitution gives Congress the authority to make laws, the president the responsibility to administer them, and the Supreme Court the right to interpret or enforce them. Separate powers are designed to make each institution independent of the others. However, each delegation of authority is qualified by other constitutional provisions so that legislative, executive, and judicial powers are shared to some extent. The same phenomenon is apparent at the state and local levels. Government institutions are as interdependent as they are independent.

The functioning of these institutions over time has accentuated this sharing and interdependence, although a considerable degree of separateness and independence persists. In addition, a variety of bureaucratic institutions have been created that wield substantial independent power over public policy. Eventually it will be demonstrated that there is more to public policy than public officials. Here, however, the focus is on legislators, chief executives, bureaucrats, and judges.

Legislators

Under the U.S. Constitution and its state-level counterparts, legislators are the principal lawmakers in the political system. To become a law, a proposal, in the form of a bill, must be approved by Congress, a state legislature, or a city council. Approval depends on coalition building, in which the support of a legislative majority is sought. Without legislative approval, no taxes can be raised, no money can be spent, and no new programs can be launched. The constitutional assumption is that the people's elected representatives should play the leading role in making public policy.

To ensure a high degree of responsiveness, legislators are accountable to the electorate every two, four, or six years. In practice, however, electoral accountability does not always result in the adoption of policies favored by the voters. One reason is that individual legislators can escape responsibility for policies adopted or not adopted by the legislature as a whole. Through casework, or constituency service, legislators can cultivate a "hard-core" of grateful constituents who will support their legislator because he or she has performed some useful service for them, such as expediting the delivery of a Social Security check or arranging a tour of the Capitol building. These norms enable legislators to pursue their own preferred policies, subject, of course, to certain constraints. A tobacco state senator probably would not tempt the fates by leading the fight against tobacco advertising or "passive" smoking.

Legislative observers would find this mode of behavior more acceptable if legislators were responsive to the chief executive or to legislative party leaders, who may take a broader view. Such responsiveness could help to integrate legislative policy making. But legislative bodies are notoriously decentralized and fragmented, at least in the United States.

In Western Europe, it is common to find parliamentary systems, in which the chief executive is also the leader of the parliament or legislative body, and "responsible party" systems, in which legislative members of the same party vote together on major issues. The United States, in contrast, has separate legislative and executive branches, weak political parties, and legislators with king-sized and queen-sized egos. Legislators in the United States enjoy a freewheeling, swashbuckling style that makes legislative coalition building difficult.

Another problem confronting legislative coalition builders is the concentration of power in the hands of legislative committees. Often referred to as "little legislatures," committees are the workshops of legislative bodies where bills are hammered out, amendments are drafted, and deals are struck. But here, too, many ideas are condemned to the dustbin of history. For that reason, committees are known as legislative graveyards; most bills die in committee, without coming to the floor for a vote.

Despite these obstacles, legislators pass an amazing number of measures. Every year, for example, state legislatures in the U.S. approve about 40,000 bills.[3] In general, legislative bodies prefer to pass bills that distribute benefits to bills that impose penalties or bills that redistribute the wealth across social classes.[4] Legislative bodies prefer bills that delegate authority to the chief executive or the bureaucracy, although they may complain about executive "usurpation." By delegating authority to others, legislators escape responsibility for difficult policy problems and for solutions that upset people. Delegation has become rampant since Franklin Roosevelt's New Deal, when the U.S. Supreme Court allowed Congress to delegate considerable authority to the executive branch. This has led some observers to wonder whether a system of checks and balances has in fact become a system of blank checks.

Chief Executives

With individual legislators marching to their own drumbeats, chief executives face a formidable task when they engage in the politics of lawmaking. Legislative deference to chief executives is far from automatic. Legislative resistance is especially likely when the legislative and executive branches are controlled by different political parties, which is the situation in twenty-eight states,[5] and which has been the case at the national level for twenty-four of the last thirty-six years.

Regardless of which party controls the legislative branch, chief executives cannot take legislative cooperation for granted. Even under the best of circumstances, the chief executive's power is the "power to persuade."[6] The chief executive cannot simply tell legislators what to do. Rather, he or she must wheedle and cajole, relying on good ideas, political pressure, personal charm, public support, and a touch of blarney. Some chief executives, such as Ronald Reagan, have made the most of the power to persuade, at least for a time. Others, such as Jimmy Carter, were far less effective at speech making and personal appeals.

If wit and wisdom facilitate persuasion, chief executives also possess other important resources that come with the office. Perhaps the most important of these resources is visibility. When the president of the United States catches cold, it makes national news. A gubernatorial runny nose is less newsworthy, but governors and mayors have no difficulty making headlines. Because of this visibility, chief executives have emerged as the leading agenda setters within government. Along with the mass media, they help to determine which issues the public thinks about and which issues the government will address. Some formal vehicles for this agenda-setting role are the president's State of the Union address and a governor's State of the State address. But chief executives can command an audience at any time, especially for crises.

Despite their best efforts, chief executives lose many legislative battles. For example, the legislature may adopt a bill, as requested by the chief executive, but with so many amendments that it is unacceptable. When this happens, the chief executive may veto the bill, in which case the legislature may vote to override. In many states, governors have what is known as the "line-item" veto for budget bills. This enables governors to delete particular line-items or programs from the budget without vetoing the entire bill—a formidable power that some presidents have coveted. However, even line-item vetoes may be overridden.

When chief executives get sufficiently frustrated with the legislative branch, they may resort to questionable means to pursue policy goals. For example, Governor Richard Thornburgh of Pennsylvania tried repeatedly to convince the Pennsylvania legislature to "privatize" the state's liquor store system. A privately run operation, Thornburgh maintained, would be less costly and more efficient than the existing government-run operation. Unable to persuade the legislature of this, Thornburgh issued an executive order abolishing the state-store system. A state court subsequently overturned the order, on the grounds that the governor had overstepped his legal authority.[7] President Reagan, frustrated by congressional reporting requirements for national security operations, issued a classified executive order instructing the head of the CIA to say nothing to Congress about the sale of arms to Iran, despite statutory requirements for congressional notification. Some chief executives, opposed by powerful legislators, have grown impatient with the constitutional system of checks and balances.

There are, however, perfectly legal ways for chief executives to have an impact on public policy when legislative cooperation diminishes.[8] As the legislative branch has delegated more authority to the bureaucracy, chief executives have recognized that they can make policy as effectively through management as through legislation. By appointing loyal, capable cabinet and subcabinet officials, they can influence bureaucratic policy making. According to one observer, governors now spend more time managing state government than they do working with the state legislature.[9] Some presidents have also demonstrated keen interest in the management side of policy making. Nixon, for example, attempted to create an "administrative presidency," with high-level bureaucrats following the president's lead on major issues. Nixon's administrative presidency was derailed by the Watergate affair, but the strategy was used effectively by Reagan.[10]

Bureaucrats

The bureaucracy's size, power, and discretion to make decisions have grown enormously. Since 1950 state bureaucracies have increased 242 percent to 3.8 million people, and local bureaucracies have expanded 191 percent to 9.3 million people.[11] Although the size of the federal bureaucracy has been more stable during this period, its influence has grown as it dispenses larger amounts of federal money. Federal bureaucrats have ample opportunities to structure the behavior of state and local governments by awarding or withholding federal grants-in-aid. Bureaucrats at all levels of government also award contracts to private sector firms for goods or services supplied to the government. There can be little doubt that the bureaucracy constitutes a "fourth branch of government."

One of the bureaucracy's jobs is to implement policy by designing programs to carry out laws. The Internal Revenue Service (IRS) implements policy when it designs tax forms to conform with congressional intent. Similarly, the Immigration and Naturalization Service (INS) implements policy when it warns employers not to hire illegal immigrants. If statutes were clear and airtight, the implementation of policy would be fairly routine, but few statutes fit that description.

The importance of the bureaucracy in policy implementation sometimes is a distraction from the role the bureaucracy plays in policy making. Many laws are in fact drafted by bureaucrats or by legislative aides with substantial assistance from bureaucrats. In addition, bureaucrats make policy openly and directly through what is known as "administrative rule making." For example, the Federal Communications Commission (FCC) voted to "deregulate" radio in 1981, dropping requirements that radio stations cover news and public affairs and allowing radio stations to run as many commercials as they wish. This policy, in the form of an administrative rule, was adopted without an explicit mandate from Congress.

The FCC is one of the independent regulatory commissions. These commissions are multimember bodies that operate relatively independent of the chief executive. The president appoints the regulatory commissioners, but they serve until their terms expire. Independent regulatory commissions are responsible for licensing nuclear power plants, resolving labor relations disputes, regulating the money supply, and setting the rates charged by public utilities.

In contrast to independent regulatory commissions, most bureaucracies are nominally accountable to the chief executive, who has the power to appoint and to fire the top officials. Most bureaucrats, however, are civil servants with considerable job security. As a general rule, they are less committed to the president's policies than are cabinet and subcabinet officials. Moreover, agencies develop strong symbiotic relationships with constituents and client groups. The Agriculture Department may be more sympathetic to farmers than to a president who wants to reduce farm price supports. In addition, chief executives do not appoint all agency heads. In state government, the people elect some agency heads, which may include the attorney general, the treasurer, the secretary of state, the auditor, and the superintendent of education. Finally, bureaucrats are accountable to other public officials, including legislators and judges. It is fair to say that the bureaucracy has many masters.

Judges

When legislators, chief executives, and bureaucrats cannot agree on appropriate public policies, controversies often must be settled in the courts. In the American system of government, judges are the ultimate arbiters of policy disputes. They decide whether a law is constitutional and whether an administrative rule is legal. They decide when the federal government may tell state and local governments what to do. They decide the meaning of phrases such as equal protection, freedom of speech, separation of powers, and due process of law.

Judges, particularly federal judges, play a central role in the policy process. Federal judges are not passive arbiters of narrowly defined disputes, but active architects of public policy. They immerse themselves in the details of technology, methodology, and administration. Increasingly, they have moved from procedural reasoning to substantive reasoning, at times functioning as legislators and managers. In specific cases, federal judges have seized control of state prisons, mental health facilities, and public schools. In addition, they have directed state legislatures to spend more money on under-funded programs. Judge

Frank Johnson required a host of costly reforms at Alabama's mental hospitals, on the grounds that the Fourteenth Amendment rights of patients and inmates were being violated.[12] Similarly, Judge Arthur Garrity took over much of the management of the Boston public schools to ensure that his school desegregation orders were faithfully carried out.[13]

Decisions by federal district court judges may be reversed by U.S. circuit courts of appeals or by the U.S. Supreme Court. However, appellate judges, as they are sometimes called, generally defer to trial judges, such as federal district court judges. They also defer to judges who preceded them on the bench. It is rare for the U.S. Supreme Court to reverse an earlier Supreme Court decision, even if today's justices would have decided the case differently. This informal norm is known as the doctrine of *stare decisis* or adherence to precedent, from the Latin phrase, "let the decision stand."

Despite *stare decisis*, courts move in new directions as new problems, such as AIDS, arise and as society takes note of changes, such as the growing number of working women. Indeed, in many policy domains, judges have been the principal trailblazers in government. The U.S. Supreme Court under Chief Justice Earl Warren took the lead in securing rights for persons accused of a crime.[14] The Court under Chief Justice William H. Rehnquist, although widely viewed as conservative, has taken steps to ensure affirmative action and to limit sexual harassment. For example, in *Johnson v. Santa Clara County*, the Rehnquist Court upheld a local government decision promoting a qualified woman ahead of a qualified man, even though the man's qualifications were slightly higher.[15]

When the Supreme Court interprets the U.S. Constitution, that interpretation is binding on other courts. However, state supreme courts are the ultimate arbiters of disputes involving state constitutions. If the U.S. Supreme Court allows searches and seizures under certain circumstances, a state supreme court may strike down the same kinds of searches and seizures, based on its reading of the state constitution. As the U.S. Supreme Court has once again become more conservative on criminal justice, state supreme courts found civil rights for criminal defendants in state constitutions.[16]

The vagueness of phrases such as equal protection and due process of law permits courts wide leeway and discretion. Constitutions constrain the behavior of judges but do not determine their behavior. Richard Neely, chief justice of the West Virginia Supreme Court, said: "Since there is hardly any question which cannot be framed in such a way as to assume 'constitutional' dimensions, for all intents and purposes every conceivable question of public policy is up for review by the courts.

Vested with this power to determine what is and what is not within the purview of their authority, courts can at will substitute their judgment for that of all the other agencies of government." [17]

Judges, however, cannot act unless a case is brought before them by litigants. Furthermore, appellate judges must reach a consensus before they can speak. But this process is far less complex in a panel of three judges or nine justices than it is in a legislative body consisting of dozens or hundreds of individuals who represent diverse constituencies. As a result, when legislators reach an impasse on controversies such as abortion, school busing, and capital punishment, judges are in a position to fill this power vacuum.

A Federal System

Federalism

Washington, D.C., has no monopoly over public policy in the United States. State and local governments are policy institutions within the federal system of government and in their own right. They are responsible for implementing most federal domestic programs, which typically leave to the discretion of state and local decision makers many basic aspects of policy.

The United States is truly a multigovernmental system. For a number of issues, state governments are virtually immune from federal supervision and control. Banking regulation, insurance regulation, and occupational licensing remain firmly in the hands of state administrative agencies. Questions concerning divorce and child custody are handled almost exclusively by state courts. Even public utility regulation is controlled largely by the states, despite sharp increases in utility bills and growing public concern.

Considerable autonomy also is exercised at the local level. Zoning decisions, which shape the character of neighborhoods and the quality of everyday life, are made by local governments, without so much as a raised eyebrow from state governments or federal courts. Inspections of housing, restaurants, and buildings, all of which are necessary for public health, are controlled by local governments with little input from other levels of government.

Intergovernmental Relations

Despite the considerable discretion exercised by state and local governments, the federal government has extended its control over them by offering the "carrot" of federal grants-in-aid in return for certain concessions. President Lyndon Johnson's War on Poverty relied heavily on such grants-in-aid. President Nixon used a different approach, which he called the new federalism. Under Nixon, the flow of federal dollars increased dramatically, while federal restrictions were loosened somewhat. President Reagan also voiced support for a new federalism, but his version combined sharp cutbacks in federal support with new responsibilities for state governments. Both Nixon and Reagan supported a shift away from categorical programs and toward greater reliance on block grants.

About 80 percent of the federal aid to state and local governments comes in the form of categorical programs, which have narrowly defined objectives, distinct statutory and budget identities, detailed planning and operational requirements, and defined target populations. The nation's principal income support strategy for the poor, Aid to Families with Dependent Children (AFDC), is a categorical grant program. AFDC's purpose is to help poor families with children maintain a minimal standard of living. Cash assistance is provided to families if they meet explicit statutory and administrative standards and regulations. Even though the states fund one-half of the costs of AFDC, federal law governs its fundamental rules.

Block grant programs—the balance of federal aid—give states and localities money for broad purposes, such as health, housing, education, and employment, but do not require that all recipients offer a specific set of programs and services. States and local governments have wide discretion to invest federal dollars as they see fit, but the federal government remains responsible for ensuring that the funds are spent for their intended purpose. For example, under the Community Development Block Grant program, mayors, governors, and their staffs may select a mix of housing services that seem well suited to the particular needs of their community.

Categorical programs still predominate, but the number of intergovernmental aid programs was cut from nearly 500 in the mid-1970s to about 400 in the mid-1980s.[18] A parallel shift took place in regulation from direct orders and "mandates" to more indirect forms of federal control, such as partial preemptions and crossover sanctions. An example of a partial preemption is the Surface Mining Control and Reclamation Act of 1977, which grants states the option of running their own strip-mining program, provided that federal standards are accepted. If a state refuses the option, the federal government exercises full preemption, running the program out of a regional office. Examples of crossover sanctions include the federal government's ability to withhold highway funds from states that refuse to set the drinking age at twenty-one years or to conform to a certain maximum highway speed limit. The federal government usually bargains with the states in the hope of achieving federal objectives.

Policy Influentials and Lobbyists

Interest Groups and Lobbyists

The fragmented, decentralized policy system described so far is highly permeable to groups outside of government. Private interest group involvement in public policy is a widely recognized and long-standing fact of American government. Interest groups work closely with legislators and bureaucrats to develop mutually beneficial policies. The specialized committee structure of Congress, which is mirrored by most state legislatures, enables interest groups to focus their efforts on the individuals and groups with power over the issues of greatest concern to them.

Clusters of people interested in the same issue—members of legislative committees and subcommittees, bureaucratic agencies that administer the policies formulated by a committee, and the groups that are most directly affected by such policies—are often called subgovernments or issue networks. These networks wield considerable influence over many policy domains, such as the financial industry, agriculture, public works, and defense contracting. Interest groups are full-fledged partners in major policy-making circles.[19]

The number and variety of interest groups in the United States is enormous. Although no one has been able to count all of them, various sources provide a rough sense of the size of the interest group population, which has grown rapidly since the 1960s. The following information was drawn from directories of interest groups and lobbyists compiled in the early 1980s.

—There are nearly 16,000 national voluntary membership organizations, and more than 200,000 state and local community groups.[20]

—More than 10,000 lobbyists are based in Washington. More than half of them are employed by groups with an economic or occupational base, such as unions, trade and professional associations, farm groups, and individual corporations.[21]

—More than 500 corporations employ lobbyists in Washington.[22]

—More than 100,000 lawyers serve as professional lobbyists for various clients.

Given the strong representation of private economic interests, it is not surprising that citizen groups have gotten into the act. More than 1,200 citizen groups may be found in Washington. Environmental groups, civil rights organizations, antipornography groups, and gun owner organizations are all examples of such citizen groups. Thousands of additional groups may be found in state capitals and other communities.

State and local government officials also hire staffs to represent them in Washington. The National Governors' Association, National Conference of State Legislatures, National League of Cities, U.S. Conference of Mayors, National Association of Counties, and others actively lobby the national government on matters of concern to states and localities. They also press legislators and administrators to act favorably on requests for financial assistance and regulatory decisions.

There is tremendous diversity in the size, resources, leadership, cohesiveness, and prestige of interest groups that participate in the policy process. Those with substantial money, committed members, strong leadership, and a favorable reputation exert considerable influence. All other things being equal, having a large membership is desirable because a group's political clout is enhanced if it speaks for many voters. But large groups have difficulty maintaining a unified membership and directing their activity toward policy goals that excite members. Therefore, small, intense, single-issue groups may be more successful than large groups.

An interest group with few members but a good deal of clout is the Business Roundtable—an organization of a few hundred top corporate executives. Although small in membership, the enormous wealth it represents enables it to compete effectively in policy arenas with labor unions, such as the American Federation of Labor-Congress of Industrial Organizations (AFL-CIO), representing nearly 14 million workers.

When interest groups approach elected officials and government administrators, they are lobbying for help either to get something done to benefit them or to stop something from happening that adversely affects them. Many people equate lobbying with arm-twisting, corrupt contributions, or pressure tactics of one sort or another. While some of these practices go on, the normal situation is considerably more complicated than that.

Effective lobbying rests on the use of information and money. When lobbyists meet with members of Congress, they supply facts about issues and political intelligence about the positions and strategies of others in Congress and the executive branch. Lobbyists testify at congressional hearings, observe committee deliberations, and perform other services for their clients. Groups sponsor professional and social gatherings to which elected officials are invited—and often paid a fee for appearing—to cement relationships. Interest groups may conduct public relations campaigns to convince voters in the member's district to support their cause. Advertising, press releases, and letter writing campaigns are all used to build a climate of support for their positions and to secure favorable treatment from legislators. And, of course, groups contribute to congressional election campaigns—more than $130 million in 1986.[23]

Interest groups also lobby executive agencies. Bureaucratic agencies are responsive to interest groups because they need political allies to advance their policy goals and to protect them from legislators or chief executives who may dislike their programs and policies. Lobbying bureaucratic agencies generally involves the same techniques used with legislators, except that campaign contributions apply only to elected officials. All major agencies have one or more constituent groups with which they maintain close and mutually beneficial alliances.

Although less visible, interest groups are active within the judicial arena. The direct contribution of money is rare because it is illegal to bribe judicial officials. But interest group budgets can be used to back legal cases that have policy significance. Suits seeking to overturn legislative or administrative decisions are a common feature of practically all important policy issues. These challenges come not just from businesses trying to protect their financial interests; civil rights groups and environmentalists have successfully pursued legal strategies that have advanced their causes. Even the selection of judges is not beyond the reach of interest groups. They lobby executives and legislators on behalf of certain court nominees, and in some states and localities interest groups try to influence election contests between candidates for the bench.

The Mass Media

Perceptions of public officials, public policies, and governments are shaped significantly by the mass media, especially television and newspapers. By focusing obsessively on the "horse race" aspects of presidential campaigns, the media do not give voters enough real help in their efforts to evaluate the candidates' issue positions. By devoting more attention to national and local politics than to state politics, the media limit public awareness of state politics. By oversimplifying and sensationalizing certain policy controversies, the media discourage rational decision making. On the positive side, the media can be credited with exposing public problems and errant public officials. Political scientists and other observers are devoting increased attention to the role of the media in politics, especially their impact on election campaigns. The outcome of electoral contests ushers in a new administration, with a new vision for the future. By influencing the outcome of elections, the media indirectly influence public policy as well.

Clearly, the media influence public perceptions of the candidates' character traits and thereby shape campaign issues. Election results frequently hinge on how well each side presents its case to the media or through the media. Jimmy Carter was unable to overcome a perceived lack of leadership ability in 1980, but Ronald Reagan did not seem to be hurt by reports that he invented or distorted facts in his political speeches. In his concession speech following an overwhelming defeat at the polls in 1984, Walter Mondale admitted that he was an anachronism—a candidate who felt uncomfortable on television in a television age. Former senator Gary Hart's 1988 presidential campaign was abruptly interrupted when newspapers ran stories suggesting marital infidelity. Senator Joseph Biden also withdrew from the presidential race following press accounts of plagiarism. For some candidates, character is the issue.

The media's influence on politics and public policy extends well beyond the electoral arena. It is pervasive, reaching citizens in the nation's heartland and the powerful in Washington. Ironically, the media's influence is often so strong and ubiquitous that it is not noticed. The readers of the *Tri-City Herald* newspaper live near a nuclear power plant and a high-level nuclear waste disposal site in Hanford, Washington. The *Herald*, which has long promoted nuclear power, runs numerous stories about the safety, reliability, and economy of nuclear power, and few stories about the dangers and unanticipated costs of nuclear energy. Stories have carried headlines such as "Radiation Linked to Good Health" and "A-Plants Don't Taint Environment." The paper's editors refer to nuclear "storage sites" rather than nuclear "dumps." [24] Exposed to such pronuclear sentiment on a regular basis, local citizens are primed to view nuclear power favorably. Unless local newspapers fairly present both sides of an issue, citizens will lack one source of information they need to make intelligent decisions.

In contrast, many newspapers encourage investigative reporting, much of it very strong. The *Washington Post*'s persistent investigation of the Watergate break-in helped bring about the resignation of President Nixon and ushered in a new era in campaign finance. The *Chicago Sun-Times*'s 1978 series on bribes, kickbacks, and payoffs accepted by city building inspectors, health inspectors, and fire inspectors had a major impact on city practices. In its zeal to catch greedy inspectors, the *Sun-Times* purchased and operated a tavern, dubbed The Mirage, for several months and documented numerous instances of corruption. Following the publication of the series, the Chicago Fire Prevention Bureau created an internal investigations unit to monitor the quality of fire inspections; the city initiated team inspections by building, fire, and health inspectors to discourage shakedown attempts; the U.S. Justice Department added new lawyers to cope with findings concerning tax fraud; the IRS assigned additional agents; and the Illinois Department of Revenue created a permanent task force, the "Mirage Unit," for systematic audits.[25]

Although the media's ability to shape public policy is rooted in its ability to shape public opinion, the elite media—the television networks, the preeminent newspapers, and weekly news magazines—shape public policy directly. Chicago's public officials reacted swiftly to the *Sun-Times*'s series on corruption, rather than waiting for public outrage to mount. One sees the same phenomenon following reports on "60 Minutes" or, in some instances, in anticipation of such reports. As a public relations exercise, public officials often react to an investigative report rather than face the firestorm of public criticism it is expected to trigger. In the process, media influence is magnified. The mere threat of a public outcry may be sufficient to alter public policy.

The Scope of Conflict

Most textbooks on American politics and public policy describe the American experiment as a "representative democracy" in which citizens elect representatives—legislators and chief executives—who in turn make public policy. Elected representatives, taking the public's views into account, pass laws and make other authoritative decisions. They also appoint bureaucrats and judges, who adopt rules and adjudicate disputes. But representative democracy is only part of the picture. Many decisions of the utmost importance are made by corporate elites, who do not have to answer to the American people. Although nominally accountable to boards of directors and/or stockholders, corporate managers are in fact free to make many decisions as they see fit. These decisions—concerning plant location, production, marketing, jobs, and wages—are private.

At the other end of the spectrum, some decisions are made, not by public officials, but by the people themselves. This is literally true when voters participate in "issue elections." It is also true, for all intents and purposes, when public opinion becomes so aroused that public officials are compelled to defer to citizens and their preferences.

What exists in the United States, therefore, is not representative democracy but "elastic" democracy. When the scope of conflict is exceedingly narrow, representative democracy gives way to private decision making, such as corporate governance. When the scope of conflict is exceedingly broad, representative democracy gives way to public decision making in the form of direct democracy (Table 1-1). The policy-making process can be thought of as a kind of rubber band, which stretches well beyond the original contours of representative democracy.

Private Decision Making

Although it is useful to view business groups as lobbyists or interveners in the policy-making process, it is necessary to view them as policy makers as well. If one considers only pressure politics, one misses the

Table 1-1   The Policy-Making Spectrum: The Scope of Conflict

Narrow	Moderate	Broad
Private decision making (corporate governance, capitalism)	Representative democracy (candidate elections, conventional lawmaking)	Public decision making (issue elections, aroused public opinion)

more worrisome side of business influence—namely, the private sector's capacity to make decisions that affect large numbers of people and the private sector's lack of accountability. Technically, such decisions are private policies; they are made by private actors such as corporate chief executive officers, vice-presidents, and board members. As a practical matter, however, such private decisions are sanctioned and legitimated by the government, for example, by court decisions upholding private property rights. Charles Lindblom has argued that business enjoys a "privileged position" in American politics.[26] The government, for better or worse, has delegated to the private sector primary responsibility for mobilizing and organizing society's economic resources. It might be said that decisions by "private governments" are often as far-reaching as decisions by the government itself.

Large corporations, the private governments under consideration here, have distinctive decision-making processes. The focal point for corporate decision making is the board of directors, which consists of top company executives and prominent business leaders from other companies. At some companies, workers have a representative on the board; at many others, however, labor is not directly represented. According to close observers, corporate boards are dominated by top corporate executives. Even if outsiders constitute a majority of board members, the strategic decisions are made by insiders and then ratified by the rest of the board.[27] This phenomenon has been referred to as "managerial capitalism." [28]

Most large corporations are free to make policy as they wish, with a minimum of government control. If a steel company decides to shut down a factory and lay off 2,000 workers, it is free to do so. In most states, companies are not even required to give their workers advance notice if they make such a decision. Corporations are also free to set prices as they see fit. A privately owned monopoly, such as an investor-owned public utility, is not free to set prices. Under an arrangement that dates back to the early twentieth century, private monopolies, such as public utilities, must accept fairly close government regulation, including price controls, in return for their monopoly status. But public utilities are exceptional. In general, government control is weak and corporate discretion pervasive.

Corporate executives argue, with some justification, that they are accountable to the public through the workings of the market. If companies are mismanaged, or their prices are too high, or their products are inferior, consumers "vote with their pocketbooks" and spend their money elsewhere. But markets do not function that perfectly. Information about companies, their products, and their finances is costly to obtain and not easily understood. Consumers are handicapped by inadequate information. Moreover, markets fail to take into account the social costs of "externalities," such as air pollution. Where externalities are substantial, market prices grossly understate the underlying costs of producing services. Finally, government subsidies disguise the real costs of producing some goods and services. It is difficult to know, therefore, whether oil companies are operating efficiently, considering the generous subsidies they receive from the federal government. Indeed, some industries, such as defense and aerospace, receive such huge subsidies that it is difficult to evaluate them at all.

Many companies are accountable to their stockholders, on whom they depend for capital, especially publicly held companies whose stock is traded in the various stock markets. As a group, stockholders are becoming more aware and more astute. Mobilized by citizen activists, such as Ralph Nader, and by "corporate raiders," such as T. Boone Pickens, stockholders have put pressure on corporate managers and corporate boards to eliminate certain investments, award higher dividends, and change other practices. For the most part, however, stockholders routinely accept the policies of corporate managers. They also typically rubber-stamp the slate of corporate directors proposed by management. If stockholders are relatively weak, workers are even weaker. Although workers can bargain through their unions over wages, benefits, and working conditions, they have virtually nothing to say about the decisions that affect the company's future and theirs. Private corporations are profoundly undemocratic in their governing arrangements. By accepting private ownership of corporate enterprises, the United States precluded economic democracy and allowed corporate oligarchies to develop. As Robert Dahl observed, "a system of government Americans view as intolerable in governing the state has come to be accepted as desirable in governing economic enterprises." [29]

Public Decision Making

If private decision making epitomizes one end of the policy-making spectrum—a narrow scope of conflict, limited accountability, and government deference to corporations—public decision making epitomizes the other end—a broad scope of conflict, high accountability, and government deference to the public at large. Some decisions are made in "the court of public opinion." When public officials sense that an issue is too controversial to be handled through normal channels, public opinion comes into play and the views of public officials recede into the background. In E. E. Schattschneider's words, the "scope of conflict" expands.[30]

Public opinion is like a slumbering giant, which, when aroused, becomes fearsome and intimidating. Under such circumstances, the public policy effects may be considerable. Public opinion has been credited with ending the war in Vietnam, sustaining the environmental movement, promoting tax relief, halting the spread of nuclear power plants, cracking down on drunk driving, and forcing presidents Lyndon Johnson and Richard Nixon from office. Public opinion also has jeopardized civil rights and civil liberties, encouraging local governments to "exclude" poor people from the suburbs and to undermine efforts to achieve meaningful school desegregation. Public opinion is the stuff of which dreams and nightmares are made.

Public decision making means, for the most part, that public officials defer to public opinion when an issue is highly salient and controversial. But the people also make policy more directly from time to time, at least at the state and local levels. They do so through mechanisms, including the initiative and the referendum, popularized by the Progressives early in the twentieth century. A referendum is a measure that has been passed by a legislature and is then placed on a ballot for voter approval or disapproval. An initiative is a measure proposed by citizens that becomes law if approved by a majority of voters. To get an initiative on the ballot, a significant number of state residents—usually 5 percent to 10 percent of those voting in the last statewide election—must sign petitions.

At the moment, thirty-seven state constitutions authorize referenda, and twenty-one state constitutions authorize initiatives.[31] Referenda outnumber initiatives by approximately three to one, but initiatives carry more weight because they enable citizens to adopt policies opposed by elected officials. Initiatives and referenda have been used sporadically since the early twentieth century, but they became popular during the 1970s, as citizens, disenchanted with government, attempted to participate more directly in the policy-making process. In 1986 roughly 200 propositions appeared on the ballot.[32]

Public decision making, whether through initiatives and referenda or through government deference to public opinion polls, is more controversial than it might seem. Many politicians believe that they were elected to make these decisions and that ordinary citizens lack the knowledge to make public policy directly. Politicians also worry about the growing influence of the mass media, which contribute so significantly to the formation of public opinion. If public opinion mirrors the views of journalistic elites, it simply magnifies media influence—a far cry from what the Progressives had in mind.

Politics and Policy

Politics varies from one issue to another because politics reflects issue characteristics such as visibility and complexity. Differences in politics in turn result in different policies and outcomes. To understand such variations, it is useful to think of six alternative "images" of the policy process. These images encompass representative democracy, but they also reflect the highly elastic nature of American democracy. They run the gamut from highly private to highly public decision making.

Following are brief descriptions of the six images to be used as a framework for analyzing the policy process.

1. Board-room politics: decision making by business elites and professionals, but with important public consequences
2. Bureaucratic politics: rule making and adjudication by bureaucrats, with input from clients and professionals
3. Cloakroom politics: policy making by legislators, constrained by various constituencies
4. Chief executive politics: a process dominated by presidents, governors, mayors, and their advisers
5. Courtroom politics: court orders, in response to interest groups and aggrieved individuals
6. Living room politics: the galvanization of public opinion, usually through the mass media

Each of these images implies a different locus of power, a different arena for combat, and a different set of participants. Each also implies a different set of outcomes, ranging from stagnation to incrementalism to innovation, from limited responsiveness to symbolic responsiveness to policy responsiveness. In short, different institutions yield different sets of policy consequences.

The six images serve as convenient bridges between issue characteristics and policy consequences. Each image of the policy process will be related to the issue characteristics that precede it and its outcomes (Table 1-2). The effects of salience, conflict, complexity, and costs— issue characteristics—on policy making and the implications of various policy processes for change, responsiveness, and other outcomes—policy

Table 1-2   Images of the Policy Process

Images	Principal actors	Common issue characteristics	Common policy outcomes
Board-room politics	business elites professionals	low salience high complexity hidden costs	stagnation limited responsiveness
Bureaucratic politics	bureaucrats professionals clients	low to moderate salience low to moderate conflict disputed costs	incrementalism limited responsiveness
Cloakroom politics	legislators interest groups executive officials	moderate to high salience moderate to high conflict disputed costs	incrementalism symbolic responsiveness gridlock policy responsiveness
Chief executive politics	chief executives top advisers	high salience high conflict disputed costs	crisis management symbolic responsiveness
Courtroom politics	judges interest groups aggrieved individuals	high conflict manifest costs	innovation policy responsiveness (to minorities)
Living room politics	mass media public opinion	high salience high conflict manifest costs	electoral change policy responsiveness innovation

consequences—will be examined. The changes that occur in issue characteristics over time and the consequences of such changes will be highlighted.

The reason for integrating process and substance is the close relationship between the kind of issue under consideration and the policy process. Consider the following propositions:

—Issues that concern large numbers of people are likely to stimulate intense public debate and draw more participants into the policy process than issues that concern only a small segment of the public.

—Complex policies and those that call for major changes in public or bureaucratic behavior are much more difficult to implement than those that can be routinely carried out through established organizational networks.

—Issues involving hidden costs are handled by the private sector, while issues involving disputed costs or manifest costs require some governmental response.

Another reason for linking politics and policy is that substantive results flow from different policy-making processes. Consider, for example, the following:

—Decisions made within the private sector and ratified by government agencies legitimate self-regulation, impose hidden costs on consumers, and preempt meaningful reform.

—Decisions made by low-level or middle-level bureaucrats tend to reflect professional norms, organizational imperatives, and standard operating procedures. Incrementalism, policy making that changes things only marginally, is the most likely result, along with "nitpicking" and other forms of rigid behavior.

—Decisions made by politicians against a backdrop of public arousal provide occasional opportunities for policy innovation. However, highly conflictive issues that do not quite reach the crisis point often result in gridlock or stalemate.

—When politicians respond to aroused citizens, they frequently make symbolic responses or substitute casework, addressing the problems of a few individuals, for broader policy action.

—Decisions made by judges may differ significantly from decisions made by other public officials, in that no effort need be made to dilute or disguise policy change. The Constitution, job security, and strong professional values protect judges from politicians, though not from politics. The courts are capable of addressing problems that paralyze other institutions of government.

An approach that highlights alternative images has several advantages. First, the policy process is dynamic but disorderly. Issues move from one arena to another over time, but they do not follow the same sequence. This observation is fundamentally different from a leading point of view in the policy literature that assumes that issues proceed in a rather orderly fashion from the agenda-setting stage to the policy formulation stage to the policy adoption stage, and so on.

Second, institutional settings matter, and they matter in somewhat predictable ways. Different branches of government and different levels of government present their own special opportunities and pitfalls. Successful political strategists are attentive to both.

Third, the policy images will demonstrate that the nontraditional areas of policy making deserve attention, that without them the picture is incomplete. The discussions of board-room politics and living room politics will shed light on actors outside of government, including business people, journalists, and citizens.

Overall, it will be established that issue characteristics constrain policy makers in significant ways, that there is no single policy process but several, that controversies shift from one arena to another over time, and that politics is a significant determinant of policy outcomes. This conception of politics involves not only the familiar institutions of government but also business elites, interest groups, the mass media, and public opinion.

Notes

1. John Poindexter, quoted on "McNeil-Lehrer News Hour," July 15, 1987.
2. Larry Martz, "Taking Blame," *Newsweek*, July 27, 1987, 14.
3. Richard Bingham, *State and Local Government in an Urban Society* (New York: Random House, 1986), 124.
4. Theodore Lowi, "American Business, Public Policy, Case Studies, and Political Theory," *World Politics*, July 1964, 677-715.
5. Council of State Governments, *The Book of the States, 1986-87 Edition* (Lexington, Ky.: Council of State Governments, 1986), 28.
6. Richard Neustadt, *Presidential Power* (New York: John Wiley & Sons, 1976), 78.
7. Gary Warner, "Despite Ruling, Future of Liquor Stores Up in Air," *Pittsburgh Press*, Dec. 30, 1986, 1.
8. Samuel Kernell, *Going Public: New Strategies of Presidential Leadership* (Washington, D.C.: CQ Press, 1986).
9. Coleman Ransone, Jr., *Governing the American States* (Westport, Conn.: Greenwood Press, 1978), 96.
10. Richard Nathan, *The Administrative Presidency* (New York: John Wiley & Sons, 1983).
11. Kenneth Meier, *Politics and the Bureaucracy*, 2d ed. (Monterey, Calif.: Brooks/Cole Publishing, 1987), 31.
12. Tinsley Yarbrough, *Judge Frank Johnson and Human Rights in Alabama* (University: University of Alabama Press, 1981).
13. J. Anthony Lukas, *Common Ground* (New York: Alfred A. Knopf, 1985).
14. *Gideon v. Wainwright*, 372 U.S. 335 (1963); *Miranda v. Arizona*, 384 U.S. 436 (1966).
15. *Johnson v. Santa Clara County*, 107 Sup. Ct. 1442 (1987).
16. Robert Pear, "State Courts Surpass U.S. Bench in Cases on Rights of Individuals," *New York Times*, May 4, 1986, 1.
17. Richard Neely, *How Courts Govern America* (New Haven, Conn.: Yale University Press, 1981), 7.
18. Randall Ripley and Grace Franklin, *Bureaucracy and Policy Implementation* (Homewood, Ill.: Dorsey Press, 1982), 62; Paul Peterson et al., *When Federalism Works* (Washington, D.C.: Brookings Institution, 1986), 218.
19. For more on subgovernments, see Randall Ripley and Grace Franklin, *Congress, the Bureaucracy, and Public Policy*, 3d ed. (Homewood, Ill.: Dorsey Press, 1984).

20. Graham Wootton, *Interest Groups, Policy and Politics in America* (Englewood Cliffs, N.J.: Prentice-Hall, 1985), 91.

21. Figures are from a directory compiled by Arthur Close, *Washington Representatives* (Washington, D.C.: Columbia Books, 1983), cited by Samuel Patterson et al., in *A More Perfect Union*, 3d ed. (Homewood, Ill.: Dorsey Press, 1985), 239.

22. Jeffrey Berry, *The Interest Group Society* (Boston: Little, Brown, 1984), 20.

23. "FEC Releases First Complete PAC Figures for 1985-86," (Washington, D.C.: Federal Election Commission, May 21, 1987), 1.

24. Cassandra Tate, "Letter from 'The Atomic Capital of the Nation,'" *Columbia Journalism Review*, May/June 1982, 31-35.

25. Pamela Zekman and Zay Smith, *The Mirage* (New York: Random House, 1979).

26. Charles Lindblom, *Politics and Markets* (New York: Basic Books, 1977), 170-188.

27. Lewis Solomon, "Restructuring the Corporate Board of Directors: Fond Hope—Faint Promise?" *Michigan Law Review* 76 (March 1978): 581-610; Victor Brudney, "The Independent Director—Heavenly City or Potemkin Village?" *Harvard Law Review* 95 (January 1982): 597-659.

28. Alfred Chandler, Jr., *The Visible Hand: The Managerial Revolution in American Business* (Cambridge, Mass.: Harvard University Press, 1977), 1-12.

29. Robert Dahl, *A Preface to Economic Democracy* (Berkeley: University of California Press, 1985), 162.

30. E. E. Schattschneider, *The Semi-Sovereign People* (New York: Holt, Rinehart, and Winston, 1960), 2-3.

31. Council of State Governments, *Book of the States, 1986-87*.

32. Austin Ranney, "Referendums and Initiatives in 1984," *Public Opinion*, December/January 1985, 15-17.

2   Political Culture, the Economy, and Public Policy

American political institutions function as parts of the larger national cultural and socioeconomic system. The actions of political institutions and, therefore, the nature of public policy are greatly influenced by these cultural and economic forces, unique to the United States. The country, as a part of the global environment, also is affected by developments in other parts of the world. But the political agenda of U.S. policy makers is not the same as that of leaders in other industrialized nations, and it is fundamentally different from those of less-developed or socialist countries. The United States has the world's most powerful economy, which is controlled for the most part by privately owned corporations. Government ownership of major industries, such as steel or transportation, is not even under consideration in the United States, but such ownership is common the world over. How to control the production of excess food is a contentious issue in the United States, but many other countries fret about how they are going to feed their citizens.

This chapter outlines some of the underlying features and tendencies in the American cultural and economic environment. Before examining the specific arenas in which public policy is formulated and implemented, one should consider the broader context within which political institutions and actors function.

Political Culture

Political culture can be defined as the attitudes and beliefs of citizens about how political institutions and processes ought to work, about fellow citizens and their place in the political process, and about the proper rules of the political game.[1] Several enduring values of the American political culture have shaped public policy from the beginning of the republic.[2] Individualism, the right of people to pursue their self-interest and to be responsible for their own well-being, is a fundamental American cultural value. Personal freedom, which is closely linked to individualism, has meant the right to pursue self-improvement and protection from government interference. Along with individualism, the sanctity of contracts and the right to acquire and own property contribute to the free market ideology that dominates the political and economic systems in the United States.

Americans also believe in democracy—the right of every citizen to participate in public affairs. Support is widespread for equal treatment under the law, political equality, and equality of opportunity. In addition to these core political values, cultural values, including religion and the centrality of the nuclear family, have very significant political implications. It must be noted, however, that in many ways the United States does not live up to its political ideals, that it is a society with racist and sexist elements. As recently as 1950, black Americans did not have equal access to public schools or the voting booth. At the close of the 1980s, after years of the government's expressed commitment to breaking down racial barriers, there are few truly integrated communities. Women did not have the right to vote in elections until the beginning of the twentieth century, and they still earn considerably less than men.

Conflicts and tensions between values and beliefs frequently have been the source of American political struggle and debate. For example, the triumph of the southerners and midwesterners, who rallied around Andrew Jackson, over the Eastern aristocratic cliques that controlled American government in the late eighteenth and early nineteenth centuries was accomplished by appealing to the public's belief in individualism, pragmatism, and equality of opportunity. Franklin Roosevelt's New Deal, which substantially expanded government management of the economy and publicly funded social welfare programs, represented a victory for democratic egalitarian values over uncompromising individualism and capitalism. Ronald Reagan's policies of the 1980s represented a swing back toward individualism, capitalism, and traditional family values. The dynamism of America's political culture stems in part from the inherent tensions between cherished, yet competing, cultural values. Political struggles that aim to change an existing balance between these values can have dramatic effects on the nature of public policy.

The Market Paradigm and Procedural Democracy

A towering presence in the American political culture is, and always has been, a world view that regards the so-called free market as the best allocator of society's goods and services. This viewpoint is that government's role is primarily one of protecting certain economic, social, and political norms, or rules of conduct, such as competitive markets, private property, representative government, and others. This world view has its roots in seventeenth- and eighteenth-century political and economic thought, found in the works of John Locke, Adam Smith, David Hume, and Benjamin Franklin, and it dominated the thinking of nearly all the framers of the Constitution.

What is a free market or the market mechanism for allocating goods in a society? It is a system that relies on voluntary exchanges between autonomous individuals to allocate goods and services in an efficient manner. Efficiency can be defined as the maximum output technology can produce with the least use of resources. In free markets producers compete with one another to satisfy consumer demand for goods and services. Consumers are assumed to be willing to give up a certain amount of what they have, usually in the form of money, for various quantities of other goods and services—what economists call a demand function. When voluntary exchanges occur between producers and consumers, both parties are viewed as better off. A producer has given away something (a chair, for example) for something (say $100) he or she values more. The consumer has given away something, the $100, for something he or she values more, the chair. As long as no coercion is involved, there is no reason to believe that these exchanges are not mutually beneficial.

In such a system those who provide the goods and services on the terms most consumers find attractive should naturally be involved in the most exchanges, while those who offer goods on unattractive terms should be involved in the least. Over time, the inefficient producers will fall out of the market. The efficiency of the system, the highest output at the lowest cost, is guaranteed by competition. Furthermore, many people benefit because their preferences ultimately determine what kinds of goods and services are provided and they buy them at the lowest possible cost.

This formulation was fully worked out in the eighteenth century and credited to Smith's seminal work, *The Wealth of Nations*, but most of the core ideas can be found in earlier works, most notably Locke's.[3] The free market formulation was enormously influential because it provided the justification for laissez-faire capitalism and representative democracy, advocates of which were fighting to free societies from the remnants of feudalism and the privileges of the aristocracy. The free market paradigm forms the basis of the individualist ethic so central to American life. The logic of the free market is compelling—give people a chance to produce what they can and those who produce what is most wanted will obtain the greatest rewards. It is both democratic and meritocratic. What more could one desire?

Before going further, however, it is necessary to carefully examine the free market paradigm. First, it is a theoretical construct, not an empirical reality. Often, a vast difference exists between actual markets and the free market ideal. Like any theoretical construct, it is based on a number of assumptions. One such assumption is that individuals and businesses behave on the basis of the rational pursuit of self-interest.

Rationality requires knowledge; therefore, to work properly, a market must contain consumers who have "perfect knowledge" of what the market has to offer. That is, people must be aware of the alternatives to make rational choices about exchanges into which to enter. Otherwise, inefficient producers might be rewarded, and various other market distortions could occur.

Other necessary conditions are open entry into a market and fair competition among producers. If potential producers are excluded from offering their products to consumers, then innovation becomes less likely and efficiency is jeopardized. Similarly, if certain companies are able to engage in unfair behavior—terrorize competitors, produce at a loss for a long period of time, misrepresent their products to consumers—the free market dynamic is upset, and both production efficiency and consumer utility are compromised. The nature of a free market is quite specific, and actual markets are easily distorted.

Another essential point about the market paradigm is that it does not prescribe outcomes. One cannot predict the mix of goods and services that will be available in a society using a free market model. One can only assume that people know what they want and then attempt to establish rules and procedures that will give society as much of what it wants as is possible within the limits imposed by resources, technology, and individual productive capacity. If markets are free and open and people know what is available, goods and services should be allocated in a way that creates the greatest happiness for the greatest number. The desired outcome, happiness or what economists call "utility," is defined by the rules and procedures through which it is realized.

For Smith, Hume, Locke, and many other seventeenth- and eighteenth-century thinkers, the free market paradigm also defined individual freedom. Freedom was having an equal chance to produce valued commodities and trading them for other items of value. This was a revolutionary idea because it ignored privilege and religion; properly understood, it is still a radical philosophy. Clearly, equality of opportunity was not a reality in the eighteenth century, but the free market paradigm convinced many political philosophers and politicians of the validity of the idea of equality of opportunity. If markets were to operate optimally, entry into them had to be free and open; if societies were to be properly ordered, opportunities had to be open to all. When Thomas Jefferson wrote in the Declaration of Independence that "all men are created equal," he meant that all men, except slaves and the indentured, should be free to compete in society for the benefits that were available.

The basic point is that the free market paradigm dominates far more than the discipline of economics and the business sector of American society; it dominates the political and legal spheres as well. (Eighteenth-century scholars did not recognize the largely artificial distinction made between politics and economics; the two were the same.) American democracy is procedural—it is defined by rules through which political leaders are chosen by citizens in elections.[4] Its bedrock values—equality of opportunity, freedom of expression, the right to vote, the sanctity of property—spring directly from the free market paradigm. The Constitution elevates these procedural values above all others. Its logic is that justice is defined by procedural guarantees and that maintaining the integrity of procedures is the main task of government.

The idea that underpins this logic is that the best way to preserve a free society is to allow people to pursue self-interest in a system, free market capitalism, that converts this pursuit into societal welfare. This reflects a view common among eighteenth-century thinkers that government should ensure the operation of free markets because it was through market activity that individuals achieve happiness and society as a whole realizes productive efficiency. The other principal components of the Constitution—separation of powers, checks and balances, and federalism—develop this view of limited government more fully, and are probably best understood as attempts to protect markets from majority power and minority privilege (see *Federalist 10*).[5]

American democracy operates like a market. Popular participation comes mainly in the form of citizens choosing between competing candidates, who are packaged like products, and of those elected making policies they hope will please as many voters as possible. Certain "rules of the game" are upheld by the judiciary, an institution over which the citizenry has little control. As these rules, procedures, and values endure, they become part of the culture and the symbolism of politics. In contemporary America most political elites and many citizens are deeply committed to the procedural view of democracy.

Procedural democracy is complex, amoral, antitraditional, and vague about certain questions, such as what happens when property rights conflict with other rights. Therefore, it should not be surprising that procedural democracy is not always implemented perfectly. Equality of opportunity, in particular, has been extremely difficult to realize in practice because capitalist societies have allowed accumulated wealth, and the advantages that go with it, to be passed from one generation to the next. Cultural biases also have been stubbornly persistent in the United States. The Constitution did not embody the full ideal of procedural democracy; under it blacks were treated as subhumans. Only three of five blacks were counted as part of the population for determining the number of representatives each state would have, and women were not recognized as full citizens. There has been a gradual recognition that the ideal espoused in this document—that *all* men, meaning all humans, are created equal—had to be confronted and obvious contradictions resolved. Still, the ultimate goals are procedural. American democracy does not stand for equality of condition, only equality of opportunity; it is decidedly inegalitarian in this sense.

Participatory Democracy

Representative/procedural democracy does not place a great deal of value on having citizens directly involved in making policy decisions. For many democratic theorists this is a critical shortcoming. Jean Jacques Rousseau, another of Adam Smith's contemporaries and acquaintances, said about representative government in England: "The people of England regards itself as free, but is grossly mistaken; it is free only during the election of members of parliament. As soon as they are elected, slavery overtakes it, and it is nothing." [6] He prescribed a much more classical form of democracy, in which citizens would make societal laws directly, submerging their self-interest in pursuit of the collective interest or "general will." Participatory democracy is an alternative to procedural democracy.

Interest in participatory forms of democracy is very much alive among contemporary democratic theorists. [7] Jane Mansbridge has written about what she calls "unitary" democracy, which envisions a common good that is separate and distinct from the outcome of the struggle between competitive interests in a political community. [8] Advocates of unitary democracy contend that community forums in which citizens meet face-to-face and work toward consensual solutions to the common problems they face are both feasible and highly desirable. In such settings issues can be framed in such a way as not to be easily divisible into "we" versus "they" dichotomies, and citizens learn how to work toward commonly desired ends.

A classic example of unitary democracy at work is a town meeting in which a question such as drinking water fluoridization is discussed. The issue affects nearly everyone in more or less the same way; advocates on both sides debate the issue face to face; most participants are looking for a consensual solution; and preferences are registered publicly without behind-the-scenes maneuvering. This form of democracy is still practiced in rural New England and holds considerable appeal for many Americans.

Benjamin Barber advocates what he calls strong democracy, which involves direct citizen participation in the resolution of all kinds of political issues. The challenge for modern societies, according to Barber, is to create forums in which people can engage in public discussions of important issues and make intelligent policy decisions. The value of civic education and community consciousness would be emphasized. Barber would like to see electronic town meetings on public television networks, national referenda on leading issues, and the registering of public opinion through interactive television, in addition to the traditional community meetings.[9]

The common element in unitary and strong democracy is the emphasis on direct participation by citizens in the policy-making process. This idea is very much a part of American culture, even though relatively few citizens practice it. Participatory democracy appeals to Americans in the abstract, but most take part only by voting for representatives. Political reality is dominated by the pursuit of private interests, by affiliations with narrow interest groups, and by legal/adversary processes and procedures.

Assessing Contemporary Political Culture

Debate about contemporary political culture usually centers on whether Americans have become more conservative. Some observers have likened the 1980s to the 1950s by pointing out the prominence of free market, religious, and family-centered values in both eras. The evidence cited most frequently that the United States has turned to the right includes Reagan's impressive electoral victories in 1980 and 1984; the growing number of Republican officeholders and identifiers; the party's fund-raising ability; the pervasiveness of conservative policy proposals such as antiabortion and school prayer amendments and tax limitation referenda; and the increased visibility of groups that espouse traditional values. The American people, it is claimed, tried liberalism in the 1960s and 1970s but found it wanting. During the 1980s they sought to establish a new equilibrium among leading political values, an equilibrium that was more traditional and conservative than that prevailing in the late 1960s and 1970s.

This argument is backed by some empirical evidence, but it is not entirely persuasive. Conservative politicians and conservative policy ideas *were* more visible and successful in the 1980s than in the 1970s. However, the cultural changes taking place appear to be much more subtle and complex than suggested by the statement that Americans are becoming more conservative.

One widely cited reason for the rise of conservatism is the alleged collapse of liberalism and its political programs, which dominated the U.S. policy agenda from the 1930s to the 1980s. Modern American liberalism is closely associated with the Democratic party. Liberalism and the Democrats rose to power in the 1930s through New Deal legislation that expanded government involvement in social welfare and the economy. Uniting workers, intellectuals, southerners, and various ethnic minorities, the Democrats enacted unprecedented social welfare programs and policies. The most conspicuous and enduring law, the Social Security Act, guarantees financial assistance to the elderly, the poor, and the disabled. During the 1960s and early 1970s large Democratic majorities in Congress worked cooperatively with Lyndon Johnson, and later combatively with Richard Nixon, to design new government programs in housing, education, welfare, health, employment, civil rights, and environmental regulation.

Criticisms of these second-wave liberal Democratic policies were voiced by politicians, researchers, and citizens from the beginning and eventually grew stronger. Academic studies of social welfare, civil rights, and regulatory programs revealed many serious flaws of theory, design, and execution. Politicians and intellectuals also questioned the morality of liberalism, especially as it applied to abortion, school prayer, sex education, criminal justice, and the threat of communism. By the 1980s few politicians willingly identified themselves as liberals. Instead, they called themselves moderates, pragmatists, progressives, or neoliberals.

While political leaders no longer labeled themselves liberal, Americans continued to support most liberal programs. Public trust in government institutions and public officials has declined since the 1960s, but support for government benefits remains high. The percentage of Americans who believe that the government will do "what is right" (always, or most of the time) slid from more than 70 percent to 25 percent between 1964 and 1982, but then rose to 42 percent in 1986.[10] Public support for Social Security, however, is very strong: nine Americans in ten cite at least one advantage of the program.[11] Despite a $200 billion federal deficit in 1984, nearly 90 percent supported the continuation of cost-of-living adjustments for Social Security beneficiaries.[12] Most Americans (75 percent) believe the government should find employment for everyone who wants to work and help people obtain low-cost health care.[13] According to the Gallup Poll, nearly 75 percent favored more government spending for social programs in 1984—the same year a conservative president was overwhelmingly reelected on a platform of reducing government outlays.[14] Since the 1950s public opinion polls consistently have found that Americans like government benefits, but do not like to pay for them. In 1987, for example, 88 percent opposed cutting federal entitlement programs, and 80 percent opposed raising taxes to make up for the deficit.[15]

Some critics of modern liberalism argue that it is not the public's distaste for government spending that undermined liberal programs; rather, the public has become disillusioned with the social and moral values spawned by liberalism. If this argument is correct, it should be reflected in surveys about attitudes on abortion, school prayer, gun control, the death penalty, racial integration, and the Equal Rights Amendment. In fact, liberal attitudes have gained support in some of these areas and lost support in others since the early 1970s. For example, support for the Supreme Court's stand on abortion, which guarantees a woman an unrestricted right to terminate a pregnancy during the first trimester, rose slightly from 47 percent in the 1970s to 50 percent in the 1980s.[16] Support for the Equal Rights Amendment rose from 58 percent to 63 percent.[17] Most Americans—more than two-thirds—oppose state laws prohibiting interracial marriages, but in 1965 only half the population opposed them. More than 90 percent of Americans believe that blacks have a right to live anywhere they see fit; in 1960 only 70 percent recognized this right.[18]

The American public has hardened its attitude toward crime and criminals. The number favoring stricter gun control laws fell 10 percent—from 69 percent to 59 percent, and those endorsing the death penalty rose markedly, from 50 percent to 72 percent.[19] Moreover, the public remains committed to certain traditional ideas. Despite the rulings of the Supreme Court, approximately eight citizens in ten support prayer in public schools—a level that has remained constant for decades.[20] The proportion of the public that views religion as "very important" in their lives rose from 52 percent in 1978 to 55 percent in 1986, but remained far below the 70 percent level of the mid-1960s.[21] Some increase in religious zeal has come in the form of support for evangelical and fundamentalist religious organizations. The Gallup Poll and *Christianity Today*, a conservative magazine connected with the evangelical movement, estimated that there were 35 million Americans in 1984 who could be considered evangelicals or fundamentalists—people who were "born again," who encouraged others to believe in Christ, and who believed in a literal interpretation of the Bible—an increase of 8 million over their 1981 estimate.[22] In a 1986 poll one-third of the respondents described themselves as born again Christians.[23]

Detailed studies of American values reveal some generational differences on issues of political culture that are closely tied to life experiences and economic conditions. Americans born after World War II are more likely to exhibit what have been labeled "postmaterialist" values. They are more apt than their elders to believe that giving people a say in government decisions, protecting freedom of speech, and improving the environment are more important than curbing inflation, fighting crime, and expanding the economy.[24] However, these values are somewhat less popular among American youth under twenty-five than they were among youth in the 1970s.[25] An annual survey of college freshmen in California showed that the percentage of those preparing for a career in business doubled from 12 percent to 24 percent between 1968 and 1987, and those indicating that preserving the environment was important to them fell from 45 percent in 1972 to 16 percent in 1987.[26]

The American public's responses to direct questions about their ideological leanings reveal a slight conservative shift. Since the 1970s there has been roughly a ten-point increase in the percentage, to 35 percent, of the public regarding itself as conservative; the number of self-identified liberals declined slightly from 21 percent to 18 percent in the early 1980s, but then returned to its 1970s level by 1986.[27] Nearly half of American adults place themselves in the middle of the ideological spectrum.[28] Caution must be used in interpreting these findings. Many conservatives express support for liberal positions such as job guarantees or gun control, while many liberals fail to support liberal positions such as affirmative action, government regulation, and increased government spending.[29] Moreover, fads play a role in ideological self-identification. It was more fashionable to be a conservative during the Reagan era than it was during the 1970s.

Changes have occurred in the percentage of Americans calling themselves Republicans, Democrats, and independents. The number of those who regard themselves as Republicans rose from 23 percent in the mid-1970s to 28 percent after the 1980 election and then to 31 percent from 1984 through 1987. Democratic party affiliation declined from the 45 percent level it held throughout most of the 1970s to 40 percent from 1984 through 1987.[30]

Evidence suggests that there was some movement in a conservative direction during the 1980s, but there were no massive or unambiguous changes in cultural and political values. The "new conservatism," to the extent that it exists at all as a cultural phenomenon, appears to consist largely of a resurgence of traditional American values, such as individualism, capitalism, distrust of government, and respect for law and order. The rapid cultural changes of the opposite sort—humanism, postmaterialism, permissiveness—that dominated the 1960s and 1970s have been arrested, but the country has not experienced a return to the value systems of earlier periods in American history.

New Political Machinery

Changes in public attitudes provide only a partial explanation for the success of the new conservatism of the 1980s. Equally important were efforts by influential individuals and organizations to convince Americans that conservative causes and politicians deserved support. Like most political movements, the new conservatism was driven by elites, and it depended heavily on money and modern communication technology. The degree of change can be appreciated by looking at the proliferation of conservative, cause-oriented interest groups and the financial strength and effectiveness of the Republican party.

Beginning around 1970 conservative Americans mounted an effective, multifaceted effort to enhance their political clout and to promote a conservative agenda. They created new organizations, reinvigorated old ones, and used new tactics and strategies to influence elections and public policy. The increasing numbers of conservative political action committees (PACs) were particularly striking. By 1984 conservative-leaning PACs outnumbered liberal-leaning PACs five to one, and they were spending twice as much money in the political process—mostly on Republican candidates.[31]

Similar growth occurred among conservative lobbying groups. By the 1980s, 2,000 trade and professional associations were headquartered in Washington, up 300 from 1977, and more than 500 corporations had offices there, nearly double the number a decade earlier.[32] A publication entitled *Washington Representatives* listed 1,300 corporate representatives in 1985, up 300 from 1981.[33] The Business Roundtable, an elite lobbying group formed in the early 1970s and composed of corporate chief executives, steadily increased its stature and influence during the 1980s. Older business lobbying groups like the Chamber of Commerce grew markedly in membership, operating budgets, and effectiveness.[34]

Conservative points of view were bolstered by scholars and policy analysts working in research institutions. Conservative think tanks experienced rapid growth in funding in the late 1970s and early 1980s. The budget of the Heritage Foundation shot up from roughly $1 million in 1976-1977 to more than $7 million in 1981-1982. The American Enterprise Institute went through a similar growth pattern, its budget eventually topping $10 million.[35] Research institutions with university bases, such as the National Bureau of Economic Research at Harvard, the Hoover Institution at Stanford, and the Center for the Study of American Business at Washington University in St. Louis, attracted corporate and foundation money to conduct scholarly work with a decidedly conservative flavor.

This does not mean that scholarly findings can simply be bought. At a minimum, however, such support influences the questions that scholars pursue and rewards scholars who share the views of the funding agencies. By supporting some scholars while excluding others, those who supply the money can enhance the credibility of a particular argument.

Being effective in Washington and in communities around the country requires ample sums of money. In 1983, when the Natural Gas Supply Association (NGSA) wanted Congress to decontrol natural gas prices, they hired a consulting group called Communications Management to stir up popular support for their position. With the help of careful canvassing methods in friendly neighborhoods, the so-called Alliance for Energy Security, as the newly created group was known, spent more than $1 million to convince thousands of people to sign printed postcards for delivery to their congressional representatives.[36] The development of extensive grass-roots organizations to reinforce their claims that the public supported their positions was one way conservative groups augmented their traditional strength in Washington. In addition, a number of corporations embarked on expensive advertising campaigns to promote the free market, antigovernment philosophy.

New Republican Political Muscle

Much has been written about the decline of parties in American political life.[37] Parties and party politicians used to be the principal mediators between government and the people. Political parties selected and groomed candidates for public office, attracted paid and voluntary campaign workers, supplied jobs to loyalists, and even served as vital social institutions. In modern politics many of these functions have been taken over by individual candidates, the mass media, or interest groups.

The Republican party adapted itself to the new political age much more rapidly than the Democrats largely because of the Republicans' remarkable ability to supply money—the common denominator of modern politics. The Republican party raised $150 million to $200 million dollars during a typical 1980s election cycle, four to five times as much as the Democrats. The abundance of money allowed Republicans to do things that Democrats could not. The Republicans maintained a large national staff, which then raised more money. They recruited strong candidates for House and Senate seats by supplying substantial amounts of "seed" money to attractive candidates. They groomed future candidates for national office by committing funds to state legislative elections. In 1978 and 1980 Republicans gained more than 500 state legislative seats nationwide.[38] The Republican National Committee conducted campaign training seminars using the latest information on campaign technology. The party financed public opinion polls, provided assistance in creating media advertising spots, and analyzed voting patterns to pinpoint areas where voter registration drives would yield more Republican voters.[39] By the mid-1980s the Democrats were performing many of these same services, but with a much smaller budget.

The Republican party also promoted its political philosophy with expensive nationwide television campaigns. One effective advertising campaign in 1980 showed an older, overweight man, a look-alike for the Democratic Speaker of the House, Thomas P. O'Neill, Jr., riding in a large black limousine. The occupants became more and more befuddled as they drove around in circles, and their car eventually ran out of gas.

The party's wealth also helped its officials coordinate their efforts with sympathetic political action committees and with state and local party organizations. Following the 1980 census, for example, the party supplied research and legal assistance to Republican-controlled state legislatures to ensure that congressional and state legislative districts would be drawn to favor Republican candidates. The party also mobilized supporters on behalf of presidential policy initiatives, such as the Reagan budget and tax proposals in 1981.[40]

In short, the political successes of conservatives in the 1980s reflected some changes in public attitudes and their decided advantage in money, organization, strategy, and attractive candidates, led by Ronald Reagan. These resources were marshaled through the efforts of a relatively small group of prominent and influential individuals. As a cultural phenomenon, the new conservatism looks less like a new vision of politics and society than a reinvigoration of traditional values that had eroded during the 1960s. America in the late 1980s is not as conservative as it was in the 1950s, but the working Democratic majority of liberals and progressives of the 1960s and 1970s has been effectively checked by a coalition of business and social conservatives working through and with an army of interest groups and an energetic Republican party.

The Economy

The central economic objectives of U.S. policy makers are quite clear and have remained fairly constant for decades: to promote sustained economic growth without price inflation, to maintain low levels of unemployment and poverty, and to bring about high standards of living for American citizens. When unemployment and inflation rise, the cost of government also goes up. A rise of one percentage point for unemployed Americans, for example, costs the federal treasury roughly $25 billion in benefit payments and lost tax revenues. But keeping unemployment and inflation low is very difficult. Since 1950, for example, the United States has experienced five recessions, periods when the economy failed to expand for several months or even years, resulting in high levels of unemployment.

The task of managing the contemporary American economy is growing more difficult. Whether and how government should intervene in the economy has always been a matter of great controversy in American politics—a central dividing line between liberals and conservatives,

Democrats and Republicans. Moreover, the economic realties of the 1970s and 1980s have shattered many of the old assumptions, increased the stakes of the game considerably, and multiplied the number and difficulty of choices policy makers face.

Government's Role in a Strong Economy

Government economic policy making was easier, and in some ways less critical, when the U.S. economy was expanding at a stable pace during the 1950s and 1960s. Consider the following indicators:

—the economy grew at a healthy rate of 4 percent annually, and per capita income increased by roughly 2 percent each year

—productivity growth—the measure of output per hour worked—was also impressive, with an average annual increase of more than 3 percent[41]

—unemployment averaged about 4 percent, and annual inflation rates were seldom more than 2 percent

—the cost of borrowing money, while gradually rising from a 2 percent interest rate in 1950, did not exceed 4 percent until 1965

—the economy was running smoothly with slightly less than 60 percent of the adult population in the labor force—more than 85 percent of American men and 35 percent of the women[42]

Government's role in the economy was fairly uncomplicated by contemporary standards. When the economy slumped, the government would enlarge the supply of money for investors and increase government spending to stimulate growth. Through these steps major recessions and accompanying unemployment could be mitigated or avoided altogether. When a recession hit in 1957-1958 and unemployment rose to a postwar high of nearly 7 percent, the federal government increased spending beyond revenues, ending the year with a deficit of $13 billion, also a postwar high. The unemployment rate dropped to 5.5 percent by the following year.

The main purpose of macroeconomic policy—increasing or decreasing the money supply, raising or lowering deficit spending—was to maintain high levels of employment by stimulating demand for goods and services. With the economic depression of the 1930s and 1940s not far behind them, policy makers were preoccupied with the problem of unemployment. Joblessness was perceived as a male problem and was closely related to the condition of manufacturing firms, which employed one-third of the workforce, compared with one-fifth in today's economy.

The absence of strong competition for consumer markets from other nations was another fact of economic life in the 1950s and 1960s, when practically all products sold in the United States were manufactured domestically. U.S. exports accounted for one-fourth of all world exports and far exceeded imports.[43]

The American standard of living surpassed that of every nation. In 1960 per capita gross national product (GNP), the money value of all final goods and services produced within a year,[44] in the United States was roughly twice that of Western Europe and six times that of Japan.[45] Economic strength and prosperity in the United States provided a model economy that the entire noncommunist world sought to emulate.

At the close of the 1980s, however, the U.S. economy was no longer the unchallenged economic powerhouse of the industrialized world. Many industrialized nations and several Third World nations had become important economic competitors. The U.S. trade deficit—the difference between imports and exports—surpassed $150 billion per year. Japanese companies sold products worth more than $85 billion in the United States in 1986, while U.S. sales to Japan totaled only $27 billion, creating the largest U.S. trade deficit with any country.[46] The diminished autonomy of the American economy revealed more clearly than ever the intimate connection between government policy and economic performance. What American policy makers decide about trade and tax policy has a direct bearing on the ability of U.S. corporations to compete in the world market against corporations that are governed by different rules.

The 1950s and 1960s were not free from economic problems. Poverty was quite severe. For more than twenty years after World War II, roughly one American in five lived in poverty by U.S. government standards. In 1960, for example, 40 million Americans—22 percent of the population—were poor. By 1973 the poverty rate had fallen to half of the 1960 level, and it remained at 11 percent to 12 percent for the rest of the decade.[47] The average American's standard of living was much lower in the 1950s and 1960s than in the 1980s. Taking inflation into account, per capita income was roughly half the level achieved in the 1980s.

By the 1960s various sectors of society, but especially blue-collar workers, the elderly, and the middle class, began to demand a larger slice of the economic pie. The federal government initiated policies aimed at improving the economic well-being of various segments of society. The domestic portion of the federal budget burgeoned as programs for the elderly, the poor, the unemployed, students, veterans, military retirees, and many other groups were either created or enlarged. At the same time, billions of dollars were being spent to fight a war in Vietnam.

Expanding Government's Role

The late 1960s and early 1970s represented a watershed in American policy making, as hundreds of new spending and regulatory programs were established. It was taken for granted that the economy would grow and produce sufficient revenues to sustain these new government endeavors. Policy makers were not spending money lavishly; indeed, many of the new programs had meager budgets. But the political climate in Washington accepted, and in many ways encouraged, the practice of defusing conflicts by creating programs or regulations to satisfy interest groups and voters. The substantial reduction in poverty during the late 1960s and 1970s can be attributed in large part to federal income transfer programs, particularly Social Security.[48]

This flurry of policy initiatives enlarged the federal budget. In 1965 the budget was just under $120 billion—roughly double the 1952 level. It took only seven years for the federal budget to double again. In another six years, by 1978, it had once again doubled. As a percentage of GNP, federal spending rose from 14 percent in 1950 to 18 percent in 1960, 20 percent in 1970, and 22 percent in 1980. Stimulated by the explosion of federal grant-in-aid programs, state and local government spending also shot up—from $50 billion in 1960 to more than $350 billion by 1980. Government was spending more and relying more heavily on individuals to pay for it. Taxpayers began to feel the pinch. Personal income taxes and Social Security payroll taxes accounted for 64 percent of federal revenue in 1963, but 77 percent in 1980.

The growth in Social Security provides an excellent example of how spending can increase dramatically over time as policy makers adjust programs even in seemingly small ways. During the 1960s and 1970s the basic program for the elderly, known as Old Age Survivors Disability Insurance (OASDI), was amended several times. More people were made eligible; benefits were increased; a cost-of-living adjustment (COLA) was added to offset the erosion in income caused by inflation; and other income security programs, including Supplemental Security Income (SSI), were created for disadvantaged groups. At the time, these actions were not regarded as radical policy decisions. They were far less controversial than the creation of the Community Action Program, the passage of several civil rights acts, or the enactment of medical insurance programs for the poor (Medicaid) and elderly (Medicare, which became part of Social Security). The cumulative effect of these "modest" adjustments in Social Security became clear later on. The federal government allocated $25 billion to Social Security programs in 1965; by 1975 outlays for Social Security and Medicare had increased to nearly $78 billion. Social Security and Medicare expenditures jumped to $150 billion by 1980; in 1988 the federal government spent a little over $300 billion on these core Social Security programs.[49]

Contemporary Political-Economic Problems

Mounting public sector spending was only one dimension of the rapidly changing American economy. More Americans were working than ever before. The labor force expanded from 70 million in 1960 to 107 million in 1980, and women's participation in the labor force increased dramatically, from one in three in 1960 to one in two by 1980. The economy shifted away from manufacturing of steel, automobiles, and heavy equipment and toward services, such as insurance, banking, and information. Between 1960 and 1980 employment in manufacturing remained fairly stable, rising to 20 million from 17 million, but service sector employment jumped to 18 million from 7 million.

Unfortunately, economic troubles began to emerge during the 1970s, as revealed by the following indicators:

—economic growth slowed to an annual rate of less than 3 percent
—annual productivity increases fell to just over 1 percent
—unemployment averaged 6.2 percent—higher than in the 1950s and 1960s
—interest rates were just about twice as high as in the previous decade
—imports exceeded exports in seven of the ten years
—economic growth and productivity in Western European countries and Japan were consistently higher than those of the United States
—the standard of living in several West European countries edged ahead of the United States for the first time in thirty years[50]

Various sectors of the economy reacted to these unfavorable developments by seeking to protect their vital interests. An ever-expanding number of interest groups pressed lawmakers for more government subsidies or protective regulations. Underlying problems in the economy and their implications were ignored. By acceding to the demands of various interest groups, national policy makers shielded society from the negative effects of a sputtering, treadmill economy. Americans were running faster—more people working, more money in circulation, higher interest rates—but the economy was going nowhere. The Federal Reserve Board expanded the nation's money supply twice as fast in the 1970s as it had done in the 1960s. Government spending consistently exceeded revenues, and the budget deficits mounted. The administrations of Richard Nixon, Gerald Ford, and Jimmy Carter adopted various government policies aimed at curbing spiraling inflation, including outright controls on wages and prices.

The unprecedented combination of high unemployment, rising prices, and mounting interest rates brought economic hardship to millions of Americans and gave rise to a new economic term—stagflation. Inflation became the most dreaded malady in this economy of sorrows, and for good reason. Prices increased by an average of 7.5 percent per year in the 1970s compared with only 2 percent per year during the 1960s. Americans shifted their concern from unemployment to inflation and its effect on their standard of living. Everyone wanted to be protected from the negative effects of inflation: unions bargained for inflation-adjusted wages; senior citizens demanded cost-of-living increases in Social Security programs; management passed price increases along to consumers; and landlords raised rents to offset rising utility bills.

Conditions were ripe for change as the 1980 presidential election approached. The extent of the nation's economic deterioration was clear: inflation surpassed 13 percent; interest rates approached 20 percent; productivity was *declining;* and 7 percent of the labor force was jobless. In this economic climate, any president would have been hard pressed to achieve reelection. Carter also suffered from a negative image resulting from the the attack on the U.S. Embassy in Iran and the taking of American hostages. And he faced a strong opponent with a new economic agenda. Reagan and the Republicans proposed tax and expenditure reductions that the American middle class found understandable and appealing.

Ironically, several of the building blocks in the Reagan administration's economic and government reform program had already been laid during the last two years of the Carter administration. The Federal Reserve system, under Chairman Paul Volcker, instituted a stricter monetary policy to choke off inflation. The Carter administration began to loosen government regulations in various sectors of the economy, including the telecommunications and transportation industries. Carter tightened efficiency measures in federally funded welfare programs. His spending priorities were a larger defense budget, freezes or cuts in domestic programs, and a balanced budget. These moderate policies reflected a consensus among national policy makers that a new economic order was needed.

There can be no doubt, however, that Reagan's election and the adoption of his economic policies by Congress in 1981 brought about major changes in America's political economy. These policies and their consequences dominated the nation's economic policy agenda in the 1980s. The twin towers of Reagan's economic strategy were the Economic Recovery Tax Act, which slashed personal income taxes by one-quarter over three years, and the Omnibus Budget and Reconciliation

Act, which increased defense spending and cut social spending in areas such as government jobs and training, education, and programs for the poor.[51]

This economic strategy was nothing less than audacious. Senate Republican leader Howard Baker called it a "river boat gamble." During the presidential primaries, rival candidate George Bush, who subsequently became Reagan's vice president, called it "voodoo economics." Reagan claimed that cutting taxes and domestic spending would invigorate the economy sufficiently to bring in the revenues needed for the continuation of other government programs and for the expansion in military spending.

These predictions were wrong. The economy plunged into the deepest recession in forty years; unemployment exceeded 10 percent, and the federal deficit increased from $60 billion in 1981 to nearly $200 billion two years later, peaking at $221 billion in 1986. The interest payments on the national debt alone exceeded $100 billion, or about 13 percent of all federal spending, by 1984.

Two major factors prevented Reagan from succeeding. First, he did not propose reductions in the domestic budget sufficient to offset the defense buildup. When the deficit mounted, he refused to increase taxes to pay the federal government's price tag; the nation continued to borrow and doubled the national debt in less than six years. Second, the restrictive monetary policies of the Federal Reserve Board choked off inflation and slowed the economy generally.

One positive result of the painful recession of 1981-1983 was that the inflation genie was put back into the bottle. Inflation fell from double digits in 1979-1981 to 6 percent in 1982 and just over 3 percent in 1983—an average that was maintained over the next four years. By the end of 1983 an economic recovery was under way—productivity improved substantially and unemployment fell steadily. In many ways the American economy of the mid- to late 1980s looked healthy, but the huge federal deficits (more than $145 billion in 1988) have imposed, and will continue to impose, a tremendous long-term burden on American citizens and policy makers.

Other problems, less obvious than the deficits, also lurked in the new economy. The poverty rate rose to 15 percent from 11 percent, which meant that there were 35 million poor Americans. The gap widened between rich and poor and between the prosperous economic regions of the country and those that were struggling.[52] These negative consequences can be traced to the deep recession in 1982 and to the Reagan administration's domestic spending cuts, which primarily affected the poor and the near poor.

Another problem was the persistence of high real interest rates—the difference between nominal interest rates and the rate of inflation—due in large part to the deficits. When individuals and corporations want to borrow money, they have to pay more for it in part because they are competing with the federal government, which is borrowing billions of dollars to pay for its activities. A significant portion—10 percent to 15 percent—of the debt is owned by foreign investors, and high interest rates make government securities and corporate bonds an attractive investment. From 1981 to 1985 the high real interest rates in the United States increased worldwide demand for the dollar, increasing the value of the dollar relative to most other currencies. As a result, foreign imports were cheaper and U.S. exports more costly and therefore less competitive. This situation led to a trade deficit of $150 billion, which became another economic concern and political issue. Declining real interest rates in 1985-1986 and government negotiations with U.S. trading partners caused the value of the dollar to fall in international currency markets by the spring of 1985. The dollar's decline was supposed to help the trade deficit, but it did not, at least in the short-term; the trade deficit in 1986 was nearly $160 billion. Further reductions in interest rates were blocked by the need to keep investment in the debt appealing to foreigners.

The Third World debt added another dimension to U.S. economic woes. During the 1970s American banks lent a great deal of money at interest rates from 15 percent to 20 percent to many African and South American countries, whose main form of collateral was raw materials, in most cases, crude oil. At that time oil prices were high and projected to stay that way. But, when the Organization of Petroleum Exporting Countries (OPEC) lost its control over crude oil supplies in the 1980s, oil prices fell precipitously, putting Third World debtor nations in a terrible position. Many of them could not even pay the interest on their loans, let alone the principal. A few Third World leaders began to talk openly about ceasing loan payments, and some in the American banking community started looking to the government for loan guarantees or assistance in negotiating new loan agreements with borrower nations.

A Comparative Perspective

The relationship between cultural values, economic conditions, and public policy is particularly apparent when one compares the United States with other nations of the world. Western industrialized nations have quite different governmental operations and public philosophies that reflect diverse cultural and economic experiences. Consider the difference between the United States and Western Europe 100 years ago. In Europe desirable land had long been held by the wealthiest segments of society, economic mobility was minimal, and a large industrial working class had formed. In the United States the government was practically giving away large tracts of land in the West, frontiers remained to be settled, and large fortunes were being made and lost quickly. An industrial working class, composed mostly of European immigrants, was beginning to form, but most parts of the country remained primarily agrarian. The history of American economic development, which is characterized by a large property-owning segment of the population, an expanding middle class, and almost no dissenters about the primacy of capitalism, accounts for some of the distinctive aspects of the modern political economy. The United States continues to be distinctive because of its large, fairly autonomous private sector, relatively modest government social welfare spending, and widespread acceptance of the values of individualism and capitalism.

The social welfare state came relatively late to the United States. Programs to aid sick or injured workers, the elderly and disabled, the unemployed, and new parents were established in Western Europe several decades before they appeared in the United States.[53] Nearly all West European countries have universal income support programs for the poor and unemployed and national health insurance systems; these have never taken hold in the United States. While growth in American social welfare spending since the late 1960s was comparable to that in Europe and Japan, other Western democratic governments are considerably more generous in providing housing assistance, unemployment benefits, vacation and maternity leaves, and income security for the elderly.[54] The data presented in Table 2-1 demonstrate that the U.S. government taxes its citizens less and spends less money on social welfare purposes—transfer payments—than most other developed nations.

Because the private sector/free market ethic continues to dominate American political culture and the U.S. economy, policy makers face choices very different from those in other countries. Unlike their European counterparts who may debate refinements in their national health care system, American policy makers appear unlikely to even adopt comprehensive health insurance. Government planning and management are integral to the economies of Japan and many West European countries, but this approach is derided by business leaders and most government officials in the United States.[55]

Although smaller than that of other industrialized nations, the American public sector is present in nearly every aspect of the nation's social and economic life. Especially influential is the burgeoning body of federal, state, and local regulatory law that governs public and private behavior. Between 1960 and 1980 the number of federal regulatory agencies doubled—from twenty-eight to fifty-six; their workforce grew

Table 2-1   Government Expenditures and Tax Revenues for Selected Countries (1984)

Country	Government expenditures as percentage of GDP	Transfer payments as percentage of GDP*a*	Tax revenues as percentage of GDP
France	49.4	33.0	48.4
Japan	27.1	17.2	30.3
Netherlands	56.5	39.7	54.8
Sweden	59.8	32.1	60.0
United Kingdom	44.9	23.0	42.9
United States	36.9	18.1	31.7
West Germany	44.2	24.1	45.6

Source: Organization for Economic Cooperation and Development, National Accounts (Paris: OECD, 1987), vol. 1; and OECD Economic Outlook, Historical Statistics (Paris).

Note: GDP = gross domestic product, the value of all goods and services produced for final use within each country.

a Includes standard transfer payments like unemployment benefits, workmen's compensation, public social welfare assistance, health care, old age and disability insurance, and payments on property income.

by 90,000; and their budgets increased threefold. The *Federal Register,* which compiles all government regulations grew from about 15,000 pages in 1946 to 87,000 pages in 1980.[56] Similar developments occurred in most states. Activities long regulated by government, such as transportation, food and drug quality, agriculture, occupational licensing, and banking, were joined in the 1960s and 1970s by regulatory efforts in consumer product safety, air and water pollution, workplace health and safety, automobile safety, and civil rights. Beginning in the late 1970s, however, the federal government began to deregulate certain industries, including trucking, banking, broadcasting, and the airlines. The Reagan administration relaxed enforcement of strip-mining legislation, affirmative action statutes, and antitrust laws. Regulatory agencies were forced to cope with leaner budgets and fewer employees. The number of pages in the *Federal Register* actually declined, as the White House discouraged new administrative rules and regulations that were opposed by the business community. The regulatory surge of the 1970s was followed by a deregulatory trend in the 1980s that reaffirmed the strong appeal of the free market paradigm.

Sharing policy responsibilities among different levels of government is characteristic of the American political system. States and localities dominate a number of important policy areas and share others with the federal government. Subnational governmental power is based on a tradition of local self-determination that is older than the country itself, protected by the Constitution, and sustained by individualistic cultural values.

American state and local governments are stronger and more autonomous than their counterparts in most other countries, but it would be a mistake to believe that only the United States vests power and authority in subnational governments. Canadian provincial governments have considerable constitutional authority, which gives them a certain measure of autonomy from the national government and superiority over the cities. Britain and Sweden have unitary, rather than federal, systems, but local governments are important political institutions. In Sweden, cities such as Stockholm have extensive taxing power. In Britain local powers come through less formal means, such as the recognition of local expertise and institutionalized bargaining over certain policy matters. Central government leaders know that they must obtain the support of an extensive network of local public officials to finance and implement education, health, housing, and welfare programs, so they must continually negotiate with local officials to secure cooperation. In both nations the absence of chief executives at the state or local levels is probably the most significant contrast with American states and localities.[57]

Relationships between national and subnational governments undergo change. The independence of state governments from the federal government, a characteristic of nineteenth-century America, was significantly altered by the New Deal of the 1930s. The liberal Democratic programs of the Great Society in the 1960s and 1970s imposed a host of new national objectives on states and localities. With these sweeping programs, the federal government asserted itself as the leading actor in the intergovernmental system. Grant-in-aid programs and regulatory mandates gave the federal government leverage to alter traditional state and local services and to convince states and localities to provide many new ones.

The trend toward greater federal control of policy and implementation abated during the 1980s. This change came about in part because of a nearly universal recognition that narrow-purpose federal grants led to fragmented and inefficient government services. Too many programs were attempting to treat related problems without any effective means of coordination. Republican presidents Nixon, Ford, and Reagan called for a "new federalism," in which states and localities would have more authority and responsibility. Many overlapping, but separately operating, federal aid programs were consolidated into block grant packages; still, most federal grant-in-aid money remained in the narrow-purpose programs known as categorical programs.

It is evident that state governments have grown in stature within the federal system. States have demonstrated their willingness and ability to raise money for public services, and state governments have become more innovative in policy making and in reforms aimed at improving management. It appears that states are emerging from a long period of dormancy to become more equal partners in the federal system.

The New Agenda

The landscape of American public policy and politics is changing, and Americans are facing unpleasant and difficult choices. The United States is the world's most powerful economy. With less than 5 percent of the world's population, the United States generates more than half of the world's GNP. But U.S. economic dominance in the world is challenged not only by its trading partners, most notably Japan, but also by less-developed Third World nations.

The problems created by a complex industrialized society and its role in the world economy are not easily handled. Many of them—health care, poverty, environmental protection, and civil rights—may not have good solutions. Resources to address public problems are finite. For some issues, such as the environment, the United States may be running out of time. Sometimes attempts to improve matters through public action succeed only in creating new and more difficult problems.

Beyond these broad economic and policy challenges, the nation is also experiencing important social changes and problems. More than 200 years since the founding of the republic, the United States is still what sociologists call a "loosely bounded culture"—one that holds together, but with ongoing and serious rifts. The nation's standard of living is the envy of most of the world, but nearly one-sixth of the population is poor by the government's definition. More than twenty years after the passage of the Civil Rights Act, blacks and whites commonly live in different neighborhoods and attend different schools. More than sixty years after obtaining the right to vote, women are still seeking equality in the labor force.

While there is a foundation of public support that makes governance possible, Americans have a deep-seated skepticism of government solutions and distrust of political institutions and politicians. The Watergate scandal, which revealed abuse of presidential power, forced President Nixon to resign. Public revelations and televised hearings about an arms-for-hostages deal with Iran, in which members of President Reagan's staff may have disobeyed the law and misled the public, increased distrust in government. The persistence of social problems and the occasional eruption of scandals erode public support for government institutions.

From the end of World War II to the mid-1970s, the United States experienced an expanding economy and government budget. It was, according to congressional scholar Allen Schick, a *distributive* era.[58] The growing economy allowed benefits—tax breaks and spending programs—to be spread around without causing friction. With the economy and revenues keeping pace, legislators could ignore difficult questions of social equity or government planning while enacting policies that conferred tangible benefits on constituent groups. The demands of organized and politically active groups were satisfied. Powerful groups were not asked to sacrifice. Government largesse was distributed to those who made a case. Initial subsidies were typically small, but they grew steadily.

The "politics of giving" was supported by both political parties because benefits could be given to important constituents without apparently hurting anyone else. Building a veterans' hospital in Wilkes-Barre, Pennsylvania, did not seem to take anything away from cattle ranchers in Colorado, because the federal government was also building water projects the ranchers wanted. Political scientist Theodore Lowi contrasted these distributive policies with redistributive policies, such as welfare, education for the children of low-income families, subsidized housing for the poor, for which the "haves" were taxed to support programs for the "have-nots." [59] Redistributive policies provoke heated conflicts among legislators and are therefore more difficult to enact. They require cohesive majorities that are concerned with social equity, but such coalitions are rare in American politics. Consequently, the consensual politics of distribution dominated the policy-making arenas of American national government.

Many aspects of the distributive era are still operating in government. Old habits die hard, but the nation is clearly entering a new era—a "politics of taking," with the government doing the taking. Sharing the pain may well be the essence of the new politics. The public pie is no longer expanding at a rate that allows for the peaceful continuation of existing commitments, let alone provides for anything new. Yet, old beneficiaries continue to demand "their share," and new groups clamor to have their problems addressed. Rather than substantially trimming government spending or raising taxes, political leaders have made up the difference between group demands and total revenue by borrowing huge sums of money.

Chronic $200 billion deficits in the government's balance sheet stimulated an unprecedented consciousness about the budget. The elevation of budget decisions to the status of high politics means that the distinction between distributive and redistributive policies is no longer very meaningful. Everyone knows that money spent in one area is money that cannot be spent somewhere else. It is no longer possible to maintain the illusion that there can be winners without losers. The budget—tax and expenditure policy—dominated the congressional agenda for most of the 1980s and will continue to do so for years to come. Legislative energy and attention have been forced away from the enactment of new policies and toward the reconsideration of the old.

Similar changes are evident at the state and local levels. Indeed, the erosion of distributive policies owes its origin as much to Proposition 13, a ballot initiative that restricted tax increases in California, and its echoes in other states as to developments in Washington. State governments, which are constitutionally obliged to balance their budgets, have not had the luxury of pondering the long-term effects of budget deficits. In the wake of the taxpayers' rebellion, they had no choice but to cut spending. In the same spirit, state legislatures have institutionalized review of existing programs; they also have made it difficult for bureaucracies to adopt new rules and regulations by providing for legislative vetoes of such rules. Even liberal Democratic governors, like Michael Dukakis of Massachusetts, found themselves endorsing fiscal prudence, cutback management, and deregulation.

Summary

This chapter briefly reviews a number of large, complicated topics. The purpose is to show how two broad forces in American society— political culture and the economy—influence politics, government, and public policy. Political culture determines what people expect of government and what role citizens and politicians play in politics. Economic well-being is the most consistently important issue in American politics, and economic performance is both a cause and an effect of government policy. Political beliefs and expectations and the economy change over time, and these changes are reflected in the policy agenda of government.

The politics of the 1980s are markedly different from those of earlier epochs in American history, and different politics means different policies. The United States seems to be entering an era in which limitations in the economy and trade-offs inherent in policy choices will have to be confronted more visibly, and one would hope, more candidly.

For example, if the government tries to control inflation by employing strict monetary policies, that move hurts the export market. A certain sector of the economy, such as agriculture, feels the effects quickly and forcefully. If the government tries to alleviate the trade deficit by taxing or limiting foreign imports, American consumers pay higher prices for many products. If the government commits large sums of money to national defense or continues to run large deficits, less will be available for retirement, medical care, and public works programs. Americans have seen different priorities come and go. During the New Deal period government spending was seen as the key to prosperity; the private sector reemerged during Dwight Eisenhower's administration. Government came back with more spending and regulation in the late 1960s and 1970s, then drew back from regulation in the 1980s. Americans may begin to insist on more straight talk from politicians about which combinations of priorities are compatible and which are not.

The American government's response to the challenges of the present and the future will be shaped by cultural and economic developments and by the actions of policy-making institutions. Understanding the peculiarities of and the distinctions among the different arenas of politics is central to the study of American public policy. These institutions and their policy-making processes are the subject of Part II.

Notes

1. See Lewis Lipsitz, *American Democracy* (New York: St. Martin's Press, 1986), 31.
2. For a more detailed discussion of American political values and beliefs see Linda J. Metcalf and Kenneth M. Dolbeare, *Neopolitics: American Political Ideas in the 1980s* (New York: Random House, 1985).
3. See John Locke, *Two Treatises of Government*, ed. Peter Laslett (New York: Cambridge University Press, 1963); and Adam Smith, *The Wealth of Nations* (New York: Random House, Modern Library Edition, 1937).
4. The concept of procedural democracy is presented and discussed at length in Ira Katznelson's and Mark Kesselman's text *The Politics of Power*, 2d ed. (New York: Harcourt Brace Jovanovich, 1979).
5. Alexander Hamilton, John Jay, and James Madison, *The Federalist Papers* (Cambridge, Mass.: Belknap Press, 1966).
6. Jean Jacques Rousseau, *The Social Contract and Discourses*, trans. G. D. H. Cole (New York: E. P. Dutton, 1950), Book III, 94.
7. See Benjamin R. Barber, *Strong Democracy: Participatory Politics for a New Age* (Berkeley: University of California Press, 1984); and Philip Green, *Retrieving Democracy* (Totowa, N.J.: Rowman & Allanheld, 1985).
8. Jane J. Mansbridge, *Beyond Adversary Democracy* (Chicago: University of Chicago Press, 1983).
9. Barber, *Strong Democracy*, ch. 10.
10. The 1964 and 1982 figures are from the Center for Political Studies at the University of Michigan. They were published in the *New York Times*, July 15, 1983, B6, and by William Crotty, *American Parties in Decline*, 2d ed. (Boston: Little, Brown, 1984), 67; the 1986 figure is from the *New York Times*, Jan. 28, 1986, A1, A14.

11. See Paul Light, *Artful Work: The Politics of Social Security Reform* (New York: Random House, 1985), 59.

12. *Gallup Report*, no. 229, October 1984, 13.

13. Crotty, *American Parties in Decline*, 67.

14. *Gallup Report*, no. 229, 13.

15. *Gallup Report*, no. 263, August 1987, 26-27.

16. George H. Gallup, *Gallup Poll 1972-1977* (Wilmington, Del.: Scholarly Resources, 1978), vol. I, April 7, 1974, 247; Gallup, *Gallup Poll 1983* (Wilmington, Del.: Scholarly Resources, 1984), 137.

17. *Gallup Report*, no. 190, July 1981, 24; *Gallup Report*, no. 229, 10.

18. See Crotty, *American Parties in Decline*, 67-68.

19. Gallup, *Gallup Poll 1972-1977*, vol. I, Oct. 30, 1974, 583; Gallup, *Gallup Poll 1983*, 114; *Gallup Report*, nos. 232/233, January/February 1985, 4.

20. *Gallup Report*, no. 177, April-May 1980, 11; *Gallup Report*, no. 217, October 1983, 18.

21. *Gallup Report*, no. 259, April 1987, 12-14.

22. *Gallup Report*, no. 236, May 1985, 11-12, 38.

23. *Gallup Report*, no. 259, 28.

24. Ronald Inglehart, "Post-Materialism in an Environment of Insecurity," in *American Political Science Review* 75 (December 1981): 880-900.

25. Ibid., 888.

26. "More College Freshmen Plan to Teach," *New York Times*, Jan. 12, 1987, A15.

27. See *Gallup Report*, no. 187, April 1981, 21; *Gallup Report*, no. 204, September 1982, 17; and *Gallup Report*, no. 230, November 1984, 23; *New York Times*, Jan. 28, 1986, A1, A14.

28. Depending on how the question is asked, different polling organizations come up with slightly different results regarding American ideological distribution. Overall, the findings of Gallup, National Opinion Research Center, and Center for Political Studies are quite similar. For an extended discussion see Crotty, *American Parties in Decline*, 61-66.

29. Ibid., 68.

30. *Gallup Report*, no. 260, May 1987, 16-17.

31. See Michael J. Malbin, ed., *Money and Politics in the United States* (Chatham, N.J.: Chatham House, 1984), 295-297.

32. Jeffrey M. Berry, *The Interest Group Society* (Boston: Little, Brown, 1984), 20.

33. Ann Cooper, "Lobbying in the '80s: High Tech Takes Hold," *National Journal*, Sept. 14, 1985, 2030.

34. Thomas Byrne Edsall, *The New Politics of Inequality* (New York: W. W. Norton, 1984), 120-128.

35. Ibid., 117-120.

36. Ann Cooper, "Middleman Mail," *National Journal*, Sept. 14, 1985, 2041.

37. See, for example, Crotty, *American Parties in Decline*; Everett C. Ladd, Jr., *Where Have All the Voters Gone?* (New York: W. W. Norton, 1978); Jeane J. Kirkpatrick, *Dismantling the Parties* (Washington, D.C.: American Enterprise Institute, 1978); and Austin Ranney, "Political Parties: Reform and Decline," in *The New American Political System*, ed. Anthony King (Washington, D.C.: American Enterprise Institute, 1979).

38. David Adamany, "Political Parties in the 1980s," in *Money and Politics in the United States*, 80.

39. Ibid., 78-85.

40. Ibid., 95-101.

41. *Business Week*, special issue, "The Reindustrialization of America," June 30, 1980, 10.

42. Unless otherwise indicated the statistics provided in this section were taken from tables in the appendices to *The Economic Report of the President*, prepared annually by the Council of Economic Advisers. The 1986, 1987, and 1988 versions of this report would include all the figures presented here. See *The Economic Report of the President* (Washington, D.C.: U.S. Government Printing Office, 1986, 1987, 1988).

43. *Business Week*, "The Reindustrialization of America," 6-7.

44. Gross national product (GNP) differs from gross domestic product (GDP), another measure of national economic output, in that GNP includes profits and income of American corporations and individuals that are operating abroad, but does not count the profits and income of foreigners or foreign-owned corporations operating in the United States. GDP does count the latter, but does not include the former.

45. Robert B. Reich, *The Next American Frontier* (New York: Penguin Books, 1983) cites Organization for Economic Cooperation and Development (OECD) data on this point in a footnote on page 285.

46. *New York Times*, Jan. 17, 1988, E4.

47. See Harrell R. Rodgers, Jr., *The Cost of Human Neglect* (Armonk, N.Y.: M. E. Sharpe, 1987), 18.

48. See Lawrence E. Lynn, Jr., "A Decade of Policy Developments in the Income Maintenance System," in *A Decade of Federal Antipoverty Programs*, ed. Robert H. Haveman (New York: Academic Press, 1977), 88-95.

49. Figures come from *The Economic Report of the President*, 1986; and the Bureau of the Census, *Statistical Abstract of the United States 1975*, 95th ed. (Washington, D.C.: U.S. Government Printing Office, 1974).

50. Reich, *The Next American Frontier*, 285.

51. See Gregory B. Mills, "The Budget: A Failure of Discipline," in *The Reagan Record*, ed. John L. Palmer and Isabel V. Sawhill (Cambridge, Mass.: Ballinger, 1984), 111-114.

52. See D. Lee Bawdin and John L. Palmer, "Social Policy: Challenging the Welfare State," in *The Reagan Record*, 194-201.

53. Rodgers, *The Cost of Human Neglect*, 104-107.

54. Ibid., 57, 103-125; and Ira C. Magaziner and Robert B. Reich, *Minding America's Business* (New York: Harcourt Brace Jovanovich, 1982), 11-27.

55. The low regard for economic planning on the part of American policy makers is documented by Ross K. Baker in "The Bittersweet Courtship of Congressional Democrats and Industrial Policy" (Paper delivered at the Annual Meeting of the Midwest Political Science Association, Chicago, Illinois, April 10-12, 1986).

56. Norman J. Ornstein et al., eds., *Vital Statistics on Congress, 1987-1988* (Washington, D.C.: Congressional Quarterly, 1987), 170.

57. Robert Lineberry and Ira Sharkansky, *Urban Politics and Public Policy*, 3d ed. (New York: Harper & Row, 1978), 33-44.

58. "The Distributive Congress," in *Making Economic Policy in Congress*, ed. Allen Schick (Washington, D.C.: American Enterprise Institute, 1983), 257-273.

59. Theodore Lowi, "American Business, Public Policy, Case Studies, and Political Theory," *World Politics*, July 1964, 677-715.

SIX IMAGES
OF THE POLICY
PROCESS

PART II

Part II is the core of the book. It uses six "images" to illustrate the process, substance, and consequences of American public policy. The goal of these chapters is to equip readers with analytical tools with which they can examine contemporary public policies and assess the behavior of political institutions. The chapters are arranged to take the reader from those institutional settings where issue salience is low and the scope of conflict narrow—board-room politics—to those where issue salience is high and the scope of conflict broad—living room politics. It may be useful to think of a spectrum, ranging from highly private decision making by corporate elites to highly public decision making by ordinary citizens, with decision making by government officials falling somewhere in between.

Chapter 3 develops the image of board-room politics as a metaphor for important policy decisions that are largely delegated to the private sector. In some cases, the existence of a government regulatory agency conceals the fact that the industry actually regulates itself with limited government oversight. In other instances, the illusion of government oversight is replaced by the illusion of competition, which conceals the existence of powerful oligopolies. Either set of circumstances means that hidden costs are imposed on consumers and workers. Low salience and high complexity permit these costs without triggering a public outcry.

Chapter 4 introduces the image of bureaucratic politics, decision making by the bureaucrats who work in and run the government's administrative agencies, both social service and regulatory. Although government agencies exist to carry out the laws, few administrative agencies are truly responsive to the general public. Instead they are most often responsive to clientele groups or those they are supposed to regulate. Indeed, responding to the public at large is less important to most bureaucrats than adhering to standard operating procedures and deeply ingrained professional norms.

Chapter 5 develops the image of cloakroom politics as a metaphor for politics dominated by Congress, state legislatures, and city councils. Legislative politics is less predictable and more volatile than other forms of politics. At different times and in different issue areas, evidence can be seen of symbolic responsiveness and policy responsiveness. Depending upon the circumstances, one observes incrementalism, small changes generally increasing government involvement in a policy area; gridlock, the failure to reach agreement on major public problems; and innovation, meaning substantial and sweeping policy change.

Chapter 6 focuses on chief executive politics as a metaphor for decision making by presidents, governors, mayors, and their advisers. The chief executive's special strengths include crisis management and policy initiation. That is not to say that chief executives consistently make good decisions in a crisis, only that they can and do make quick decisions. Chief executives' policy initiatives frequently are responsive to majority preferences, but they can encounter stiff opposition on the road to enactment. Chief executives try to shape majority preferences when possible, relying on symbolic responsiveness to provide a protective shield when their personal values do not coincide with the apparent values of the general public.

Chapter 7 develops the image of courtroom politics or judicial policy making. Most court rulings are not policy-making actions, but responses to grievances between two parties. Judges occasionally make policy, however, and when they do, their decisions are often innovative, creative, and costly. Unlike the legislative branch, courts are political institutions capable of redistributing benefits without concealing the magnitude of the costs, capable of innovating without concealing the magnitude of change. Minorities frequently are the beneficiaries of judicial intervention, although it is worth noting that minorities may include not only women, blacks, and the handicapped, but also private corporations, criminals, and extremists.

Chapter 8 explores the image of living room politics as a metaphor for the interplay between the mass media and public opinion on highly salient and highly conflictual issues. The argument will be advanced that public opinion, when aroused, must be satisfied. The termination of U.S. involvement in Vietnam and the resignation of President Richard Nixon are events that ultimately reflected public disenchantment with the behavior of the president of the United States. Ballot initiatives and referenda in pursuit of tax reductions or restraints on nuclear power show how citizens also can motivate significant state policy changes. Although living room politics is reserved for a select number of issues, it is an extremely powerful force. Without living room politics, politicians would be less responsive to majority preferences than is currently the case.

3   Board-Room Politics

Social scientist Harold Lasswell once defined politics as "who gets what, when, and how." [1] By that definition, many private sector decisions are as political as those made by government officials. When a steel company shuts down a coke oven, the consequences for workers, their families, and the local community can be devastating. When a paper mill discharges poisonous chemicals into the atmosphere or a nearby stream, the consequences for public health may be severe. When a hospital decides to invest in expensive lifesaving equipment, such as emergency helicopters, the hospital may save many lives, but it may also raise its prices. When a business chooses to donate 5 percent of its pretax profits to charity, numerous nonprofit organizations may benefit, but the government may collect less tax money. In each of these cases, private organizations decide who gets what, when, and how.

To describe private decision making that has public consequences, the metaphor "board-room politics" will be used. Board-room politics means decisions made by private organizations, usually corporations, with limited government control. Some of these decisions are literally made in corporate board rooms; others are made at lower levels by corporate managers, subject to constraints by a board of directors. The private sector is not monolithic in its structure, norms, or purposes. There are important differences between publicly held and privately held companies, nonprofit and for-profit organizations, big corporations and small businesses, monopolies and competitive entities. Despite these differences, one fact is true of all private corporations: they have an enormous impact in the daily lives of all Americans.

Charles Lindblom wrote that the role of the private sector is vital not just in the United States but in all market-oriented societies. "Corporate executives in all private enterprise systems . . . decide a nation's industrial technology, the pattern of work organization, location of industry, market structure, resource allocation, and, of course, executive compensation and status." [2]

The role of the private sector is especially significant in the United States. The private sector accounts for 62 percent of the gross domestic product (GDP) in the United States or the sum total of all goods and services produced. In contrast, the private sector accounts for 54 percent of the GDP in the United Kingdom, 48 percent in France, and 46 percent in Italy.[3] The overwhelming majority of Americans, 82 percent, are employed by the private sector. Other Western democracies are less reliant on private employment: in the United Kingdom, 69 percent of all workers are privately employed; in Sweden, 62 percent (see Table 3-1). In the United States, many vital industries are controlled primarily or exclusively by the private sector. These include railroads, airlines, electric companies, telephone companies, oil producers, automobile manufacturers, and mail delivery companies. In Western Europe many of these industries are controlled by government.

Moreover, the private sector in the United States is growing as a result of privatization and deregulation. Privatization, the transfer of service delivery functions from the public sector to the private sector, is spreading at the state and local levels. For example, approximately 35 percent of U.S. cities contract with private companies for refuse collection.[4] In some states, this particular practice is extensive. In New Jersey more than half of the municipalities contract for refuse collection; nearly as many arrange to have road construction and maintenance and solid waste disposal provided by private companies.[5] Contracting for social services, usually with nonprofit organizations, is also widespread. Almost half of the states contract for mental health services; in some states 90 percent of mental health funds are spent this way.[6] Other social services are also provided through contracts, including employment services, child abuse centers, nursing homes, day care centers, drug abuse clinics, and half-way houses for parolees. Privatization has advanced more slowly at the federal level, despite strong support from Ronald Reagan's administration.

Deregulation, the relaxation of government standards and requirements, has proceeded much more rapidly at the federal level. During the Carter administration, Congress took steps to deregulate the airline, trucking, and financial industries. The Civil Aeronautics Board (CAB) was abolished, barriers to entry into the trucking industry were reduced, and savings and loan institutions were given greater freedom, for example, to issue credit cards and make consumer loans. Congress also deregulated the price of oil and natural gas. The Federal Communications Commission (FCC) relaxed government regulation of the broadcasting industry by eliminating limits on commercial time and by issuing licenses for longer periods of time. The FCC's role in regulating AT&T was reduced, as a result of an antitrust settlement that permits AT&T to compete with IBM and other computer companies in the lucrative data-processing market. More broadly, the Reagan administration discouraged government regulation by requiring, for example, that

Table 3-1   Public Employment in Six Western Nations

Country	Public employees/ all employees	Private employees/ all employees
France	32.6%	67.4%
Italy	24.4	75.6
Sweden	38.2	61.8
United Kingdom	31.4	68.6
United States	18.3	81.7
West Germany	25.8	74.2

Source: Richard Rose et al., *Public Employment in Western Nations* (New York: Cambridge University Press, 1985). Reprinted by permission.

administrative agencies submit cost-benefit studies to the Office of Management and Budget (OMB) before adopting major rules and regulations. This requirement is often waived when an agency proposes a deregulatory rule. In this way, the administration discouraged administrative rule making except for the purpose of reducing controls on the private sector. As a result of these trends, the power of the private sector in American politics has grown. The private sector is freer than ever to decide who gets what, when, and how.

Corporate Concerns

An agenda, whether corporate or governmental, consists of items or issues thought to warrant serious attention. The building blocks of corporate agendas differ from those of government agendas. The question that faces a private corporation is not whether to make changes in health policy or energy policy or transportation policy, but whether to focus most of its efforts on finance, management, or public relations. Within these broad categories, further choices must be made: whether to concentrate on earnings, costs, disbursements, or profit margins; or on diversification, modernization, product quality, expansion, or labor relations; or on advertising, customer relations, community relations, or government affairs. While the typical business carries on all these activities at once, the emphasis given to one area or another reveals not only the company's issue priorities but also its values.

The Bottom Line

Corporate priorities may be inferred from corporate behavior, but executives also speak for themselves. When they do so, they reveal a preoccupation with profits, the proverbial "bottom line." As *Fortune* magazine discovered in its survey of 500 chief executive officers, corporate heads think mainly about financial matters and far less about product quality, customer relations, or employee relations (see Table 3-2).[7] They also think more about higher profits than about market share, although this undoubtedly varies from corporation to corporation. It is difficult to escape the conclusion that corporate executives have their eyes on short-term, rather than long-term, goals.

To say that corporate executives care mainly about profits is not to say that they ignore other goals. Corporate agendas are not limited to a single issue, any more than legislative, judicial, or executive agendas are. But in the private sector, as in the public sector, one issue drives out another. Consider the case of U.S. Steel, now known as USX. During the 1950s and 1960s steel executives concentrated their attention on profit margins and labor relations. Instead of opting for modern techniques, such as continuous casting and basic oxygen furnaces, U.S. Steel retained open-hearth furnaces and traditional production methods that were becoming obsolete. The Japanese, setting long-term goals, made the most of new technologies. U.S. Steel's capacity to compete with the Japanese grew so poor that it decided not to manufacture steel any longer but to concentrate on oil and gas. Seventy-three percent of U.S. Steel's revenues came from steel in 1978, but that figure plummeted to 33 percent in 1985.[8] The company, once the mightiest steel company in the world and a symbol of American know-how, is now only halfheartedly committed to the steel business. The company's name change, from U.S. Steel to USX, dramatically symbolizes this shift.

Some companies neglect certain issues because they are preoccupied with other matters; other companies neglect issues because they doubt their importance or see no advantage in involvement. For example, many companies neglect the mental and physical health of their employees because they fail to perceive a connection between employee health and productivity. As union membership declined, from approximately 19 million in 1977 to about 17 million in 1987, the ability of organized labor to sensitize companies to employee concerns also diminished. Some companies neglect environmental impacts, despite laws to the contrary, because they do not wish to incur the costs of cleanup efforts. As punishment, they may pay a fine, but only if the government discovers the violation and vigorously enforces the law.

The mass media occasionally bring neglected issues to the public's attention, but the media try not to portray the communications industry in an unfavorable light. Consider, for example, the question of "cross-media ownership," the joint ownership of a newspaper and a broadcasting station in the same community. In January 1975 the FCC announced a major decision, allowing most newspaper-broadcasting

Table 3-2   *Most Important Objectives of Chief Executive*
Officers (CEOs)

Objective	Percentage of CEOs citing objectives
Improve profits, earnings	36.7
Growth	21.9
Improve returns to shareholders	11.1
Employee development	8.8
Long-term planning, strategy	6.4
Control costs, improve productivity	4.5
Improve product/service quality	3.9
Restructure company	3.9
Provide for management succession	3.7
Other	27.8

Source: Maggie McComas, "Atop the Fortune 500: A Survey of C.E.O.'s," *Fortune*, April 28, 1986, 29. Reprinted by permission.

combinations to remain intact despite concerns that cross-ownership undermines diversity in the flow of news. Many of the nation's leading newspapers failed to report this story. Those that covered it often failed to mention that their newspaper owned a local broadcasting station.[9] Clearly, some issues will remain buried when companies find it convenient to ignore them.

Agenda Determination

Corporate executives are the principal determiners of corporate agendas. As long as the company prospers, corporate managers are free to chart a course for the future. When earnings decline or a crisis erupts, board members intervene in an effort to get the company back on track. Board meetings provide opportunities for members to establish new priorities. However, the board meeting typically is the final step in a long, protracted process. Like a congressional debate, a board meeting is the culmination of a long series of discussions, of maneuvers and countermaneuvers, bargains, double crosses, and power plays. The meeting may be only a formality because the "decision" has been made. When the board of the Penn Central Railroad met on June 8, 1970, the die was already cast. In informal discussions it had already been determined that the chief executive officer, the chief operating officer, and the chief financial officer must go. Not long thereafter, the company went bankrupt.

Prior to important board meetings, managers may attempt to mobilize support to stave off a policy change or a coup d'état. An embattled

Steve Jobs, chairman of Apple computers, threw a dinner party in the spring of 1985, with an influential board member as the guest of honor.[10] Jobs, whose position was in jeopardy, hoped to persuade the board member to rally to his cause. When the board member merely picked at his whole-wheat pizza, Jobs began to see the handwriting on the wall. A Silicon Valley board member with no appetite for whole-wheat pizza is like a steel worker who turns down a beer; it does not happen unless something is fundamentally wrong.

Corporate agendas are also influenced by the policies, schemes, and strategies of their rivals. Ford Motor Company decided to offer a five-year/50,000-mile warranty, and Chrysler Corporation had to swallow its pride or up the ante. Chrysler opted for one-upmanship, offering a seven-year/70,000-mile warranty. When one company hits upon a successful marketing strategy, as the Wendy's hamburger chain did by asking "Where's the beef?" its competitors must react. Until they solve this problem by coming up with a snappy response or another scheme, marketing will be high on their agenda. Corporations also have thrown each other into a tizzy by staging take-over attempts. If unwelcome, they are referred to as "hostile" takeovers. Ted Turner proposed to take over CBS, forcing a transformation in the network's agenda. For weeks CBS was preoccupied with preventing the takeover. CBS eventually succeeded but later found it necessary to undertake a major management shake-up and massive layoffs.

Corporate agendas also may be shaped by government officials. President Lyndon Johnson issued Executive Order 11246 in 1965 and placed affirmative action on the agendas of businesses throughout the nation. Johnson's order prohibited discrimination by government contractors and established a compliance office to ensure cooperation. Because most sizable companies do some business with the government, Johnson's executive order guaranteed that affirmative action would receive serious attention in corporate board rooms across the land. By offering lucrative contracts to companies willing to design and develop new weapons systems, the Defense Department also has been successful in shaping corporate agendas and in influencing university agendas. Corporate scientists and academics throughout the United States are engaged in research on the Strategic Defense Initiative (SDI), also known as "star wars," funded by the Defense Department.

Ordinary citizens do not play a significant part in setting corporate agendas, but they have been responsible for a number of highly visible agenda-setting efforts. By mobilizing activist shareholders, concerned citizens have attempted to shape corporate agendas through proxy resolutions that address important social issues—civil rights, corporate responsibility, apartheid in South Africa.[11] One highly publicized effort was Campaign GM, organized by Ralph Nader. With the support of the Securities and Exchange Commission (SEC), Campaign GM placed two proposals before the GM board: to increase the size of the board and to create a shareholders committee. The hope was that these reforms would increase consumer influence at GM. Neither proposal was adopted; indeed, no public interest proxy proposal opposed by management ever has passed. Nevertheless, in several instances, corporate managers have made modest concessions in return for an agreement by shareholder activists to withdraw their proxy resolutions.

The Public-Private Spectrum

So far corporations have been considered as a class. There are, however, differences among corporations, and these differences, apparent in policy making, are also apparent in agenda setting. Some businesses "affected with a public interest" [12] are more vulnerable to public pressure than most; other businesses, whose stock is not publicly traded, are less vulnerable than most. In between are those corporations with which the public is most familiar—corporations whose stock is traded but which are free to set prices as they please (see Table 3-3).

Public utilities, at one end of the spectrum, are businesses affected with a public interest. These are usually natural monopolies, or companies that can supply services more efficiently if they face no competition. The rates of natural monopolies are set by government officials to keep prices at a reasonable level. Examples of natural monopolies are electric, natural gas, and telephone companies; the rates they charge customers are determined by state public utility commissions. A new industry, cable television, also was treated like a utility, with city councils setting rates, until 1984, when Congress decided that cable television companies should be allowed to set their own rates. In effect, Congress said that cable television is no longer to be treated as a public utility.

The agendas of public utilities are subject to control by government officials because government regulators have considerable influence over their revenues, allowable costs, and profit margins. Regulators decide whether to grant a utility company's rate hike request in full or in part. A "stingy" public utility commission, in effect, places revenue requirement issues on a company's agenda; a "generous" commission enables a utility company to concentrate on other issues, such as expansion or diversification.

At the other end of the public-private spectrum are privately held companies, whose stock is not publicly traded but is held by family members and/or employees. These companies have considerable discretion in what they do and when they do it. In contrast to other compa-

*Table 3-3   The Public-Private Spectrum: Degree of Government
Influence*

Very low	Fairly low	Fairly high	Very high
privately held firms and foundations (Cargill, Inc., the Ford Foundation)	publicly held firms: competitive firms and oligopolies (the funeral industry, the auto industry)	publicly held firms: monopolies (investor-owned public utilities)	government corporations (TVA, U.S. Postal Service, municipal utilities, etc.)

nies, privately held companies need not hold an annual public meeting and need not submit extensive financial data to the SEC. Even more important, they need not respond to the currents and crosscurrents of Wall Street. Privately held companies account for approximately one-half of the total employment in the United States.[13]

Foundations, which exist to dispense money to favored causes, constitute a small subset of private organizations that have extraordinary flexibility in setting their agendas. Although bequests sometimes impose constraints, foundations are usually free to set priorities and to change direction rapidly. The Ford Foundation, for example, announced in 1966 a major effort to promote equal opportunity for blacks in politics, education, employment, and housing. Over the next two decades, Ford supported civil rights litigation through grants to the Lawyers' Committee for Civil Rights under Law, the NAACP Legal Defense Fund, and other groups. Ford also supported a variety of educational and advocacy efforts aimed at improving conditions for black Americans.

Many citizen groups owe their origins to "seed money" from foundations. Political scientist Jack Walker noted that 39 percent of citizen groups formed during the postwar era received foundation grants at the time of founding.[14] Without the timely support of leading foundations, many civil rights groups and environmental groups probably would not exist; others would have vanished by now. Many conservative think tanks also depend upon foundation support. Think tanks such as the American Enterprise Institute, the Heritage Foundation, and the Reason Foundation have helped to place deregulation, privatization, and a variety of other conservative causes on the government's agenda. Through grants to nonprofit organizations, foundations also have transformed the agendas of city councils, state legislatures, and Congress.

Corporate Governance

Board-room politics is more hierarchical than cloakroom politics, more competitive than bureaucratic politics, and more volatile than courtroom politics. It is less visible than chief executive politics and living room politics but more pervasive than both. The scope of conflict—or the extent of public involvement—is relatively narrow, not because the stakes are low, but because the issues are regarded as being outside the government's jurisdiction and the public eye. As former White House chief of staff Donald Regan once put it, "Businessmen, for the most part, are not used to the glare of publicity." [15] In fact, there is a dramatic gap between the importance of board-room politics and the degree of public involvement it receives. Although board-room politics has become more visible and more controversial since the 1960s, it is still largely the province of the private sector.

Who Has the Power?

American corporations wield considerable power and enjoy substantial autonomy. Nevertheless, no corporation is an island. Public utilities operate under constraints imposed by government regulators. Publicly held corporations take the interests and demands of their stockholders into account. Even privately held companies must be somewhat sensitive to market forces. During times of upheaval, corporations find themselves responding to social movements, if only to deflect them. During times of crisis, corporations respond to appeals by political leaders that the "national interest" or the "public interest" requires their cooperation. During World War II, for example, corporations stopped producing consumer goods and mobilized to build ships, tanks, and aircraft.

Increasingly, corporations must be sensitive to the wishes and machinations of certain investors, including institutional investors and corporate "raiders." Institutional investors include banks, insurance companies, universities, and other entities with substantial stock portfolios. These institutional investors, more aware and active than ever before, wield power by threatening to sell their stock unless corporate policies change. Corporate raiders, such as Carl Icahn and T. Boone Pickens, have become powerful players. If raiders let it be known that they intend to take over, they can create waves within their targets and throughout the stock market. In addition, takeover artists have resorted to "greenmail" as part of an "unfriendly" takeover attempt: the raiding company offers to sell its stock, in a deal not offered to other stockholders, to the target company. In return for this lucrative buyout, the raider agrees to drop the hostile takeover bid. Raising cash to prevent a hostile takeover is not an easy matter, and corporations pay a price for doing so. To foil James Goldsmith's takeover attempt, Goodyear was forced to sell its energy operations. CBS had to reduce its staff because it had spent so much money fighting Ted Turner's takeover attempt.

Despite pressure from investors and public officials, corporations have considerable autonomy in the practice of American politics. Corporations have legal rights that protect them from politicians, bureaucrats, and judges. Moreover, corporate power is concentrated. A relatively small number of corporations control a relatively high percentage of certain markets. Highly concentrated industries include automobiles, tires, synthetic rubber, metal cans, organic fibers, explosives, beet sugar, flat glass, and others.[16] Moreover, power within corporations tends to be concentrated in the hands of a few individuals. These individuals include the company's chief executive officer, chief financial officer, president, and board chair.

The archetype for sociologist Max Weber's hierarchical model of organization was the government bureaucracy, but the modern corporation comes closer to his ideal type than the modern government bureaucracy. As previously noted, the bureaucracy's "chain of command" is blurred by the fact that it has multiple sovereigns. In addition, the bureaucracy's political executives must bargain with career executives; they cannot simply issue an order and wait for it to be carried out. Top corporate officials can behave more autocratically if they wish to do so. Private corporations normally operate with a clear chain of command and fixed responsibilities.

Wizards and Whales

There is no such thing as a corporate leader for all seasons because corporations differ in their dependence on sound management, creative experimentation, public favor, and government support. Some corporations require leaders who can play an "insider" game, that is, people who excel at organizational management. Others require leaders who can play an "outsider" game, that is, those who excel at public relations. If demand for a product or service is stable and a company's market share is secure, an inside game may be sufficient. A more volatile situation may require greater reliance on an outside game.

There are different types of outside games. In some instances, corporate leaders must win the support of customers; in others, they must curry the favor of government officials. Public utilities do not have to worry a great deal about marketing strategies because the demand for their product is fairly stable; but they must be mindful of their image in the regulatory community, for regulators determine what rates they may charge. In contrast, television stations, partially protected by the

First Amendment, are subject to rather light-handed government regulation, but they must constantly be concerned about their market share, because advertising revenue is directly dependent on market share or ratings.

Corporate leadership styles are highly diverse. Whitney MacMillan, chief executive officer and chairman of the board of Cargill, the largest grain company in the world, maintains a very low profile outside the company. He is, by choice, a rather mysterious figure, a sort of Wizard of Oz—one hears about his great deeds and accomplishments but seldom sees the man in the flesh. As the head of a privately held company, MacMillan is free to refuse requests for press conferences, interviews, and public apologies. Henry Hillman, president of the privately held company that bears his name, cultivates the same leadership style. In a rare interview, Hillman explained why he seldom grants interviews: "A whale is harpooned only when it spouts." [17]

Other corporate executives spout all the time. Lee Iacocca, Chrysler's chairman, personifies the corporate executive as impresario. More visible than any other corporate leader in America, Iacocca routinely takes to the airwaves with a direct message: "If you can find a better buy than Chrysler, buy it!" Iacocca's style is bold, direct, forceful, and flamboyant. In part, his style reflects Iacocca's irrepressible personality; it also reflects Chrysler's brush with bankruptcy at the beginning of the 1980s. Iacocca faced a special challenge because he had to inspire confidence in investors on Wall Street and in consumers on Main Street.

Other corporate executives, who head large publicly held companies, have found that it is useful to be respected but not necessary to be liked. David Roderick, chairman of the board of USX, would rather be perceived as a shrewd businessman than as a favorite uncle. Roderick, who has been trying to ease his company out of the steel business, combines Iacocca's high visibility with a tough, take-no-prisoners approach. This leadership style has not helped Roderick's image in steel communities facing high unemployment, but it may have boosted his image on Wall Street, where investors are often skeptical of a "bleeding heart." Roderick is no bleeder. As he said when announcing the shutdown of the Duquesne Works in Pennsylvania's Monongahela Valley: "We want to be friendly, but we're not Santa Claus." [18]

Roderick and Iacocca may represent special cases because of their companies' central importance to the American economy and because of the difficulties they faced as Japanese products made inroads into their markets. Some observers perceive a trend toward low-profile chief executive officers who resist the "cult of personality." [19] If so, the inside game will become more common as a corporate leadership strategy.

Decision Making

Within corporations many decisions are made by managers, with minimum input from boards of directors; other decisions are made by boards, despite opposition from managers. As a general rule, managers are free to make strategic decisions as long as the "bottom line" is favorable. When the corporation begins to flounder, board members intervene. In short, corporate boards are most active in times of crisis.

If boards are seldom dominant, they are nevertheless more important than they used to be. Corporate boards were once regarded as little more than "rubber stamps"; decisions were made by top managers and then simply ratified by members of the board. The role of the board, it seemed, was to legitimate management decisions and to convince investors that the corporation was in fact being guided, or at least monitored, by a distinguished panel of leading citizens.

This practice has begun to change, not dramatically perhaps, but noticeably. First, boards are much more diverse demographically. Women and minorities now sit on boards in growing numbers, which means a greater variety of viewpoints and more lively debates on topics such as affirmative action. A lone black on a corporate board may not be able to win a showdown vote, but, as most boards prefer to operate by consensus, the first response to a protest by a minority board member is likely to be a search for a compromise.

Second, boards have given greater representation to outsiders—bankers, lawyers, and others who do not work for the company. According to one estimate, about 65 percent of corporate directors are outsiders,[20] meaning that managers occupy fewer seats than before. Although many of these outsiders are handpicked by the managers, the potential for dissent is greater than it used to be.

A third trend is to place limits on interlocking directorates in which board members are selected from institutions that have official dealings with the company, such as banks, insurance companies, or law firms. The collapse of Penn Central raised questions about such interlocking directorates because a number of Penn Central board members were bankers and shippers with potential conflicts of interest. A different board might not have saved the hapless Penn Central, but a truly unbiased board might be able to head off disaster for another company in the future. A number of companies, such as J.P. Stevens, have done away with interlocking directorates.

The significance of these trends is that corporate boards, more than ever before, are in a position to voice vigorous dissent, to challenge management decisions, and to identify the corporation's best interest without regard to personal circumstances. These trends increase the potential leverage of boards over managers.

Often, however, the board chair is also the principal manager. Even in this situation it is not uncommon for boards to challenge the chair. For example, the board of Marquette Electronics, a medical electronics firm, voted five to one to remain in Milwaukee rather than to move two of its four operating divisions to Florida. The chairman of the board, Michael Cudahy, cast the sole dissenting vote.[21] Although the chairman probably had the authority to make the move anyway, he declined to do so, respecting the wishes of other board members.

Like other institutions important in American politics, corporate boards have found it useful to delegate certain tasks to committees, which then make recommendations to the full board. This practice conserves time and permits some board members to develop enough expertise to challenge managers. Corporate boards also have established audit committees, compensation committees, and nominating committees that exercise growing influence in decision making. For example, RCA's compensation committee, disenchanted with Chairman Robert Sarnoff, recommended that he receive no salary. The board agreed. Sarnoff, correctly perceiving this as an insult, promptly resigned.[22]

To understand the role of corporate boards in corporate decision making, it is useful to imagine a situation in which the U.S. president's cabinet, selected by the president, is then vested with the authority to make policy for the federal government, to fire White House aides, and ultimately to fire the president. Such an arrangement would probably encourage the president and his aides to be more mindful of cabinet opinions. Similarly, corporate boards can influence decisions without having to resort to the ultimate weapon of dismissal.

Strategies and Policies

Adaptability

If corporations are to prosper in a competitive environment, they must be able to adapt to changing circumstances and trends. The question is not whether corporations are capable of changing but whether they are capable of changing in time. A business tottering on the edge of bankruptcy is desperate enough to try something drastic; a corporation whose strategic decisions will lead to trouble in five to ten years may not perceive the need for a new approach.

The Ford Motor Company ignored the handwriting on the wall—the growing popularity of small economical foreign cars—preferring instead to continue the old, familiar pattern of large cars and large inventories. Surprised by the OPEC oil embargo of 1973-1974, Ford decided to weather the storm rather than to change course. Company executives proposed a shift to smaller cars, but Henry Ford II rejected such suggestions, dismissing small cars as "little shitboxes." [23] The company missed other golden opportunities as well; it developed a marvelous rust-proofing process in 1958 but moved very slowly to use it. Ford was familiar with the technology for front-wheel drive but was slow to pursue it. Ford had a chance to purchase Honda but declined to do so.

The basic problem at Ford was the unwillingness of top managers to take a long-term perspective. Many other companies suffer from the same affliction. Unable to demonstrate a favorable return on investment in a few years, they routinely reject proposals for risky innovations. An exception is Allen-Bradley, a Milwaukee manufacturer of industrial controls. Heavily reliant on assembly lines, Allen-Bradley introduced a new technique, computer-integrated manufacturing, which permits the manufacture of different versions of a product at mass-production speeds in lots as small as a single unit. In effect, this technique combines the advantages of assembly-line speed and customized production. According to conventional accounting principles, which stress short payback periods, this was an unwise strategic decision. At the beginning, the costs of computer-integrated manufacturing outran the profits. In the long run, however, the process is likely to establish Allen-Bradley as a world leader in industrial controls.

Corporations differ in their inclination and their ability to shift gears quickly. According to economics professors Walter Adams and James Brock, size is a factor—big companies are more conservative and more bureaucratic than small companies.[24] H. Ross Perot, who attempted to change General Motors's policies from within, would probably agree. According to him, changing GM's corporate culture was like "teaching an elephant to tap dance." [25] Frustrated, Perot turned to other pursuits.

Competition is another factor. Public utilities, which face limited competition for customers, have been notoriously slow to change. Only strong pressure from state public utility commissions in the 1970s persuaded electric utility companies to build fewer plants and redesign their rate structures to promote energy conservation. In contrast, companies that face tough competition adapt more quickly to changing circumstances.

Symbols and the Corporate Image

A positive corporate image is a tremendous asset, and a negative image a major liability. A drug company that symbolizes safety and reliability is likely to prosper; if the same company is suddenly seen as careless or dishonest, sales plummet. Clever company executives appreciate the close connection between symbols and their company's image.

They also recognize that symbols may reinforce or undermine company policy.

A corporate symbol may be a building, a press release, a charitable contribution, a logo, an advertisement, a Christmas bonus, or an appointment. When U.S. Steel changed its name to USX, the company was sending an unmistakable message to investors that a new era had begun: a steel company was becoming a diversified conglomerate. Chrysler appointed Douglas Fraser, the head of the United Auto Workers, to sit on its board of directors, extending an olive branch to workers. The intention was to encourage a new cooperative spirit in labor-management relations as Chrysler attempted to step back from the brink of bankruptcy.

There is no doubt that corporate executives care about symbols. Often, however, they fail to recognize what kind of symbol they are creating. For example, when the ill-fated Penn Central railroad was born, the red boxcars of the Pennsylvania Railroad were integrated with the green boxcars of the New York Central. Stuart Saunders of the Pennsylvania Railroad was named chairman of the board, and Alfred Perlman of the New York Central was named president. Like two jealous children, Saunders and Perlman quarreled about how many boxcars would be painted red and how many would be painted green.[26] In the meantime, the merged railroad was sinking deeper into debt. The colors came to symbolize their struggle for power and their inattentiveness to the business.

Some corporate executives have a blind spot about the impact of certain symbols on important constituencies. When General Motors announced that it was laying off 29,000 workers and then awarded fat bonuses to top executives, the company projected an image of arrogance and insensitivity. Anticipating this announcement, Perot said, "If in fact, they pay the big bonuses, it would be exactly as though the generals at Valley Forge in our revolution had decided to go out and buy new uniforms for themselves, when the troops were fighting in the snow barefooted."[27]

Another negative symbol is the "golden parachute," which became common during the early 1980s as corporate mergers swept the country. A golden parachute is a contractual clause that offers top corporate executives a generous severance payment if they are fired as part of a successful takeover. The executive simply pulls the rip cord and floats gently to the ground as the old corporation goes up in flames. The stated rationale for golden parachutes is that they discourage managerial resistance to hostile takeovers that will ultimately benefit investors. On the other hand, golden parachutes represent extraordinary selfishness in the highest ranks of leading corporations. Harvard University professor

Robert Reich said the golden parachute suggests that "the only way shareholders could trust corporate executives not to feather their nests at the shareholders' expense was to provide them a pre-feathered nest at the shareholders' expense." [28]

Two Views of Profitability

All corporations pursue higher profits, but they differ significantly in the time they set to reach their goals. A recurring question that companies face is how to balance short-term costs and long-term benefits. For example, Johnson and Johnson decided to recall Tylenol products after several people were killed by poisoned capsules in 1982. The recall and subsequent design and production of tamper-proof packaging was very costly. In the long run, however, the decision enhanced Johnson and Johnson's credibility in a market that depends on consumer confidence. After losing a hefty share of the painkiller market to its competitors, Johnson and Johnson rebounded to its previous market share within a few years.

In contrast to Johnson and Johnson is the case of the Firestone Tire and Rubber Company, whose steel-belted radial tires were prone to blowouts, tread separations, and other dangerous defects. Despite considerable evidence that the tires were hazardous, Firestone continued to manufacture and sell them to unsuspecting consumers. Pressed by the National Highway Traffic Safety Administration (NHTSA) for performance data, Firestone refused and went to court to prevent the agency from releasing to the press the results of a consumer survey. Eventually, after months of controversy, Firestone agreed to a massive recall. By that time, however, the company's reputation had been badly damaged by hundreds of accidents, at least thirty-four deaths, and a public image of greed and defiance.[29]

Most people would applaud Johnson and Johnson and condemn Firestone. Confronted by evidence that a product is unsafe, a company should act swiftly to withdraw the product or improve it. But the issue is not so clear cut. When does a product become unsafe? All automobiles are unsafe to some extent and could be made safer, for example, by installing airbags, which cushion the impact of a collision. Should companies make their products as safe as they can be? Should companies make some products safer, others cheaper, so that consumers have a choice? If so, why not allow one company to produce a relatively safe product, while another company produces a relatively cheap product? Should consumers be free to place cost above safety? And who should define safety, the companies or the government?

At a minimum, the public might insist that companies be honest about their products' virtues and vices. But does this require that they go out of their way to reveal flaws and problems? The question arose when the Federal Trade Commission (FTC) proposed that used car dealers be required to inform consumers of any known major defects of cars on their lots. The proposal did not seem particularly onerous, but used car dealers persuaded Congress to veto it. The same question also arises when health experts recommend that cigarette advertising be banned or that tobacco subsidies be eliminated. Time and again, the powerful tobacco industry has resisted policies that would discourage smoking or protect nonsmokers from the hazards of "passive" smoking.

After the Board Has Met

Implementation Problems

The implementation of corporate policies is seldom automatic. Just as governments depend on corporate cooperation to implement a policy such as environmental protection, corporations depend on government cooperation to carry out policies such as plant construction. Many businesses have been unable to expand because of antipollution laws that forbid new plants in "nonattainment" areas if a new plant would degrade air quality. Many electric utility companies have been unable to build nuclear power plants because of government disapproval either from the Nuclear Regulatory Commission (NRC) or from a state agency. A corporate policy is often the first step in a long chain of problematic events. At any rate, this is true of public utilities and publicly held industrial corporations.

The implementation of corporate policies is especially tricky in an intergovernmental setting. Pacific Gas and Electric (PG&E), a San Francisco-based utility company, needed the approval of the NRC and the California Energy Conservation Commission to build a nuclear plant. Although the approval of the NRC was assured, that of the Energy Conservation Commission was not. Citing a California statute banning new nuclear power plants in the state until a safe means of nuclear waste disposal had been found, the Energy Conservation Commission rejected PG&E's request. The decision was subsequently upheld by the U.S. Supreme Court, which ruled that state governments are free to object to nuclear plants on economic grounds, even when such objections are closely related to safety concerns.[30]

Implementation is also highly problematic in corporations characterized by high decentralization, strong professionalism, or both. When a newspaper or magazine owner leans too heavily on a reporter or editor, the journalist may resign rather than submit to censorship. When a hospital administrator instructs doctors to cut costs to improve the hospital's financial picture, doctors may cite the Hippocratic oath—and a few other oaths as well—as grounds for refusal. Multinational corporations face special challenges in implementing policies across a far-flung empire. Indeed, this was Union Carbide's defense when it tried to explain a poisonous gas leak that killed an estimated 2,000 people in Bhopal, India. According to Union Carbide headquarters, its foreign subsidiary failed to conform to company safety policies, with catastrophic results.

Despite these difficulties, there are several reasons why corporate policies are more easily implemented than bureaucratic rules and regulations. First, in the private sector it is easier to fire people who are not performing well than it is in the public sector. White-collar corporate employees may be dismissed virtually without cause. In contrast, government regulations controlling civil service employment have established procedures and appeal rights to protect employees. Second, the private sector has access to considerable financial resources that help to remove obstacles. Corporate lobbyists directly intervene in government decisions, and corporate political action committees (PACs) remind politicians that reelection is easier if corporations are on their side. Third, the private sector is gifted at public relations when mass persuasion is necessary. Indeed, the leading media experts in American politics are the advertising wizards of Madison Avenue—guns for hire, whose services are available for the right price. Corporations, like government bureaucracies, face obstacles when they propose controversial policies, but they have more power to remove such obstacles from their path.

In Search of Golden Eggs

To many politicians, corporations are geese that lay golden eggs. This observation is especially true at the state and local levels, where politicians perceive corporations as sources of jobs, taxes, economic development, and prosperity. To convince corporations to settle within their boundaries, state and local politicians offer special subsidies and tax breaks, and, if these overtures are successful, the politicians can take credit for a coup. Governor Martha Layne Collins took considerable pride in announcing that Toyota would build an assembly plant in Georgetown, Kentucky, and Governor Tommy Thompson expressed elation when computer whiz Steve Chen agreed to build supercomputers in Eau Claire, Wisconsin.

Pioneering corporations offer benefits not just to particular states and communities but to society at large. Consider, for example, Bell Laboratories, the most celebrated industrial lab in the United States. Among its many achievements, Bell Labs significantly reduced the costs of long-distance communication by developing coaxial cable transmission and microwave radio relay. In addition, Bell developed the transistor, which laid the groundwork for portable radios, space flight, and computers. From 1925 to 1975 scientists from Bell Labs acquired an astonishing 18,000 patents. [31]

Other companies also have developed technologies whose benefits extend far beyond a single community or state. For example, in 1986 IBM scientists published a paper concluding that superconductors could be made from ceramics without the costs of working at extremely low temperatures. This breakthrough, which sent ripples of excitement throughout the scientific community, holds the promise of substantially reducing the costs of generating electricity.[32]

Many communities owe their revitalization to public-spirited corporate leaders. During the 1950s the Mellon family joined forces with the Democratic "machine" to clean up the air in Pittsburgh; in addition, they spearheaded the Pittsburgh renaissance, which included the construction of picturesque skyscrapers and public parks in the city's Golden Triangle. Following a second renaissance some years later, Rand McNally hailed Pittsburgh as the most livable city in America.[33] In Minneapolis the Downtown Council, a business coalition, supported an extensive downtown revitalization program in the 1950s, including pedestrian skywalks that protect shoppers from Minnesota's harsh winters. Since then, Minneapolis has been praised for its favorable business climate, progressive government, and cultural amenities. It is no coincidence that a number of leading corporations are headquartered in Pittsburgh and Minneapolis. In general, local owners demonstrate greater community spirit than absentee owners.

Corporations demonstrate a sense of social responsibility by donating money to charity, but they differ dramatically in their generosity. Most corporations give less than 1 percent of their pretax profits to charity.[34] However, some give 5 percent, which is the maximum tax-deductible contribution allowed by the IRS. Corporate giving can become contagious in cities that foster a strong sense of community and solidarity. In the Twin Cities, for example, sixty-two companies gave 5 percent of their pretax profits to charity; another twenty-one gave 2 percent or more.[35]

Although a significant expenditure, charitable contributions pale in comparison to big ticket corporate decisions such as wage settlements, plant modernization, diversification, dividend payouts, and compliance with government regulations. Moreover, these decisions often resemble a zero-sum game in which one party's gain is another's loss. Corporations often must choose between higher profits or higher wages, expansion or environmental protection, higher dividends or a secure future for the company. The natural instinct of all corporations is to pursue higher profits, and the natural instinct of all managers is to pursue better perquisites. As a result, the most frequent beneficiaries of corporate decisions are the investors and managers. The largest beneficiaries of Chrysler's rehabilitation were managers, who enjoyed significant bonuses, and investors, whose holdings increased substantially in value as the firm recovered.[36] Employees also benefit, but they may lose their jobs in hard times; and consumers benefit, but their welfare is not high on the list of corporate priorities. As noted earlier, chief executive officers rank improvements in product or service quality much lower than improved profits and corporate growth.

Shattered Dreams

Corporate policies can have devastating consequences for workers, taxpayers, and consumers. One of the most common consequences of corporate policies is unemployment. The steel industry's policies resulted in a steep decline in its work force. In 1978 U.S. Steel had 166,800 employees; by 1984 that number had plunged to 88,753.[37] Unemployment is a bitter pill to swallow. Unemployed workers experience self-doubt, guilt, shame, depression, and despair, which often affect their physical and mental health. Alcoholism, child abuse, spouse abuse, and suicide are occasional side effects. In American society, as in many others, a person's self-image is intimately connected to his or her job. This is especially true of men, who have been taught to think of themselves as breadwinners. Moreover, unemployment almost always has serious consequences for a family's economic well-being. Even if another member of the household works, one income may not be sufficient.

The effects of unemployment are especially harsh in certain communities and certain segments of society. Small towns, long dependent on a particular industry, may have difficulty coping when a company decides to mothball a plant. Restaurants and shops may close their doors forever, and city services may decline as the city's tax revenue drops. A virtual ghost town may result. Black Americans are disproportionately affected by unemployment, and the black community suffers acutely when unemployment increases. Black teenage unemployment is alarmingly high—two black teenagers out of five are out of school and not working.[38] These conditions are breeding grounds for crime and drug abuse. A society that tolerates high unemployment pays a high price in other ways.

Unemployment need not be tragic if it is temporary and if it leads to a new, better job. In fact, society benefits from a more productive use of its human resources. Many Western countries have retraining programs that facilitate transition from one job to another. West Germany, for example, offers every adult up to two years of full-time training or retraining. A number of other countries provide vouchers that workers may use for on-the-job training wherever they wish. In contrast, job-training programs in the United States are severely limited in scope and focus. Most private job-training is geared to a particular job rather than a broader set of marketable skills. The U.S. government conducts job-training programs, but they are generally restricted to the unskilled, and there are few programs to retrain people with obsolete skills or those who wish to improve their skills. Moreover, government outlays for job training have been cut back as a result of budget constraints and disillusionment with the results of the Comprehensive Employment and Training Act (CETA). For all these reasons, the consequences of unemployment in the United States are worse than they need be.

Bankruptcy is another possible consequence of corporate policies, though it is a far less common solution to business problems than laying off employees. From a societal point of view, the occasional bankruptcy is not alarming if it is caused by changing market conditions or technological advances in related industries. But the collapse of a pivotal company can be disturbing, especially if the company is part of a complex web of other companies. Society can ill afford the bankruptcy of major companies in industries that are heavily concentrated or that are central to commerce or national security. As a result, taxpayers are often asked to mop up after a corporate disaster.

Thus, Congress agreed to bail out Chrysler, at a cost of $1.2 billion, when bankruptcy seemed imminent. The demise of Chrysler would have made a highly concentrated industry even more concentrated, and it would have devastated many communities where Chrysler plants are located. The federal government also came to the rescue following the collapse of Penn Central. To preserve a national rail service, Congress created Conrail for freight transportation and Amtrak for long-haul passenger service. Although Conrail was sold in 1987, Amtrak still is heavily subsidized by the federal government. From time to time state governments also find it necessary to rescue businesses. To keep state savings and loan associations from declaring bankruptcy, Ohio was forced to contribute as much as $120 million in state funds.[39] The cost of a bailout can be very high indeed.

Taxpayers pay in still another way for corporate mistakes. Many industries, especially defense and aerospace, are heavily subsidized by taxpayers. More than 85 percent of the National Aeronautics and Space Administration's (NASA) budget goes to contracts awarded to aerospace industries.[40] When these industries are wasteful and inefficient, the costs ultimately are borne by taxpayers. Although the government is partly to blame for awarding these contracts in the first place and for tolerating huge cost overruns, corporations bear primary responsibility.

If taxpayers pay for some corporate mistakes, consumers pay for others. Consider the case of the Dalkon Shield, an intrauterine birth control device marketed by the A. H. Robins company between 1970 and 1974. The shield was used by approximately 2 million women, and approximately 90,000 of them reported pelvic infections, sterility, or involuntary abortions. The deaths of at least twenty-one women can be traced to use of the device.[41] It is impossible to estimate the costs of this disaster in terms of shattered dreams and shattered lives. These costs are especially hard to bear when one considers evidence that Robins was aware of these dangers months before the product was marketed.

Other companies also have inflicted health disasters on consumers—sometimes wittingly, sometimes unwittingly. Eli Lilly's Oraflex, an arthritis drug, caused an estimated twenty-seven deaths in the United States alone. Ford's Pinto, with its notorious exploding gas tank, resulted in injuries and deaths. Johns Manville's asbestos brought about numerous health-related problems.

Sometimes an entire industry must shoulder the blame for policies that adversely affect consumers. In the late 1970s and early 1980s, insurance companies sharply reduced premiums and agreed to take on poor risks in order to generate revenue to invest. Their aim was to take advantage of temporarily high interest rates. When interest rates declined and numerous claims came due, insurance companies found themselves short on cash, and they again raised their rates. Motivated by greed, the insurance industry paved the way for a liability insurance crisis that makes it difficult for doctors, municipal governments, and others to secure insurance. In some communities, doctors will not deliver babies because of the high cost of malpractice insurance. Cities have closed public skating rinks and limited access to public parks because they cannot afford insurance coverage.

Redemption

Corporations do learn from their mistakes. Under new management, Ford Motor Company makes small cars and cars with front-wheel drive, and it maintains small inventories. Ford now produces the cars consumers want, in quantities that match demand, and confidence in Ford has soared. The Ford Escort is the most popular car in the world. Ford also has taken steps to rustproof its cars, so that cars with good engines need not be condemned to the scrap heap years before their time.

Electric utility companies also have learned from their mistakes, thanks in part to pressure from public utility commissions and citizen groups. After years of overbuilding, they have opted for more creative ways of meeting customer demand, relying on time-of-day rates, seasonal rates, and other rate structures that encourage energy conservation. These policies have paid off for investors. From 1972 to 1987, two-thirds of America's major electric utilities returned to investors more profits on the average with less risk than did the nation's industrial giants.[42] No longer on the ropes, the electric utilities are thriving.

If companies learn from their mistakes, they also learn from the successes of risk-taking pioneers. The "diffusion of innovations," [43] apparent in the public sector, also shows up in the private sector.

For example, newsrooms have installed cathode ray tubes for computerized editing and production, and other newsrooms have done likewise. Grocery stores have stamped bar codes onto packaged foods to reduce congestion at checkout lines. Utility companies have delegated telephone hookup and meter-reading tasks to customers, thereby cutting costs.

In more abstract terms, companies also alter management strategies in response to exhortations from academics and market analysts. U.S. corporations are scrambling to emulate Japanese corporations, with their emphasis on teamwork between management and labor. They are also attempting to move toward flexible-system production, as in the case of Allen-Bradley. Although such learning is generally good, there is a danger that corporations will respond too quickly to the latest fad. At the moment, corporations seem to be heeding Thomas Peters and Robert Waterman's admonition to stick to their knitting and concentrate on what they do best.[44] Yet this new strategy would be unnecessary if corporations had not earlier responded to another adage: hedge your bets through diversification. Perhaps the best kind of corporate learning is that which recognizes the importance of frequent experimentation. This permits corporations to move in new directions, but one step at a time.

Summary

The distinction between public policy and private policy is a cultural artifact. Most Western democracies regard industrial policy as public policy; in the United States, industrial policy is private, with some governmental supervision. Most Western democracies view rail transportation, steel production, electricity, and telecommunications as public enterprises; in the United States, these are, for the most part, private. Most Western democracies rely on the government to employ a substantial number of people and to retrain employees when necessary; in the United States, the private sector provides employment and training.

In E. E. Schattschneider's words, we have "privatized" conflict by removing certain issues from public debate.[45] The privatization of conflict limits participation in the policy-making process, but it does not limit policy effects. As a result, there is a mismatch between the importance of many private decisions, the stakes, the degree of public involvement, and the scope of conflict. Most citizens are bystanders and spectators when these critical decisions are made. Although ordinary people are not completely powerless, their ability to affect corporate decisions is quite limited.

During the 1970s the government intervened more forcefully in the private sector to promote goals such as affirmative action, environmental protection, and consumer protection, which will be discussed in the chapters that follow. It must be noted, however, that government intervention has diminished once again as a result of deregulation and privatization. At any rate, that is true of the federal government, where employment levels have stabilized and where pressure to reduce government spending is intense.

This trend leaves more decisions in the hands of corporate managers and corporate boards. The metaphor "board-room politics" is used to describe this phenomenon not because boards are more important than managers but because the major decisions are made by a relatively small group of people who are tied in some fashion to the corporation. As for the relative importance of managers and board members, the managers usually dominate the decision-making process until a crisis erupts; then the board intervenes to save the day.

In making strategic decisions, officials at publicly held corporations are influenced by investors and their perceived interests. Because investors are impatient and concerned about the bottom line, publicly held corporations tend to pursue short-term profits, even if this is not in the company's long-term best interest. Privately held corporations have greater flexibility in these matters, but even they are judged by their short-term accomplishments. As a result, strategic planning takes a back seat to producing a favorable bottom line.

This shortsightedness has resulted in some spectacular mistakes, such as the U.S. auto industry's inability to meet consumer demand for small, fuel-efficient cars until it was too late. Similarly, the U.S. steel industry failed to modernize and alter production techniques in a timely manner. Companies do learn from mistakes, but they learn slowly. In the meantime, the nation pays a heavy price for their errors.

Employees are the most obvious victims of corporate mistakes; layoffs inflict economic and psychological damage. Moreover, neither the government nor the private sector goes very far to ensure that displaced workers will land on their feet. The United States does little to cushion the blow of unemployment and to prepare workers for new jobs.

Consumers also suffer when corporations make mistakes. Despite the work of government agencies such as the Consumer Product Safety

Commission, the Food and Drug Administration, the National Highway Traffic Safety Administration, and the Occupational Safety and Health Administration, companies still produce defective automobiles, tires, birth control devices, drugs, insulating materials, and power plants. Some of this is understandable; life has its risks. Yet all too often corporations manufacture products that they know to be unsafe.

Finally, taxpayers are harmed by poor corporate judgment. A substantial percentage of government expenditures consists of subsidies to private industries, such as defense, aerospace, and agriculture. The government usually receives something in return, but widespread cost overruns suggest that taxpayers are not getting their money's worth. Taxpayers also suffer when a company goes bankrupt or when government intervention is necessary to avert bankruptcy.

The intention in evaluating board-room politics is not to be overly harsh. The government bears partial responsibility for many corporate mistakes. In appraising board-room politics, one must ask not whether it is perfect but whether it is superior or inferior to other political processes, where the scope of conflict is broader. By examining these other political processes, one will be able to make useful comparisons.

Notes

1. Harold Lasswell, *Who Gets What, When, How* (Cleveland: Meridian Books, 1958).

2. Charles E. Lindblom, *Politics and Markets* (New York: Basic Books, 1977), 171-172.

3. International Monetary Fund, *World Economic Outlook* (Washington, D.C.: International Monetary Fund, April 1985), 109.

4. E. S. Savas, *Privatization: The Key to Better Government* (Chatham, N.J.: Chatham House, 1987), 131.

5. Eagleton Institute of Politics, *Alternative Methods for Delivering Public Services in New Jersey* (New Brunswick, N.J.: Rutgers University Press, 1986), 7.

6. Mark Schlesinger et al., "Competitive Bidding and States' Purchase of Services: The Case of Mental Health Care in Massachusetts," *Journal of Policy Analysis and Management* (Winter 1986): 245-259.

7. Maggie McComas, "Atop the Fortune 500: A Survey of CEOs" *Fortune*, April 28, 1986, 26-31. The Fortune 500, compiled annually, includes the 500 publicly held U.S. industrial companies with the largest sales.

8. John Portz, "Politics, Plant Closings, and Public Policy: The Steel Valley Authority in Pittsburgh" (Paper presented at the Annual Meeting of the Midwest Political Science Association, Chicago, Illinois, April 9-11, 1987).

9. William Gormley, Jr., *The Effects of Newspaper-Television Cross Ownership on News Homogeneity* (Chapel Hill, N.C.: Institute for Research in Social Science, 1976), 51.

10. Bro Uttal, "Behind the Fall of Steve Jobs," *Fortune*, Aug. 5, 1985, 20-24.

11. Proxy resolutions are proposals introduced by shareholders and voted on by shareholders. If adopted, they become corporate policy.

12. *Munn v. Illinois*, 94 U.S. 113 (1877).

13. Lisa Mesdag, "The 50 Largest Private Industrial Companies," *Fortune*, May 31, 1982, 108-114.

14. Jack Walker, "The Origins and Maintenance of Interest Groups in America," *American Political Science Review* 77 (June 1983): 390-406.

15. Donald Regan, quoted on "McNeil-Lehrer News Hour," April 16, 1987.

16. Walter Adams, "Public Policy in a Free Enterprise Economy," in *The Structure of American Industry*, ed. Walter Adams (New York: MacMillan, 1977), 483-516.

17. Mesdag, "The 50 Largest," 114.

18. Ralph Nader and William Taylor, *The Big Boys* (New York: Pantheon Books, 1986), 58.

19. Steven Prokesch, "Remaking the American CEO," *New York Times*, Jan. 25, 1987, C1.

20. Victor Brudney, "The Independent Director—Heavenly City or Potemkin Village?" *Harvard Law Review* 95 (January 1982): 599.

21. Jack Norman, "Marquette Electronics Considered Florida Move," *Milwaukee Journal*, March 5, 1987, 1.

22. Lee Smith, "The Boardroom is Becoming a Different Scene," *Fortune*, May 8, 1978, 150-170.

23. David Halberstam, *The Reckoning* (New York: William Morrow, 1986), 462.

24. Walter Adams and James Brock, *The Bigness Complex* (New York: Pantheon Books, 1986).

25. Eric Gelman, "GM Boots Perot," *Newsweek*, Dec. 15, 1986, 56-58.

26. Joseph Daughen and Peter Binzen, *The Wreck of the Penn Central* (Boston: Little, Brown, 1971), 338-339.

27. H. Ross Perot, "Perot to Smith: GM Must Change," *Newsweek*, Dec. 15, 1986, 59-60.

28. Robert Reich, "Enterprise and Double Cross," *Washington Monthly*, January 1987, 17.

29. Arthur Louis, "Lessons from the Firestone Fracas," *Fortune*, Aug. 28, 1978, 44-48; Stuart Feldstein, "How Not to React to a Safety Controversy," *Business Week*, Nov. 6, 1978, 65.

30. *Pacific Gas & Electric Co. v. State Energy Resources Conservation and Development Commission*, 461 U.S. 190 (1983).

31. John Brooks, *Telephone* (New York: Harper & Row, 1976), 12-16.

32. Dale Russakoff, "A High-Tech, High-Stakes Race Begins," *Washington Post National Weekly Edition*, June 15, 1987, 10.

33. Two of your authors, who grew up in Pittsburgh, heartily agree. The third agrees with Frank Lloyd Wright, who, when asked what should be done about Pittsburgh, thought for a moment and replied, "Abandon it!"

34. William Ouchi, *The M-Form Society* (Reading, Mass.: Addison-Wesley Publishing, 1984), 16-31.

35. Ibid.

36. Reich, "Enterprise and Double Cross," 17.

37. Nader and Taylor, *The Big Boys*, 58.

38. Robert Reich, *The Next American Frontier* (New York: Penguin Books, 1983), 204.

39. Saundra Saperstein, "The S&L Crisis is Over, but It Won't Go Away," *Washington Post National Weekly Edition*, Sept. 2, 1985, 33-34.

40. Stuart Diamond, "NASA Wasted Billions, Federal Audits Disclose," *New York Times*, April 23, 1986, 1.

41. Robin Henig, "Behind the Shield of Deception," *Washington Post National Weekly Edition*, Dec. 2, 1985, 35.

42. "Regulators See Utilities' Return on Stock as Good-news, Bad-news Situation," *Milwaukee Journal*, March 13, 1987, C7.

43. Jack Walker, "The Diffusion of Innovations in the American States," *American Political Science Review* 63 (September 1969): 880-889.

44. Thomas Peters and Robert Waterman, *In Search of Excellence* (New York: Warner Books, 1982), 292-305.

45. E. E. Schattschneider, *The Semi-Sovereign People* (New York: Holt, Rinehart, & Winston, 1960), 1-19.

4   Bureaucratic Politics

The federal government employs 2.8 million civilians. State and local governments account for roughly 13 million additional public employees.[1] Congress, the presidency, and the courts, with their supporting coterie of staff, advisers, and patronage appointees make up about 2 percent of the federal total, and their institutional counterparts at the state and local levels claim a similarly small share of their public workforces. Therefore, most government employees work in executive branch agencies administering programs or providing services to citizens; these workers are referred to as bureaucrats. The American bureaucracy or the "administrative state" is often said to constitute a fourth branch of government.[2]

These bureaucrats work in the Internal Revenue Service (IRS) office in Philadelphia sorting tax returns, entering information into computers, and shipping computer tapes to the IRS Center in West Virginia.[3] They work for the Nuclear Regulatory Commission (NRC) as field investigators reviewing plant construction plans with engineers from the Texas Power and Light Company and negotiating agreements on contested issues having to do with power plant construction standards. They are highway patrol officers enforcing speed limit laws.

Sometimes bureaucrats have to make very controversial decisions. In 1986 the New York State commissioner for agriculture had to decide whether to allow a dairy in New Jersey to sell milk in New York City, knowing it would charge less than the five other dairies licensed to sell milk in the city. Granting a license to the New Jersey dairy would have saved consumers money, but also would have thrown the city's dairy market into turmoil.[4]

Central to the political world of bureaucratic agencies are the statutes authorizing their existence and specifying their structure, activities, and budgets. Also central are the relevant congressional committees and citizens whose lives are affected by the particular bureaucracy. Many agencies carry out policies based on broad, vague statutes. The Interstate Commerce Act, for example, gave the Interstate Commerce Commission (ICC) the mandate to regulate railroad rates to ensure that they were "reasonable and just." The Wagner Act created the National

Labor Relations Board (NLRB) and instructed it to control "unfair labor practices." [5] Even more detailed statutes, such as environmental or social service laws, give agencies significant discretion in determining how a policy will be implemented. After all, legislators cannot anticipate all the contingencies of policy implementation, and in many cases they do not even know what they want out of policies. This discretionary power is a vital component of bureaucratic politics.

The size, structure, and resources of an agency are also essential to its identity. Large staffs and budgets generally carry a certain measure of power and influence and consume the time of the legislatures that debate how agencies should be organized, to whom they should report, and how much money they should receive. The range of variation in staffing and resources is enormous (see Table 4-1). Figure 4-1 depicts the organizational structure of a typical bureaucratic agency.

Contrary to popular belief, bureaucrats do not try to be obstructionist or unpleasant. Indeed, they are very attentive to the concerns and preferences of certain individuals and groups—the occupational or categorical groups they serve, the industries they regulate, and the ideological groups with whom they share an affinity; these private sector groups are often referred to as an agency's "clientele." Bureaucrats are also attentive to congressional committees and high-ranking executive branch officials. Having and maintaining supporting coalitions both within and outside of government is often the key to agency strength and survival.

Internal forces represent another aspect of bureaucratic politics. Government agencies typically put many knowledgeable and well-trained individuals to work on highly complex problems, and these individuals soon acquire expertise and develop preferred ways of dealing with problems. Expert knowledge and standard operating procedures simplify daily decisions and help to protect an agency from outside criticism. In addition, skillful leadership within the bureaucracy is necessary because an agency's success depends in part on positive relationships with other government elites.

Issues and Bureaucrats

Agenda Content

American bureaucracies have two major functions—regulation and service delivery—and the issues of bureaucratic politics fall into these categories. Virtually every administrative agency was created either to regulate private sector industries or to provide services to citizens, including the monthly cash payments made by the Social Security Administration (SSA) and unemployment insurance programs. Many large

*Table 4-1   Outlays and Employees of Federal Departments and
Selected Agencies (1988)*

Agency	Outlays (in billions)	Full-time employees
Agriculture	$ 50.7	99,085
Commerce	2.3	41,049
Defense	311.4	1,065,347
Education	14.7	4,500
Energy	10.2	15,950
Health and Human Services	361.3	119,099
Housing and Urban Development	13.9	12,438
Interior	4.4	70,400
Justice	5.8	76,920
Labor	25.4	18,060
State	3.6	26,658
Transportation	24.6	59,868
Treasury	187.3	146,188
Veterans Administration	27.0	216,709
Small Business Administration	−0.3	4,227
Environmental Protection Agency	4.6	14,323
NASA	9.5	22,425

Source: Office of Management and Budget, *The Budget of the United States, FY 1988*
(Washington, D.C.: U.S. Government Printing Office, 1987).

agencies or departments perform both functions. The distinction between the two is obvious when one contrasts, for example, the regulation of food and drug quality with the provision of food stamps or
medical care. But, it is also obvious that all government service delivery
and cash transfer programs must also have regulatory components that
identify eligible recipients, outline procedures, and prohibit certain
actions. The distinction between regulatory and service delivery policy
is not hard and fast.

Regulatory policy occupies an important place in American history.
Federal laws passed in the late nineteenth century to regulate railroad
pricing and corporate mergers were a central part of the Populist/Pro-
gressive reaction to the arbitrary practices of big business. They represented precedent-setting government interventions into the private sector and were quite controversial. The present scope of government
regulation is enormous, encompassing advertising, agriculture, air and
water pollution, aviation safety, banking, consumer products, corporate
mergers, food and drug quality, hospitals and medical practice, nuclear
energy, radio and television, transportation, utility pricing, and many
other areas of private sector activity. And, regulation is still a controver-

Figure 4-1 The Department of Justice

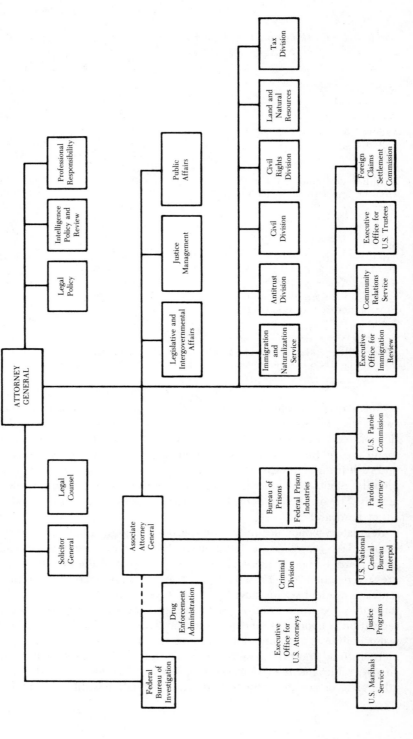

Source: *Washington Information Directory, 1988-1989* (Washington, D.C.: Congressional Quarterly, 1988), 404.

sial enterprise. Regulatory statutes provide aggrieved parties with the right to appeal agency decisions, which means that many of these issues are resolved through formal judicial procedures either within the agency or in the court system. Therefore, two characteristics of regulatory issues are their focus on the actions of private industry and their highly legalistic nature.

Service delivery issues typically involve categorical groups of citizens and public sector organizations—veterans and the Veterans Administration (VA), welfare recipients and state departments of social services, state and local governments and the U.S. Department of Housing and Urban Development. The issues are usually distributive or redistributive in nature. Should education grants received by welfare recipients be counted as income when determining future benefits? How should local in-kind contributions figure into matching-funds requirements in federal urban development programs? How should garbage pickups be scheduled in different city neighborhoods? The appeals of agency decisions on such matters are likely to be directed at legislatures or chief executives, not the courts. Service delivery issues can be contrasted with regulatory issues in that they are confined largely to the public sector and are usually resolved through political rather than legal channels.

Because regulatory policy is aimed at private sector organizations, such as businesses and unions, regulatory issues often reflect the concerns of these groups. Bankers are usually the first to react to Federal Home Loan Bank Board (FHLBB) rules, and the same is true with radio and television stations and Federal Communications Commission (FCC) decisions, meat packers and drug companies and the Food and Drug Administration (FDA), unions and the NLRB. However, the rules promulgated by regulatory agencies and the adjudicative decisions they make also stimulate questions and criticisms from many quarters. Citizen groups, legislative committees, other agencies, the media, and ordinary citizens all contribute to the ongoing chorus of commentary about regulatory actions or the need for them. Regulatory issues spring largely from this commentary.

Most service delivery issues originate in much the same way. Services are delivered, and various individuals and groups react. The commentary and subsequent bureaucratic response to it lead to the definition of problems for which solutions must be sought. Like regulatory policy, government-sponsored social service programs in the United States had a slow, halting start, but are now extensive.[6] The government provides a vast array of cash and in-kind assistance programs to the poor, the elderly, the unemployed, the disabled, the handicapped, veterans, farmers, migrant workers, and many other categories of needy individuals. (Federal human service spending for 1986 amounted to roughly

$450 billion; state and local spending in the human service category added about $340 billion to the federal total.)[7] Governments at all levels also supply traditional public services such as highway construction and maintenance, water and sewers, electrical power, police and fire protection, parks and recreational facilities, and others. The programs through which all these services are provided are subject to varying degrees of scrutiny, as are the agencies that administer them; and issues arise among those who are watching and those who are receiving.

This chorus of commentary includes bureaucratic and other government participants. Issues may arise from the observations of the investigators, monitors, and inspectors that agencies employ. Professionals within the bureaucracy are another fruitful source of policy ideas. Because their primary loyalty and orientation is to their professional discipline, they may have a nonbureaucratic perspective and a willingness to express their ideas.[8] Advisory groups, usually composed mainly of professionals with a few citizen representatives, sometimes provide a forum for the development of new ideas and issues for their agencies.[9] For state and local administrative agencies, actions taken by the federal government, such as the issuance of new standards for automobile emissions, agricultural chemicals, welfare benefits, or Medicare reimbursements, create issues.

In both areas of bureaucratic politics there are overarching issues that must be resolved either by the chief executive or the legislature. For example, the question of whether certain longstanding areas of regulation should be deregulated, or whether basic approaches to regulation should be changed are not decided by the regulatory agencies themselves. Action on these basic questions comes from the larger political arena. Administrative officials are very much aware that such issues exist, and they may contribute to their resolution by offering advice on policy options, but the major decisions are made by elected officials or, in some cases, judges.

Shaping Agendas

Administrative agencies have an almost instinctual reaction to issues that are raised about their performance, and that is to try to define them in nonthreatening ways and to process them through established channels. If welfare rights advocates are complaining about bureaucratic insensitivity, contradictory and self-defeating regulations, and meager social welfare budgets, the likely response from federal or state agencies would be to define the issues in very specific terms. Should case loads be decreased by a certain percentage? Should day care allowances be increased to $75 from $50 per week? In the regulatory realm, complaints about testing requirements for chemical pesticides, for example, would be whittled down to very specific questions about the number and kinds of tests that have to be completed, the time allowed for test results to show up, and the physical and procedural safeguards that should accompany the use of the chemicals. These are the kinds of questions and issues bureaucratic agencies can deal with effectively. Broad questions about fairness, equity, sensitivity, and the like are usually matters of statutory law and, therefore, have to be decided by legislative and executive authorities.

As issues are defined and selected by administrative agencies, bureaucratic and political considerations come into play. Bryan Jones and several colleagues at Wayne State University conducted a detailed study of three agencies, the Sanitation Department, the Division of Environmental Enforcement, and the Department of Parks and Recreation, in Detroit in the early 1970s. They attempted to determine the extent to which political—trying to keep the neighborhoods and groups happy—rather than bureaucratic criteria—providing services in accordance with standards of efficiency—affected the distribution of services in the city.[10] Overall, they found that professional and bureaucratic criteria dominated, but that political considerations ran a close second.

Agendas set by federal bureaucracies reflect and change with the politics of the administration. One can look at the Civil Rights Division of the Justice Department for instruction. During the Carter administration the Justice Department actively pursued affirmative action by arguing on behalf of numerical hiring goals for blacks, women, and Hispanics in cases involving public agencies, most notably police and fire departments, that were being sued for discrimination. The department's position on affirmative action changed dramatically under the Reagan administration. Justice began entering employment discrimination cases on the other side, arguing against numerical systems that earlier federal efforts had established. In cities like Detroit, Indianapolis, and New Orleans affirmative action plans for police and fire departments, which local officials had finally accepted after years of resistance and many rounds of negotiation with federal officials, were challenged by the Justice Department.[11]

The argument put forth here is that the agenda of bureaucratic politics is determined by the interaction of the major "process streams"—problem identification, the formation of policy proposals, and politics—that run through government.[12] Problems are being identified all the time by individuals and groups affected by bureaucratic actions, by legislators, by the media, by agency personnel, and by other levels of government. Problems for which politically and bureaucratically acceptable solutions are available receive attention, and the rest are ignored. Agendas change when these major process streams, particularly the political, change. Long lists of identified problems and potential solutions for them are continually circulating around legislative, bureaucratic, and academic communities; those that dominate the agendas of bureaucracies at any given time tend to fit best with the prevailing political climate.[13] Because the chief executive is the most powerful agenda setter, an agency like the Office of Management and Budget (OMB), which performs the central clearinghouse and oversight functions for the president, plays a major role in determining what fits or does not fit with the administration's politics. Internal bureaucratic forces, such as standard procedures, expertise, and control of information, can offer considerable resistance to changing political winds, but they cannot shield an agency's agenda from the effects of political forces generated at the top.

Politics and the Bureaucracy

The preceding discussion demonstrates that two commonly held beliefs about bureaucracy—that bureaucrats do not make policy and that bureaucrats are not involved in politics—are no longer acceptable.[14] It seems likely that most people recognize a certain political element in bureaucratic behavior, but bureaucratic politics are not easily understood because they are usually obscured from public view. An investigation of the politics of policy making in the administrative state reveals typical political behavior: individuals and groups struggling for power over policy; consultation, bargaining, and sometimes subterfuge as means of resolving conflict; larger forces and events structuring, but not completely determining the outcomes of political competition (individuals *can* make a difference).

Power

Power in the world of bureaucratic politics comes in a variety of forms. Career bureaucrats, especially professionals and administrators, have power because of what they know and what they do. Their expertise is based in part on access to and control over specialized information that their organizational superiors may not be able to process on their own.[15] Engineers for the Army Corps of Engineers or the National Aeronautics and Space Administration (NASA), for example, help to shape the practices and policies of those agencies with their specialized training and knowledge. The same is true, but to a lesser extent, of program analysts and managers in departments such as Labor or Health and Human Services. Clearly, the rarer the expertise, the greater the power that goes with it.[16]

In addition to power based on expertise there is power conferred by authority. The officials who are placed at the top of bureaucratic hierarchies have a certain amount of formal authority to impose their will on an agency or department. Independent regulatory commissioners have the authority, as specified by Congress, to promulgate rules and adjudicate cases involving the industry practices they regulate. Secretaries of state, attorneys general, and local fire chiefs have a great deal of formal authority over the procedures and policies of their organizations. However, this power is not always as straightforward as it might first appear. There are many areas of overlapping jurisdiction and numerous conflicting claims to authority within the administrative state. This is especially true in the intergovernmental arena, where local, state, and federal agencies frequently compete for power over policy.

A third kind of bureaucratic power comes from outside political alliances, affiliations, and connections. Strong agencies usually have strong constituencies, the client groups they serve or other groups that identify with the agency. Reciprocal relationships between bureaucratic organizations and outside interest groups, in which the groups try to protect the agency from hostile citizens or elected officials in exchange for favorable policies, are common at all levels of government. Notable examples include veterans' groups and the VA and farmers' organizations and the U.S. Department of Agriculture (USDA). How a policy option affects client groups is a very important consideration in agency policy making, a consideration that can both guide and constrain action. However, courting interest groups is not as easy as it once was; the number of groups an agency must be concerned about has proliferated, and they often strongly disagree about policy.[17] For example, the Environmental Protection Agency (EPA) tries to keep environmental groups satisfied without alienating business groups.

Power Struggles

Policy making is a continuous enterprise in most bureaucracies. Line bureaucrats, those in direct contact with clients and problems, investigators, and policy analysts supply a steady stream of policy ideas to legislative staffs for drafting into agency regulations or statutory language. These policy proposals move up through the organizational hierarchy, and high-level officials either accept them or reject them.[18] Top administrators play a pivotal role in the bureaucratic policy-making process because they stand between agency personnel and the central administration and have alliances on both sides. They try to satisfy politicians and career staff by making sure the careerists see some of their ideas put into practice while preventing conflicts with chief executive preferences. Central administrative units—budget and policy offices—are now used by nearly all chief executives to review agency regulations and legislative proposals before they go to the legislature, as a further check on policy entrepreneurs or renegades within the bureaucracy.

The most common form of power struggle within an agency occurs between the careerists who have standard routines, turf, and interests to preserve and protect and agency heads with partisan or ideological agendas they seek to promote. Normally, outright conflict is avoided through "mutual accommodation." [19] Agency heads often have considerable substantive knowledge of the policy issues they confront and experience with the organization they direct, and they try, for the most part, not to threaten bureaucratic values. On the other side, careerists are accustomed to seeing leaders come and go—the average term of office for top-ranking bureaucratic officials is twenty-two months[20]—and are willing to make certain concessions to appease the leadership of the moment.[21]

When internal bargaining and accommodation procedures break down, which occurs most often when a markedly new policy direction is being imposed from above, bureaucratic conflict ensues. This situation is generally unpleasant; conflicts attract outsiders—interest groups, the media, legislators, and chief executives—and their entry fundamentally changes a bureaucratic political struggle. The power, influence, and authority of these outsiders usually overwhelms the bureaucratic combatants and shifts the dispute into the larger political arena. An occasion of this sort represents a failure of administrative politics. In this larger arena almost anything can happen; indeed, it is likely that unusual actions will take place: firings, resignations, or dramatic policy changes or reversals. Shifting policy disagreements to this level is very risky, yet it is sometimes seen as necessary by threatened bureaucratic actors.

A typical scenario for bureaucratic conflict occurs when careerists work through interest groups, legislative committees, and/or the courts to bring to light unwelcome actions or policies of agency heads. A well-publicized example is the controversy over the EPA during Ronald Reagan's first term. Reagan appointed Anne Gorsuch (later Burford) to head the agency, and she and her top staff, who had little knowledge of or experience with agency procedures or practices, began making major changes—new regulations and personnel and budget alterations. Before long, congressional committees, at the prodding of environmental groups and veteran agency employees, began looking into EPA activities. They discovered what appeared to be overt attempts to circumvent environmental statutes.[22] Several resignations resulted, including Burford's, and the president replaced the agency's leadership with a group of experienced EPA administrators headed by William Ruckelshaus.

The discovery of illegalities and improprieties was a major factor in the shake-up at EPA. Rita Lavelle, an EPA official, was convicted of perjury and sentenced to jail for lying to Congress about her role in settling a hazardous waste suit involving her former employer. Bureaucratic fraud, waste, and abuse are salient items in the political world, and they are often what enable outsiders, usually with some inside help, to succeed when they attack an agency.

The normal state of a bureaucratic agency is low visibility politics, unchallenged authority over a certain policy and program domain, and support from outside groups and legislative committees. Under these circumstances, internal administrative norms, tempered by statutes and the policy preferences of agency heads, determine policy. Bureaucratic conflict disrupts normal procedures and relationships. When an agency's authority to make certain decisions is challenged, control can be lost to outside institutions—the legislature, chief executive, or the court. This situation is obviously something agencies try to avoid.

Leadership

Leadership in bureaucratic politics consists of strategies and tactics for gaining and maintaining a powerful and autonomous role for bureaucratic actors in the policy process. Bureaucratic officials exercise influence over a certain realm of policy in large part because they are able to use organizational tools to mask the extent of their power. Plainly, certain administrative officials are more successful in this endeavor than others. Robert Moses, who planned and saw through to completion much of New York City's present infrastructure of highways, bridges, tunnels, and parks, was a strong leader. Another was Admiral Hyman Rickover, who, despite the misgivings of most other Navy leaders, led the Navy into the nuclear era by showing that nuclear reactors could be designed to run submarines. J. Edgar Hoover, who built the Federal Bureau of Investigation (FBI) in his image and became powerful enough to challenge presidents, was a leader of almost mythic strength.[23] Analyses of the careers of these and other bureaucratic leaders suggest that leadership in the administrative state revolves around three basic ingredients: motivation, context, and personal ability.

Anthony Downs describes five bureaucratic types based on differences in motivation. There are climbers, who are interested only in power, money, and prestige; conservers, who seek "convenience and security" above all else; zealots, who vigorously promote certain ideas and policies and seek power to advance these ideas; advocates, who promote somewhat broader organizational interests and policies and seek power as a way of advancing or elevating their organizational functions; and statesmen, who promote the public interest, and seek power to steer government in a direction that is advantageous to the society as a whole.[24]

The kind of bureaucratic leadership that emerges depends on the political context an agency faces. Young agencies, for example, usually need advocates, and maybe a few zealots, to establish a reputation and power base in policy-making circles. Sargent Shriver's vigorous promotion of the Peace Corps in the early 1960s is cited as a classic example of effective advocacy on behalf of a fledgling agency. Rickover was essentially a nuclear power zealot, and he fought to establish his own organizational domain within the Navy's Bureau of Ships to get his projects under way.

Advocates, but also conservers, can be effective defenders of agencies during periods of budget stringency, a time when more statesmanlike behavior might result in dramatic agency losses. Zealots come to the fore when functional crises hit, when dams break, power plants fail, satellites explode, or reserve stockpiles overflow, because such circumstances place a premium on ideas and people who are sure of their ideas. Robert Moses, Rickover, and Hoover were always sure of their ideas, and they rose to prominence during crises, the Great Depression, World War II, and the cold war.

Many effective bureaucratic leaders are entrepreneurs who extend their organizational domain and become more powerful. Moses used his base as president of the Long Island State Park Commission and chairman of the New York State Council of Parks during the early 1920s to become the head of more than ten city, state, and metropolitan commissions and authorities at the peak of his career in the late 1950s.[25] Entrepreneurs like Moses exhibit the characteristics of advocates and climbers; they aggressively promote their organization and themselves. However, bureaucratic imperialism is not always possible or even desirable. When the climate of opinion, elite and public, toward an agency is unfavorable, bureaucratic leaders often try to consolidate rather than extend their authority.[26]

The need for statesmanlike leadership is most evident in mature administrative organizations and during times of national crisis, when it is important to offset the myopic inclinations of advocates and conservers. Hoover was discredited in part because his zealous leadership was no longer appropriate in a mature and established FBI. One of the most serious problems in the administrative state is not having a leadership that is flexible enough to adapt to changing political environments, and one of the major impediments to flexible leadership is that the most consistently rewarded bureaucratic motives—those of advocates, zealots, and conservers—are not particularly conducive to flexible leadership.

Effective administrative leadership also requires individual ability. Studies of bureaucratic organizations have identified a consistent set of attributes, behavioral patterns, and outlooks associated with successful leaders. Leadership in administrative politics demands intelligence, especially the ability to acquire substantive knowledge and to use organizational processes; the will to achieve or succeed; highly developed interpersonal skills; the willingness and ability to listen and learn from others; and the inclination to enjoy organizational and political work and the exercise of power.[27] Leaders are quick to identify the wielders of power and know how to deal with them in various situations. They are capable of thinking in unusual ways, of solving difficult problems, and of resolving internal conflicts. They appreciate the normative and symbolic aspects of their decisions and actions and take seriously their role as teachers and promoters of esprit de corps. They must also know how to make effective use of the media when circumstances require it or when opportunities present themselves. Hoover was a pioneer in this area.

How Bureaucracies Decide

The literature on political and organizational decision making is emphatic about the tendency of public bureaucracies to make only marginal changes in existing policies in any given round of decision making, a practice known as incrementalism.[28] Administrative decision makers rarely consider problems in their entirety. They restrict themselves to a specialized slice of the problem, react to feedback about the success or failure of current policy by considering a limited number of alternative approaches, and choose options that seem to satisfy all or most of the major interests in their political environment.[29] Past policy decisions serve as the highly valued base for subsequent decisions precisely because of their political character—they represent the best compromise decision makers could devise in the past, and, in the absence of overwhelming evidence to the contrary, there is no reason to believe that the problems or the attendant politics have changed enough to require a radically new approach.

Incremental decision making is in many ways a result of bureaucratic inertia, the adherence to standard operating procedures and/or professional norms, and internal support for longstanding policies, which has a powerful conservative effect on administrative decisions.[30] The specialized knowledge and information that exists in the middle and lower levels of the bureaucracy is often effectively used to protect internal interests. From his study of information transmission in the military, Morton Halperin identified eleven different ways information can be packaged to influence decisions.[31] Some of them are: report only those facts that support the stand you are taking; structure the reporting so that senior participants will see what you want them to see and not other information; request a study from those who will give you the desired conclusions; advise other participants on what to say; direct the facts if necessary and if you can get away with it.[32] Michael Lipsky's study of police and other "street-level" bureaucratic behavior notes that police often exaggerate the danger connected with their jobs to reduce the likelihood that superiors will impose sanctions on those who take certain "threat-reducing" actions, in other words, tough treatment of suspected criminals.[33]

The link between bureaucratic politics and incrementalism does not entirely eliminate the importance of rational or analytic factors in bureaucratic decision making. The so-called "rational" model of decision making would have administrators look at problems comprehensively and employ certain analytic techniques to evaluate policy options with precision. Rational decision making can be distinguished from incremental/political decision making in that a wider range of alternatives for achieving policy objectives can be considered—nonincremental options are not ruled out automatically—and because decision makers search for solutions that provide the most benefits at the lowest cost rather than for solutions that satisfy as many interests as possible.[34] Rational decision makers use techniques like cost-benefit analysis in identifying the best solutions to policy problems.

The Army Corps of Engineers was probably the first government agency to make consistent use of cost-benefit analysis in determining the best water projects to undertake and in justifying the projects to Congress. For example, a proposal to build a dam on a particular river to create a lake would be evaluated by listing all the costs and benefits of the project and then attaching dollar values to them. The costs would include items such as the value of the land that would be flooded, the cost of relocating families whose homes would be destroyed, the value of lost recreational opportunities, and the cost of construction. The benefits would include new hydroelectric power, irrigation water for farmers, new recreational opportunities, and reduced damage from floods.[35]

Market prices commonly are used in assigning dollar amounts to costs and benefits. Where no market values apply, as with questions regarding the preservation of natural habitats or the psychological and social turmoil associated with destroying communities, imagination and creativity must be put to use. The basic rule is that projects whose benefits are larger than their costs should be pursued, and future costs and benefits have to be discounted to their present value to make this determination. When there are many potential projects from which to choose and a limited amount of money that can be spent, as is the case in any real-world setting, the projects offering the largest net benefits, often expressed by benefit-to-cost ratios, are preferred.[36] As this brief sketch of cost-benefit analysis illustrates, the technique provides decision makers with fairly clear-cut choices. But many assumptions—that market prices accurately reflect the social value of different outcomes, for example—and a good deal of guesswork, especially in projecting future costs and benefits, go into the final calculations.

The problem with rational approaches to decision making is that most administrators find them difficult to use because of the cognitive demands they impose, such as evaluating long lists of alternatives and sorting through highly technical analyses, and economic pressure caused by the amount of staff time needed to complete all the analytic chores. Moreover, the rational approaches are often politically irrelevant— legislators are usually more interested in how popular programs are with constituents than in their cost-benefit ratios. However, because rational/analytic decision-making processes do not necessarily give preference to existing policies, and are therefore capable of producing nonincremental results, they have gained a certain political appeal among those who seek to make dramatic changes in administrative policy and practices. Jimmy Carter tried to make executive agencies more efficient by insisting that they employ a new, nonincremental budgeting procedure known as zero-based budgeting, and Ronald Reagan pursued regulatory reform by creating a White House unit that subjected all new regulations proposed by executive agencies to cost-benefit tests.[37]

Overall, the influence that analytic procedures have on administrative decisions varies according to the nature of the problem and the dispositions of decision makers. Highly technical matters invite analytic solutions, but most of the questions administrators confront are too political to be answered wholly, or even primarily, by analysis. Among bureaucratic officials there are many who dislike and distrust analysis, but a growing number are comfortable with it.[38] Many see mastery of policy planning and analytic activities as a path to greater power and influence in decision-making circles because analysis has become an accepted part of the process through which most organizational decisions are made. Unless the interests associated with policy decisions have numbers to back up their views, they operate at a disadvantage.

Rules and Regulations

Bureaucratic policies come in a number of different forms. First, there are written rules and regulations that have wide applicability and carry the force of law. Second, there are adjudicatory decisions that settle, through court-like procedures, disputes between antagonistic parties, usually an agency and a business accused of violating an administrative rule or regulation. Third, there are guidelines, policy statements, and advisory opinions that convey to interested parties an agency's thinking or intentions about various matters, but do not have the full legal force of formal rules and regulations. Fourth, there are informal means of settling disputes that do not entail full adjudication. Finally, there are the actions that line bureaucrats take that define the meaning of regulatory or service-delivery policy in practice.

Administrative agencies have developed a mountain of rules and regulations that specify the meaning of legislative statutes. These are published in the *Federal Register* and the *Code of Federal Regulations* and in comparable documents in the states and localities. The adoption of such rules and regulations at the federal level takes place in accordance with procedures spelled out in the Administrative Procedure Act (APA), and similar statutes exist in most states. When an agency wants to develop rules to enforce provisions of statutes, which Congress has authorized them to do, the APA requires (1) that a public notice, carried in the *Federal Register,* be given specifying the time, place, and nature of the rule-making proceedings; (2) that interested parties be given the opportunity to submit written, and in some cases oral, arguments and facts relevant to the rule; and (3) that the statutory basis and purpose of the rule be indicated. After rules are promulgated, thirty days' notice is required before they take effect.[39] These procedures, known as informal rule-making, are designed to give everyone a chance to participate in this essentially legislative activity.

APA rule-making procedures can be much more formal and cumbersome when a statute requires rule making "on the record after a formal hearing." Under such circumstances agencies must conduct proceedings that resemble trials; witnesses present testimony and submit data or other evidence, there are opportunities for cross-examination of witnesses, and interested parties are prohibited from contacting agency officials during the proceedings. After the hearings, time is set aside for further evidence to be submitted, and agency officials must go over the entire record and carefully document their reasons for issuing a rule. Such hearings often last for weeks or even months. Although agencies are seldom enthusiastic about this degree of formality, they may use this procedure even when they are not required by statute to do so. They do this to blunt criticism of the rules and to bolster their position with the courts, which see adherence to formal procedures as one of the justifications for allowing agencies to exercise rule-making power. Reliance on rules and formal rule-making procedures by agencies increased during the 1970s and 1980s.

Administrative adjudication has a narrower focus than rule making. When there is a disagreement between a company and a union about labor standards, or between the Social Security Administration and a recipient about eligibility for certain benefits, or between a utility company and the NRC about a plant safety issue, a settlement can be reached through adjudication. The procedures are similar to those in a court of law—formal notifications to appear are given to all parties, public records are kept, only certain kinds of evidence are admissible, and each party gets a chance to cross-examine adverse witnesses.[40]

To conduct these proceedings, the bureaucracy employs specially trained personnel, called administrative law judges, who bring with them impartiality and legal and substantive knowledge.[41] The judges apply administrative law to the particular case and either issue "orders" or, in other words, make a decision, or submit recommendations for a decision to commissioners or chief administrators. In virtually every case, appeals to federal courts are guaranteed. Adjudicated decisions provide a clear guide about agency policies within the confines of the issues raised in particular cases, but, unlike rules and regulations, they do not establish policy that can be applied with confidence to similar cases.

Bureaucratic agencies also make policy statements and issue advisory opinions (courts refrain from issuing these), but these pronouncements, usually made informally, are not as authoritative as rules and regulations. Statements and advisory opinions enable agencies to tell individuals or companies how the agency intends to react to certain actions or conditions, or what an agency's operating policy is, with the understanding that such statements do not bind the agency and are subject to full review by the courts, which regard such guidelines as less deserving of deference than formal rules or adjudicatory decisions. An example of a policy statement is the 1974 Federal Power Commission statement about the priorities it would use in curtailing natural gas delivery in a time of shortage.[42] Businesses of all sorts seek advisory opinions from agencies like the Federal Trade Commission (FTC), the Securities and Exchange Commission (SEC), the Labor Department, or the EPA on matters ranging from whether certain employees are subject to provisions of the Fair Labor Standards Act to whether certain air pollution devices will satisfy Clean Air Act requirements.

Advisory opinions often are issued to head off litigation. In fact, most of the disputes about policy enforcement that could lead to litigation or to formal adjudication are resolved through informal agreements between agency personnel and the other parties involved—the Labor Department and a company agree that an outside arbiter should meet with its employees to discuss their grievances or a utility company promises the NRC that it will make certain changes in plant safety procedures. These informal agreements are another attempt to cope with reality because agencies cannot possibly use formal adjudication to resolve all the disagreements they encounter about matters of fact and policy application.

The day-to-day actions taken by bureaucratic officials in their efforts to administer statutory law represent a final large piece of the policy picture. As incredible as it may seem, the thousands and thousands of pages of administrative rules and regulations still leave many real-life situations ambiguous, and on-the-spot bureaucratic discretion is needed. Street-level bureaucrats, such as policemen and welfare case workers, are continually faced with the need to make judgments in ambiguous situations—when to make arrests for certain crimes and when not to, when to insist upon or waive certain evidentiary requirements for benefits or special assistance.[43] Although the use of such discretion may seem inevitable, many argue that the police and others who engage in selective enforcement should establish more rules and follow them in more situations.[44] Policy that is determined through direct action or informal agreement tends to be unsystematic, inconsistent, and variable; but there are limits to what can be specified and, in certain circumstances, advantages for the agency and its clients in acting informally.

Symbolism

At first glance bureaucratic politics would not seem to provide fertile ground for symbolism. After all, it is the bureaucracy that has to translate the often ambiguous and symbolic statutes enacted by legislatures into concrete rules and activities. Bureaucrats cannot fudge the details; they have to make decisions about who gets what, where, and how. When an individual is granted public assistance or a firm is fined for polluting a river, that means the administrative state has acted in a tangible, substantive manner. Rules, regulations, and adjudicative decisions allocate benefits, specify administrative procedures, and prescribe certain public or private sector behaviors; none of these would seem to be a symbolic exercise. Furthermore, most administrative officials do not conceive of their activity as symbolic. They see themselves as executing the will of the legislature—defining problems, designing solutions, and evaluating the effectiveness of past actions.

However, a number of scholars who have written about bureaucracy have emphasized its symbolic aspects. At one extreme, some argue that the administrative state exists largely to carry out symbolic functions.[45] Regulatory policy is said to provide reassurance to the citizens that certain decisions, transportation and utility pricing, for example, are being made with an eye toward their interests, even though the results of the decisions may not benefit them. Regulatory policy also serves notice to elite interests, the regulated industries, that punitive steps may be taken if they engage in excessively selfish behavior, even though such steps rarely are taken. For social welfare agencies the symbolism argument is that their administrative policies are designed to indicate to the lower classes that they are not entitled to government assistance, even though many of them are, while suggesting to the middle class that assistance is available to anyone who really needs it, even though it is not, and finally to reassure the upper classes that traditional values of individualism and self-reliance are not being abandoned.[46] The thrust of such arguments is that administrative policies, either purposefully or unwittingly, are designed not to solve problems, but to appease and/or legitimate certain interests and to provide an institutional forum in which recognized interests can compete for influence over policy.

One can find symbolism in other administrative behaviors. Federal and state commissions may hold hearings to gather citizen input or to grant agenda status to issues raised by grass-roots groups, but then continue to formulate policies in accordance with bureaucratic or industry preferences, thereby revealing the purely symbolic nature of their public actions.[47] Highway patrol officers send a symbolic message when they allow motorists to exceed the speed limit by ten miles per hour. Inspectors of restaurants, nursing homes, or even nuclear power plants also send symbolic messages if they routinely ignore certain "minor" violations. Whether bureaucratic officials recognize it in their actions, symbolism is an unavoidable aspect of policy implementation and enforcement.

Change

Bureaucracies depend on continuity. Most agencies prefer to build up a solid base of effective policies and then work carefully and patiently to extend that base as they confront new problems. This way of working is the incrementalism described in the previous section. However, administrative agencies are capable of change and innovation, and this observation applies not only to young agencies, where one might expect some novelty, but also to older, established agencies. Politics, not incrementalism, is the constant in bureaucratic life. When political developments convince bureaucratic leaders that change and innovation are necessary, they can bring them about.

During the 1970s significant changes took place in administrative policies, especially in regulation. These changes can be traced to the growing consumer and environmental movements that brought together previously unorganized interests to exert pressure at all levels of government.[48] Regulatory agencies and policies, which were notorious for favoring the industries being regulated, were a primary target for consumer and environmental groups. Over time these reformers were able to achieve an impressive number of victories over regulatory dragons. Ralph Nader's breakthroughs on automobile safety regulations helped to pave the way for many other reform efforts.[49] State public utility commissions all over the country began eliminating reduced rates for high volume industrial users after citizen groups armed with the analyses of economists argued convincingly that such pricing schemes discouraged conservation, caused unnecessary strain on generating facilities, and penalized homeowners and the poor. The solutions they proposed—peak-load and marginal cost pricing and lifeline rates—were widely adopted.[50] New leadership and supportive political environments also led to the reinvigoration of the FTC as a protector of consumers in the early 1970s and even to a major change to a more environmentally sensitive philosophy within the Army Corps of Engineers.[51] New forces were pushing their way into the political environments of government agencies and stimulating policy change.

Because not all of the changes sought by reform groups become policy, it is important to identify the circumstances that favor change in administrative policies. Political strength is one factor; consumer and environmental groups were solidly grounded in the middle class, and some of the issues they raised had widespread appeal. Movements with this kind of constituency base can strike effectively where politicians feel it most—at the voting booth. Many elected officials at the local, state, and national levels quickly became sympathetic to some of the demands coming from consumer and environmental groups.

Elected officials appoint bureaucratic officials, so the changes in the political landscape during the 1970s soon had effects inside the bureaucracy as consumerists and environmentalists went to work at a growing number of agencies. William Gormley's study of public utility commissions emphasized the role of agency staffs and what he called "proxy advocates" in bringing about changes in utility pricing policies.[52] Proxy advocates are public officials, such as attorneys general, and consumer councils who work on behalf of the citizenry across a range of policies and decision-making settings. Gormley found that the combination of a sympathetic and knowledgeable staff and a dedicated proxy advocacy effort was a potent source of policy innovation and change.

It is also necessary to consider the distributional effects of policy changes. In most of the cases mentioned above earlier policies provided substantial benefits to a few (industry) with the cost being thinly distributed among the many. When the many became organized and began to feel strongly about the benefits to be gained from policy change, they found many elected officials who sympathized with their arguments for policy change. Where the advantages of policy change are less obvious from a political standpoint, in a situation in which costs and benefits are borne by antagonistic groups of similar size and strength, one would not expect politicians to be inclined to make policy changes.[53]

Finally, political developments influence policy. The energy crisis in the 1970s made conservation a popular, compelling cause, and environmentalists used it to great advantage, especially in areas such as utility pricing and natural resource policy. The near meltdown at Three Mile Island, which shook up the NRC, led to major changes in policy and outlook among nuclear power regulators.

Change and innovation are sometimes short-lived. The recent history of the FTC is instructive. As was mentioned, the FTC was an important part of the proconsumer shift in federal policy during the 1970s. With a supportive Senate Commerce Committee headed by Warren Magnuson, D-Wash., in the early 1970s, new personnel, strong statutory backing, and, after Carter's election, Michael Pertschuk, a forceful consumer advocate as its chairman, the FTC set out to make capitalism fair and safe for the American people. Between 1976 and 1980 it took on the American Bar Association, the insurance industry, the sponsors of children's advertising on television, used car dealers, and funeral home directors, but it lost as many of these battles as it won. Congress voided a number of the FTC's major rulings and imposed a host of restrictions on it beginning in 1977. Sentiment in the House and Senate Commerce committees had shifted noticeably back toward industry, and the FTC fought an uphill battle for change until Pertschuk was replaced by James Miller, a Reagan conservative.[54]

Winners and Losers

It is commonly alleged that regulatory policies primarily benefit the regulated industries, and that social service policies primarily benefit the bureaucrats who administer them. These rather cynical observations can serve as a useful starting point for a discussion of who benefits from administrative politics.

In the regulatory realm the so-called "capture" theory is often put forward.[55] The basic argument is that over time regulated industries come to dominate regulatory agencies. This capture takes place because after the fervor for reform, usually stimulated by callous industry behavior, has resulted in the creation of a regulatory entity, it quickly becomes apparent that the expertise, interest, and dependable political support the regulatory agency needs to sustain itself resides mainly in the regulated industry. As time passes a symbiotic relationship—the movement of personnel back and forth and shared interest in each other's priorities and policies—develops between the two, and the capture process is well on its way. This analysis has been applied fairly convincingly to the ICC and the railroads, the Federal Power Commission (FPC) and the natural gas industry, the Civil Aeronautics Board (CAB) and the airlines, and several other pairs.[56] According to economist George Stigler, industries come to see regulation as a benefit, mainly because most forms of regulation restrict entry into regulated markets, thereby reducing competition.[57]

There is no doubt that the capture concept is apt for a number of different regulatory situations past and present, but it is also true that not all regulatory agencies are captured, that captured agencies do not necessarily stay captured, and that some regulatory legislation is intended to promote and protect industry. There are also important differences in regulatory realms that need to be taken into account. The capture theory was typically applied to regulatory agencies that focused on a single industry and/or a limited number of companies and to situations in which regulatory objectives were primarily economic. Many current regulatory agencies oversee more than one industry and have social objectives, such as environmental protection, health and safety in the workplace, and civil rights. The multifaceted political environments these agencies face make any simple influence model implausible. One would expect these agencies to pursue various objectives—serving the public, accommodating industry, ensuring their own survival—with the emphasis given to each changing over time in accordance with external and internal pressures.

Gormley's differentiation of regulatory policies according to complexity and conflict provides a useful framework for sorting out expectations about beneficiaries.[58] Regulations that are not terribly complex, such as seatbelt rules, procedures to cut off utilities for nonpayment of bills, or smoking bans in public facilities, give various groups some say in policy because unusual expertise is not required to exert influence. If citizen advocacy groups are active and skillful, there is a good chance that the public will benefit from the policies or at least that some conception of the public interest will be considered in policy making. If public advocacy groups are not present, self-interested groups will dominate. For technically complex policies—for example, the use of genetically altered material, securities fraud, or banking regulations—a proxy advocate is usually needed to secure policies beneficial to the public. In such cases the specialized expertise and political muscle needed for an effective challenge to objectionable industry behavior may not be available except in a government agency.

The argument linking bureaucrats and social service policies is similar in some ways to the capture theory. Concern about poverty in the

1960s brought into being some hastily designed programs that were not nearly strong enough to solve the problem, but did create a certain number of jobs for those interested in administering social services. Some alleged that black community organizers were the primary beneficiaries of many War on Poverty programs because community groups were enlisted to implement programs, and known minority leaders were hired to administer them. The actual subsidies and services provided by the programs were said to be too meager or too difficult to obtain for the truly needy to benefit, and unnecessary or even harmful for many of those who did receive them.[59]

The systematic research that has been done on social service programs does not completely refute the arguments just presented, but it suggests that they are simplistic and misleading. Food stamps have helped to reduce malnutrition among America's poor; Medicaid has allowed many poor people to receive medical treatment previously unavailable to them; job training programs have helped people find jobs; and Head Start and Upward Bound have enabled many minority students to complete high school and college.[60] However, it is also true that Medicaid has resulted in expensive and in some cases unnecessary treatment, that some of those who benefited most from job training programs were not especially disadvantaged, and that the largest welfare programs—Aid to Families with Dependent Children (AFDC), food stamps, Medicaid, and housing subsidies—do not encourage self-sufficiency or reward industry and entrepreneurship. A more accurate appraisal of the beneficiaries of social service programs, therefore, would be that recipients of services as well as bureaucrats benefit from the programs, but there is clearly a need for ongoing programmatic reform.

Distinctions among service delivery programs also should be noted. The War on Poverty programs are often referred to as "social welfare" programs. As the term connotes, these programs aim to improve the lives and aspirations of poor and disadvantaged citizens. But many American social service programs are not aimed at the poor; they have a middle-class clientele. Veterans' benefits or farm subsidies are prime examples, as well as Social Security and Medicare. Another category of service programs—highways, mass transportation, water and sewer construction projects—benefits the public as a whole, as well as contractors and their employees. Overall, more money is spent on these nontargeted, middle-class programs than on programs designed to help the poor. In 1984 roughly $120 billion of the $450 billion federal human service budget went for targeted assistance. Social Security, Medicare, and unemployment insurance accounted for about $260 billion of the remainder, with the rest going to other nontargeted cash transfer programs and public works projects.[61]

Actions and Effects

This examination of policy consequences begins with sketches of two programs and then discusses how they illustrate the main themes associated with bureaucratic implementation and impact. To reflect the variety of implementation settings, one of the examples is a state regulatory policy carried out by a commission, and the other is a federal program implemented through an intergovernmental service delivery network.

California Coastal Commissions

The Pacific Ocean is one of California's greatest natural resources, and the policy for land use in coastal areas is of great interest to its citizens. Until the 1970s city and county zoning boards governed the coastal areas within their jurisdictions, which in most cases meant that conservation had a lower priority than development. As the environmental movement took hold in California, activists began to call for state control of the coastal zones. After the state legislature failed to pass regulatory legislation in 1970, 1971, and 1972, an initiative effort was undertaken in 1972, and Proposition 20, the Coastal Initiative, was enacted by voters in November.[62]

The initiative called for the creation of a state coastal commission and six regional commissions, which had the exclusive right to review and approve all forms of development within 1,000 yards of the shore. The regional commissions had an equal mix of local officials and public representatives appointed by the governor and the legislature, and the state commission combined representatives from each of the six regional commissions with six public members.[63] The idea was neither to ignore local interests nor to allow them to dominate. Staff for the commissions was guaranteed by a $5 million appropriation that went with the initiative.

The commissions' mandate was fairly clear: "preserve, protect, and, where possible, restore the resources of the coastal zone," and this environmental tone was not compromised by language invoking economic considerations.[64] The initiative set forth strict timetables for making decisions regarding the granting of development permits, and it called for advance publicity of, and public participation in, commission hearings and decisions. All major development projects required two-thirds approval of the regional commissions, and all important regional commission decisions could be appealed to the state commission and from there to the state superior court. In short, the commissions were responsible for protecting the coastline from construction projects that would produce deleterious environmental, recreational, or scenic effects.

Although they dealt mainly with insignificant cases, the commissions were generally tough on environmental issues in the bigger cases. The record shows that in well over 50 percent of the cases involving statutory issues, such as improving public access to beaches, enhancing scenic resources, or protecting wildlife habitats, the commissions either denied the permit or imposed significant new conditions. Some philosophical variation among them was reflected in their decisions; the South Coast Commission in San Diego was the most permissive, and the North Central Commission in San Francisco the most restrictive. The state commission was definitely restrictive in its rulings, denying permits or imposing conditions on 75 percent of the cases it heard where statutory issues were raised.[65] Very few of its decisions were overturned in court.[66]

Because the commissions reviewed projects that had already been approved by local governments and other state agencies, their decisions to deny construction permits or to impose additional requirements on contractors had very real impact. Not surprisingly, denials of proposed projects sometimes created a furor among developers, construction unions, and some local governments. A frequently imposed requirement in Southern California was that land be set aside for public access to the beach. But the commissions could not require anyone to develop and maintain such pathways; they could only hope, usually to no avail, that local governments or another state agency would do so. Not all of the requirements imposed by the commissions, therefore, had the desired effect. Commission decisions almost completely halted construction on or near wetlands areas, which had been disappearing at an alarming rate before the initiative was passed. This shutdown was probably the most notable short-term impact of commission actions. Another anticipated, but nevertheless problematic, impact of the initiative and its implementation was a rise in housing costs, estimated at $4,000 on the average for houses in the coastal zone and $1,000 for those in the areas bordering it.[67]

The state and regional commissions' staffs also solicited a great deal of expert advice on methods of preserving coastal resources and in 1975 completed the Comprehensive Coastal Plan, as required by the initiative. The plan was used to formulate the 1976 California Coastal Act. This legislation provided for a permanent state coastal regulating body and called for some state acquisition of environmentally sensitive coastal lands, a power the earlier commissions had lacked. However, the approval process for development projects was altered significantly to give local government more control and to incorporate economic considerations into the decision-making process. The change resulted from political pressure on legislators from unhappy developers.

Public Employment and the Labor Department

One of the clearest policy differences between Jimmy Carter and Gerald Ford during the 1976 presidential race was that Carter promised to spend money to combat unemployment if he were elected. Carter pushed Congress to appropriate about $20 billion for jobs in 1977. More than half of this money went to implement the Comprehensive Employment and Training Act (CETA), and most of the CETA money went into its public service employment (PSE) programs. These programs provided state and local governments and nonprofit agencies with money to hire full-time employees, who, it was hoped, would gain the training and work experience to qualify for regular jobs. The number of people holding PSE jobs stood at around 300,000 in June 1977, but was slated to jump to 725,000 in just nine months. The Department of Labor (DOL) in conjunction with 450 agencies of state and local governments, known as prime sponsors, were responsible for implementing the jobs initiative.[68]

The normal difficulties of such a rapid expansion were compounded because the supplemental public service employment money carried a number of new restrictions on participant eligibility and program design. Some state and local governments had begun to practice what is known as substitution. Through questionable layoffs and rehirings on CETA payrolls, or the tranfer to CETA of openings created by attrition, the state and local governments were using PSE funds, but not creating new jobs for the unemployed. Concern over substitution led to the stricture that new money was to be used only for special projects lasting no longer than a year. The DOL strongly encouraged prime sponsors to funnel a large portion of their new PSE money to nonprofit groups, which were less prone to indulge in substitution. New eligibility requirements increased the duration of unemployment necessary to qualify for PSE jobs from fifteen days to fifteen weeks.

Early in 1977, at the prodding of the new administration, the DOL sent prime sponsors a series of urgent directives instructing them to perform various tasks, such as assessing community needs and assembling pools of eligible applicants, that would lead to a smooth and effective expansion. However, in May, about the time the appropriation was passed, the department again changed a number of definitions and directives concerning projects and eligibility, thereby making earlier plans meaningless. As a result, the preparation process fell apart, and the DOL emphasized an easier priority: the prime sponsors were to hire as many people as quickly as they could.

And hire people they did. About 450,000 new PSE jobs were created in the nine-month period. In some localities the job creation and hiring process was conducted in a carnival-like atmosphere. Organizations of every conceivable variety submitted project proposals and received funding. Although some order and rationality prevailed over proposal review in most prime sponsorships, there was little direction or long-term purpose reflected in the decisions. The principal motivation was to get people on board quickly and to spend the money in accordance with DOL timetables.

The results, not surprisingly, included the creation of many projects of questionable value, the enrollment of many ineligible participants (about 20 percent of the total), and the neglect of other aspects of CETA, such as job training and youth programs. Perhaps most damaging of all was the growing suspicion among citizens and the press about the wisdom of using public funds in this way. *Reader's Digest* touched a raw nerve in Congress and throughout the CETA establishment when it published an article entitled "CETA: $11 Billion Boondoggle," which featured descriptions of "nude body sculpting workshops" and "body drumming classes" operating under CETA auspices.[69]

By 1978 fraud, waste, and abuse in CETA had become the overriding issue in unemployment policy. Congress enacted a major reauthorization of the law, which carried an unambiguous message for the DOL: find and stamp out the abuse. The department quickly imposed a series of new record-keeping requirements and liability sanctions on the prime sponsors, and then sent people into the field to investigate and audit prime sponsor operations. When the results were tallied, the DOL set the illegal expenditure rate in CETA programs at .5 percent.[70] Congressional critics were not convinced by this finding and chided the department for not looking harder for abuses.

At the prime sponsor level, staff resources shifted toward regulatory compliance—documenting the legality of expenditures—and away from program operations. The DOL was now reviewing all aspects of prime sponsor operations and handing out harsh criticisms and punishments, forcing some localities to pay back illegally spent funds. Administering PSE programs became so burdensome and unpleasant that few administrative or elected officials wanted them. Less than two years after the 1978 reauthorization, Congress eliminated PSE programs, which, during a ten-year history had spent $20 billion.

Implementation

These two examples illustrate how statutory language contributes to successful or unsuccessful implementation. When the objectives of a policy are stated without ambiguity, administrators can design regulations and settle disputes in ways that further those objectives. California's Proposition 20 had clear environmental objectives, and the state coastal commission was faithful to these goals. In the case of CETA's public service jobs, some objectives were in conflict—hire people quickly, but find those most in need—and the DOL gave the prime sponsors inconsistent signals about priorities. This inconsistency led to confusion at the state and local levels.

Successful implementation also depends on the right set of characteristics within the agency. Is the agency capable of executing the duties assigned to it? Does it have knowledgeable staff and enough people and money? California's Proposition 20 included a staffing appropriation that allowed the commissions to hire top-notch people without approaching the legislature for funds. The commissions' staffs achieved most of the major objectives of the initiative. The Department of Labor did not add to its operations and liaison personnel during the massive expansion of PSE in 1977, and this certainly contributed to sloppy implementation. At the prime sponsor level, the differences in the staff capability were quite apparent to field researchers and were seen as one of the main reasons for uneven performance.[71]

Staff capability alone does not ensure successful implementation; attitude and leadership also count. The ideal combination is a capable staff, philosophically committed to the goals of the program, and effective leaders. In California, the commissions were solidly behind the goals of the coastal initiative, and Mel Lane, the chairman of the state commission, provided strong competent leadership.[72] The CETA situation was quite different. There were few committed to public service employment within the Labor Department, and nothing that would qualify as outstanding leadership came from the department during the 1976 expansion. However, skillful leadership did exist in many prime sponsorships, and its presence was the most reliable predictor of effective implementation.

Effective communication is also necessary for implementation, particularly when more than one level of government is involved. During the CETA period, the DOL issued massive planning documents to state and local prime sponsors in conjunction with changes in policy. Prime sponsor staffs often were overwhelmed by the volume of communications flowing from the department, and their reaction was to ignore most of it.

Administrative agencies frequently are restricted in their enforcement capacity. To fully protect California's coast the commissions would have needed the power to force the cooperation of other state and local agencies and the money and authority to buy wetland habitats and construct the beach pathways. They did not have such power. The CETA program suffered from a different problem. Stricter accountability and more aggressive enforcement led to considerable unhappiness at state and local levels, as elected officials objected to DOL auditors breathing down their necks. The burden of implementation eventually led to the refusal of state and local elected officials to defend the program when it was on the congressional chopping block, and their silence certainly contributed to its demise.

Impact

The California Coastal Initiative had a fairly clear antidevelopment impact—a slowdown in construction in the coastal area and a halt to development in wetland areas. Not surprisingly, these substantive results also had political effects. Construction and development interests were not at all shy about expressing their unhappiness with the commissions' policies in 1975 and 1976 when new coastal legislation was being formulated in Sacramento.[73] The new law reflected the tug-of-war between environmental interests and the construction industry by providing for the completion of pathways to the beach and the protection of wetlands, but also by returning to local governments primary responsibility for approving most construction projects in the coastal zone. It is common for programs that produce noticeable effects to also stimulate political opposition.

Public service employment provides an excellent example of why many social services are controversial: their impacts are difficult to document or demonstrate, and they are subject to various interpretations. The desired results were a reduction in unemployment, assistance for economically disadvantaged people, and additional public services for communities. This attractive combination of benefits ensured the program's popularity among legislators in the 1970s, but there were always good reasons for questioning whether these benefits were actually realized.

For the problem of reducing unemployment, the main difficulty arose from the practice of substitution, which, to the extent it took place, nullified the effects of PSE. Policy analysts disagreed on the most accurate way to measure the phenomenon, and substitution estimates ranged from 15 percent of PSE jobs to 90 percent.[74] If all the PSE positions had been newly created jobs, every 500,000 jobs would have represented a .5 percent reduction in the unemployment rate. An educated guess is that roughly 25 percent of the PSE jobs were substituted jobs, and, because the cost of a 500,000-job program was more than $4 billion, the program lost about $1 billion through substitution.

Evaluating public service was equally complicated, ambiguous, and controversial. Many questioned the wisdom of having public service employees working on arts projects, on the numerous cleanup campaigns started around the country, or in many of the social service agencies that secured CETA funding. Most of the studies pronounced the bulk of PSE projects worthwhile, but this did little to deter critics.[75]

The typical PSE participant was a white male of prime working age with a high school education who was not receiving welfare. This discovery cast doubt on the claim that the program was serving the neediest. The point is underscored when program participants are compared to the population eligible for PSE. The participant group includes a substantially smaller percentage of high school dropouts and welfare recipients.[76] The program helped many needy people get on their feet, but its benefits were disproportionately enjoyed by the less disadvantaged among the unemployed.

Learning

It seems reasonable to expect bureaucratic agencies to learn from their experiences and to incorporate that learning into their implementation policies and practices. Most people would regard this development as central to effective administration. However, it is also understood that many bureaucratic actors are creatures of habit and others are tuned in mainly to political messages; therefore, internal and external factors sometimes limit an agency's openness to new ideas and responsiveness to new developments.

The California Coastal Commission is a classic case of an agency ready and able to learn. The combination of a young, committed staff and a clear mandate to undertake a comprehensive analysis of coastal issues was ideal for bureaucratic learning. The initiative also protected the commission from legislative interference while it developed the coastal plan, and this protection reduced some of the political pressures, especially from development interests. The coastal plan captured the principal lessons the coastal commission experience had provided, and many of these lessons found their way into the 1976 coastal legislation.

The CETA public service employment situation was different in nearly every respect. The Employment and Training Administration (ETA) of the Department of Labor was not particularly young, committed, capable, well funded, or well led; the agency suffered from high turnover among its top officials. One might conclude that the department learned from the PSE expansion that strict regulatory compliance was necessary to make CETA programs effective, but in fact Congress more or less forced this posture on the department, with dubious consequences. The DOL inhabited a political world that was intrusive and volatile, and department officials learned to react quickly to changing political winds. But, it is not at all clear that these reactions included much learning about effective program administration or policy design.

Overall, several observations about learning in bureaucratic politics seem warranted. First, an openness to new personnel, new ideas, and new approaches is critical in enabling agencies to learn. Second, leadership and learning go hand in hand. Without encouragement and guidance from high-level administrative officials, bureaucrats are unlikely to learn constructive lessons from their experience because they may have difficulty seeing the big picture; top officials should have it in plain sight. Third, the political context must be considered. Agencies with a solid base of political support and a reputation for competent administration among policy makers have the time to learn from their mistakes. Agencies that are subject to constant attention and frequent criticism from elected officials tend to become so paranoid that learning is virtually impossible.

Summary

The Constitution has very little to say about the administrative state. The president is given primary authority over the executive branch, and therefore the bureaucracy, but Congress has the power to create, abolish, organize, and reorganize executive agencies. Congress also can specify authority relationships between the administrative entities it creates and the other branches of government. Any bureaucratic agency can be rendered powerless by Congress, and most of them can be severely crippled, if not paralyzed, by the president or the courts. For bureaucratic agencies, the exercise of power is mostly a matter of having the backing and support of interest groups and other branches of government that have the political influence or constitutional authority they lack.

This support is by no means automatic. Chief executives frequently try to reshape agencies whose policies they oppose. When an attack of this sort occurs, career bureaucrats may fight back by using sympathetic interest groups, the legislature, and the courts to help them protect their domain. If the assault comes from the legislature, a different coalition must be assembled. Agencies can sometimes compete effectively in the high-stakes, high-visibility arenas of politics by playing one branch of government off against another. This skill is part of what has enabled the bureaucracy to become a fourth institutional force in American government.

Clearly more important than their ability to resist incursions from other institutions is the fact that administrative agencies generally remain outside of the political limelight. Their influence over policy is greatest when other institutional powers are not watching too closely. Because their policy-making power is derivative, it is always subject to review and alteration: legislatures can abolish agency rules, adjudicative decisions can be overturned by the courts, administrative regulations can be changed in the offices of chief executives. But these kinds of checks are used sparingly; the normal environment of bureaucratic agencies permits them to exercise considerable power over public policy precisely because the other branches want the bureaucracy to make the tough unpopular decisions. The bureaucracy is one of the places in government "where the rubber meets the road."

Notes

1. U.S. Bureau of the Census, *Statistical Abstract of the United States: 1986*, 106th ed. (Washington, D.C.: U.S. Government Printing Office, 1985), 294, 322.

2. Emmette S. Redford, *Democracy in the Administrative State* (New York: Oxford University Press, 1969).

3. Kathy Sawyer, "The Mess at IRS," *Washington Post Weekly Edition*, Nov. 11, 1985, 6.

4. "State Limits Jersey Dairy's Access to City Market," *New York Times*, Dec. 12, 1986, A1, B4.

5. For more on the ICC see Marver Bernstein, *Regulating Business by Independent Commission* (Princeton, N.J.: Princeton University Press, 1955); on the NLRB see Benjamin J. Taylor and Fred Whitney, *Labor Relations Law*, 4th ed. (Englewood Cliffs, N.J.: Prentice-Hall, 1983).

6. See Harrell R. Rodgers, Jr., *The Cost of Human Neglect* (Armonk, N.Y.: M. E. Sharpe, 1982), chaps. 3 and 4.

7. Computed from data published by the U.S. Bureau of Census in *Statistical Abstract of the United States: 1987*, 107th ed. (Washington, D.C.: U.S. Government Printing Office, 1987), 257, 292.

8. Francis E. Rourke, *Bureaucracy, Politics and Public Policy*, 3d ed. (Boston: Little, Brown, 1984), 137-143.

9. Ibid.

10. Bryan D. Jones et al., "Service Delivery Rules and the Distribution of Local Government Services," in *Readings in Urban Politics*, 2d ed., ed. Harlan Hahn and Charles H. Levine (New York: Longman, 1984), 224-248.

11. See Philip Shenon, "U.S. Acts to Stop Quotas in Hiring It Backed in the Past," *New York Times*, April 30, 1985, A1, A29; and John L. Palmer and Isabel V. Sawhill, eds. *The Reagan Record* (Cambridge, Mass.: Ballinger, 1984), 204-208.

12. John W. Kingdon, *Agendas, Alternatives, and Public Policy* (Boston: Little, Brown, 1984), 92.

13. Ibid., chap. 6.

14. See *From Max Weber: Essays in Sociology*, ed. and trans. Hans H. Gerth and C. Wright Mills (New York: Oxford University Press, 1946), chap. 8; or Luther Gulick and Lyndall F. Urwick, eds., *Papers on the Science of Administration* (New York: Institute of Public Administration, Columbia University, 1937).

15. Rourke, *Bureaucracy, Politics and Public Policy*, chap. 3.

16. Ibid., chap. 4.

17. See Lance de-Haven Smith and Carl E. Van Horn, "Subgovernment Conflict in Public Policy," *Policy Studies Journal* 12 (Summer 1984): 627-642.

18. See Robert S. Gilmour, "Policy Formulation in the Executive Branch: Central Legislative Clearance," in *Cases on Public Policy-Making*, ed. James E. Anderson (New York: Praeger, 1976), 80-96.

19. Charles E. Lindblom, *The Intelligence of Democracy* (New York: Free Press, 1965).

20. See Hugh Heclo, *A Government of Strangers: Executive Politics in Washington* (Washington, D.C.: Brookings Institution, 1977), 103.

21. Rourke, *Bureaucracy, Politics, and Public Policy*, chap. 3.

22. See Norman J. Vig and Michael E. Kraft, eds., *Environmental Policies in the 1980s* (Washington, D.C.: CQ Press, 1984), chaps. 5, 7, 8, 17; and Palmer and Sawhill, *The Reagan Record*, 146-151.

23. See Eugene Lewis, *Public Entrepreneurship* (Bloomington: Indiana University Press, 1980).

24. Anthony Downs, *Inside Bureaucracy* (Boston: Little, Brown, 1967), 88-89.

25. Lewis, *Public Entrepreneurship*, 214-215.

26. Rourke, *Bureaucracy, Politics, and Public Policy*, 118-119.

27. Laurence E. Lynn, *Managing Public Policy* (Boston: Little, Brown, 1987), 119-125.

28. See Herbert A. Simon, *Administrative Behavior: A Study of Decision-Making Processes in Administrative Organizations* (New York: Macmillan, 1957); James G. March and Herbert A. Simon, *Organizations* (New York: John Wiley & Sons, 1964); Richard M. Cyert and James G. March, *A Behavioral Theory of the Firm* (Englewood Cliffs, N.J.: Prentice-Hall, 1963); Aaron Wildavsky, *The Politics of the Budgetary Process*, 3d ed. (Boston: Little, Brown, 1979); Charles E. Lindblom, "The Science of Muddling Through," *Public Administration Review* 19 (Spring 1959): 79-88.

29. Lindblom, "The Science of Muddling Through."

30. Rourke, *Bureaucracy, Politics and Public Policy*, 29-35.

31. Morton H. Halperin, "Shaping the Flow of Information," in *Bureaucratic Power in National Politics*, 3d ed., ed. Francis E. Rourke (Boston: Little, Brown, 1978), 102-115.

32. Ibid., 102-110.

33. Michael Lipsky, "Toward a Theory of Street-Level Bureaucracy," in *Bureaucratic Power in National Politics*, 135-157.

34. For a modern version of the rational perspective, see Charles J. Hitch, *Decision-Making for Defense* (Berkeley: University of California Press, 1965); or E. S. Quade, *Analysis for Public Decisions* (New York: Elsevier, 1975).

35. A more complete discussion of this example can be found in B. Guy Peters, *American Public Policy: Promise and Performance*, 2d ed. (Chatham, N.J.: Chatham House, 1986), 297-309.

36. For an excellent discussion of the principles and techniques of cost-benefit analysis, see Edith Stokey and Richard Zeckhauser, *A Primer for Policy Analysis* (New York: W. W. Norton, 1978), chaps. 9 and 10.

37. The basic idea of zero-based budgeting is to offer decision makers information in a form that allows them to make choices based on effectiveness, rather than on past funding levels. First, agencies are divided into "decision units," which should correspond to the program operating entities within the agency. Each decision unit prepares "decision packages" that indicate which

programs and activities they would continue at higher or lower funding levels. The packages then move up the agency hierarchy and are used to establish priorities at each level until an overall agency budget request is assembled. The process is supposed to identify the programs that work best so that they can be continued or expanded, and those that are not working well can be cut back or eliminated. For a full discussion, see Fred A. Kramer, ed., *Contemporary Approaches to Public Budgeting* (Cambridge, Mass.: Winthrop, 1979), chap. 4.

38. Lynn, *Managing Public Policy*, 187.

39. See Kenneth Culp Davis, *Administrative Law of the Seventies,* supplementing Davis's *Administrative Law Treatise,* (Rochester, N.Y.: Lawyers Co-Operative Publishing, 1976), 170; and A. Lee Fritschler, *Smoking and Politics,* 3d ed. (Englewood Cliffs, N.J.: Prentice-Hall, 1983), 79.

40. See Davis, *Administrative Law of the Seventies*, chap. 8.

41. See Fritschler, *Smoking and Politics*, 93-98.

42. Davis, *Administrative Law of the Seventies*, 141.

43. Lipsky, "Toward a Theory of Street-Level Bureaucracy."

44. See Davis, *Administrative Law of the Seventies*, chap. 4.

45. See Murray Edelman, *The Symbolic Uses of Politics* (Urbana: University of Illinois Press, 1964), chap. 3.

46. See Frances Fox Piven and Richard A. Cloward, *Regulating the Poor* (New York: Vintage Books, 1971); or Piven and Cloward, *Poor People's Movements* (New York: Vintage Books, 1979).

47. William T. Gormley et al., "Potential Responsiveness in the Bureaucracy: Views of Public Utility Regulation," *American Political Science Review* (September 1983): 704-717; and William T. Gormley, Jr., *The Politics of Public Utility Regulation* (Pittsburgh: University of Pittsburgh Press, 1983), 113-130.

48. See Andrew S. McFarland, *Public Interest Lobbies* (Washington, D.C.: American Enterprise Institute, 1976); or Jeffrey M. Berry, *Lobbying for the People* (Princeton, N.J.: Princeton University Press, 1977).

49. See Mark V. Nadel, *The Politics of Consumer Protection* (Indianapolis: Bobbs-Merrill, 1971); and Kenneth J. Meier, *Regulation* (New York: St. Martin's Press, 1985), 96-97.

50. Gormley, *The Politics of Public Utility Regulation;* and Douglas D. Anderson, "State Regulation of Electric Utilities," in *The Politics of Regulation,* ed. James Q. Wilson (New York: Basic Books, 1980), 3-41.

51. See Meier, *Regulation*, 106-113, on the FTC; and Daniel A. Mazmanian and Jeanne Nienaber, *Can Organizations Change?* (Washington, D.C.: Brookings Institution, 1979), on the Army Corps of Engineers.

52. Gormley, *The Politics of Public Utility Regulation*.

53. See *The Politics of Regulation*, chap. 10.

54. See Meier, *Regulation*, 106-113; and Michael Pertschuk, *Revolt Against Regulation* (Berkeley: University of California Press, 1982).

55. See Bernstein, *Regulating Business by Independent Commission;* Theodore J. Lowi, *The End of Liberalism*, 2d ed. (New York: W. W. Norton, 1979); Grant McConnell, *Private Power and American Democracy* (New York: Alfred A. Knopf, 1966); and George Stigler, "The Theory of Economic Regulation," *Bell Journal of Economic and Management Sciences* (Spring 1971): 3-21.

56. See Bernstein, *Regulating Business by Independent Commission;* Bradley Behrman, "The Civil Aeronautics Board," in *The Politics of Regulation*, 57-120; and David Howard Davis, *Energy Politics,* 3d ed. (New York: St. Martin's Press, 1982), 130-165.

57. Stigler, "The Theory of Economic Regulation."

58. Gormley, *The Politics of Public Utility Regulation*, 152-159.

59. For evaluations of American social welfare programs from authors with contrasting ideological perspectives see Piven and Cloward, *Regulating the Poor*, and Charles Murray, *Losing Ground: American Social Policy 1950-1980* (New York: Basic Books, 1984).

60. See Robert H. Haveman, ed., *A Decade of Federal Antipoverty Programs* (New York: Academic Press, 1977); John E. Schwarz, *America's Hidden Success* (New York: W. W. Norton, 1983); Karen Davis and Kathy Schoen, *Health and the War on Poverty* (Washington, D.C.: Brookings Institution, 1978); and Robert Taggart, *A Fisherman's Guide: An Assessment of Training and Remediation Strategies* (Kalamazoo, Mich.: W. E. Upjohn Institute for Employment Research, 1981).

61. These figures come from Sheldon Danziger and Daniel H. Weinberg, eds., *Fighting Poverty* (Cambridge, Mass.: Harvard University Press, 1986), chap. 1.

62. Our account of the California Coastal Commissions was taken from Daniel Mazmanian and Paul Sabatier, *Implementation and Public Policy* (Glenview, Ill.: Scott, Foresman, 1983), 218-265.

63. Ibid., 224.

64. Ibid.

65. Ibid., 233.

66. Ibid., 227.

67. Ibid., 246.

68. This discussion of public service employment is based on a similar account in Donald C. Baumer and Carl E. Van Horn's, *The Politics of Unemployment* (Washington, D.C.: CQ Press, 1985), chaps. 4-5.

69. Ralph Kinney Bennett, "CETA: The $11 Billion Boondoggle," *Reader's Digest*, Aug. 8, 1978, 72-76.

70. Baumer and Van Horn, *The Politics of Unemployment*, 133.

71. See Randall B. Ripley et al., *The Implementation of CETA in Ohio*, Employment and Training Administration, U.S. Department of Labor, R&D Monograph No. 44 (Washington, D.C.: U.S. Government Printing Office, 1977); or Ripley et al., *CETA Prime Sponsor Management Decisions*, Employment and Training Administration, U.S. Department of Labor, R&D Monograph No. 56 (Washington, D.C.: U.S. Government Printing Office, 1978).

72. Mazmanian and Sabatier, *Implementation and Public Policy*, 229.

73. Ibid., 250.

74. For estimates of substitution, see Alan Fechter, *Public Employment Programs* (Washington, D.C.: American Enterprise Institute, 1975); National Planning Association, *An Evaluation of the Economic Impact Project of the Public Employment Program* (Washington, D.C.: National Planning Association, 1974); George Johnson and James D. Tomola, "The Fiscal Substitution Effects of Alternative Approaches to Public Service Employment," *Journal of Human Resources* 12 (Winter 1977): 3-26; and Richard Nathan et al., *Public Service Employment: A Field Evaluation* (Washington, D.C.: Brookings Institution, 1981).

75. See William Mirengoff and Associates, *CETA: An Assessment of Public Service Employment Programs* (Washington, D.C.: National Academy of Sciences, 1980); or Nathan et al., *Public Service Employment*.

76. Baumer and Van Horn, *The Politics of Unemployment*, 116.

5   Cloakroom Politics

Much of American politics and policy making takes place in the cloakrooms, committee rooms, and chambers of city councils, state legislatures, and the U.S. Congress. Legislative institutions are often perplexing and frustrating to members and citizens alike. Describing and assessing the way legislatures operate is a little like retelling the story of the blind men who try to say what an elephant is by describing what they can feel. The impression one gets depends on where one is standing.

Legislatures are highly democratic, open institutions that are also responsive to narrow, specialized interest groups. Legislatures are powerful actors in the policy process, but they delegate responsibility for many significant decisions to other political institutions. Legislatures are the most responsive political institutions and in some ways the least responsible. To many observers, legislative policy making is both appealing *and* appalling.

Compared with most other brands of politics, cloakroom politics is perhaps the most visible, democratic, chaotic, and human. Only chief executives command more public attention; only living room politics is more democratic. Legislatures embody a fundamental urge in the American experience—to have a place where the conflicts of public life are debated, deliberated, and decided in full view.

Legislatures are a focal point for the inside players. Government administrators, lobbyists, citizen activists, and journalists have easy access to the legislative chambers and committee rooms and offices. Legislators do not dominate the policy process, but they insinuate themselves into all aspects of public policy. They raise important issues, allocate public goods and services, and influence public and private behavior even when they delegate decisions to others.

Although Americans admire what Alexis de Tocqueville called, "this ceaseless agitation" [1] of legislatures, citizens often are frustrated by the chaos of legislative life. Legislatures reflect not only democratic impulses, but also the interests of the powerful. At times legislatures courageously tackle the tough issues of the day; at other times they seem to cower before the challenges that face them. Sometimes legislative actions make the situation worse; when legislatures do nothing, sometimes things get better. Legislatures mirror the conflicts that exist in American society. Consensus is achieved slowly, and it can evaporate quickly.

The Crowded Agenda

The scope of cloakroom politics is incredibly broad. It includes economic affairs, environmental protection, defense and foreign policy, and health, education, and welfare issues. Every year members of legislatures cast hundreds of votes on public laws and resolutions. Countless issues receive attention from committees, subcommittees, and individual members. The scope of cloakroom politics is illustrated by the issues considered by Congress over just two years, 1987 and 1988. Table 5-1 presents a partial list, but it conveys the incredible breadth of Congress's responsibilities and public policy interests. As American legislatures go, Congress is not unusual in having a far-reaching policy agenda. State legislatures also have extremely varied agendas. During a recent session, the California legislature held hearings and passed legislation covering topics as diverse as urban economic development, insurance reform, child care, health services for senior citizens, and hazardous waste policies.

At first glance one might conclude that legislatures, their committees, and members consider practically everything imaginable. Open and democratic as they are, however, legislatures do not respond to everyone who knocks on their doors. Legislatures are collections of many smaller organizations—the offices of the senators and representatives and legislative committees. Most issues are handled first by subcommittees and committees, especially in the U.S. Congress, and never considered by other members. Committees and subcommittees have wide latitude to conduct hearings, investigate, and review legislation within their jurisdictions. Legislatures as a whole take major policy action on relatively few items each year. Many of the votes that members make are simple yes or no choices structured by the committee work that has gone before.

Most legislative activity is debate and discussion rather than lawmaking, and legislatures can influence policy without making laws. Legislatures often engage in protracted considerations of issues without making decisions because, unlike other institutions, they are important democratic and political forums—where symbolism can be just as important as substance. A great deal of time and energy is spent raising issues, seeking publicity, educating the public, helping political supporters, and embarrassing opponents.

*Table 5-1   Selective List of Issues Considered in the 100th Congress,
1987-1988*

AGRICULTURE: farm bank relief, farm credit, price supports, subsidies

BANKING: savings and loan bailouts, securities dealers, nonbank banks

DEFENSE: Strategic Defense Initiative, arms control, Pentagon procurement,
SALT II limits, war powers

ECONOMIC AFFAIRS: appropriations bills, Gramm-Rudman-Hollings deficit limitation, balanced budget amendment, debt ceiling increase, oil import
fee, insider trading on Wall Street, product liability

ENERGY/ENVIRONMENT: acid rain, nuclear power, clean water bill, water projects, wild and scenic rivers, endangered species, ozone layer

FOREIGN POLICY: foreign aid, Iran-contra investigation, Saudi arms sale,
Iran/Iraq war, Persian Gulf shipping, aid to contras of Nicaragua

GOVERNMENT OPERATIONS: federal pay, ethics in government, creating
a cabinet department of veterans' affairs, special prosecutor law, line-item
veto for president

HEALTH, EDUCATION, WELFARE: day care for children, child nutrition, long-term health care, AIDS, catastrophic health insurance, student
financial aid, welfare reform

HOUSING/COMMUNITY DEVELOPMENT: public housing, urban development grants, local government problems

LAW ENFORCEMENT/JUDICIARY: antitrust laws, civil rights, immigration reform, nominees for Supreme Court and appellate courts, fair housing

SCIENCE/TECHNOLOGY: space programs, super collider, technology
transfers

TRADE: trade deficit, global trade talks, retraining assistance for workers
displaced by foreign trade

TRANSPORTATION: airport safety, highway projects, 55-mile per hour
speed limit, smoking on airplanes

Source: Congressional Quarterly Weekly Reports, 1987-1988.

There is an intense struggle to get a vote onto the floor of the House
or Senate or in some instances to keep the institution from voting on a
policy question. If a problem is not already on the institution's agenda,
it is difficult to get it there. One scholar noted that the bulk of
Congress's time is consumed considering matters that recur each year.[2]
During the Ninety-ninth Congress, for example, more than half of the
roll call votes dealt with budget resolutions and appropriations bills. By
examining the trillion-dollar federal budget, Congress touches practi-

cally everything the government does, but few components receive close scrutiny.

Legislatures frequently must revisit past policy actions or deal with unfinished business from previous Congresses. Many of the items listed in Table 5-1 were passed by Congress ten or even forty years ago, but in a different form. For instance, farm price supports, weapons procurement, borrowing money, product safety, tax reform, toxic substances, clean water, welfare reform, and nuclear power were debated and voted upon in the Ninety-fourth Congress.[3]

Another large chunk of legislatures' limited time is consumed by crises. Legislatures are quick to respond to pressing international, national, and state events. A space shuttle disaster, famine in Africa, arms for hostages, bank failures, stock manipulation on Wall Street, an oil spill, scandals, and other problems command the immediate attention of elected representatives.

Many features of cloakroom politics keep the doors open to a broad range of advocates: power is dispersed, and there are many ways to gain access to the institution's agenda. Legislatures respond to the concerns of a wide range of outsiders, including presidents and governors, executive agencies, interest groups, and individual citizens, but the response is not the same in kind or degree.

Legislative agenda setting occurs on three distinct levels—the individual member, the subcommittee and committee, and the institution. Because issues follow different routes to each level, different interests are represented at each level. The attention of a single representative may be easily gained, but not an institution's.

Members

The issue agendas of individual legislators are strongly influenced by the concerns of citizens and organizations from their districts. Dealing with constituency problems consumes the time of members and their personal staffs. Representatives use their influence to speed up grants for sewer projects, obtain tax breaks for a steel mill, or fight for more financial aid for students. Collectively, the concerns of constituents play a strong part in shaping the policy activity of legislatures.

When legislators stand for reelection every two, four, or six years, they must account, however loosely, for their action or inaction on important matters. Voters and journalists, who shape evaluations of legislators, like to ask, "What have you done for us lately?" Despite the fact that nine members of Congress in ten who seek reelection win their contests, most "run scared" even in districts that appear safe for the incumbents. Indeed, one reason so many seats are safe is that members work so hard at reelection.[4]

Committees and Subcommittees

The agendas of legislative committees are shaped by a different cast of characters. Committee chairs exercise a great deal of power. They control the committee's resources and direct its policy focus. Nonetheless, they are responsive to concerns expressed by the executive branch. Indeed, many of the issues considered by legislative committees originate in administrative agencies.

Organizations and industries that are affected by the laws within a committee's jurisdiction are also agenda setters. Outside interest groups influence legislators because the groups supply the milk and honey of politics—money and grateful voters. Running for office costs a great deal of money; Senate campaigns run to millions of dollars. The quest for campaign funds compels legislators at least to listen to the concerns of their contributors. To some extent, then, the interests of campaign contributors become the interests of officeholders.

Organizations with money employ several methods to get consideration from subcommittees and committees. They hire lobbyists to monitor legislation, meet with members and staff, and pay legislators to speak at group meetings. Organizations that cannot deliver money or votes have a much tougher time getting attention.

Legislators use their committee status in creative ways to raise campaign contributions. Senator Robert Packwood, R-Ore., and Senator Lloyd Bentsen, D-Texas, the chairmen of the Senate Finance Committee in the 99th and 100th Congress respectively, formed "breakfast clubs" to raise cash. Club members were invited to weekly breakfasts with the chairman, provided they made contributions to the senator's campaign. Breakfast with Packwood cost $5,000; Bentsen collected $10,000. After journalists criticized Bentsen, he returned more than $500,000.[5]

Organizations also pay members for just looking at their problem. For example, a large Virginia coal company provided a dozen members concerned with mining legislation with a private jet and paid them $2,000 apiece for attending a discussion of energy issues and visiting a coal mine.[6]

Legislators use their committee and subcommittee positions to focus attention on scandals or government mismanagement and fraud. Investigations throw light on the members as well as the issues. A typical congressional probe was launched in early 1987 after a New York-bound Amtrak train traveling faster than 130 miles an hour rammed a Conrail freight engine. Sixteen people were killed, more than 150 people were injured, and train service between Washington, D.C., and New York City was disrupted for days.

Under existing law, the Federal Railway Administration (FRA) and the National Transportation Safety Board (NTSB) began investigating the accident. Within days, they determined that Conrail engineers had ignored signals on the track and had taped shut a whistle that would have warned them to stop. Safety officials also disclosed blood and urine tests that suggested the Conrail crew might have been impaired by the use of marijuana.

Before the administrative investigations were complete, Senator Frank Lautenberg, D-N.J., chairman of a Senate transportation subcommittee, called a hearing on the causes of the accident. Before television cameras and the print media, the chairman and his colleagues grilled witnesses from the railroads, the unions representing the engineers, and officials of the safety agencies. Assuming the role of judge and jury, Republican senator Alfonse D'Amato of New York concluded that drug abuse by the crew caused the accident and demanded random tests of all train operators.

Little dramas like the train accident investigation occur dozens of times each year. An event arouses media and public concern. Administrative officials are summoned to appear before a legislative committee where they are criticized—often with justification. The legislators then move onto the next issue, while the administrators return to their tasks a little chastened, but seldom wiser for the experience. Although the laws are not often rewritten, administrative practice may change substantially. By poking into administrative actions, legislators advance their electoral ambitions because the process increases the legislators' visibility back home.

Subcommittee and committee agendas are also shaped by legislators who have strong policy views. Known as "policy entrepreneurs," these legislators have a keen interest in advancing a cause, an idea, or a new program. That interest, combined with their extraordinary ambition, makes them very influential. As they seek legislative accomplishments or perhaps higher office, they push new items onto subcommittee agendas. They respond quickly to national and international events and mass media reports. For instance, a well-known U.S. senator assigns an aide to watch the television show "60 Minutes" so that he can offer legislative proposals on related topics the following week.

Policy entrepreneurs do not necessarily want to expand government spending programs. For example, Senator Phil Gramm, R-Texas, who led the charge for reductions in federal spending, is no less an entrepreneur in the policy arena than Senator Edward Kennedy, D-Mass., a longtime advocate of expanded public health insurance programs.

Committees listen to outsiders, especially chief executives, but their entrepreneurial instincts also bring new ideas to the agenda. In one session, for example, congressional committees made sweeping changes in national immigration policy, passed a massive highway building and rehabilitation program, revised the clean water act, and imposed economic sanctions on the South African government. None of these policies was promoted by the president; some were actively opposed.

Legislative staff are another fertile source of subcommittee and committee policy proposals. Congress employs an army of professional analysts, lawyers, and political advisers—more than 14,000 personal and committee staff.[7] Another 25,000 work for support agencies, including the Congressional Research Service (CRS), the General Accounting Office (GAO), the Congressional Budget Office (CBO), and the Office of Technology Assessment (OTA). Two-thirds of the GAO audits and investigations are initiated by the agency rather than by elected representatives.[8]

The Institution

Issues that dominate the attention of the entire legislature are broad societal concerns and/or issues advanced by presidents, governors, or legislative leaders. Take the issue of tax reform, for example. President Ronald Reagan's proposal in 1985 launched the months of hearings, debates, and committee and floor votes preceding a major overhaul in 1986. Even though various tax reform bills had been introduced as early as 1982 by Senator Bill Bradley, D-N.J., and Representative Richard Gephardt, D-Mo., not much happened until the president got involved.

The mere mention of a policy initiative by the president or a governor stimulates legislative activity and may yield new laws. In his 1987 State of the Union message, for example, Reagan highlighted three legislative priorities: welfare reform, catastrophic health insurance, and making the United States more competitive in the world economy. Immediately, these issues leaped atop Congress's agenda, even before specific proposals were produced to flesh out each idea.[9]

Legislative leaders occasionally can turn the spotlight on policy issues even when they do not percolate up from committee and subcommittee power centers. For example, new antidrug legislation appropriating nearly $2 billion was adopted in late 1986, yet the traditional sources of policy proposals—committees, executive agencies, major interest groups—were not advocating major legislation at the year's beginning. Why did this happen so swiftly? Two well-known athletes—a college basketball star and a professional football player—died of cocaine overdoses. Despite the absence of reliable statistics showing an increase in drug use, opinion polls revealed increasing public anxiety about drug abuse among young people, especially the use of crack cocaine. The *New York Times* reported: "Antidrug bills that have lingered in committees for months or years are now passing out 'in minutes.' . . . Cost doesn't seem to be an object now." [10]

Debating and Deciding

Although legislatures can engage in policy debates and focus public attention at will on social and economic problems, it is much harder for them to take decisive action. Deliberation and debate can be carried on by individual members and committees, but making *laws* requires collective action by several majorities. When legislators want to make policy, they must deal, bargain, and compromise. Moreover, cloakroom politics is molded by the contemporary political and economic environment: legislatures do not function in hermetically sealed chambers.

Suppose someone asked for an explanation of why a landmark tax law was passed in 1986 but not in 1980 or 1988. One might begin by sketching the basic features of the political landscape. The presidency and the U.S. Senate were controlled by Republicans, the House of Representatives by Democrats. With public opinion polls revealing widespread displeasure with the tax system's complexity and favoritism, a popular president advocated a major overhaul. Democrats were loath to bear any blame for blocking reform because their 1984 presidential nominee, Walter Mondale, had promised a tax increase and had lost in all but one state. Seeking desperately to retain control of the U.S. Senate, the Republicans needed a tax bill before the 1986 election.

Painting tax reform politics in such broad brush strokes, however, conceals important nuances. To get a bill through, committee chairs, legislative leaders, and the president were obliged to satisfy the parochial demands of dozens of legislators and interest groups. Passage was threatened by potential defections by House Republicans. As noted in the following excerpt from the *Washington Post*, the bill's fortunes were reversed by doling out favors.

President Reagan may have wanted to talk taxes when he invited Rep. Steven Gunderson to the Oval Office last week, but the young Republican from Wisconsin wanted to talk cows. . . . By the time the session was over, both men had what they wanted: Gunderson knew Reagan would sign the farm bill sought by his rural district; Reagan knew that Gunderson would vote for the tax-overhaul legislation in the House. . . . Says Gunderson, "I think that's a sensible way for adults to do business." And that's the way business was done up and down the Republican and Democratic aisles of the House.[11]

Similar politics molds hundreds of bills that do not make headlines. In the cloakrooms of every capitol building, politics is characterized by fragmented power, bargaining and compromise, deadlines, and legislative and executive leadership.

Fragmented Power

No one controls or commands legislatures. At times it seems that there are 535 leaders on Capitol Hill and no followers. House and Senate *elected* leaders retain their positions only as long as the members support them. Unlike bureaucracies where there is a chain of command, a hierarchy of authority, legislatures are collections of independent contractors. No one tells a member how to run a committee or how to vote. Environmental Protection Agency (EPA) regulations governing auto emissions standards are issued by the administrator who may seek advice from staff, industry, and the public, but the final decision on many matters rests with the administrator. When Congress writes laws governing air pollution, 535 members have some say in the outcome.

Legislatures are not without organization. Committees and subcommittees are the heart and soul of legislative policy making. Writing about Congress in 1885, political scientist, later president, Woodrow Wilson referred to its committees as "little legislatures." [12] What Wilson observed then is no less true today. Committees are powerful vehicles for policy deliberation and action. In fact, a legislature's ability to shape public policy is vastly expanded by the division of labor and development of expertise made possible by the committee and subcommittee system.

Congress is divided into hundreds of little legislatures. In 1988 the House had 22 major legislative committees and 140 subcommittees; the Senate had 16 committees and 84 subcommittees. Because subcommittees are chaired by members of the majority party, more than half of the Democrats in the House chaired a subcommittee. Each majority party senator chaired at least one subcommittee and sometimes two.[13] Two examples of committee and subcommittee organization, the Senate Labor and Human Resources Committee and the House Agriculture Committee, are illustrated in Table 5-2.

In fact, power is so widely dispersed in legislatures that the media and the public have trouble keeping track of the star players in each legislative ball game. Even powerful groups, such as the House Ways and Means Committee, which handles tax matters, trade policy, Social Security, and health programs, among others, are practically invisible to the public. Most committees and subcommittees are more obscure. Few people outside of Washington, D.C., know that the House Appropriations Subcommittee on Labor, Health and Human Services, Education, and Related Agencies appropriates more than one-third of the entire federal budget. Fewer still have heard of the Subcommittee on Surface Transportation or the Subcommittee on Commerce, Consumer Protection, and Competitiveness, let alone have the foggiest idea about what they do.

Table 5-2   The Organization of Two Congressional Committees

Subcommittees of the Senate Committee on Labor and Human Resources

> Aging
> Children, Family, Drugs, and Alcoholism
> Education, Arts, and the Humanities
> Employment and Productivity
> Handicapped
> Labor

Subcommittees of the House Committee on Agriculture

> Conservation, Credit, and Rural Development
> Cotton, Rice, and Sugar
> Department Operations, Research, and Foreign Agriculture
> Domestic Marketing, Consumer Relations, and Nutrition
> Forests, Family Farms, and Energy
> Livestock, Dairy, and Poultry
> Tobacco and Peanuts
> Wheat, Soybeans, and Feed Grains

Source: Washington Information Directory 1988-1989 (Washington, D.C.: Congressional Quarterly, 1988), 842-843, 888.

The policy issues handled by each subcommittee give rise to "issue networks" that include members of Congress and staff, executive agencies, interest groups, journalists, and academics. Many important policy decisions, which go unnoticed by the public, are made within this subcommittee-centered power structure. The fragmented system satisfies legislators because it permits more of them to exercise power, and the various organizations affected by the subcommittee contribute to the members' campaigns. Interest groups and executive officials are pleased because they gain access and attention to their concerns. If tobacco companies want to weaken government regulations about smoking, the Subcommittee on Tobacco and Peanuts, whose members hail from tobacco-producing states, swings into action and gives the industry an opportunity to press its case in a public forum. When the fishing industry is upset about environmental regulations, the Subcommittee on Fisheries, whose members are from coastal areas, tries to grant relief.

Subcommittees also create power bases for promoting innovative policies. The chairman and subcommittee chairmen of the House Energy and Commerce Committee, for example, have used their platforms to launch investigations and formulate sweeping changes in health policy, environmental protection, and telecommunications. According to Chairman John Dingell, D-Mich., the jurisdiction of the committee is "anything that walks and anything that thinks about walking." [14]

The formulation of the Asbestos Hazard Emergency Response Act of 1986, which established guidelines for cleaning up asbestos in the schools, demonstrates subcommittee-based entrepreneurship. The bill's principal sponsor was Representative James Florio, D-N.J., chairman of the Subcommittee on Commerce, Transportation, and Tourism. An archetypal policy entrepreneur, Florio uses his subcommittee to advance legislation in areas as diverse as hazardous waste policy and railroad regulation. Notice that the words "schools" and "health" do not appear in the title of his subcommittee. Florio, who has aspired to the governorship of New Jersey, captured the asbestos issue because the chairman of the House Education and Labor Committee, Augustus Hawkins, D-Calif., did not seize it for his committee.

The meshing of politics and public policy is readily apparent in this episode. Florio's asbestos law served diverse audiences. Parents and teachers no longer worried about the health risks, and school board members were relieved because cleanups could get under way. The asbestos industry was grateful because limits were placed on their liability for health effects, and the EPA was pleased to have federal policy clarified on a serious health hazard. Such legislative victories can be translated into future electoral rewards. This victory may enhance the perception of Florio's power and increase the flow of contributions from political action committees (PACs).

Bargaining and Compromise

Because power is widely dispersed, bargaining and compromise are central to legislative politics. Fragmentation enhances the power of members and subcommittee leaders, but it makes reaching consensus more difficult; a few determined individuals can stall the process. Legislatures may fail to make progress on important policy issues for months or even years. At times, the legislative process moves at a snail's pace. Yet, when agreement is reached and the deals are struck, legislatures can move with blinding speed.[15]

A majority of legislators must support a bill repeatedly before it reaches a chief executive's desk for signature. Majorities must be obtained in subcommittees, committees, and in the entire House and Senate. If there are disagreements between House and Senate—and there usually are—a temporary conference committee is appointed to iron out the differences and then seek yet another majority in each chamber.

Although members often take cues from party leaders and the president, majorities assembled to pass one law may not stick together for the next battle. As new issues arise, majorities must be put together at all stages of the legislative process—one vote at a time. Building coalitions is painstaking work that often resembles Monty Hall's "Let's Make a Deal." David Stockman, Reagan's first budget director, called the task of pulling coalitions together in Congress the "politics of giving."

An actual majority for any specific bill had to be reconstructed from scratch every time. It had to be cobbled out of the patchwork of raw, parochial deals that set off a political billiard game of counter-reactions and corresponding demands. The last ten or twenty percent of the votes needed for a majority in both houses had to be bought, period.[16]

If presidents and governors prefer "wholesale" politics—good ideas— legislators prefer "retail" politics—rewards for one's district or state. A House leadership aide put it simply: "No matter how members ask the question it always comes down to one issue—how will it affect me." [17] Crafting laws requires many different types of agreements. Deals may involve one member agreeing to vote yes on a bill with the understanding that the favor will be returned. Or legislation may include a higher appropriation, lower taxes, or favorable treatment for an industry in a member's district as the price for a positive vote.

Some observers regard the horse-trading, compromise, and vote swapping that characterize legislatures as distinctly unsavory. To these critics, the German chancellor Otto von Bismarck was correct in saying, "Politics is like sausage. Neither should be viewed in the making." But the nature of representative democratic institutions makes it unlikely, and even undesirable, for them to behave otherwise. To fashion laws in an open democratic institution, a broad consensus must be achieved and sustained. "Good" policy benefits, or at least does not harm, the people and interests represented by elected officials.

Deadlines

This underlying dynamic helps explain why legislatures often procrastinate until the last possible moment before reaching a decision. Just before adjournment or an election, legislatures often rush through hundreds of bills. In one marathon session that lasted eighteen hours, the New Jersey Assembly voted on more than 100 bills before recessing.

Why does a legislature act like a football team executing a two-minute drill—quickly and efficiently moving the ball down the field for a touchdown when before they seemed unable to move it two feet? Why does a legislature not always act as if the deadline was fast approaching? Action is postponed primarily because everyone waits until the end to get the best deal. Knowing that decisions on major legislative initiatives and tax and spending bills may not be made until the eleventh hour encourages everyone to hold off their commitments.

Legislators also delay action in the hope that unfavorable political conditions will improve. Perhaps public opposition to a controversial policy will soften; maybe the governor will take a different position; perhaps the next election will bring more like-minded individuals to the legislature. Without deadlines, legislatures may not be able to make decisions. The end of a fiscal year, the expiration of a law's authorization, an impending election, or adjournment force legislatures to act, whether they are ready or not.

Leadership

Fragmented power and the need for compromise increase the importance of leadership to put things together.[18] Legislative leaders assemble coalitions and set priorities for the institution. But leaders derive their power from the members and must defer to their wishes to keep their support. The positions that legislative leaders take on policy issues are heavily influenced by the views of other legislators in their party.

According to Randall Ripley, a perceptive student of American politics, congressional leaders perform five policy-related tasks.

—help determine who sits on the most powerful committees
—help decide when legislative business will come to the floor of the House and Senate
—help organize votes on the floor of the House and Senate by contacting—whipping—members to attend and vote
—communicate leadership preferences and collect information on member needs and preferences
—serve as focal points for contact with the White House and the press

But a leader's most important power is to persuade his or her colleagues to follow.

Majority and minority leaders exercise more influence on procedural matters—when a bill is considered or how an issue is framed for a vote—than they do on the substance of legislation, its policy objectives and strategies.[20] Leaders package issues so that fellow party members can cast votes that help them with their constituents or interest groups. When Robert Dole, R-Kan., was Senate majority leader, he arranged for Republican senators seeking reelection to introduce budget amendments restoring proposed cuts in popular programs in their states. Senators from urban states called for increases in urban development grants and mass transit aid. Senators from tobacco states asked for decreases in the cigarette tax. Senators from agricultural states demanded higher price supports and so on. The value of such techniques has been magnified by television coverage of House and Senate proceedings.

Members are most likely to play follow-the-leader when it advances their electoral goals. But members have an iron clad excuse for ignoring a leader's requests: "I can't vote with you because it could cost me reelection." Even leaders themselves sometimes resort to this defense. House Majority Leader Jim Wright, D-Texas, opposed his party's tax reform bill in 1986 because it was not sufficiently generous to the Texas oil and gas industry. Wright did not suffer for his defection; he was elected Speaker of the House a few months later.

Congressional leaders are the essential glue for holding coalitions together, yet they rarely advance legislation independently. Consider this assessment of former senator Howard Baker, R-Tenn., widely regarded as one of the most effective Senate leaders in history.

Like most leaders in both houses Baker had no particularly identifiable policy vision to offer. In the minority he is best remembered for helping President Carter and then Majority Leader Byrd engineer Senate approval of the Panama Canal treaties. In 1981 he simply worked for the Republican President's preferences.[21]

Leaders in state legislatures can be more influential than congressional leaders. Presiding officers in state legislatures often appoint the members and chairs of standing committees, decide which committee will consider legislation, determine when bills will be "posted" for a vote, and closely oversee deliberations on the floor of the chamber. They may also promote substantive programs and persuade standing committees to enact those programs. Alan Rosenthal, a leading authority on state legislatures, wrote:

On some issues ... leaders are inclined to play a prominent role. On revenue policy, the shots are likely to be called by legislative leaders. In the field of education ... leaders in over half of the states play a significant role.

Even in the states, however, Rosenthal concluded: "Aggressive policy leadership is probably the exception rather than the rule."[22]

Ironically, leadership from within the legislature may be more difficult to achieve than leadership from chief executives. Presidents and governors can go directly to interest groups and the public upon whom legislators depend for support. As a result, chief executives are often the most effective "legislative leaders." They not only set the legislative agendas, but also formulate policies and then push them through to final adoption. "Whatever the precise sources of policy formulation," Rosenthal wrote, "the processes by which proposals make the agenda, receive serious consideration, and get adopted may depend considerably on executive leadership."[23]

Presidents and governors have political powers that are unavailable to members of Congress and state legislatures (see chapter 6). Chief among these is the ability to be heard above the clamor of voices. Representative David Obey, D-Wis., said, "The President has the only megaphone in Washington." [24] Presidents and governors attract media and public attention and can exert pressure on legislators to go along with their wishes. Ripley summarized the inherent shortcomings of legislative institutions: "A single individual with considerable formal power can inevitably declare a position and follow through on it more skillfully and rapidly than a multiheaded body like Congress." [25]

Forging Consensus

The characteristics of cloakroom politics profoundly influence what legislatures do. What does this mixture of individual needs, fragmented power, compromise, and leadership produce in the way of public policies?

Symbols over Substance

Symbol often triumphs over substance in cloakroom politics. Much legislative activity involves talk, not action. Hearings are held, bills introduced, speeches delivered, but no legislation passes. Significant policy results are hard to achieve because they mean that legislatures must wield the coercive power of government to regulate public and private behavior—in other words, do something unpopular such as reallocating benefits, or raising taxes, or imposing restrictions on industry or individuals. Making the wrong move can cost members their jobs.

Sometimes primarily symbolic laws are passed to reassure politically aroused groups.[26] Without offering tangible benefits, the legislature addresses the concerns of aggrieved parties with policy pronouncements that mollify them. Groups that are not sophisticated or well organized are more likely to be satisfied with purely symbolic action. Disadvantaged groups, such as the unemployed and the poor, seldom have sufficient political clout to hold elected officials accountable.[27]

Legislatures often adopt policies that are long on goals but short on the means for carrying them out. Such policies may strike only a glancing blow at the problem. The gulf between rhetoric and reality frequently is exposed by the difference between authorizing language and appropriations bills. Authorizations set out the objectives and strategies for ameliorating a problem; appropriations bills supply money for programs and benefits to people. The Housing and Community Development Act is a policy with lofty goals but little cash. Its avowed goals are to create "viable urban communities by providing decent housing and a suitable living environment for persons of low and moderate income." [28] Congress's $3 billion annual appropriation may seem generous, but it falls short of achieving the law's ambitious objectives. In fact, during the mid-1980s more public housing units were destroyed than were built.[29]

Actions taken for symbolic reasons still may have important consequences. Public concern over the degradation of the environment was met with the National Environmental Policy Act (NEPA), which announced the government's intention to protect the environment. Although it began as a symbol, NEPA became an important policy instrument because it requires federal agencies to prepare environmental impact statements. Working through the courts, environmental activists use this requirement to block projects with effects detrimental to the environment.

Incremental Change

The drawn-out policy process and fragmented power often yield only minor policy changes. When legislatures finally act, problems typically are addressed in small, manageable steps—modest departures from past practice. The stabilizing forces holding back substantial change are very powerful indeed. Agendas are crowded with proposals; only a few receive serious attention. Legislators have abundant opportunities to veto or water down proposals.

Policy issues are rarely considered comprehensively. Legislatures slice up broad policy domains into many pieces so that a large number of members serving on committees and subcommittees can participate. Rather than structure a governmentwide policy on health care, for example, Congress divides health-related issues into discrete programs.

Fear of the unknown also inhibits rapid and radical change. In contrast to business persons, who tend to be risk takers, legislators avoid risks. When they vote for a law they want to be certain that it will not make things worse. Under these circumstances they choose to tinker with solutions, through trial and error, rather than to embrace innovative approaches with the potential of disastrous consequences. Reconsiderations are practically guaranteed; most laws have three- to five-year life spans so that a legislature can look at the issue again and change its mind.

Future policy directions often are molded by past decisions. Legislators find that the compromises reached by their predecessors serve as useful guides. Because lawmakers want to avoid controversy and conflict during a drawn-out process, they find it politically feasible and prudent to seek modest changes in current policy. Opposition from others is less likely when changes from the status quo are minor and nonthreatening to other vested interests.

Congressional policy making on the annual budget demonstrates incrementalism at work. Congress usually makes minor adjustments from year to year. Major departures, such as the substantial increase in defense spending during the 1980s, are rare; they take place only if accompanied by strong presidential leadership. The budget under consideration usually equals last year's budget, plus or minus a small percentage.[30] Battles occur over what seem like inches of territory to the outside observer. Will spending increase by 2 percent or 3 three percent? Will formulas governing grant-in-aid programs benefit smaller cities with less than 25,000 residents? The competition is fierce, but the public rarely understands what, if anything, is at stake. To insiders, these battles are important because they are, quite literally, the principal policy issues before the legislature.

Pork-Barrel Policies

Legislators want to deliver benefits, sometimes known as pork-barrel programs, to people, businesses, and communities in their states and districts. The desire to parcel out "particularized benefits" produces what are called distributive policies.[31] Members of Congress are not the only ones who want to participate in the politics of giving and credit claiming. To justify expanding the fleet in the 1980s, the secretary of the Navy announced a policy of "strategic dispersal." Rather than keeping ships in the few ports where they had been berthed for decades, he proposed several new port facilities, creating thousands of jobs in the chosen cities. But critics, including former naval officers, said it was a blatant attempt to curry political favor. "It can't be justified in strategic terms, except for strategic politics." [32]

Pork-barrel politics was evident when Congress overrode President Reagan's veto and enacted the Water Quality Act of 1987, which was loaded with special projects for more than 400 congressional districts and every state in the nation. James Weaver, a maverick Democratic representative from Oregon, tried in vain to eliminate questionable projects. He proposed cutting Oregon's Elk Creek Dam, deemed costly and unnecessary by the Army Corps of Engineers and the GAO, but Representative Robert Smith, R-Ore., objected. "We should deal with this project as the member representing the area desires," he said.[33] The Elk Creek Dam survived.

Organized interests benefit from this system of handing out government largess. The economically disadvantaged and politically unorganized usually lose when their interests conflict with those of more powerful groups. For example, Reagan convinced Congress to drop public jobs programs for the long-term unemployed and poor people. But Congress refused to terminate the Economic Development Administration (EDA)—a program characterized by Stockman as a "boondoggle" and "demonstrably useless." The difference? EDA distributes low-

interest loans and other assistance to businesses and construction companies in 80 percent of the country. Public service job holders did not have
a political action committee; the construction industry did.[34]

Innovation

Occasionally, public policy undergoes radical change. Landmark
laws may increase government involvement in matters previously left to
the private sector, such as health insurance for the elderly. The Social
Security Act, which guaranteed government support for senior citizens,
the Civil Rights Act of 1964, which forbade discrimination against
minorities and other groups, and across-the-board tax and spending cuts
enacted in 1981 represent fundamental innovations in public policy.

From time to time, conditions fostering innovation by legislatures
arise. According to political scientist Charles Jones, significant policy
shifts may occur when a well-organized and vocal public unites and
demands government action or when policy makers achieve a temporary consensus around unprecedented proposals.[35] Strong political leadership, often from the president or governor, and favorable economic
and political conditions are also powerful agents of policy innovation.
President Lyndon Johnson championed the Civil Rights Act of 1964.
Major changes in the tax system and federal spending priorities were
achieved with effective leadership from President Reagan. Governor
Bruce Babbitt of Arizona was able to break a forty-year deadlock over
water conservation policy in his state with effective public and private
leadership. Governor George Deukmejian of California played a central
role in convincing the legislature to overhaul the state's welfare system.

Legislators usually follow, rather than lead, but there are exceptions.
Senator Edmund Muskie, D-Maine (1959-1980), galvanized the environmental movement in promoting the Clean Air Act of 1970 and other
environmental laws. Senator Alan Simpson, R-Wyo., led the fight to
reform the nation's immigration laws, and in 1987 Speaker Wright
shepherded through Congress a law to aid homeless Americans.

Events, political conditions, and the state of the economy all affect
the degree of innovation. When federal budget deficits are high, opportunities for greater federal spending are severely restricted, but other
innovations, such as deregulation and privatization of public services,
become more likely. Conversely, when federal revenues exceed projected expenditures, as was the case in the mid-1960s, new programs are
born. Johnson started the War on Poverty and promised both guns for
the war in Vietnam and butter—domestic spending programs. And
when state governments realized a revenue bonanza during the late
1980s, major reforms in education and economic development strategies
were quickly put in place.

Significant policy breakthroughs inevitably create problems, but once new government initiatives are established, the fundamental questions are no longer discussed. Instead legislators try to fix and refine—to "rationalize" policies created by breakthroughs. Political scientist Lawrence Brown makes a useful distinction: breakthrough policies are highly partisan, ideological, contentious, and visible, and rationalizing policies are less partisan and contentious and concern relatively fewer citizens or interest groups. Debates about incremental changes revolve around perceptions of the success or failure of programs and the need for them at a particular point in time rather than ideological preferences.[36]

Federal programs dealing with unemployment follow this general pattern to a large extent.[37] There have been two major policy innovations in unemployment programs since the 1930s. The first and most important occurred during President Franklin Roosevelt's administration when the government provided assistance to the jobless through unemployment insurance and job creation programs. Since then, the unemployment insurance program has been modified dozens of times—extending or shortening benefit payments, expanding categories of program recipients—but it has never been seriously threatened with elimination. It is the largest and most durable government strategy for helping the unemployed, and between 1974 and 1984 the expenditures averaged more than $16 billion annually.

In contrast, federal job creation programs have been alternately embraced and rejected by U.S. politicians over the years. The Depression-era public works programs vanished during World War II when unemployment declined. During the 1970s federal jobs programs averaged more than $3 billion annually. In 1981 the jobs programs were terminated but reappeared two years later when unemployment exceeded 10 percent.

The second major breakthrough in employment programs was the War on Poverty, which offered job training programs to the long-term unemployed. Since then federal funds have supported a second chance training system for thousands of people who have not obtained an adequate education or training in school. Basic policy objectives and expenditures remained stable, but programs and service delivery have been altered repeatedly since the 1960s.

Gridlock

When legislatures deal with extremely controversial policies, the policy process gets stuck in a gridlock of opposing viewpoints and power. Representative David Price, D-N.C., observed: "Congress is often difficult to mobilize, particularly on high-conflict issues of broad scope." [38] Legislatures have ground to a halt over civil rights policy, aid to education, and other issues in the past, but things seem to be getting worse.[39] "Congress now has difficulty legislating because the role demanded of it by economic conditions is not congruent with the type of legislation encouraged by its organizations and behavior," congressional budget scholar Allen Schick wrote.[40]

Congress's handling of the acid rain problem is instructive. Since the early 1970s, scientists have warned that the buildup of sulfur dioxide and other substances in the atmosphere, caused primarily by the burning of coal, was damaging trees, crops, and drinking water. But no significant laws were enacted to correct this damage; members of Congress representing regions where industry caused the pollution were unwilling to force expensive cleanup technology on those industries. The pollution continues; the debate drags on.

The federal budget deficit is another typical gridlock. From 1981 to 1985 Congress debated deficit reduction strategies without taking strong action. By 1985 the budget deficit had swollen to $200 billion. The deficit deadlock stemmed not so much from disagreements over whether the problem was serious, but over which course to pursue. Most Democrats favored tax increases and lower defense spending. Most Republicans preferred no tax increases and less domestic spending. No matter which party prevailed, meaningful deficit reduction required one or more unpleasant policy actions—hiking taxes or slashing popular programs.

While Congress groped for answers, the deficit problem worsened, and the options became fewer and more painful. Reluctant to adopt sufficient program cuts and tax increases, the president and Congress decided to borrow huge sums of money. By the end of 1985, the public debt had risen above $1.8 trillion—more than double what it was at the beginning of 1981. This spectacular growth in the nation's debt brought about an even more spectacular growth in interest payments to service the debt—from $53 billion in 1980 to approximately $130 billion in 1985.[41]

The gridlock was eventually finessed when Congress adopted the Gramm-Rudman-Hollings (GRH) deficit reduction act—named after its sponsors, senators from Texas, New Hampshire, and South Carolina, respectively. Passed in 1985, GRH mandated reductions in federal spending that promised a balanced budget by fiscal year 1991. Unlike previous budget-balancing resolutions, it empowered the president to make automatic, across-the-board spending cuts should Congress fail to reach specified reductions by the beginning of each fiscal year. Social Security benefits, existing contracts for defense and other projects, programs for poor people, and interest on the national debt were excluded. House Budget Committee counsel Wendell Belew said, "It's a kind of mutual assured destruction theory of fiscal policy. What they're doing is creating a kind of artificial crisis . . . an action forcing mechanism."[42]

Shortly after GRH's enactment, the U.S. Supreme Court ruled that portions of it were unconstitutional, and the law was modified. In GRH's early days, deficit reduction targets were met by resorting to one-time gimmicks, accounting tricks, and sales of government assets. It was not until the stock market meltdown in 1987, when the Dow Jones industrial average lost more than 500 points, that Congress was willing to swallow the strong medicine of tax increases and real spending cuts that amounted to more than $33 billion in deficit reductions.

Delegation

Legislative lawmaking is often a blunt instrument for addressing public problems. The surgical precision with which courts and the executive branch can sometimes perform, is rarely evident. Broad, vague, and sometimes contradictory policies are a direct byproduct of the need to reconcile competing claims and preferences. Consequently, many public laws contain ambiguous statements that a majority of the legislature can endorse. The task of translating aspirations into programs and services is delegated to government administrators, other levels of government, courts, private businesses, and citizens. Indeed, the more controversial the policy, the more likely that legislatures will ask others to make the tough choices.[43]

When legislators delegate hard decisions to others, they can garner political rewards while shifting the wrath of aggrieved parties elsewhere. Delegating authority to others also gives legislators leeway to blame federal agencies or other governments for failing to fulfill legislative intent and to take credit for correcting faults through constituent case work.[44]

The most common form of policy delegation occurs when Congress or a state legislature defines a problem in legislation and then mandates federal or state agencies to solve it. Recognizing and defining a problem are important, but the responsibility for deciding precisely how to cope with it is likely to be much more difficult. Consider the problem of hazardous waste management. State legislatures around the country have required the construction of safe facilities for the storage and disposal of dangerous wastes generated by chemical plants. The choice of *where* to locate facilities is up to environmental protection agencies or special commissions.

New Jersey's Hazardous Facilities Siting Act is typical of these state laws. It established criteria for siting three to five incinerators and landfills for handling hazardous waste. A nine-member commission appointed by the governor was supposed to decide in whose backyard to build the facilities. When the commission selected eleven possible sites, strong public opposition in those communities formed instantly. Commission meetings were packed with outraged citizens; community groups threatened civil disobedience and violence; state and local elected officials attempted to block the commission's staff from taking soil and water samples; law suits were filed to block the process; and state legislators introduced new legislation to overturn the process.

Legislators also impose difficult policy tasks on individuals and businesses. Affirmative action hiring policies are carried out by private organizations that decide whether to follow the letter and spirit of the law or to ignore it. Responsibility for enforcing immigration laws rests with private employers who must verify an individual's citizenship or permit to work in the United States. Failure to do so can result in a substantial fine. Often the courts must rule on whether congressional intent has been followed by private firms.

Congress also hands complicated problems to state and local governments, and state legislatures may pass tough issues on to local governments. Legislatures may mandate changes in policies and programs at other levels of government without providing adequate resources and then hold them accountable. Congress may order state and local governments to upgrade the education of young children, reform their welfare systems, enhance air and water quality, and improve highway safety. Congress may authorize funds to support new programs and agency staff, but the funding may not permit the realization of policy goals and expectations.

Establishing the Ground Rules

The nature of cloakroom politics influences not only laws and policy objectives but also the results. Even when legislatures delegate authority, they establish the ground rules for who gets what, when, and how from government. Legislatures are often the final arbiters of how much government spends on important societal goals and from whom money will be raised to pay for those commitments. Few individuals, institutions, and organizations are untouched by legislative action or inaction.

The legislatures' unique task is to make policy, rather than implement it. That task helps explain much of cloakroom politics. To legislate is to set a goal, define a problem, raise an issue. Lawmaking is the beginning of a long process of delivering public goods, services, and regulations. Making laws guarantees neither positive results nor the realization of intended consequences; at times there is a wide gulf between policy intent and the actual results achieved in society.

Legislators are held accountable for policy positions, not for policy results. Indeed, if they were responsible for the consequences of public policies, legislators would probably enjoy considerably less electoral success. They are typically more interested in and capable of discussing policy problems than in crafting solutions, and they are usually less interested in policy implementation and impact than in debating policy. These preferences are understandable given their objective, which is reelection; the style of legislative politics, which is compromise; and the difficulty of collective action.

Policy Implementation

Laws are seldom written with potential implementation problems in mind. Because it is so difficult to reconcile competing interests, legislators expect administrative agencies and others to figure out how to put laws into effect. In fact, excessive legislative goals are often regarded as an effective method to achieve change. The authors of the Clean Air Act of 1970 are proud of their achievement, even though it quickly became obvious that the law's air quality standards would not be met and still have not been met.[45] They reasoned that setting high standards stimulated the auto industry to work harder to reduce pollution. In fact, the method worked; the deterioration of air quality stopped, and there have been some significant improvements.

Nevertheless, a disregard for potential implementation difficulties can reduce the likelihood of achieving positive results. Public laws are sometimes endorsed without legislators ever carefully defining the problems the laws are supposed to address. Policy entrepreneurs who perceive a need for government programs may not be sure how to translate their aspirations into workable laws. The know-how to "solve" problems like minority youth unemployment or drug use may not yet be available, but legislators seize opportunities to advance innovative policies on these issues when they arise.

Ignoring implementation issues when laws are crafted may erode respect for government. To get laws enacted, legislators (and chief executives) may exaggerate not only the problem but also the potential effectiveness of the remedy under consideration. Then, if the problem fails to go away, the public and legislators may falsely conclude that it cannot be remedied with government programs or that the policy approach was misguided. Repeated rounds of hyperbole and rising expectations followed by disappointment and condemnation undermine public support for governmental solutions.

The fate of the youth employment initiatives passed during the early months of the Carter administration illustrate this theme. The Youth Employment Demonstration Project Act (YEDPA) embodied a collection of legislative impulses that proved extremely hard to carry out. Moving on a legislative fast track, President Jimmy Carter convinced Congress to add $1 billion in youth programs in less than four months. Unable to choose among the dozens of approaches reflected in the House and Senate bills, Congress essentially adopted a grab-bag strategy and decided to experiment with all of them.

Within three years most of YEDPA's programs had vanished. Federal, state, and local administrators struggled to carry out dozens of new initiatives simultaneously. There were simply too many programs, too many objectives, and there was too much money. Worthwhile programs were mounted, but it was hard to sort these out from the ensuing mess and chaos. Program managers were hard pressed to demonstrate positive outcomes. By 1981 Congress was no longer enamored of youth employment experiments, especially those without successful performance records.

Who Benefits?

Legislators tend to be concerned about the distribution of program benefits provided by law and with the efficient application of administrative regulations. Generally, they assume that programs or policies will be helpful to people if implemented properly—even though this view may be highly inaccurate. For example, a member of the House Education and Labor Committee may believe that spending more money on education is an end in itself. The ultimate results of education programs may not show up for years, and are difficult to gauge. Lawmakers may not be around long enough to see them. This perspective on policy impacts not only influences lawmaking; it also has consequences for the distribution of benefits in society.

Government benefits come in many different forms: tax breaks for companies, grants to fund social service programs or to build bridges, regulations that protect domestic industries from foreign competition, income-support payments for the unemployed, poor, and retired, and so on. Underlying all tax and expenditure decisions, regulations, and policies is the struggle over who benefits and who does not.

Legislative policy often favors the haves over the have-nots, the organized over the unorganized, the middle class over the lower class.[46] Those with money and resources have an advantage because they can use the leverage afforded by campaign contributions and lobbyists to press their point of view. Unemployed people and the poor can not support lawyers to prowl the halls of the Capitol, let alone fund reelection campaigns.

Even when programs set out to serve the disadvantaged, legislators can expand them to help the better-off segments of society, too. As originally conceived in 1965, the EDA grants program was supposed to help chronically depressed regions, such as Appalachia. But by the 1980s aid formulas had been revised to include most of the country. Social Security and senior citizen health care programs, originally intended to care for needy individuals without alternative means of support from pensions or families, now pay benefits to millions of older Americans who are quite well off.

In fact, most programs that serve low- and moderate-income Americans contain substantial benefits for others. Subsidized health care programs, such as Medicare for the aged and Medicaid for the poor, supply physicians with a substantial portion of their income. Residential training programs for disadvantaged youth benefit several large corporations that run the facilities. Nutrition programs for low-income citizens support agricultural industries and food stores. Grants for low-income college students benefit the schools they attend.

Indeed, when government programs try to serve poor Americans exclusively, the programs generally do not survive. During the 1970s federal lawmakers doled out billions of dollars through the Comprehensive Employment and Training Act (CETA). State and local governments were given funds to create jobs for the unemployed, but many of those hired were essentially middle-class workers who had recently been laid off. Stories abounded of well-heeled and well-connected federally funded jobholders. In an effort to serve the truly needy, Congress sent an unambiguous message to local officials: hire only the long-term unemployed and the poor. Two years later, practically every participant met the standards, but achieving the new objectives was purchased at a high cost. When President Reagan proposed eliminating the program in 1981, state and local elected officials stood by and watched it die.

Effective lawmaking depends upon finding the delicate balance of benefits that holds the majority together long enough for passage. The balance is particularly difficult to achieve when, as often happens, the legislation pits one advantaged group against another: the middle class against industry, manufacturers against service providers, the public against the chemical, insurance, and banking industries. It is considerably harder to find the right balance when everyone participating is able to make a strong case and exact a price for the "wrong" decisions.

The political art of balancing costs and benefits can be found in many laws, but it is perhaps nowhere more apparent than in the tax code. Affecting virtually every American who has any income, federal tax policy embodies compromises and trade-offs in benefit distribution like no other law. Benefits received by one group must be paid for by raising money somewhere else. The tax reform debate of 1985-1986 brought these trade-offs into full view. The resulting bill was a master stroke by the House Ways and Means Committee and the Senate Finance Committee. Important middle-class benefits, such as deductions for interest paid on home mortgages were retained, but others, like deductions for consumer interest loans, were phased out. Corporate tax rates were reduced, but benefits for certain industries, such as oil and gas, were eliminated or curtailed.

Policy Impacts

There are times when compromise is neither possible nor desirable: when costs and benefits are not easily balanced and when the costs of a new policy are obvious and controversial. In such circumstances, legislators prefer to wait for chief executives, the courts, or public opinion to spur them on. The history of civil rights and civil liberties policies illustrates the problem. Innovation in legislatures generally has occurred only in response to outside forces.

No matter how they came about, the civil rights laws have had significant impact. The Voting Rights Act of 1965 stripped away local election laws that had formally disfranchised minority voters, and it attacked informal practices, as well. Black registration in the seven states of the deep South covered by the law increased by more than 1 million between 1964 and 1972, an increase to 57 percent from 29 percent of eligible voters. Effective implementation of the law depended on federal officials and the courts, but congressional initiative was critical to making progress.[47]

The failure of legislatures to grapple with difficult problems also can have serious consequences. The problems created by harmful chemicals in the nation's water supply and by worldwide air pollution can be traced to careless and unregulated industry practices. Strong federal regulations were not legislated until the 1970s, and decades of neglect meant slow progress on enhancing environmental quality. The failure of state legislatures to take strong action against drunk drivers until the mid-1980s probably resulted in thousands of unnecessary deaths. Congress's inability to curtail the federal deficit during the 1980s imposes a heavy burden of debt on future generations of Americans.

Oversight and Learning

Legislative policy making can be a crude enterprise. As elected representatives grope for solutions to difficult problems, such as cleaning up toxic waste dumps, or ameliorating poverty, or curbing the AIDS epidemic, they often approve politically appealing but poorly designed policies. Legislators typically do not concern themselves with the details of program administration unless bureaucrats and private citizens run into trouble and people start complaining. But political institutions can and do learn from experience. Feeble and misguided attempts can be reshaped through trial and error. After several attempts, Congress successfully revised and strengthened education programs for disadvantaged youngsters. It took more than a decade, but compensatory education programs have clearly defined objectives and programs better suited to achieve them.[48]

Legislators form their impressions of program performance from what they hear from constituents and interest groups, from reports in the news media, from testimony at hearings, and from evaluations conducted by government agencies and others. Over time, members acquire pictures of success or failure that become the basis for intervening in program administration and for major legislative reforms.[49]

Objective evaluations of how programs work are difficult to achieve, expensive to conduct, and are sometimes distrusted by legislators. Many systematic studies do not yield unequivocal answers because it may not be possible to establish cause and effect relationships for government programs or policies. Suppose, for example, that one needed to determine whether the multibillion dollar food stamp program improves the nutrition and health of the eligible population. One would have to monitor the health and eating habits of people before and after they received aid, track similar groups of people who did not receive it, and compare the results.

But when evaluations provide clear evidence that a program works or does not work, the data are quite persuasive. For example, the Reagan administration could not persuade Congress to eliminate employment and training programs for the disadvantaged that are run through the Job Corps because there was strong evidence gathered through systematic evaluations that the program worked.

In making up their minds about programs, legislators use whatever information they can get. The problem is that unsystematic and anecdotal information often is more available and influential than careful systematic evaluations. Impressions about policy success or failure enter the policy process through many channels. Senior citizens write members of Congress to complain about exorbitant fees for routine visits to the doctor, or CBS's "60 Minutes" exposes fraud in contracts for highway construction, or the *Washington Post* reports alarming increases in airline safety violations. A legislative staffer in Arizona described the impact of a carefully selected anecdote.[50] During a hearing on licensing procedures for beauticians, a woman with bright orange hair, originally brown, complained about the incompetence of unlicensed practitioners. Her vivid portrayal convinced lawmakers to stiffen state requirements and monitoring efforts. Such evidence may be inconclusive or unrepresentative, but it exerts a powerful influence on a legislator's judgments about government programs.

Legislative oversight into public policies can be harmful, especially if the legislators reach inaccurate conclusions. The resulting criticism heaped on administrators can be demoralizing and, more important, dealing with it may distract them from essential tasks. Some observers argue that Congress and state legislatures do not conduct effective oversight because members are more interested in taking positions and claiming credit for helping those who demand it than they are in the effects that public laws generate in society.[51] Elected representatives are punished and rewarded for their votes on policies, not according to whether the laws "solve" problems. Moreover, if the laws are subsequently judged ineffective, then Congress can easily blame the bureaucracy and obtain additional rewards from those seeking corrective action.

When the policy process is competitive and diverse points of view are fully expressed, legislatures may be able to learn from their mistakes. For example, careful scrutiny of environmental laws has been ensured by continuing public health fears and the high degree of controversy surrounding proposed solutions. The Superfund toxic waste cleanup law passed in late 1980 turned out to be anything but super. Hundreds of millions of dollars later, only about 30 of the nation's 950 toxic waste dumps had been cleaned up by 1987, according to the EPA. Intense oversight efforts by the law's original sponsor, Representative Florio, and dozens of other legislators with toxic dumps in their districts led to a much stronger cleanup law in 1986.

There is an interesting paradox in legislative politics and policy. Widespread consensus is usually required to enact innovative policies, but some amount of disagreement and conflict is necessary to refine them. Too much consensus in the policy environment either supports the status quo—however effective or ineffective it may be—or fosters gigantic expansions in government power and spending that have little chance of succeeding.[52] When conflict and disagreement are too severe, efforts to revise policy may deadlock. Institutional learning is most likely when partisans and interest groups advance diverse policy remedies for the problems of program implementation.

Summary

No major government activity can be undertaken without the consent of legislatures, whether federal or state. No money can be taxed, borrowed, or spent unless the elected representatives willingly consent to the request of the president or a governor. No executive agency or top administrator can function for long without legislative support. The ground rules for the distribution of public goods, services, and regulations are established by legislatures, which may attempt to influence program implementation at any time.

Congress and the state legislatures are responsive to the changing mood of public opinion and to the views expressed by constituents, interest groups, and chief executives. But the desire of legislators to serve the public and curry favor with potential voters and supporters creates problems. Legislative institutions are subject to fads and whims and tend to respond to the loudest, most persistent demands. Legislators are easily manipulated by outsiders who can stir up public support for a position or raise campaign contributions. Groups that are already powerful tend to get what they want.

The desire to be responsive and democratic also shapes the organization and practices of American legislatures. The dispersal of power across committees and subcommittees creates opportunities for legislators to influence public policy and gain the gratitude of potential supporters who will keep them in office. But because they are fragmented and operate by consensus and compromise, legislatures seldom speak with a clear and consistent voice when making public policy. The need to accommodate diverse political interests often produces confusing public policies or no policy at all. Legislatures sometimes are unable to look ahead, and they are unwilling to address controversial issues or to act decisively.

Legislative indecision and timidity reflect deep cleavages and uncertainty in society. Legislatures have no trouble moving swiftly to clean up the environment, to crack down on drug dealers, or to raise the legal drinking age, if there is a strong and clear public demand for action. Except on rare occasions, legislatures will not set the nation's agenda or provide policy leadership. Their greatest strength lies in acting as a forum where the nation's controversies are debated in public. Legislatures are at their best when they educate the public, provide an outlet for the expression of diverse viewpoints, and forge consensus around new directions for public policy.

Notes

1. As quoted by Charles O. Jones, *The United States Congress: People, Place and Policy* (Homewood, Ill.: Dorsey Press, 1982), 13.

2. Jack L. Walker, "Setting the Agenda in the U.S. Senate: A Theory of Problem Selection," *British Journal of Political Science* 7 (1977): 423-445.

3. *Congressional Quarterly Almanac, 1976* (Washington, D.C.: Congressional Quarterly, 1977).

4. Thomas Mann, *Unsafe at Any Margin* (Washington, D.C.: American Enterprise Institute, 1978).

5. *Washington Post National Weekly Edition*, Feb. 16, 1987, 12.

6. *Washington Post National Weekly Edition*, Oct. 6, 1986, 13.

7. Roger Davidson and Walter Oleszek, *Congress and Its Members*, 2d ed. (Washington, D.C.: CQ Press, 1985), 237.

8. Frederick Mosher, *The General Accounting Office* (Boulder, Colo.: Westview Press, 1979), 178.

9. Beth C. Fuchs and John F. Hoadley, "Reflections from Inside the Beltway: How Congress and the President Grapple with Health Policy," *PS* (Spring 1987): 212-220.

10. Joel Brinkley, "Competing for the Last Word on Drug Abuse," *New York Times*, Aug. 7, 1986, 10.

11. Dale Russakoff, "Deals Are Struck, Hands Are Held—and the Tax Bill Sneaks By," *Washington Post National Weekly Edition*, Dec. 30, 1985, 10.

12. Woodrow Wilson, *Congressional Government* (New York: Meridian, 1956).

13. Randall B. Ripley, *Congress: Process and Policy*, 3d ed. (New York: W. W. Norton, 1983), 161.

14. Interview with authors, Washington, D.C., Nov. 19, 1984.

15. John F. Hoadley, "Easy Riders: Gramm-Rudman-Hollings and the Legislative Fast Track," *PS* (Winter 1986): 30-36.

16. David Stockman, *The Triumph of Politics* (New York: Harper & Row, 1986), 250-251.

17. Interview with authors, Washington, D.C., Dec. 10, 1984.

18. Legislative leaders in this sense are individuals elected by their respective party memberships. In Congress the leadership is the Speaker of the House, the majority and minority leaders, assistant leaders (sometimes called party whips), and the party caucus officers in the House and Senate.

19. Ripley, *Congress*, 229-230.

20. Barbara Sinclair, *Majority Party Leadership in the U.S. House* (Baltimore: Johns Hopkins University Press, 1983); and Randall B. Ripley, *Majority Party Leadership in Congress* (Boston: Little, Brown, 1969).

21. Ripley, *Congress*, 229-230.

22. Alan Rosenthal, *Legislative Life* (New York: Harper & Row, 1981), 167-168.

23. Ibid., 266.

24. Interview with authors, Washington, D.C., May 29, 1985.

25. Ripley, *Congress*, 325.

26. Murray Edelman, *The Symbolic Uses of Politics* (Urbana: University of Illinois Press, 1964).

27. Randall B. Ripley and Grace Franklin, *Congress, the Bureaucracy, and Public Policy*, 3d ed. (Homewood, Ill.: Dorsey Press, 1984).

28. Carl E. Van Horn, *Policy Implementation in the Federal System* (Lexington, Mass.: D. C. Heath, 1979), 106.

29. John Herbers, "Outlook for Sheltering the Poor Growing Ever Bleaker," *New York Times*, March 8, 1987, 1.

30. Aaron Wildavsky, *The Politics of the Budgetary Process*, 3d ed. (Boston: Little, Brown, 1979).

31. David Mayhew, *Congress: The Electoral Connection* (New Haven, Conn.: Yale University Press, 1974); and Theodore Lowi, *The End of Liberalism*, 2d ed. (New York: W. W. Norton, 1979).

32. Michael Weisskopf, "A Ship in Every Port, A Vote in Every Committee," *Washington Post National Weekly Edition*, Sept. 16, 1985, 13.

33. Cass Peterson, "Despite Gramm-Rudman Diet, The House Still Likes Its Pork," *Washington Post National Weekly Edition*, Nov. 25, 1985, 13.

34. Stockman, *Triumph of Politics*, 209.

35. Charles O. Jones, "Speculative Augmentation in Federal Air Pollution Policy-Making," *Journal of Politics* 36, no. 2 (May 1974): 438-464.

36. Lawrence Brown, *New Policies, New Politics: Government's Response to Government's Growth* (Washington, D.C.: Brookings Institution, 1983).

37. The following discussion is drawn from Donald C. Baumer and Carl E. Van Horn, *The Politics of Unemployment* (Washington, D.C.: CQ Press, 1985).

38. David E. Price, "Congressional Committees in the Policy Process" in *Congress Reconsidered*, 3d ed., ed. Lawrence C. Dodd and Bruce I. Oppenheimer (Washington, D.C.: CQ Press, 1985), 211-222.

39. James MacGregor Burns, *The Deadlock of Democracy* (Englewood Cliffs, N.J.: Prentice-Hall, 1963).

40. Allen Schick, "The Distributive Congress," in *Making Economic Policy in Congress*, ed. Allen Schick (Washington, D.C.: American Enterprise Institute, 1983), 258.

41. U.S. Congress, Joint Economic Committee, *Annual Report on the Economy*, 99th Cong., 1st sess., May 15, 1985, 47-49.

42. Jonathan Rauch and Richard E. Cohen, "Budget Frustration Boiling Over," *National Journal*, Oct. 12, 1985, 2138.

43. Lowi, *End of Liberalism*.

44. Morris Fiorina, *Congress: Keystone of the Washington Establishment* (New Haven, Conn.: Yale University Press, 1977), chaps. 7 and 8.

45. Charles O. Jones, *Clean Air: The Policies and Politics of Pollution Control* (Pittsburgh: University of Pittsburgh Press, 1975).

46. Ripley and Franklin, *Congress, the Bureaucracy, and Public Policy*.

47. Charles S. Bullock III and Charles V. Lamb, *Implementation of Civil Rights Policy* (Monterey, Calif.: Brooks/Cole, 1984), 20-54.

48. Michael Kirst and Richard Jung, "The Utility of a Longitudinal Approach in Assessing Implementation: A Thirteen-Year View of Title I, ESEA," in *Studying Implementation*, ed. Walter Williams (Chatham, N.J.: Chatham House, 1982), 119-148.

49. Baumer and Van Horn, *Politics of Unemployment*, 53.

50. Telephone interview with authors, June 1, 1987.

51. Mayhew, *Congress: The Electoral Connection*; and Fiorina, *Congress: Keystone*.

52. Jones, "Speculative Augmentation."

6   Chief Executive Politics

Americans have always preferred politics with a personal touch, making heroes and villains out of public figures and evaluating politicians on the basis of human qualities such as integrity, leadership ability, and attractiveness. It is rare for the American public to be mobilized by ideological debate or to be interested for very long in institutional deliberations and actions. Political interest typically focuses on individuals, and in most cases this means chief executives—presidents, governors, and mayors. Chief executives are the most visible, and in many ways the most important, actors in American government.

The prominence of chief executives in American politics is commonly attributed to the modern media. The media, especially television, find that covering powerful individuals in government is much more appealing and manageable than following developments in legislative, judicial, or bureaucratic institutions. The visibility of chief executives contributes to the public perception that politics and government are principally about what they do.

But media atttention is only part of the reason that American politics centers around chief executives. The system of governance set up by the federal and state constitutions also helps to explain the phenomenon. The United States is notable in the world for the number of independent, elected chief executives in government. Presidents have a nearly exclusive claim to a national electoral constituency and, unlike the case in parliamentary governments, they are independent of the national legislature. Governors and "strong" mayors have a somewhat less distinctive electoral position, but they are also independent of the legislatures in their jurisdictions and the national government.[1] Chief executive-centered politics is not simply a cultural oddity encouraged by media that seek above all else to sell more corn flakes; rather, it reflects in many ways the intentions of constitution writers at the national and state levels.

The term "chief executive politics," as used here, is not meant to encompass the full range of policy-making activity of American chief executives, but only those aspects that are most exclusively attributable to these public officials. What will be explored are the more visible and important positions taken, decisions made, and policies enacted by chief executives—the public record by which they are judged. These records have two main components: decisions made by chief executives during crises and policy initiatives or innovations sponsored by chief executives. Chief executives also are involved in a great many routine policy actions, most of which are covered in the chapter on bureaucratic politics.[2]

Rulers of the Agenda

Chief executives dominate the agenda-setting process in the United States. More often than not they are able to transform policy ideas from items of discussion among a few to items of discussion among the many. Because they have the public's attention, they force other politicians to pay attention to the matters they think are important. This gives them a tremendous advantage over any rivals in defining the issues for the public, and, ultimately, for other politicians. In short, chief executives typically set the terms of debate about political issues at the national, state, and local levels. This is not to say that chief executives are always, or even usually, successful in securing enactment of the policies they prefer. Indeed, it must be understood that chief executives are more impressive in the issue creation and agenda-setting process than in policy formulation and adoption.[3]

Modern presidents are expected to be opinion leaders. Their unique relationship with the national electorate gives them a certain flexibility in choosing issues and policies that other national policy makers do not have. Woodrow Wilson championed the League of Nations, Franklin Roosevelt pushed the New Deal, Lyndon Johnson began the Great Society, Richard Nixon made a breakthrough with China, and Ronald Reagan launched an antigovernment crusade. Chief executive politics ranges over the entire spectrum of policy types including distributive, redistributive, regulatory, social and moral, intergovernmental, intragovernmental, economic, foreign, defense, and national security.

Chief executives dominate certain issue domains more than others. At the national level, presidents traditionally have dictated American foreign and military policy. This power has enabled presidents to shape public opinion about America's proper role in the world; indeed, recent presidents have regarded the international scene as a vast set of "opportunities" for improving their popularity at home, especially around election time. Nixon was an adept exploiter of these international opportunities, coming up with the SALT I agreement and Henry Kissinger's pledge that "peace was at hand" in Vietnam as he faced reelection in 1972, and taking trips to the Middle East and the Soviet Union as the Watergate scandal heated up.[4]

International crises and foreign and military policy adventures also have caused big problems for presidents. Since the Vietnam War, negative responses by the national media, Congress, and the public have become a more common reaction to statements presidents have made and actions they have taken in the international arena. Jimmy Carter's and Ronald Reagan's presidencies were damaged by festering foreign policy problems (Carter's handling of the hostage crisis in Iran and the Soviet invasion of Afghanistan and Reagan's trading of arms for hostages with Iran and his support of Nicaraguan contras). International affairs continue to offer opportunities for presidents to mold public opinion, but there are limits to the inclination to believe what presidents say about the world and America's place in it.

Within their respective jurisdictions most governors and many mayors take the lead on issues and policies. Just like presidents, the combination of the media attention and their formal powers makes them substantially more visible and influential than other state and local politicians. The public and other policy makers look to them for new ideas and new proposals, and they have a flexibility in articulating policy concerns and proposing remedies that elected officials with narrower constituencies do not share. In his successful race for the governorship of California in 1975, Jerry Brown boldly rejected the policy positions of his popular predecessor, Ronald Reagan, and made liberal social and environmental reforms the centerpiece of his campaign. Governor Richard Lamm of Colorado established a national reputation during the 1970s and 1980s for speaking candidly about a wide range of controversial issues including environmental protection, Western rights, and the right to die. Madeleine Kunin ignored the conventional wisdom about avoiding new spending proposals and made toxic waste cleanup an issue in winning the governorship of Vermont in 1984.[5] Governors and mayors even have an analogue to foreign policy in intergovernmental relations, which, among state and local officials, is uniquely theirs to exploit.

Choosing the Issues

Although chief executives have a good deal of freedom to choose their issues, there are limits to this freedom. Occasionally, an issue in the form of a crisis is thrust upon the chief executive. The hostage episode in Tehran was a crisis that demanded an immediate, and then prolonged, presidential response. American diplomats were being held by militant "students," and a policy needed to be formulated at once. Philadelphia mayor Wilson Goode was faced with a crisis in 1985 when a radical group called MOVE refused to leave a condemned row house, leading to a confrontation with the police.

Not all crises are as compelling as the examples just cited, but chief executives have considerable latitude in labeling an event a crisis or a noncrisis. Carter tried to make the oil shortages of the 1970s into a crisis when he made his famous "moral equivalent of war" declaration to promote his energy policies. Reagan often portrayed the presence of the Sandinista government in Nicaragua as a national security crisis to convince Congress to aid the contras. Many regard the plight of the homeless in the United States as a crisis, but few politicians are responding to this issue as such. In part, crises exist in the eyes of the beholders, and presidents are able to open or close those eyes.

Table 6-1 depicts some of the relationships between issues, stages in the agenda-setting process, and chief executive discretion or range of choice. The table shows that crisis situations tend to involve problems that are very difficult for chief executives to ignore, but they usually give executives a good deal of flexibility in defining the nature of the problem for other policy makers and the public and in choosing a response. For issues that chief executives *choose* to promote, what happens at the different agenda-setting stages follows the opposite pattern. Chief executives have a wide choice in the selection of problems to address and they have a strong position from which to define the nature of these problems; but their ability to enact innovative responses is limited because they must take into account the preferences of the many other actors in the policy-making process, most of whom defer to chief executives during crises.

Available evidence suggests that governors and mayors may have somewhat less discretion than presidents in choosing issues to emphasize. For these politicians there are certain perennial issues, reflecting the basic services that state and local government provide—education, streets and highways, law enforcement and prisons, and social services—and these are nearly always addressed by leading candidates and officeholders.[6] Taxes frequently dominate all other issues, sometimes to the point of ensuring the end of the political careers of incumbents who have raised taxes and giving other candidates no real choice about how to position themselves.[7] Decisions made in Washington sometimes command the attention of state and local officials because intergovernmental grants-in-aid represent about 20 percent of state and local revenue. Domestic spending cuts made during the first Reagan term forced many states to assess their budget priorities as they had to decide whether and how to replace lost federal funds. In short, the leading issues for states and localities often are "givens" that represent long-standing or pressing problems.

Presidents and other chief executives are rarely, if ever, whimsical or freewheeling in their choices about what issues to emphasize; too much

Table 6-1 Issues, Agendas, and Chief Executive Discretion

	Problems/issues	Agenda stage	
		Problem definition	Specification of policy alternatives
CRISIS SITUATIONS	American hostages seized in Iran	Moslem extremism American weakness Russian meddling	diplomacy military action international sanctions
	MOVE occupies building in Philadelphia	radicals threaten law and order poverty breeds militancy neighborhood in peril	confrontation negotiation postponement strategies
Level of chief executive discretion	low	moderate	moderate/high
NONCRISIS SITUATIONS	tax reform	high tax rates for middle class low tax rates for the wealthy corporate give-aways	change tax rates eliminate deductions increase corporate taxes
	education reform	declining literacy in society low pay for teachers teacher union resistance to innovation	improve educational facilities adopt performance-based pay system increase teacher salaries across-the-board
Level of chief executive discretion	moderate/high	moderate	moderate/low

is at stake for decisions to be made haphazardly. Presidential scholar Paul Light stated, "All presidential decisions are purposive. Presidents select issues on the basis of their goals." [8] He listed the principal goals as reelection, historical achievement, and good policy.[9]

Most chief executives want to be reelected and therefore choose issues they think will help them garner votes. In general, they believe their positions on issues matter; indeed, that success or failure can hinge on issue stances and policy pledges.[10] This belief does not mean that chief executives are always aggressive in taking positions on a wide range of issues. It means that most perceive a need to address some important issues and to act in a way consistent with what they have said, even if vigorous follow-up is lacking. With all the media hype and money that go into contemporary campaigns, chief executives with reelection in mind are likely to be listening to their political advisers, media consultants, and public opinion pollsters more than their policy specialists. Policy agendas are often formed around issues that are evocative and remedies that are thought to be popular, rather than based on a serious effort to diagnose what is wrong and to find viable solutions.

Not all chief executives are concerned with reelection. In fact, some of them—presidents in their second term, governors who have reached the legal limit of their tenure in office, or others who decide they do not wish to run again—do not have to think about it at all. For most presidents, governors, and mayors, elections are a means to some larger and more substantive end, such as initiating good public policies, not an end in themselves. Chief executives want to leave a favorable historical legacy, and most of them recognize that sponsoring noteworthy and effective public policies is the best way to achieve this goal. The goals of historical recognition and good policies typically blend into one effort. Fortunate chief executives have knowledgeable advisers with ideas that are worthy of consideration. Chief executives who succeed in getting these ideas made into policy are recognized and remembered.

Sometimes chief executives use their positions to promote particular ideologies, and ideological expression cannot be neatly subsumed under the categories of reelection, historical recognition, or good public policy. Chief executives emphasize certain issues that have strong ideological content, even though some of them are not particularly popular, as part of a larger effort to build, maintain, or repudiate a dominant ideological coalition. Lyndon Johnson, who had not been a strong supporter of civil rights policies, became in the mid-1960s a champion of programs for poor and minority citizens in an effort to defend and expand the liberal Democratic ideology (and political coalition) that his predecessor, John Kennedy, had begun to build. Reagan led an effort to destroy this coalition and replace it with one built around conservative causes. He attacked all of the most ideologically loaded policy legacies of the Kennedy/Johnson era—public school busing, affirmative action, social welfare programs, reduced military spending, prohibitions on school prayer, intrusive regulations, and others.[11]

In every administration there is tension among those who are concerned about issues that contribute to short-term popularity, those who seek to promote ideological principles, and those who are interested in establishing policies of long-term effectiveness. Achieving a balance between these forces is one of a chief executive's main tasks, and some are better at it than others. Roosevelt offered ideas that brought not only electoral success but also historical recognition for his policy accomplishments and his ideological leadership.

Chief executives, particularly presidents, rarely are at the cutting edge of new issues or policy ideas. In a strict sense, they do not initiate agenda issues or lead the way to innovative approaches to problems. The real initiators are likely to be political activists, interest groups, researchers, or even legislative staffers or bureaucrats.[12] Most new issues and policy ideas have humble beginnings as the number of people interested in them is small. Some of these ideas, however, attract the attention of more visible spokespersons, become widely discussed, and eventually attract coalitions of supporters.[13] At any given time there are streams of acknowledged problems and potential solutions—policy proposals—flowing around and through policy-making institutions.[14] Chief executives and their policy advisers pick out those that fit with their philosophy and direction and promote them.

Obviously, many considerations figure into choosing issues, among them the political costs associated with certain ideas and the fit between the new ideas and the other positions taken by a chief executive.[15] Political parties add another voice to the process of selecting issues. Every four years the parties' platforms give various groups and advocates the opportunity to debate policy ideas, thereby helping chief executives determine those that have broad support.[16] Typically, chief executive policy leadership does not consist of a flash of inspiration and a headlong rush to legislative action; most often it is a set of cautious, purposive decisions made by executives and their advisers after surveying the ideas and proposals circulating among the politically active and aware.

Neglected Issues

Compared with other American policy makers, chief executives raise an exceptionally wide variety of issues. As tribunes of the people they are free to discuss just about any policy question they wish. Still, there is no doubt that certain kinds of issues are systematically neglected or excluded from their policy agendas; the spectrum of chief executive politics may be wide, but it is far from unlimited. With two major parties each striving to assemble majority coalitions, there is an undeniably centrist bias to American politics. Like the parties, and usually as leaders of them, chief executives need majorities to support them. Therefore, they aim most of their political pitches at the largest sector of the electorate. Because most Americans are middle class, U.S. politics tend to revolve around issues that most directly affect the middle class. A serious socialist agenda, therefore, is irrelevant, and few, if any, conservative leaders seriously challenge the New Deal reforms. Although it may be difficult to pin down, there is a kind of majority consensus that defines the acceptable range of political discourse in the United States, and successful chief executives remain within this range.[17]

Generalizations such as the one just offered are deliberately imprecise and can be easily misinterpreted. Our emphasis on middle-class/centrist politics does not mean that minorities and the poor are neglected altogether. The political history of black Americans—that of neglect by the white majority for many years, followed by selective attention as their political significance was recognized—confirms the basic thrust of the claim about the forces that dominate agendas, but also demonstrates that the trends can change. Significant events, media attention, and effective advocacy coalitions can turn a neglected issue into a salient issue in a fairly short time. By the same token, an issue may remain submerged indefinitely if no one with political muscle chooses to promote it. There are no absolutes in the issue creation process. Societies change, sometimes rapidly, and policy ideas that seemed outlandish at one time can become serious agenda items at another. Economic, technological, and environmental developments are not the only causes of these societal changes; human beings may be the agents of social and political change. Chief executives can and do change the nature of political discourse by daring to explore new directions.

Formulating and Persuading

The presence or absence of crisis conditions is of overarching significance in explaining the politics associated with chief executive policy making. During crises normal politics is suspended, and the power to decide comes to rest in the hands of chief executives and those they choose to advise them. Policy is determined in a centralized, hierarchical manner. This is one of those matters about which there is nearly universal consensus among legislators and other policy makers. Presidents are expected to lead during times of crisis, and other political elites recognize that presidents need room to maneuver if they are to do this effectively. With this unilateral power goes the responsibility for the decisions that are made. Crises test a chief executive's leadership and decision-making ability in an arena where the stakes are very high.

The classic example of crisis decision making is the Cuban missile crisis of 1962. Reacting to intelligence reports that the Soviet Union had placed missiles in Cuba, President Kennedy declared an emergency and called his top military and political advisers together. These meetings, and Kennedy's dominant role in them, have become something of an American legend because they have been written about and depicted on television many times. Kennedy's group gave little thought to consulting with Congress, or anyone else, as the confrontation approached. The United States and the Soviet Union stood on the brink of nuclear war, and the president was the unquestioned decision maker. The advice offered by those the president had assembled clearly had some influence, but Kennedy did not have to cajole or persuade anyone; he simply had to decide what course the country would follow. For those thirteen days in October virtually all the power of American government rested in his hands.

In noncrisis situations chief executives have to employ different political skills. Their ability to act unilaterally is greatly diminished, and their most important asset becomes the capacity to persuade others that their policy ideas deserve consideration and action. One aspect of this political skill is working with advisers and executive officials to put together an attractive program of policies. The other is the selling of the program to the legislature or the bureaucracy. In general, the government apparatus is stacked against chief executives who seek to innovate. There are many competing power centers that can frustrate the designs of chief executives if they are ignored or dealt with improperly. To be successful in normal politics, chief executives have to demonstrate the ability to be a leader among equals.

The missile crisis stands in sharp contrast to President Reagan's tax reform effort in 1986. Reagan and his economic advisers, intrigued by the prospect of offering the American public even lower tax rates, which had been cut in 1981, made tax reform the top domestic policy objective of his second term. If successful, this tax cut would make history. But history also taught that tax policy was one of the most, if not the most, prized of congressional prerogatives. Both the House Ways and Means Committee and the Senate Finance Committee would have strong views about the nature of any tax reform. Moreover, special interests save some of their biggest political guns for battles over tax policy, and their power and influence would somehow have to be nullified if meaningful tax reform was to be enacted. In short, many powerful people were unwilling to defer to the president on this matter, and he had to fight, bargain, cajole, and broadcast appeals to the public over an extended period of time to get a tax reform bill enacted. The package that finally emerged after two years of negotiation and compromise differed in several significant respects from what Reagan originally had proposed. One of the distinctive features of normal politics is that no one gets exactly what he or she wants.

Power

Richard Neustadt's enormously influential book, *Presidential Power*, provides a useful framework for understanding how chief executives exercise power.[18] Neustadt points out that executive power in American government is both protected and restricted by the Constitution. Presidents have a great deal of authority over the implementation of laws passed by Congress and over foreign affairs and military matters, but their domestic policy-making authority is limited. However, certain presidents—Franklin Roosevelt was always uppermost in Neustadt's mind—have exerted tremendous influence over both foreign and domestic policy.

This observation leads to one of Neustadt's major points: executive power is largely potential. Actual power depends on the ability of chief executives to leverage their formal powers and to stretch their influence over as many aspects of government as possible. Success implies that chief executives have convinced other government actors that going along with the plans and policies of the chief executive is in their best interest. Because this kind of governing entails extensive bargaining, Neustadt's primary and best-known conclusion, therefore, is that presidential power lies mainly in the ability to persuade.

State and local chief executives need the same talent. The governorships in most states have evolved in a way that closely parallels the presidency; the once largely ceremonial offices are now the engines of state politics. But the formal powers of governors are constrained in many important ways, which makes bargaining skills even more necessary. Governors may face tougher persuasive tasks than presidents because in most states certain cabinet officers are elected by the voters, not appointed by the governor. It is not unusual for these officials to be political rivals or opponents of the governor. No matter which, their political independence is a virtual certainty. Big-city mayors face a similar situation in that major bureaucratic officials are either elected by the citizens or selected by boards or commissions and, therefore, the mayors may have a difficult time persuading these officials to support their policies. Governors and mayors operate in smaller arenas than presidents, which reduces somewhat the number of powerful political actors with whom they must contend. But they do not have as much formal authority over their executive branches as presidents.[19]

Chief executive power is clearly elastic. Chief executives with similar or identical formal powers exert widely varying degrees of influence within the governments they inhabit. Part of this variation can be attributed to larger political or economic factors, such as the presence or absence of crises, which would foster centralized leadership. There can be no doubt, however, that the aspirations and abilities of chief executives also influence how much power they wield. Pierre du Pont made more of the Delaware governorship both in personal terms, leaving office in 1984 with an 86 percent approval rating, and policy terms, advancing environmental protection and economic development, than his predecessors, Sherman Tribett and Russell Peterson.[20] At the national level, President Carter's inability to gain control over the different facets of government during his administration, despite the presence of solid Democratic majorities in both houses of Congress, reveals him to have been considerably less adept at the power game than Roosevelt or Johnson.

However, comparisons between the most recent presidents and those whose served in the 1940s, 1950s, or 1960s should leave the student of contemporary politics somewhat uneasy. Political conditions have changed, and these changes have affected the way chief executives exercise power. Probably the most important changes have come in the number of active participants in the political process and the relationship between politicians and their constituents.

In the days of Franklin Roosevelt and Dwight Eisenhower (the background for *Presidential Power*) there were a limited number of truly powerful interest groups, and like-minded groups often worked together so that deals could be struck with the leaders who represented broad segments of society, such as business, labor, agriculture, and a few others. Party leaders exercised a great deal of influence over their ranks, which simplified presidential negotiations with Congress. There were some strong and independent executive branch officials and military leaders that had to be taken into account, but, Neustadt emphasized, one man with sound management ability, great interpersonal skills, knowledge of politics, and a clear direction could hold the various pieces of government together through the bargaining process.

By the 1970s many presidential scholars had begun to doubt whether anyone could do what Roosevelt had done.[21] The increasing number and variety of interest groups, the staunch independence of elected officials, the accompanying erosion of party cohesion, and the persistent institutional conflict and competition seemed to produce an unmanageable pluralism. It was and is unmanageable if the chief executive uses traditional bargaining strategies. Reagan, like Carter, Ford, Nixon, and Johnson, encountered tremendous resistance to his policy initiatives from the many power centers of national government, but he showed that power can be amassed in a significant new way. Reagan did not rely on bargaining with political elites; instead he took his message directly to the people, using his weekly radio broadcasts and speeches on television to persuade his supporters to pressure political officials to endorse his initiatives. The mass media emerged as the most potent weapon in a president's arsenal, and Reagan, the "Great Communicator," used it to his advantage. In the mass media age it may not matter very much whether political power brokers admire a chief executive's political acumen, as long as they have sufficient respect for, or fear of, the chief executive's ability to arouse the public through direct appeals.[22]

Increased use of direct appeals to the public as a way of enhancing chief executive power is well suited to contemporary political reality, just as bargaining was an appropriate strategy to pursue in the political environment of the 1950s. The independence of other elected officials comes from their certainty that they have established, and can maintain, a favorable image with voters. These relationships hinge more and more on money and the use of advanced communication technology. To the extent that chief executives can break into these relationships, the independence of other political actors is threatened. Legislators pay close attention to constituent opinions, and chief executives who use the media effectively can influence these opinions.[23] When this kind of influence occurs, or when politicians think it is occurring, resistance to a chief executive's policy preferences dissipates, and persuasive power has been exercised.

Tax reform again provides a good illustration. Shortly after his reelection, President Reagan set out to sell the idea of tax reform directly to the public. In 1985 he spoke on behalf of tax reform wherever and whenever he had a chance. The issue has natural political appeal, but the barriers to meaningful tax reform from political elites were legendary. Political action committee (PAC) contributions to the most influential members of the House Ways and Means and Senate Finance committees were, and still are, very generous, which only begins to suggest the difficulties associated with overhauling the tax code.[24] Nevertheless, the chairman of Ways and Means, Dan Rostenkowski, D-Ill., gave tax reform a push by reporting a bill out of his committee. In addition to trying to influence the content of any tax reform package that Congress might approve, Rostenkowski was also interested in denying Reagan the opportunity to pillory the Democrats during the 1986 election season for killing tax reform. To be sure, traditional bargaining also was at work—Rostenkowski and Treasury Secretary James Baker spent time together on Capitol Hill and on local golf courses—but everyone close to the process acknowledged the effectiveness of Reagan's appeals to the public. The interests that had the most to lose from tax reform were too strong to be overcome by pluralist bargaining. The only way to break their hold on legislators was to send a message through constituents.

The ability to persuade is still the major determinant of chief executive power. However, political persuasion is a multifaceted enterprise; it can be accomplished through traditional political bargaining among self-interested parties, through momentum-building appeals to the public, or by some combination of the two. Where opportunities for "going public" are plentiful, such as in contemporary national politics, one should expect extensive use of this tactic by telegenic politicians.[25] But bargaining and other customary political skills will continue to dominate where direct appeals to voters are difficult, where chief executives lack media appeal, or where there is a manageable number of ranking participants in the policy process.

Leadership

Most of those who have written on the subject seem to agree that the acquisition of power is the *sine qua non* of executive leadership.[26] Without power, leadership is virtually impossible. The fragmented nature of American government at all levels makes coherent action difficult; therefore, the essence of chief executive leadership is providing government with a direction or purpose. Implied in this conception of leadership is change. Leaders need to produce tangible results, and typically these come in the form of identifiable changes in government organization or policy.[27] Planned changes that are effective and long-lasting and decisive action in crises are the hallmarks of effective leadership.

The essential ingredients of chief executive leadership are both personal and institutional. Judgments about personality or character are highly subjective and, therefore, difficult to generalize, but personality seems more important than ever in the age of media politics. James David Barber, who has made a career of studying the role of personality in politics, points out that some chief executives derive positive feelings, such as satisfaction, exhilaration, and joy, from their political activity, while others experience mostly negative feelings, such as paranoia, resentment, and sadness.[28] Exhibiting some sort of positive disposition is part of effective leadership. Advisers, subordinates, and even rivals and opponents are at their best when they are driven by a forceful and inspiring personality.

The institutional side of executive leadership is concerned with the selection of advisers, analysts, political operatives, public relations specialists, and the others who are part of an administration. Most chief executives are able to surround themselves with a sizable cadre of loyalists, and their success at channeling the energies and skills of these individuals on behalf of their objectives is critical in determining their ultimate effectiveness as political leaders. Once the appointees are in place, the chief executives make the most critical choices: whose advice to take and when. And their range of options is quite large. They can rely on many advisers or few; they can make great or little use of cabinet officials, outside specialists, or members of their personal staff; or they can establish hierarchical, competitive, or collegial relationships among their advisers. There are no proven formulas for success, but the experiences of several presidents provide useful insights into this aspect of chief executive politics.

Having many close and able advisers who represent various perspectives is widely regarded as a prudent practice, although relatively few presidents have followed it. Roosevelt and Kennedy usually get the highest marks on this score. Nixon's complete reliance on three or four advisers during his second term is regarded as a reason for his downfall and should serve as a warning to other presidents of the dangers of inaccessibility.[29] Despite the Nixon precedent, concerns about leaks of politically sensitive information to the press and the natural unpleasantness associated with hearing things one does not like limited the openness of the Ford, Carter, and Reagan presidencies.

Eisenhower arranged his advisers hierarchically with the cabinet officers at the top. By all accounts, however, his regular cabinet meetings were not terribly productive. Carter revived the idea of regular cabinet meetings during his first year, but then gave up on them because they were unproductive. The basic problem with cabinet meetings is that too much of the discussion is disingenuous, as the officials present are primarily concerned about protecting their bureaucratic turf or impressing the president. Cabinet meetings can be useful for symbolic purposes or to solidify a consensus about a position or a policy, but not for policy development or even serious issue discussions.[30]

Kennedy and Johnson created a number of special task forces, composed of trusted advisers and outside intellectuals or policy specialists, to develop innovative proposals. Since the Kennedy and Johnson years presidents have established a great many similar policy groups, most of which consist of department or agency officials, generalists from the White House staff, and specialists from Executive Office agencies, to formulate policies that cut across traditional institutional or program boundaries. Another often-used means of policy development is the creation of presidential commissions, which invite respected outsiders to study a problem and recommend solutions. These groups also help presidents deflect criticism and avoid the responsibility for making controversial decisions.[31]

Effective congressional liaison is another important facet of policy leadership. Kennedy and Carter's difficulties and Johnson and Reagan's successes demonstrate the need for knowledgeable and experienced legislative liaisons. Finally, the number and importance of presidential advisers who are primarily responsible for public relations has grown steadily as the media role in politics and governance has become more pervasive. The media role is both a cause and effect of the propensity of presidents to communicate directly with the public.

Governors and mayors tend to take organizational leads from presidents, whose leadership challenges are well known. Governors' staffs grew significantly in the 1960s and 1970s, reaching an average of thirty-four members in 1979.[32] Nearly all governors employ political advisers, legislative liaisons, bureaucratic liaisons, press secretaries or public relations specialists, legal advisers, and budget experts.[33] Using teams of agency officials and political advisers to develop policy initiatives is common. Most governors regard selling their policy ideas to the legislature as one of their most difficult tasks, a true test of their leadership.[34] Mayors also need this kind of assistance. Bureaucratic liaisons, often called chief administrative officers, help mayors handle challenges from independent-minded bureaucratic agencies.[35] Depending upon how extensive their appointment power and resources are, mayors may also employ political advisers, press secretaries, and budget specialists.

Decision Making

The crisis/noncrisis distinction is of great help in simplifying the enormous variation in the characteristics and determinants of chief executive decision making. At one end of the spectrum are visible and threatening crises in which the number of participants in the decision-making process is small, advice consists mainly of substantive information and analysis, and chief executive decisions are authoritative. At the other end are controversial domestic initiatives in which the number of active participants is large, political advice and calculations are usually more important than substantive/analytic information, and chief executives and legislatures vie with one another over an extended period of time to determine the nature of policy. The power of chief executives obviously is greatest during crises, but other aspects of these situations are dangerous and unpleasant. What most chief executives would prefer is to have the characteristics of crisis decision making present in noncrisis situations; in fact, a good deal of the politics of chief executive policy making centers around efforts to achieve such a state of affairs.

The chief executive sets the basic outline of policy action in campaign promises and other statements. Translating these ideas into concrete policy proposals is the job of advisers and policy development groups. The personal involvement of chief executives in the formulation process varies in accordance with their personalities and abilities: some try to master most of the details, while others content themselves with sketching the big picture; some are rigid and doctrinaire, and others flexible and accommodating. Reagan and Carter offer illustrative contrasts. Carter impressed other politicians with his command of the details of policy options, but he could never chart a clear direction with the policies he promoted. Reagan's knowledge of policy was quite general, in some cases mostly anecdotal, but many of his pronouncements inspired successful and significant policy actions that reflected the conservative philosophy he championed.

In times of crisis chief executives have the power to make policy with little or no outside approval. For noncrisis policy initiatives the path from executive formulation to adoption can be tortuously long. Once a preferred approach has been devised, chief executives and their staffs turn their attention to eliminating the many barriers to enactment. The outcome of this effort is determined largely by the level of aggregation they can achieve. If the multiple interests that have a stake in a policy decision can be herded into a few identifiable groups and agree to be bound by the bargains their leaders strike, policy enactment is likely. Without aggregation, initiatives get shredded in the fragmented governmental machinery.

Successful aggregation indicates that power has been exercised. Chief executives have an array of persuasive devices that can be deployed on behalf of their initiatives—the invocation of party loyalty, direct appeals to the public, the dispersal of special favors, political trades and promises, the real or threatened use of a veto—and these are commonly used in this high stakes arena of power and politics.

President Reagan's twin tower successes of 1981—the three-year, 25 percent tax cut and the budget bills containing defense increases and domestic spending cuts—demonstrate effective aggregation and use of presidential power. Budget director David Stockman hastily assembled the budget proposals in the early months of the administration and moved them quickly to Congress to take advantage of the president's impressive election victory. His plan was to bring a budget package directly to the floor of Congress for up or down votes. If approved, such legislation would first direct the various authorizing committees to change the provisions of programs that obligate the government to assist the unemployed, the elderly, the handicapped, the poor, and others to bring about specified spending reductions, a budget process called reconciliation, and then to enact these collective changes into law. In the Senate, the objections of Budget Committee chairman Pete Domenici, R-N.M, were stifled by Majority Leader Howard Baker, R-Tenn., to whom Reagan made direct appeals, and the administration's budget bills, reconciliation, and the final budget resolution were passed by May. In the House a group of mostly southern Democrats, nicknamed "boll weevils" and led by Stockman ally Phil Gramm of Texas, joined with Republicans. In May and June they proposed administration-approved substitutes for the bills brought to the floor by the Democratic-controlled Budget Committee and passed them both. The committee process, the cornerstone of legislative fragmentation, was circumvented in both chambers in the enactment of these budget packages, which the administration considered vital. The success of the budget bills paved the way for the tax cut, which, as a result of a few rounds of negotiation between Reagan and leaders of the coalitions just described, was enacted a month later.[36]

The success of Republican Louie B. Nunn, governor of Kentucky, in getting a new sales tax bill through a Democratic-controlled legislature in the late 1960s illustrates the importance of political trading and special favors in the exercise of chief executive leadership. Coleman Ransone's study of governors quotes liberally from a *Louisville Courier-Journal* article entitled "Legislators Explain Nunn's Fiscal Arm Twisting" to make this point.

During the five hours of oratory yesterday, Rep. Norbert Blume, D. Louisville, explained how 57 Democrats can match votes with 43 Republicans and lose:

"Last night, many an arm was twisted."

One that was twisted is fastened to Rep. William Cox, Democratic freshman from Madisonville. He drew applause from both parties when he took time to explain on the floor how the power of the Governor's office is traditionally used in Kentucky to capture key votes in the legislature.

Tuesday, Cox supported the food-medicine-clothing amendment to the sales tax bill (the Governor opposed amendments). Yesterday in a vote to reconsider the amendment, he opposed it. He explained why:

"Today each of us must vote for what we think are the best interests of our people," Cox said. "Yesterday I let my emotion and dedication to my Democratic colleagues override my sense of responsibility to my district."

Cox represents Hopkins County. He told the House that buried among the thick pages of appropriations in Nunn's $2.47 billion budget are projects for Hopkins County that total some $1 million. . . .

Although Cox did not say it, all the legislators know the governor holds the power of "line-item veto" over the budget that will cross his desk. He can approve the whole document by signing it, but he can also veto any simple appropriation with a short pen stroke.

"When you receive much, much must be given," Cox said. "While I know the enactment of a 5 percent sales tax will impose a considerable burden on some of my constituents, I know they are the ones who will benefit most from this budget." [37]

Mayor Harold Washington of Chicago (1983-1987) faced consistent opposition from a majority bloc of twenty-nine aldermen during his first few years in office. He eventually convinced a federal judge that seven of Chicago's wards had been gerrymandered to dilute the black and Hispanic vote. As a result of a special election, Washington picked up four more supporters on the city council to match the opposition, twenty-five to twenty-five. When there is a tie on a council vote the mayor votes to break it. Washington was then able to make a number of organizational and policy changes he had long advocated. Washington followed an unusual path to achieve a working majority, without which a chief executive cannot act decisively. [38]

Programs and Policies

The variety of chief executive policies can be overwhelming; it is therefore useful to break them into three categories: (1) international and intergovernmental policies and actions; (2) economic and budget policies; and (3) domestic "quality of life" policies. This scheme has descriptive and analytic utility, and separates policies in a common and easily understood way. [39]

As the international economy becomes more extensively interwoven, states and cities are having more frequent direct dealings with foreign nations. But foreign policy is still a more or less exclusive realm for presidents. Modern presidents usually make foreign policy their highest priority because they have more power to determine policy in this area and they cannot ignore international crises. Economic and budget policies come next for presidents, who recognize that perceptions about the success or failure of their administrations hinge on the economy. Domestic policies tend to come last because breakthroughs are so difficult to achieve. [40] For governors and mayors budget and domestic policy matters dominate; these are the areas of greatest constituent interest. Economic crises—plant closings, bank failures, strikes by municipal workers—are not uncommon, and when they occur, chief executive policy leadership is expected.

The notable constant among these categories for all chief executives is budget policy. The budget embodies the priorities of government, and, because executives prepare budgets for their legislatures, they are in a position to influence their governments' priorities. [41] Budget preparation affords chief executives the opportunity to assert their preferences on nearly every aspect of policy. Although legislatures show a marked preference for making only marginal changes in existing spending levels for policies and programs when they enact a new budget, many chief executives use the budget as a powerful policy weapon, as the Nunn story illustrates. Since 1980 budget decisions have overshadowed all others at the national level as Congress has scrambled to cope with huge deficits. Washington insiders speak of the "budget driving the policy process," by which they mean that substantive policy questions are subordinated to budget considerations, such as not exceeding spending levels specified in budget resolutions, when new programs are authorized or, more commonly, when old programs are reauthorized. Although chief executives often fail to get what they want out of the budget process, they consider it a major part of policy leadership.

Substance versus Symbolism

Presidents, governors, and mayors inhabit worlds heavily laden with symbolism. Aside from the many ceremonial functions associated with these offices, symbolic rhetoric is used to build consensus on matters of general principle or for specific policies. For example, President Reagan continually invoked certain themes and slogans in relation to his policies. Tax cuts and regulatory reform were ways of "getting government off the backs of the people"; large military budgets and new weapon systems helped to "make America strong"; and aid to Nicaraguan "freedom fighters" kept communists away from U.S. borders. When the policies of a chief executive are enacted, often they are described in highly symbolic terms, typically portraying the chief executive as above parochial politics and working in the larger interest of the nation, state, or city.

Political scientist Jeff Fishel has studied the relationship between presidential rhetoric and policy actions in great detail, and has compiled some interesting data (see Table 6-2).[42] For the most part these data support the conventional wisdom about the inclinations of recent presidents toward rhetoric and action. Kennedy made many promises, followed up on most of them, but had some trouble with Congress. Johnson's 1964 campaign was high on rhetoric and very low on specific promises, but he was exceptionally effective in getting what he wanted from Congress. Nixon had trouble with the Democratic-controlled Congresses with which he had to work. Carter made more specific promises and took action on a higher percentage of them than his predecessors, but he never managed to gain control of Congress. Reagan stands out for making only a few specific policy pledges and for neglecting most of them; his overall record with Congress was mediocre, although his success rate during 1981-1982 was quite high. These data also under-

Table 6-2 *Presidential Promises, Action, and Policy*

	Kennedy (1960)[a]	Johnson (1964)[a]	Nixon (1968)[a]	Carter (1976)[a]	Reagan (1980)[a]
Number of identifiable campaign promises[b]	133	63	153	186	108
Percentage of campaign promises calling for concrete action[c]	64	60	64	67	36
Percentage of campaign promises for which full or partial executive action was taken[d]	67	63	60	65	43
Percentage of congressional dependent promises for which executive action was taken and which were enacted[e]	53	62	34	41	44

Sources: The categories first appeared in Gerald Pomper, *Elections in America* (New York: Dodd, Mead, 1968); data for Johnson and Nixon compiled by Fred I. Grogan in "Candidate Promises and Performances, 1964-1972" (Paper presented at the 1977 meeting of the Midwest Political Science Association); the rest of the data presented by Jeff Fishel in *Presidents and Promises* (Washington, D.C.: CQ Press, 1985), 33, 39, 42.

[a] Year in which promises were made.

[b] The figures for Johnson and Nixon include some foreign policy promises (14 for Johnson, 36 for Nixon). All the others include domestic policy promises only.

[c] Fishel uses four categories of campaign promises: pledges of continuity, expression of goals and concerns, pledges of action, and detailed pledges. The latter two comprise this category.

[d] Fishel uses seven categories of executive action: proposals that were fully or partially comparable to promises, token action, contradictory action, no action, mixed action, and indeterminate. Categories one and two are collapsed here for these low percentages.

[e] The total from which these percentages were calculated is slightly lower than the number of promises because some promises were not dependent on congressional actions (for example, orders and unclassifiable promises).

score the frequency of deadlock. Nixon, Carter, and, to some extent, Reagan tried to translate their rhetoric into policy proposals, but they often were thwarted by Congress at the policy enactment stage.

Nonrhetorical symbols also contribute to the leadership mystique of chief executives. By wearing blue jeans, playing softball, and having outdoor barbecues at the White House, Jimmy Carter sought to distinguish his administration from the "imperial" presidency of Richard Nixon. Jerry Brown made a point of not living in the governor's mansion, keeping an austere apartment instead, which appealed to younger, nontraditional constituents. Wisconsin's former governor Lee Dreyfus had a favorite red vest that became his trademark. Projecting a compelling image can be crucial to effective political leadership.

It is not uncommon for political observers to assert, usually in a critical tone, that certain chief executive policies are merely symbolic. This charge has often been leveled against policies in areas like civil rights, welfare, environmental protection, and foreign policy, where rhetoric usually exceeds action by a large margin. The civil rights statutes of 1957 and 1960 and executive orders dating back to 1950 did little to reduce the various forms of discrimination at which they were directed. Eventually, however, they led to stronger and more efficacious statutes, the Civil Rights Act of 1964 and the Voting Rights Act of 1965, and executive orders in 1965 and 1969 that produced significant changes in black employment and voting.[43] Given the serial nature of American policy making, initial steps that are high on symbolism and low on substance are often necessary to pave the way for policies that produce real change.

Symbolism also plays a major role in crisis decision making. How much of President Gerald Ford's aggressive military response to the seizure of the Navy ship *Mayaguez* by the Cambodians after the U.S. defeat in Vietnam was an attempt to bolster a sagging national morale and to send a message to potential adversaries that America was still willing to fight to protect its vital interests? Was the 1983 Grenada invasion a response to a real threat to American lives and national security, or was it a symbol of a new resolve to assert American hegemony in the Western Hemisphere?

These examples point up how difficult it is to make definitive judgments about symbolism and substance, particularly with regard to the high-visibility policies of chief executive politics. Chief executives sponsor policies for both symbolic and substantive reasons; the balance between the two probably is best judged after the results of such policies have surfaced and been analyzed.

Change

The conservative inclinations of American government are likely to be embodied in chief executive policies. Nevertheless, the elective institutions of American government can make innovative decisions, and, when they do, it is almost always chief executives who provide the driving force. Presidential scholar James Ceaser pointed out that "presidents have an important role to play in covering the struggle of self-interest [that pervades American politics] with a veneer of poetry and calling at certain moments for sacrifice for the common good." [44]

A crisis creates an opportunity for a chief executive to pursue innovative policies. Wars permit all sorts of unusual measures—industry seizures, rationing, strict wage and price controls, and plans for world government. The Great Depression brought forth the New Deal programs and the beginning of the welfare state. It is difficult to overstate the significance of agencies like the Rural Electrification Administration (REA) or the Tennessee Valley Authority (TVA) for the millions of rural Americans who lived in primitive conditions until the New Deal brought them electrical power, or of minimum wage and labor relations laws for the millions of blue-collar workers of that era. Policies that produce changes of such magnitude have longstanding political force and enshrine the leaders who sponsored them. They also encourage other chief executives to aspire to similar accomplishments.

It would be a mistake, however, to equate crises and innovation in American politics. One of the most significant revelations of a crisis like the depression is that centralized policy action *is* possible; it simply requires nothing more than working legislative majorities. It is not altogether unusual for such majorities to exist, at least for certain kinds of policies. Therefore, many chief executives have some opportunity for originality. President Johnson supervised a Democratic majority that shared a broad consensus on the need to alleviate poverty, and they worked together to enact innovative policies. During the 1980s there seemed to be a widening coalition in Washington that was willing to support innovative economic policies like tax reform and nearly any kind of pricing deregulation, while opposing anything that resembled a public employment program. Governors around the country have spearheaded sweeping education reforms with an unusual amount of legislative cooperation. The status quo constrains but does not dictate the actions of American policy makers, especially chief executives.

Working majorities do not simply appear out of the blue. They come about because popular chief executives make an effort to assemble them. Policies and politics are inseparable: innovative policies are most often the product of an evolutionary process that involves an awareness among politicians of widespread public concern about certain problems, the selection by a chief executive of popular solutions, and the use of persuasive techniques to build a policy majority among legislators. Chief executives can easily stumble over any of these steps, but they can also succeed; their successes are policies that produce change.

Beneficiaries

Chief executives are fond of claiming that their policies benefit all members of society. In a sense this is true. To the extent that macroeconomic policies contribute to overall economic growth, there are widely shared gains. When threats to national security are effectively rebuffed, everyone benefits. When bureaucracies are reorganized to function more efficiently or law enforcement is improved to reduce crime, the whole society is said to be better off. However, analysis easily uncovers variations in the benefits different population segments or geographical areas realize from policies. And, not surprisingly, these variations have political roots.

Like most elected officials, chief executives pursue policies that benefit their main constituents. This support is not always a matter of narrow partisanship or cynicism about doing what is best for the collectivity. For most chief executives there is a natural merging over time of their views about what is best for society and their preference for policies that disproportionately benefit their supporters. New Deal Democrats, for example, tended to view the world in terms of the struggle of workers and other ordinary citizens to use government to curb the abuses of big business. The policies of Franklin Roosevelt and Harry Truman were aimed primarily at helping white male workers, who became the core of the Democratic party as their lives improved during the 1940s and 1950s. In the early 1960s John Kennedy presided over an increasingly fragile Democratic majority coalition that needed the votes not only of blue-collar whites but also of blacks to control national elections.[45] This need led to the serious pursuit of civil rights policies and programs to aid the poor, but always with an eye toward not alienating white, middle-class Democrats. Since the 1960s black Americans have been the most cohesive Democratic voting bloc.[46] Reagan's antigovernment policies aimed to please the middle and upper classes from which the Republican party draws its strength.

The meshing of chief executive policies and constituent preferences is by no means complete. The policy universe is too crowded and complicated for chief executives always to help their friends and hurt their enemies. Carter lost the support of organized labor because he did not push minimum wage and national health insurance legislation hard enough to suit union leaders.[47] New York mayor Ed Koch angered his core Democratic constituencies, the racial and ethnic minorities and the city employees, by taking tough fiscal austerity measures during his first term (1977-1981).[48] Republican governor John Spellman of Washington committed that almost unforgivable political sin of going back on a 1980 campaign promise not to raise taxes, and it cost him his post in 1984.[49]

It is not uncommon for a chief executive to contradict one of his or her publicly stated positions rather than to pursue policies that displease important voting blocs. Reagan often changed his mind at politically opportune moments, making adept adjustments in his positions on Social Security, farm subsidies, public works programs, and import restrictions. A most striking example of a chief executive adjusting to a changing constituency is Governor George Wallace of Alabama. The leading symbol of southern racism in the 1960s, Wallace successfully courted Alabama's black voters in his 1982 gubernatorial bid. Ironically, political leaders sometimes have to follow changes in the political wind in order to stay in charge.

Promise and Performance

Chief executive policies are born out of grand promises and often generate great expectations about societal change. Invariably the results fall short of what was promised, but what is accomplished may be quite significant nonetheless. The true results of chief executive policies are realized over an extended period of time as programs and procedures become institutionalized and policies are modified. Studying the consequences of such policies reveals many examples that confirm the essentially political nature of the implementation process and underscore how difficult it is to make precise judgments about the impacts of public policies.

In 1967 Lyndon Johnson came up with an idea for helping the poor with one of their most pressing problems, the lack of decent, affordable housing. The deplorable conditions in many cities had led to rioting, and no one seemed to know how to improve matters. Johnson remembered that the federal government owned land in most cities and could more or less give the land to builders who would construct low-cost housing. With federal help the cities could build "new towns in-town." [50] Johnson brought together the relevant agency heads and a program was launched. Four years later the program had produced almost no new housing in the seven cities chosen to demonstrate its viability. Why?

By now the problems encountered during the implementation of the new towns program are well known to students of public policy. Local political opposition; inadequate federal resources, incentives, and guidance; poor communication between federal and local implementers; and a faulty program design conspired to derail this program.[51] What struck Johnson as a great idea made a number of community groups hot, left local elected officials cold, and kept bureaucrats confused. The more general lesson is that pluralism and federalism make chief executive initiatives in domestic policy areas like urban redevelopment extremely difficult to implement. Many well-intentioned programs have floundered because of the difficulties associated with getting bureaucratic agencies, elected officials, and citizen groups to work cooperatively.

Implementation problems are by no means limited to domestic policies; they also occur in foreign policy, even during crises. The most common difficulties are the same as in the domestic area: presidential intentions may be poorly communicated; implementers lack the resources necessary to carry out directives; and implementers sometimes resist doing what they are told.[52] The State Department and the military are notorious for their adherence to standard procedures, perhaps the most common form of bureaucratic resistance to orders from above (see chapter 4). At critical times during the Cuban missile crisis President Kennedy ordered the Navy to move its blockade closer to Cuba, and not to act belligerently toward the first few Soviet ships it encountered after the quarantine had been declared. Evidence indicates that the Navy did not move its quarantine line as the president ordered, and a long argument ensued between Secretary of Defense Robert McNamara and Navy Admiral George Anderson about how intercepted Soviet ships would be treated. It ended with Anderson waving the *Manual of Navy Regulations* at McNamara and then remarking, "Now Mr. Secretary, if you and your Deputy will go back to your offices, the Navy will run the blockade." [53] The Navy's reluctance to depart from standard operating procedures in the midst of this type of crisis shows that even when the president is directly involved, and the need for effective action is obvious, implementation is by no means automatic.

The existence of problems should not obscure the fact that some policies are effectively implemented with little apparent difficulty. Social Security, for example, is mainly a matter of eligibility determination and the issuance of checks, and the government seems to be capable of executing these tasks quite well. Similarly, even a major change like the 1986 tax reform can be implemented without too much difficulty because it mostly requires that the Internal Revenue Service (IRS) make a series of fairly specific changes in the tax code, which is something that agency is experienced at doing. Comparing policies that are difficult to implement with those that are implemented rather easily leads to the identification of a number of variables that help to explain or predict the observed differences. These variables are the same as those commonly used to analyze the policy-making process.

The chances of encountering major problems during the implementation of chief executive policies are largely dependent upon: (1) the amount of societal and/or organizational change the policy seeks to generate; (2) the complexity of the implementation process—how many different bureaucratic agencies and elected officials are involved; and (3) the level of consensus among the principal implementation actors about the desirability and feasibility of making planned changes.

Policies that seek to bring about great change are difficult to implement successfully because they call for widespread modification in behavior, and the government usually has only limited resources for encouraging it. However, the degree of difficulty associated with implementing high-change policies also is affected by the complexity of the implementation process and the level of consensus among the implementers. High-change policies, such as tax reform, carried out through a simple organizational network in which those involved understand and support programmatic goals have a good chance of succeeding. Complex implementation arrangements and competing priorities among implementers are almost certain to distort the original goals of high-change policies such as the new towns project and other intergovernmental social welfare and economic development programs.

For policies aimed at producing limited change the expectations are quite different. In general, such policies are likely to be implemented with reasonable effectiveness. However, they can be derailed by a cumbersome implementation process or fundamental disagreement among implementers. The new towns program was not dramatically new in what it sought to accomplish, but the organizational network required to implement it was complex and clumsy, and the consensus among implementation actors was decidedly low. These two factors accounted for the program's minimal success.

Impacts

In an interesting and revealing study, political scientist Lester Salamon examined the effects of a New Deal program thirty years after it had been terminated. The program, known as the Resettlement Program, authorized the federal government to purchase nearly 2 million acres of land in 200 different locations and to supervise specially designed agricultural or industrial communities that would make use of the land.[54] A common way of implementing the agricultural program was for the government to break large plantations up into family-size parcels and sell them under lenient terms to tenant farmers, regardless of their race. Because black land ownership in the South was uncommon, and black poverty pervasive, this program, although small in scale, represented a "bold experiment in social reform." [55] Not surprisingly, the program had many critics, primarily white southern legislators, and it was killed in 1943 after nine years. The fact that it was terminated led to the general view that the program had been a failure. Salamon's analysis of the program's impacts in 1973, however, documented a solid record of land retention by the black families it had assisted. The families had moved out of poverty into the middle class. They owned cars, television sets, and refrigerators. Their children obtained white-collar jobs, and the people were active in political and community organizations and causes. The effects, which Salamon called "sleepers," took many years to emerge in a discernible form.[56]

The pattern of impacts observed in the Resettlement Program is significant because it means that ambitious and innovative programs often have effects that can be clearly identified only many years after they are implemented. Head Start, a product of Johnson's War on Poverty, did not seem an unqualified success during its first major evaluation, which was conducted four years after the program's inception; but recent studies have documented long-term positive effects for the participants.[57] Much the same pattern has held for other major social welfare programs like job training, food stamps, and Medicaid.[58]

The main problem with sleeper effects is that they do nothing to relieve the pressure chief executives feel to produce visible, short-term results from the policies they sponsor. Because of this, chief executives favor programs that have more immediate payoffs. Policies that cannot survive by demonstrating quick positive results must maintain a certain level of political popularity during the time it takes for definitive impacts to emerge.

Chief executive policies often produce unintended results, and these, like latent or sleeper effects, muct be considered if the full impact of a policy is to be accurately assessed. The iron curtain was an unanticipated result of Truman's effort, known as the Marshall Plan, to rebuild the economies of Western Europe after World War II. Kennedy's determination to land a man on the moon by 1970 resulted in many technological breakthroughs that have had a tremendous influence on the commercial electronics industry and the way of life in the United States. Acid rain in New England and Canada is widely believed to be caused in part by coal burned in the Midwest, a practice furthered by the Carter administration's energy program that sought, through subsidies for coal conversion, to reduce the industrial use of crude oil and natural gas. It should be clear that chief executives do not always get the results they expect from the policies they sponsor.

Even more basic than the uncertainties introduced by time and unanticipated results is the problem of establishing cause-and-effect relationships between policies and outcomes. This is particularly true for chief executive policies because they often aspire to significant changes in society, but such changes almost always have complex causes. The Reagan administration's monetary and fiscal policies—the tax cut and stricter control of the money supply—frequently are credited with reducing inflation during the 1980s. However, increasing foreign competition in certain core industries and lower energy costs may have had as much to do with keeping prices down as did government policy. State reforms in education have been praised, but linking changes in teaching techniques, approaches to discipline, or working conditions in the schools with student aptitude and achievement test scores is a notoriously complex task.[59]

Foreign policies and subsequent developments also are difficult to connect. How much did the allegedly "soft" foreign policy of the Carter administration have to do with the Soviet invasion of Afghanistan? How much did the more belligerent Reagan foreign policy affect the willingness of the Soviet Union to sign meaningful arms control agreements? It should be emphasized that politicians show little reluctance to assert that positive cause-and-effect relationships exist between policies they support and favorable outcomes or that the opposite is true for policies they oppose.

Some chief executive policies and results have fairly straightforward relationships. It is possible to determine precisely the amount of money elderly recipients receive from Social Security and then to measure the impact of such payments on poverty, defined as a monetary threshold, among the elderly.[60] Decisions about the size, accessibility, and location of state highways have undeniable impacts, such as changes in population, property values, and commercial sales, that can be determined with considerable accuracy. Precise, carefully defined relationships between certain policies and their impacts can be correctly assessed, but many chief executive policies are so broad that the results and their causes are unclear.

Deferred Learning

Organizational management and policy administration are core responsibilities for chief executives. However, the pressures and incentives to take the lead in setting the policy agenda and pushing for the enactment of policies are such that few chief executives have the time or the inclination to oversee the implementation of the policies they have championed. Bureaucratic agencies and legislative committees deal with policies over the long term, and they react to implementation problems and program evaluations. Therefore, most of the institutional learning resulting from the implementation of chief executive policies takes place in bureaucracies or specialized legislative committees. At this point chief executive politics gives way to bureaucratic or legislative politics.

Efforts to reorganize the executive branch are perhaps the most common form of chief executive activity that reflects institutional learning. Bureaucratic resistance to chief executive initiatives has been recognized as a problem at least since the turn of the century. Roosevelt, Truman, Nixon, and Carter all sponsored executive branch reorganizations aimed at establishing more rational bureaucratic structures and enhancing central control. The results usually fell short of expectations, mainly because Congress and the interest groups that were tied into the existing subgovernmental networks effectively opposed the changes presidents have sought.[61] In state government, reorganizations have been common since the 1950s. Their goals are basically the same as those of federal reforms: establishing clear chains of command and making public service delivery more economical and responsive to central control.

Through the Civil Service Reform Act of 1978, President Carter tried to shake up the bureaucracy starting with individual employees. The act provided incentives for high-ranking civil servants to take on special tasks at the request of the president or cabinet officer, and it made the hiring, firing, and transfer of civil servants somewhat easier. Many governors also have pushed for higher standards in the hiring and retention of government employees, the inclusion of more jobs in civil service or merit systems, and the improvement of in-service training.[62] Taking a different approach to bureaucratic resistance, the Reagan administration showed unmistakable boldness about using its appointment power to install doctrinaire conservatives in the executive branch. The president was attempting to change bureaucratic politics from within through ideological leadership.

Chief executives are not reluctant to get involved with implementation problems if questionable results become public concerns. In fact, chief executives who successfully sponsor policy innovations—either their own or those inherited from their immediate predecessor—are likely to assign a high priority to certain matters of program delivery. A common reaction to implementation problems is to propose program reform. Many of the War on Poverty programs were designed to avoid reliance on entrenched federal and state bureaucracies and to restrict state discretion because the policy formulators in the Kennedy and Johnson administrations doubted the commitment of these bureaucratic and political officials to the programs' goals. Not surprisingly, these policies generated their own implementation problems, such as duplication of service, lack of coordination among related programs, and state and local political resistance, which Republican presidents Nixon and Reagan used to justify proposals for a "new federalism." The result of new federalism reforms is a modified intergovernmental program delivery system that includes fewer separate programs and a greater state role in implementation decisions. Because big government has become a highly charged political issue, one would expect to see chief executives at all levels of government use implementation problems to their own advantage.

Summary

Chief executive politics commands the attention of almost every American. More than any other politicians, chief executives create and articulate the leading issues of the day and propose policy solutions. Much of what they say and do is covered by the media and becomes the focus of discussion among citizens. Their visibility and their formal powers give chief executives enormous political influence.

Their political strength is clearly evident in their ability to create issues and set agendas. The concerns they choose to address become issues for the entire political community. They can force others to pay attention to their priorities and accept their definitions of issues. Their domination of the political agenda gives them a tremendous advantage in policy development.

However, when specific policy proposals are advanced, gigantic government machinery—pluralism—begins to stretch its many tentacles. Chief executive proposals frequently fail to gain the approval needed to become policy, which diminishes the political strength of the leaders who offer them. Chief executive power and policy effectiveness, therefore, are highly variable and depend for success on the ability of the individuals who occupy high office to convince the public and other political elites that their proposals are the correct course. When the quality of chief executives' leadership is widely questioned, their political muscles atrophy. Overcoming the obstacles imposed by the pluralist octopus can push chief executives into the realm of the legendary; they become the leaders others try to emulate.

These reputations for leadership are, for the most part, deserved. The rhetoric surrounding high office in this country has become so inflated with grandiose promises that all chief executives have long lists of important policy proposals they hope to enact. If they are successful, people are affected and have a tangible basis for evaluating chief executive performance. Concrete policy accomplishments are a valuable form of political currency. Established politicians display a strong allegiance to the status quo, but the values of the public are continually shifting. Chief executives, taking advantage of their unique relationship with the public, frequently have acted as agents for change in American politics.

All the time and energy chief executives devote to voicing public concerns and securing new policies naturally limit the attention they can devote to matters of administration and policy implementation. Still, because new policies tend to breed implementation problems, issues of program design and delivery frequently command the interest and concern of chief executives.

When crises occur nearly every aspect of chief executive politics changes. Media and public attention become a hindrance rather than an asset, while other political actors become much more cooperative and deferential. The power to act usually belongs unambiguously to chief executives, but the repercussions of ill-advised action can be severe. But effective crisis management is, in addition to policy entrepreneurship, an avenue to renowned chief executive leadership.

Notes

1. Most governors have formal powers that are similar to those of presidents. They serve four-year terms and can run for reelection at least once. They can appoint high-ranking state officials, although on this point there is a good deal of variation as state legislatures share this power and some state officials are elected. Governors have considerable control over the budget process and have a veto over legislative actions, in some cases a line-item veto. Strong, as opposed to weak, mayors are those who have formal powers much like presidents and governors. The characteristics of a strong mayoralty are: terms longer than two years, the power to appoint heads of executive departments, veto power over city council actions, and a large role in the budget process. Most major cities have a strong mayor-council form of government. For more details, see Thad C. Beyle, "Governors," in Virginia Gray et al., *Politics in the American States*, 3d ed. (Boston: Little, Brown, 1983), 193-203; Larry Sabato, *Goodbye to Good-Time Charlie*, 2d ed. (Washington, D.C.: CQ Press, 1983); Robert C. Lineberry and Ira Sharkansky, *Urban Politics and Public Policy*, 3d ed. (New York: Harper & Row, 1978), 161-169.

2. Paul Light provides a specific delineation of the president's agenda by categorizing executive branch proposals in a way that isolates those that are classified by the Office of Management and Budget as in accordance with the president's program and that have been mentioned in a State of the Union address. This scheme would be an appropriate way to distinguish issues and policies that we regard as proper to chief executive politics from those that are more appropriately viewed as part of administrative politics. See Paul C. Light, "Presidents as Domestic Policy Makers," in *Rethinking the Presidency*, ed. Thomas E. Cronin (Boston: Little, Brown, 1982), 351-370.

3. See John Kingdon, *Agendas, Alternatives, and Public Policies* (Boston: Little, Brown, 1984), 26.

4. James K. Oliver, "Presidents as National Security Policy Makers," in *Rethinking the Presidency*, 396-397.

5. See *National Journal*, Nov. 10, 1984, 2156, on Kunin.

6. See Beyle, "Governors," 211.

7. See Sabato, *Goodbye to Good-Time Charlie*, 105-110, 115-116.

8. Light, "Presidents as Domestic Policy Makers," 361.

9. Ibid., 362-364.

10. Jeff Fishel, *Presidents and Promises* (Washington, D.C.: CQ Press, 1985).

11. Stephen Skowronek discusses the intellectual and practical aspects of several efforts to build and then reform national government in *Building a New American State: The Expansion of National Administrative Capacity 1877-1920* (New York: Cambridge University Press, 1982).

12. See Thomas Cronin, "On the Separation of Brain and State: Implications for the President," in *Modern Presidents and the Presidency*, ed. Marc Landy (Lexington, Mass.: Lexington Books, 1985), 54.

13. Ibid., 54-58.

14. Kingdon, *Agendas, Alternatives, and Public Policies*.

15. Light, "Presidents as Domestic Policy Makers," 365.

16. Fishel, *Presidents and Promises*, 26.

17. For a discussion of bias in presidential agendas, see Fishel, *Presidents and Promises*, 20-22. For more general treatments of this subject see E. E. Schattschneider, *The Semi-Sovereign People* (Hinsdale, Ill.: Dryden Press, 1960; revised 1975); Peter Bachrach and Morton S. Baratz, *Power and Poverty: Theory and Practice* (New York: Oxford University Press, 1970); and Steven Lukes, *Power* (London: MacMillan Press, 1974).

18. Richard E. Neustadt, *Presidential Power: The Politics of Leadership from FDR to Carter* (New York: John Wiley & Sons, 1980).

19. See Duane Lockard, *The Politics of State and Local Governments*, 3d ed, (New York: Macmillan, 1983), chaps. 7 and 8.

20. Michael Barone and Grant Ujifusa, *The Almanac of American Politics, 1984* (Washington, D.C.: National Journal, 1983), 218-221; *National Journal*, Nov. 10, 1984, 2158.

21. See Bert A. Rockman, *The Leadership Question* (New York: Praeger, 1984).

22. This argument is presented more fully by Samuel Kernell in *Going Public* (Washington, D.C.: CQ Press, 1986).

23. Ibid., chap. 6.

24. See Elizabeth Drew, *Money and Politics* (New York: Macmillan, 1983), 67-76.

25. Kernell, *Going Public*, 1986.

26. See Rockman, *The Leadership Question;* James MacGregor Burns, *Leadership* (New York: Harper & Row, 1978); and Neustadt, *Presidential Power*.

27. Rockman, *The Leadership Question*, chap. 2.

28. See James David Barber, *The Presidential Character*, 2d ed. (Englewood Cliffs, N.J.: Prentice-Hall, 1977).

29. Arthur M. Schlesinger, Jr., *The Imperial Presidency* (Boston: Houghton Mifflin, 1973).

30. See Thomas Cronin, *The State of the Presidency*, 2d ed. (Boston: Little, Brown, 1980), chap. 8; Erwin E. Hargrove and Michael Nelson, *Presidents, Politics and Policy* (New York: Alfred A. Knopf, 1984), chap. 6; Norman E. Thomas, "Presidential Advice and Information: Policy and Program Formulation," in *The Presidency in the Contemporary Context*, ed. Norman E. Thomas (New York: Dodd, Mead, 1975), 160-192.

31. Hargrove and Nelson, *Presidents, Politics and Policy*, chap. 6; Thomas, "Presidential Advice and Information."

32. Larry Sabato, *Goodbye to Good-Time Charlie*, 85.

33. Coleman B. Ransone, Jr., *The American Governorship* (Westport, Conn.: Greenwood Press, 1982), 109-111.

34. Ibid., 114.

35. Lockard, *The Politics of State and Local Government*, 242.

36. David Stockman, *The Triumph of Politics* (New York: Harper & Row, 1986).

37. Ransone, *The American Governorship*, 153.

38. E. R. Shipp, "Three Years Later, Chicago's Mayor Is Turning the Corner," *New York Times*, Aug. 17, 1986, E5.

39. These categories are a slightly modified version of those used by Cronin in *The State of the Presidency*, 145-153.

40. See Cronin, *The State of the Presidency*, 145-153.

41. There is some variation by state and among municipalities in the role the chief executive plays in the budget process, but in most cases it is similar to that of the president: budget preparation for the legislature and efforts to preserve executive priorities during legislative consideration of the budget. For details see Ransone, *The American Governorship*, 128; Beyle, "Governors"; and David A. Caputo, *Urban America: The Policy Alternatives* (San Francisco: W. H. Freeman, 1976), 108-110.

42. Fishel, *Presidents and Promises*, 30-45.

43. See Harrell R. Rodgers, Jr., and Charles S. Bullock III, *Law and Social Change* (New York: McGraw-Hill, 1972), chaps. 2 and 5; Phyllis Wallace, "A Decade of Policy Developments in Equal Opportunities in Employment and Housing," in *A Decade of Federal Antipoverty Programs*, ed. Robert H. Haveman (New York: Academic Press, 1977).

44. James C. Ceaser, "The Rhetorical Presidency Revisited," in *Modern Presidents and the Presidency*, 33.

45. See Frances Fox Piven and Richard A. Cloward, *Regulating the Poor* (New York: Vintage Books, 1971).

46. For specific figures on black voting for Democratic presidential candidates, see Herbert B. Asher, *Presidential Elections and American Politics*, 3d ed. (Homewood, Ill.: Dorsey Press, 1984).

47. See Fishel, *Presidents and Promises*, 93.

48. Lockard, *The Politics of State and Local Government*, 124-125.

49. Ann Cooper, "Statehouse Reshuffle," *National Journal*, Nov. 10, 1984, 2156.

50. Martha Derthick, *New Towns In-Town* (Washington, D.C.: Urban Institute Press, 1972).

51. Ibid., 82-102.

52. Morton H. Halperin, "Implementing Presidential Foreign Policy Decisions: Limitations and Resistance," in *Cases in Public Policy Making*, ed. James E. Anderson (New York: Praeger, 1976), 208-236.

53. Graham T. Allison, *Essence of Decision* (Boston: Little, Brown, 1971), 132.

54. Lester M. Salamon, "Follow-ups, Letdowns and Sleepers: The Time Dimension in Policy Evaluation," in *Public Policy Making in a Federal System*, eds. Charles O. Jones and Robert D. Thomas (Beverly Hills, Calif.: Sage Publications, 1976), 257-283.

55. Ibid., 267.

56. Ibid., 263.

57. The original Head Start evaluation was done by Westinghouse Learning Corporation and Ohio University, *The Impact of Head Start: An Evaluation of the Effects of Head Start on Children's Cognitive and Affective Development*, report to the Office of Economic Opportunity, July 12, 1969. For subsequent research, see Irving Lazar, *Summary: The Persistence of Preschool Effects*, Community Service Laboratory, New York State University College of Human Ecology at Cornell University, October 1977. For a bibliographic summary, see Ada Jo Mann, *A Review of Head Start Research Since 1969* (Washington, D.C.: George Washington University, 1978).

58. On the impact of federal training programs, see Robert Taggart, *A Fisherman's Guide: An Assessment of Training and Remediation Strategies* (Kalamazoo, Mich.: W. E. Upjohn Institute for Employment Research, 1981); for a summary see Michael Borus, "Assessing the Impact of Training Programs," in *Employing the Disadvantaged*, ed. Eli Ginzburg (New York: Basic Books, 1980); on the impact of food stamps see U.S. Senate, Subcommittee on Nutrition, Committee on Agriculture, Nutrition and Forestry, *Hunger in America: Ten Years Later*, 96th Cong. 1st sess. 1979; also Congressional Budget Office, *The Food Stamp Program: Income or Food Supplementation?* (Washington, D.C.: U.S. Government Printing Office, 1977); on Medicare see Karen Davis and Cathy Schoen, *Health and the War on Poverty: A Ten Year Appraisal* (Washington, D.C.: Brookings Institution, 1978).

59. See Egon G. Guba, "The Failure of Educational Evaluation," in *Evaluating Action Programs*, ed. Carol H. Weiss (Boston: Allyn & Bacon, 1972), 250-266; or James S. Coleman, "Problems of Conceptualization and Measurement in Studying Policy Impacts," in *Public Policy Evaluation*, ed. Kenneth M. Dolbeare (Beverly Hills: Sage Publications, 1975), 19-40.

60. For an excellent example see Laurence E. Lynn, Jr., "A Decade of Policy Developments in the Income Maintenance System," in *A Decade of Federal Antipoverty Programs*, 55-117.

61. For a discussion of presidential reorganization efforts see Hargrove and Nelson, *Presidents, Politics and Policy*, 249-265.

62. Thad L. Beyle, ed., *State Government: CQ's Guide to Current Issues and Activities, 1985-1986* (Washington, D.C.: CQ Press, 1985), 119.

7   Courtroom Politics

It is sometimes said that courts implement policies made by other branches of government. But for a number of issues—abortion, capital punishment, search and seizure, school prayer, and school desegregation—the opposite is true: the courts make policy, and other political institutions respond to their lead. When politicians are silent or ambiguous, judicial action cannot be described as policy implementation; there may be no policy to implement until the courts act. For a wide variety of other issues, such as the environment, welfare, and communications, the courts, although circumscribed, have considerable discretion. Judges do more than resolve disputes in accordance with the law. Through their decisions, they also create law every bit as much as legislators do.

The policy-making role of U.S. courts arouses considerable controversy because it is unique. In Great Britain judges are better described as technicians than policy makers. With a few exceptions, their role is to dot i's and cross t's.[1] U.S. courts are more powerful than other courts in the Western world, and their power is growing. Law professor Donald Horowitz wrote, "The courts have tended to move from the byways onto the highways of policy making."[2] Although from time to time politicians object to the growing power of the courts, the main force driving judicial policy making is the abdication of responsibility by elected officials.

Many courts make policy, including federal courts and state courts. As the highest federal court, the U.S. Supreme Court is the ultimate arbiter of legal controversies. However, the Supreme Court's preeminence should not be construed to mean that other courts play a minor role. In fact, the Supreme Court resolves only about 150 cases each year. In contrast, the other courts combined handle millions of cases annually, and many of these cases have far-reaching policy implications.

Cases and Controversies

The issues confronted by courts are rich and diverse. Many of them, classified as private law, involve disputes between private parties. This category comprises contracts (Is an agreement legally binding?); prop-

erty (Has property been illegally damaged or confiscated?); and torts
(Have people or property been harmed?). In public law cases, government officials are parties to a legal dispute. Under this category are
questions of constitutional law (Are decisions by government officials
constitutional?); statutory law (What is legislative intent?); and administrative law (Are administrative decisions constitutional, legal, and consistent with past decisions?).

These categories overlap in all sorts of ways (see Figure 7-1). Antitrust actions by government officials often involve public and private
components. For example, government officials function as prosecutors,
but the charge is that one company has engaged in anticompetitive
behavior against another. Torts become public when a private party
sues a government official or agency for malfeasance or nonfeasance.
Overlaps within categories are even more common. In many administrative law cases, the key is legislative intent; in many constitutional law
cases, the constitutionality of a statute is questioned; in both instances,
statutory law is involved.

Because the concern here is public policy, the focus is on public law
cases, which have broader implications for society than do private law
cases. If one sues a neighbor over a barking dog, the world does not
anxiously await a verdict. If an administrative agency proposes a
change in welfare eligibility rules, the verdict may affect many thousands of people. Examples from administrative law and constitutional
law are cited to illustrate differences in judicial behavior. Although
administrative law occasionally overlaps constitutional law, each more
often overlaps with statutory law. In administrative and constitutional
law, questions of statutory interpretation are seldom far from view. A
review of the dynamics of administrative and constitutional law inevitably touches on statutory interpretation.

Constitutional Law

Constitutional law raises questions involving civil liberties, states'
rights, interstate commerce, and other protections guaranteed by the
U.S. Constitution or the constitutions of the states. The questions are
enormously varied. Under what circumstances is evidence gathered by
police admissible in a criminal proceeding? Under what circumstances
may state governments provide financial assistance to parochial schools?
What conditions may states impose on abortions? Should states be free
to execute persons found guilty of murder? When must an individual's
right to privacy yield to freedom of the press? When must freedom of
the press yield to an individual's right to a fair trial? May insurance
companies charge male drivers higher rates than female drivers? May
employers specify the sex of applicants in want ads?

Figure 7-1 Branches of Law

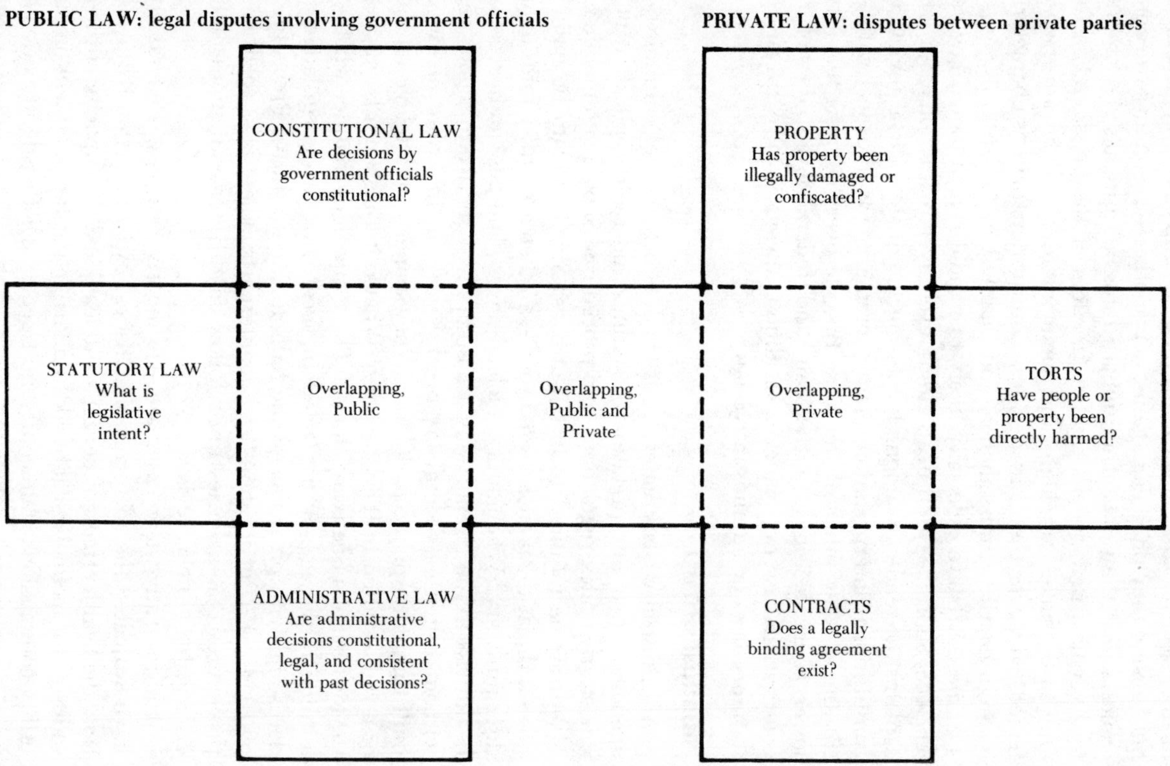

PUBLIC LAW: legal disputes involving government officials

PRIVATE LAW: disputes between private parties

CONSTITUTIONAL LAW
Are decisions by
government officials
constitutional?

Overlapping,
Public

ADMINISTRATIVE LAW
Are administrative
decisions constitutional,
legal, and consistent
with past decisions?

STATUTORY LAW
What is
legislative
intent?

Overlapping,
Public and
Private

PROPERTY
Has property been
illegally damaged or
confiscated?

Overlapping,
Private

CONTRACTS
Does a legally
binding agreement
exist?

TORTS
Have people or
property been
directly harmed?

As these questions illustrate, constitutional law involves some of the most vexing dilemmas facing society. These issues of social policy are difficult, not because they are technically complex (although some are) but because they pit values against one another—a woman's freedom of choice versus the rights of an unborn fetus, a criminal's right to a fair trial versus a newspaper's right to freedom of the press, and so forth. Obviously, stakes are high, and some interests will be adversely affected, whatever the court decides. Constitutional law is characterized by high conflict, high salience, and manifest costs.

Some courts are especially likely to handle constitutional law cases. The U.S. Supreme Court deals almost exclusively with such cases, which explains the tendency among laypersons to equate judicial review with constitutional interpretation. State supreme courts also deal with constitutional issues much of the time. But the overwhelming majority of lower court decisions, at the state and federal levels, do not raise constitutional issues. These cases almost always involve private law, statutory law, or administrative law.

Administrative Law

Administrative law cases focus on the behavior of administrative agencies—their interpretation of statutes and their application of administrative rules, regulations, and procedures. Should automobile manufacturers be required to install airbags? Should a dam be built if it poses a threat to an endangered species? When are utility rates unjustly discriminatory? When does a nuclear power plant pose an unacceptable health risk to the public? May a hospital deny service to a poor person without forfeiting federal tax breaks? May an interstate highway be built through a public park? May a newspaper own a television station or a radio station in the same city? What criteria should be applied to the location of a "halfway" house? These questions consider whether an administrative agency has acted in accordance with legislative standards and with provisions of the federal Administrative Procedure Act of 1946 (APA) or its state-level counterparts. These laws spell out the procedures that agencies must follow in different situations and the criteria for judicial review.

Administrative law cases are enormously complex. Federal courts have evaluated the adequacy of statistical experiments on foam insulation, the health effects of benzene and lead, and the capacity of the auto industry for technological breakthroughs. In passing judgment on public utility commissions, state courts must decide whether depreciation rates have been properly calculated, whether the utility's rate base should include plants under construction, whether a given rate of return allows the utility to compete for capital. One judge, exasperated by such complexities, decided to narrow the focus of the case to a single issue, rate of return.[3] Otherwise, he argued, the court's task would be hopeless, and the case interminable.

Administrative law cases are decided initially by administrative agencies. If they are appealed, many administrative agency decisions at the federal level may go directly to the circuit courts of appeals, bypassing federal district courts. Some circuit court decisions on administrative law are appealed to the U.S. Supreme Court, but most never go that far. For all intents and purposes, circuit courts are final arbiters of many administrative decisions. Among circuit courts, the D.C. Circuit, in particular, handles a higher percentage of administrative law cases than other circuit courts.[4] The D.C. Circuit Court of Appeals has sometimes been called the second most powerful court in the land. On questions of administrative law, it is, in practice, the most powerful. At the state level, administrative law cases are handled by intermediate appeals courts and further appealed to state supreme courts.

Neglected Issues

Courts seldom address issues in two important policy domains: foreign policy (responses to international crises or the use of armed forces abroad) and macroeconomic policy (taxing and spending decisions). The failure of courts to address these issues is due more to self-restraint than to a lack of plaintiffs. Many taxpayers would love to take Uncle Sam to court, if only they were permitted to do so. Although the courts have lowered barriers to standing—the right to sue—by consumer advocates and environmentalists, they have refused to facilitate taxpayer suits.[5] Taxpayers often wind up in court as defendants, with the Internal Revenue Service (IRS) or its state counterpart as plaintiff, but they seldom appear as plaintiffs in taxation cases.

On the rare occasions when the courts address questions of macroeconomic policy, they normally defer to elected officials, especially when elected officials are in agreement. When Congress granted President Richard Nixon the authority to impose wage and price controls in 1970, a special federal district court panel upheld the statute as a constitutional delegation of power to the president.[6] Similarly, the U.S. Supreme Court has upheld congressional delegations of authority to the president in foreign affairs.[7] Justice William H. Rehnquist wrote in *Dames & Moore v. Regan* (1981), "Presidential action taken pursuant to specific congressional authorization is supported by strongest presumptions and widest latitude of judicial interpretation, and the burden of persuasion rests heavily upon anyone who might attack it." In plain English, even the Supreme Court is reluctant to second-guess politicians in foreign policy.

Selection of Cases

Unlike other public policy makers, judges can address only those issues that come before them. Although courts are alike in their inability to initiate cases, they differ in their freedom to ignore them. As a general rule, supreme courts have more discretion than other courts. Federal district courts and circuit courts of appeals are supposed to hear all cases within their jurisdiction that come before them.[8] The agenda of the U.S. Supreme Court is largely discretionary. With the exception of a few kinds of cases, which seldom arise,[9] the Supreme Court may decline to hear cases. Even the Court's mandatory agenda is less mandatory than it seems to be. The Court may use devices such as the summary decision or a denial of leave to file to evade the requirement that certain cases be heard.

A similar pattern prevails at the state level, although state supreme courts differ in their discretion. In some states, the supreme court must hear appeals from trial courts; in others, the supreme court is free to choose only "significant" cases if it wishes. The variations can be explained by the existence in some states, but not others, of intermediate appeals courts. In general, supreme courts have more discretion over their caseload in states with such courts. The assumption is that one appeal from a trial court decision should be available to all parties, but that two may be excessive.

The Politics of Judging

It is sometimes said that the courts are more independent than other institutions of government. This is true in one sense but not another; judges are remarkably independent of politicians, but they are not independent of politics. Indeed, partisan politics is a significant factor in judicial recruitment and judicial behavior. Once appointed to office, federal judges are independent of the politicians who put them on the bench. Although federal judges may be impeached by the House and convicted by the Senate for "high crimes and misdemeanors," this cumbersome machinery has been used successfully only five times in U.S. history. State judges are also independent of politicians, but not always of the electorate. In thirty-six states, judges may be removed from office by the voters through regular elections or through retention elections in which the judge runs unopposed but may be unseated through a vote of no confidence. Unpopular judges are unseated from time to time—Rose Bird, the former chief justice of the California Supreme Court, for example—but the overwhelming majority of judges who must face the voters are reelected.

Judges are not immune from partisan politics. Most federal judges belong to the party of the president who appointed them, and the same is true of state judges and the governors who appointed them. Furthermore, judges remain remarkably faithful to their party while in office. Although this loyalty may vary from issue to issue, party identification is the single best predictor of judicial voting behavior.

Diffuse Power

Many textbooks on American government portray the courts as a pyramid, with the U.S. Supreme Court at the apex. This image conveys a false impression, implying a hierarchical route that in reality very few cases follow. Most lower court decisions are never reviewed by higher courts. The majority of federal district court decisions are not appealed to the circuit courts; the majority of circuit court decisions are never appealed to the U.S. Supreme Court; and most circuit court decisions appealed to the Supreme Court are not accepted for review. The situation at the state level is much the same.

State supreme court decisions are usually final. Although decisions raising constitutional questions may be appealed to the U.S. Supreme Court, the Court hears no more than fifty such cases in any given year. Even if the Court reverses the state supreme court and returns the case for further proceedings, the state supreme court may reiterate its basic conclusion, while modifying some of the specifics. Although state and federal court systems intersect, they are more independent than is commonly supposed (see Figure 7-2).

When a higher court declines to review a lower court decision, that does not necessarily imply approval. Rather, it may mean that although the higher court would have decided the case differently, it cannot say that the lower court made a mistake. It may mean that the higher court is not prepared to address a certain legal issue, or it may mean that the higher court has too many other cases to hear.

All cases are not created equal, and the more important cases tend to be heard in the higher courts. Nevertheless, many critical decisions have been made by federal district court judges. For example, Judge Arthur Garrity desegregated Boston's public schools; Judge Frank Johnson, Jr., reformed Alabama's prisons and mental hospitals, and Judge John Sirica sent numerous Watergate conspirators to prison. These cases illustrate the degree to which judicial power is dispersed throughout the United States.

Leadership Styles and Strategies

When a federal district court judge issues a decision, he or she acts alone. Higher courts are characterized by collective decision making. Intermediate appeals court decisions usually are made by three-judge

Figure 7-2   The Structure of the Judicial System

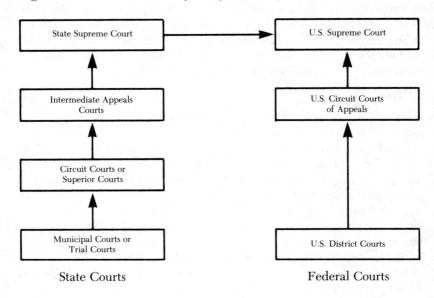

State Courts   Federal Courts

panels, while supreme court decisions are made by all the members. Coalition building is essential in such courts. Before a case is decided and the opinion written, a majority of judges must agree on the outcome and on the reasoning behind it. This consensus requires leadership—a mysterious but not altogether incomprehensible quality.

Within the courts there are three forms of leadership: political, institutional, and intellectual. Political leaders are those who can build coalitions, and the task of political leadership often falls on the shoulders of the judge assigned to write the opinion. To satisfy other members of the court, the opinion writer inserts new phrases and deletes others, with the goal of securing as many votes as possible in support of a coherent opinion. The opinion writer also seeks to discourage dissenting opinions, which convey judicial fragmentation. Centrists or "swing voters" are strategically situated to exercise political leadership because they hold the balance of power, especially when a court is ideologically divided, as was the Burger Court and is the Rehnquist Court.

Institutional leaders are those who defend the courts against various external threats and who attempt to develop the courts as institutions. When Chief Justice Charles Evans Hughes denounced President Franklin Roosevelt's attempt to "pack" the Supreme Court, he was exercising institutional leadership.[10] Chief Justice Warren Burger led the battle to add judges to the federal bench and for more discretion in case selection, which he thought would protect the Supreme Court from "overload." Various state judges also have exercised institutional leadership when they fought to modernize the courts, to reorganize the judiciary, or to reform judicial selection procedures.

Intellectual leaders are those who influence their colleagues—and subsequent generations—through the force of their reasoning and the power of their ideas. Harlan Stone's argument that "discrete and insular minorities" warrant special protection under the Constitution—an argument buried in a footnote in the 1938 case *United States v. Carolene Products*—provided the rationale for broad interpretations of the Fourteenth Amendment by subsequent courts. Hugo Black's strong views on civil liberties provided the intellectual underpinnings for many of the decisions of the Warren Court. Judges on other courts also have exercised intellectual leadership. Judge Harold Leventhal of the D.C. Circuit Court of Appeals articulated the "hard look" doctrine of administrative law, which justifies careful judicial scrutiny of the reasoning behind administrative decisions. His colleague, David Bazelon, is credited (or blamed) for the view that the mentally ill have a right to treatment under the Constitution. The reverberations from these ideas continue.

Although courts are less hierarchical than other government institutions, the chief justice or chief judge has certain powers. The chief justice of the United States presides at the Supreme Court conferences and is the first to speak. If the chief justice votes with the majority, he (or she) assigns the opinion to a particular justice. Because the reasoning behind a decision often has a longer lasting impact than the decision, chief justices exercise power even when they choose not to write. The chief judges of other federal courts are more constrained. The chief judge of a federal district court assigns cases to other judges, but randomly. The chief judge of a federal circuit court of appeals assigns the opinion when the court sits en banc, or all together, provided he or she is in the majority. However, most circuit court of appeals cases are decided by three-judge panels, and the cases are assigned randomly.

At the state level, there appears to be considerable variation in the leadership potential of chief judges. In states where supreme court judges are elected, partisan conflict often is intense enough to thwart attempts at leadership. In states where supreme court judges are appointed, the opposite is true.[11] At the local level, chief judges have the authority to assign cases.[12] Because the chief judge of local courts usually is selected by peers, he or she must be careful not to offend sensitive colleagues.

Decision Making

If leadership is a variable that adds an element of surprise to the judicial process—the "wild card" in the judicial deck—there are four more predictable elements of judicial decision making. They are law, evidence, party identification, and judicial philosophy.

Law. In resolving constitutional disputes, judges get a good deal of guidance from the constitution itself, whether federal or state. A constitution is not a legal cookbook, but neither is it a Rorschach test. Perhaps it is best to say that a constitution establishes a set of presumptions or burdens of proof. The U.S. Constitution does not define phrases such as freedom of the press, freedom of speech, or freedom of religion, but these phrases are laden with meaning from years of precedents, prior decisions that command respect. Although precedents are seldom determinative, they serve as guideposts to judges as they wrestle with difficult problems. In general, courts pay more attention to their own precedents and to those of higher courts than to the precedents of other courts.

Constitutions have less relevance for administrative law because most administrative law cases do not raise constitutional questions. Precedents are scarcer in administrative law; the administrative state is only about fifty years old, and higher courts offer less guidance on administrative law than on constitutional law. As judges evaluate administrative law cases, their guides are the federal APA and state administrative procedure acts. If administrative procedures are informal, the courts ask whether the agency acted "arbitrarily and capriciously." If administrative procedures are relatively formal, the courts ask whether the agency's decision is based on "substantial evidence" in the record. The latter is a more exacting form of judicial review. Agencies face a higher burden of proof as formality increases.

Evidence. Whether a case involves constitutional law or administrative law, courts base their decisions on evidence submitted by litigants. For the most part, evidence consists of historical facts, such as who did what to whom. Courts also look at social facts, the probable consequences of decisions. Courts have been guided by empirical research on the effects of segregation on blacks (*Brown v. Board of Education*, 1954), the effects of teacher experience on pupil performance (*Hobson v. Hansen*, 1967, 1968), and the effects of judicial procedures on the rehabilitation of juvenile offenders (*In re Gault*, 1967).

Some litigants have a distinct advantage in presenting evidence. In particular, the "haves," who tend to be repeat players who know how to use the court system, usually are better at the game than the "have-nots," who tend to be one-shot participants.[13] This gap has narrowed as a result of court decisions granting certain have-nots the right to counsel in criminal cases (*Gideon v. Wainwright*, 1963) and the creation of legal aid societies, which represent the poor in civil cases. Public interest groups use their experience and resources to represent the disadvantaged or the public in court. The National Association for the Advancement of Colored People (NAACP) has filed numerous school desegregation suits, and the American Civil Liberties Union (ACLU) many First Amendment suits. Environmentalists have been represented in court by the Natural Resources Defense Council, the Environmental Defense Fund, the Sierra Club, and other groups. These public interest groups have won a wide variety of cases protecting wilderness areas and wetlands and securing enforcement of antipollution laws. In some instances the federal government has reimbursed them for the costs of successful lawsuits—a practice known as "intervenor funding."

Party Identification. Few judges would cite party identification as a factor in their decisions. Indeed, many judges would take umbrage at the implication that partisanship enters into judicial decision making. Nevertheless, it is well established that Democratic judges and Republican judges decide certain kinds of cases differently. Democratic state supreme court judges are much more liberal on worker's compensation cases than are their Republican counterparts,[14] and they are more supportive of the claims of criminal defendants, the disadvantaged, and individuals alleging deprivations of civil liberties.[15]

This pattern holds at all levels of the federal judiciary: Democratic judges tend to be more liberal and Republican judges more conservative.[16] Therefore, it is a matter of some consequence whether a Democrat or a Republican sits in the White House. Federal district court judges appointed by President Ronald Reagan have acquitted criminal defendants only 14 percent of the time; the record is 52 percent for President Jimmy Carter's appointees.[17]

A president's ideology also matters, especially in the case of Supreme Court nominees. Despite Reagan's failure to place staunch conservatives Robert Bork and Douglas Ginsburg on the Supreme Court, he was successful in appointing one staunch conservative—Associate Justice Antonin Scalia—and two moderate conservatives—Associate Justices Sandra Day O'Connor and Anthony Kennedy—to the nation's highest court. He also designated the most conservative member of the court, William Rehnquist, as chief justice. Other presidents also took ideology into account in their Supreme Court appointments.

Judicial Philosophy. Judges differ in the extent to which they allow their personal values to decide the outcome of a case. Felix Frankfurter, who professed to be an unswerving civil libertarian, dissented against Warren Court decisions protecting individuals against the government.

Frankfurter believed the courts should defer to other branches of government under most circumstances. Oliver Wendell Holmes took a similar view. As he saw it, judges should uphold laws even though they epitomize economic mistakes or futile experiments.[18] This point of view is sometimes referred to as the doctrine of judicial restraint. Other judges have been much more willing to overturn statutes. William Douglas and Hugo Black, avid civil libertarians, routinely voted to void statutes that diminished First Amendment liberties. Black and Douglas were also judicial activists, who believed that the courts should not defer to other branches of government, especially when First Amendment rights are at stake.

In constitutional law a critical question for judges is whether to override the legislative branch; in administrative law, they must decide whether to overrule administrative agencies. During the 1970s the Supreme Court was more likely than ever before to overturn state and local laws as well as acts of Congress.[19] The U.S. Circuit Courts of Appeals were more likely to overturn administrative agencies.[20] Since then, evidence suggests that the pendulum is swinging back. However, swings of the pendulum are seldom equal. Although the courts in the late 1980s are perhaps less activist than they were in the 1970s, they are far more activist than at the beginning of the twentieth century.

Rulings from the Bench

Judges, like other policy makers, are attentive to appearances, but judges are less likely than other public officials to substitute symbolic action for substantive action. Very few court decisions are purely symbolic. Unlike other public officials, judges do not avoid difficult problems or unpopular solutions. Instead, they confront many of society's most vexing problems, and, having done so, they then rely on symbols to legitimate their decisions.

Two norms confirm judicial attentiveness to symbols. First, judges seek to avoid public feuding, viewed as unseemly and detrimental to the image of the courts; in contrast, public feuding is a popular legislative sport. Second, judges try to convey the impression of an unbroken line of precedents, dating back to the Founding Fathers, while politicians are forever talking about new ideas, new deals, and new American revolutions. Judges care about two symbols: unity and continuity.

Unity and Continuity

The school desegregation rulings of the Warren Court demonstrate the commitment to unity. Since the decision in *Brown v. Board of Education* (1954), the Court has struggled to maintain the appearance of unity on this extraordinarily divisive issue. During the Warren years, the justices were remarkably successful. Despite deep divisions, they managed to issue a series of unanimous decisions, which sent an important message to recalcitrant school boards, especially in the South: desegregation is the law of the land.[21]

School desegregation cases also demonstrate the commitment to continuity. The *Brown* decision reversed *Plessy v. Ferguson* (1896), a ruling that upheld the constitutionality of segregated facilities and services. While reversing *Plessy* as untenable in a modern age, the Court cited a wide variety of precedents that supported a broad interpretation of the Fourteenth Amendment. In subsequent cases the federal courts have portrayed court-ordered busing as a logical outgrowth of *Brown* and the Fourteenth Amendment. Politicians serve old wine in new bottles, but judges prefer to serve new wine in old bottles. This modest deception legitimates policy making by public officials who, according to a narrow reading of the Constitution, are not supposed to be making public policy.

Innovative Decisions

The commitment of courts to continuity may be good for the republic, but it obscures the extent to which judges are innovators in American politics. It also conveys a false impression that judicial policies differ only incrementally from earlier policies. Although most court decisions, like most decisions of other political institutions, are incremental, a remarkably high percentage of decisions made by the highest courts are innovative, especially when the issues are divisive and the decisions will have far-reaching effects.

It is widely acknowledged that the Warren Court was innovative. Its decisions on school desegregation, criminal justice, school prayer, and other matters transformed the Bill of Rights into a blueprint for economic and political equality. Other Warren Court decisions, on less visible topics, were equally revolutionary. For example, in *New York Times v. Sullivan* (1964) the Warren Court ruled that public figures must demonstrate actual malice to win a libel suit against a newspaper. This decision, which overruled 175 years of settled legal practice, virtually immunized the press against libel suits.[22]

Scholars are beginning to recognize that the Burger Court was also remarkably innovative.[23] In *Furman v. Georgia* (1972) the Burger Court found existing capital punishment statutes unconstitutional, which triggered changes in these statutes throughout the country. In *Roe v. Wade* (1973) the Burger Court established different ground rules for abortion during the three trimesters of pregnancy and ruled that a woman's right to privacy, while not absolute, is a constitutionally protected right. The Burger Court also was innovative in a wide variety of other areas, such as commercial free speech, sex discrimination, procedural due process, and freedom of the press.

A number of state supreme courts also have blazed new trails in public law. The New Jersey Supreme Court outlawed the use of the property tax as the sole basis for local school financing, established a right-to-die procedure for permanently comatose patients, and held hosts liable for drunk-driving accidents if they knowingly serve alcohol to an intoxicated person. In *Southern Burlington County NAACP v. Township of Mt. Laurel* (1975), a landmark decision, the New Jersey Supreme Court ruled "exclusionary zoning" unconstitutional. The court said that local governments have an affirmative duty to provide housing opportunities for lower-class persons, even if they do not already live in the community. If applied to zoning ordinances in other states, this decision would truly revolutionize residential patterns and practices.

A number of state supreme courts have taken the lead on civil liberties questions. Eleven states now bar school-financing formulas based exclusively on local property taxes, despite a U.S. Supreme Court ruling that such formulas are compatible with the U.S. Constitution (*San Antonio Independent School District v. Rodriguez*, 1973). State supreme courts in Alaska, California, Massachusetts, Michigan, New York, and Pennsylvania have gone beyond the U.S. Supreme Court in protecting the rights of criminal defendants.[24] The Supreme Judicial Court of Massachusetts ruled in 1985 that the standard for obtaining a search warrant is higher under the state constitution, which "provides more substantive protection to criminal defendants" than the U.S. Constitution. The same year the Alaska Supreme Court said that the state constitutional guarantee against unreasonable searches and seizures is broader than the Fourth Amendment to the U.S. Constitution, even though the wording is almost identical.

State supreme courts can go beyond the U.S. Supreme Court because the federal court sets a floor, not a ceiling, on constitutional rights. If state supreme courts find that state constitutions provide stronger protection than the U.S. Constitution, they are free to follow the state constitution, provided their conclusion is based primarily on state law (*Michigan v. Long*, 1983). According to one estimate, from 1970 through 1985 state courts handed down 300 published opinions declaring U.S. Supreme Court guarantees of civil liberties to be insufficient.[25]

State court procedures also have shown innovation. For example, state courts have been pioneers in allowing electronic and photographic media coverage of court proceedings, including criminal proceedings.[26] In 1981, twenty-seven states allowed television, radio, and photographic coverage of certain judicial proceedings. By contrast, federal courts still bar the use of cameras in court. Many observers believe that state courts have managed to promote freedom of the press without inhibiting constitutional rights to a fair trial.[27] Indeed, even the U.S. Supreme Court has conceded that television coverage of a criminal proceeding does not automatically violate a defendant's constitutional right to a fair trial (*Chandler v. Florida*, 1981).

Minorities as Beneficiaries

Students who take courses in constitutional law and administrative law must wonder whether their professors are talking about the same judicial system. Constitutional law students see the courts as liberal; administrative law students see them as conservative. Constitutional law students see the courts as champions of the underprivileged; administrative law students see them as protectors of special interests. These impressions are not without foundation: the fact is that constitutional law and administrative law benefit different groups in society.

The argument may be summarized as follows: (1) courts adopt policies favorable to minorities, despite opposition to such policies; (2) in constitutional law, the courts adopt policies that benefit disadvantaged minorities such as blacks, the handicapped, and the mentally ill; and (3) in administrative law, the courts adopt policies that benefit advantaged minorities, for example, utility companies, insurance companies, and transportation companies.

Constitutional Law. Because the U.S. Supreme Court is preeminent in matters of constitutional law, scholars interested in assessing the beneficiaries of constitutional law decisions have focused on this court. Most recent studies of the Court find considerable support for disadvantaged minorities in its decisions.[28] Of the twenty-eight cases in which the Court overturned a congressional statute between 1958 and 1974, twenty-seven upheld minority rights, as guaranteed by the Bill of Rights or the Fourteenth Amendment.[29] The principal beneficiaries in these cases were blacks and other disadvantaged minorities.

Some scholars assert that these studies give too much weight to the Warren Court (1954-1969), whose strong commitment to civil liberties is universally acknowledged. Political scientist Robert Dahl found that most Supreme Court decisions overturning congressional statutes through 1957 actually harmed minorities.[30] According to Dahl, the Court reinforces majoritarian decisions made by Congress. In 1985 law professor Geoffrey Stone noted that 85 percent of the Court's "noneasy" (not unanimous) civil liberties decisions during the 1983-1984 term were decided against minority rights.[31] In his view, the Burger Court launched a new era of "aggressive majoritarianism."

But the Burger Court's reputation as majoritarian in a conservative era can be traced directly to its criminal procedure decisions. In this area the Burger Court was more sensitive to public safety than to minority rights. In *Michigan v. Long* (1983), for example, the Burger Court upheld protective searches of the passenger compartment of a car if police have a reasonable belief that the suspect is dangerous. In *New York v. Quarles* (1984) the Burger Court ruled that the police may postpone the reading of a defendant's Miranda warnings until they have investigated a potential threat to public safety. The Court also upheld vehicle searches by border patrol officials, provided that circumstances are suspicious and that intrusions on privacy are limited (*United States v. Brignoni-Ponce*, 1975; *United States v. Cortez*, 1981). Despite these decisions, a fair appraisal of the Burger Court's record, not just its criminal procedure rulings or the decisions of a single term, must acknowledge a general pattern of support for minority rights.

Even the Rehnquist Court, widely expected to be conservative, has handed down a number of decisions favoring minorities. It voted to extend the reach of the Voting Rights Act (*City of Pleasant Grove v. United States*, 1987) and to allow special job protections for pregnant workers (*California Federal Savings and Loan Assn. v. Guerra*, 1987). On affirmative action the Court ruled in *United States v. Paradise* (1987) that a judge may order agencies to use promotion quotas temporarily when there is a history of "egregious" racial bias. In *Johnson v. Santa Clara County* (1987) the Court ruled that employers may give special preferences to women in hiring and promotion decisions even if no prior discrimination existed.

Although less is known about other courts, a study of federal district court decisions on education policy confirms a strong tendency for judicial support of disadvantaged minorities. The study of sixty-five education policy decisions between 1970 and 1977, sixty-four of which involved constitutional issues, found that minority plaintiffs were successful 71 percent of the time.[32] Plaintiffs in these cases included blacks, Hispanics, American Indians, aliens, women, the handicapped, the poor, the elderly, and nonconformists such as long-haired students. These findings are especially interesting because the authors deliberately excluded school desegregation cases from their sample. Their findings do not simply reiterate the well-known conclusion that school desegregation cases have been decided in favor of minorities.

What accounts for the strong support of courts for disadvantaged minorities in constitutional law cases? In particular, what caused the noticeable shift in the disposition of the courts that began in the mid-1950s? One possibility is that judges are more liberal than they used to be, and this liberalism may be attributed to changes in judicial selection practices at the state and federal levels. Consultation with bar associations prior to appointment to the bench may have encouraged the selection of judges who share the bar's commitment to civil liberties, and the appointment of more women and blacks may have further sensitized courts to minority rights.

Changes outside the courtroom—in the political and legal culture—probably explain more than changes inside the judiciary. The U.S. Constitution and the state constitutions provide a formidable arsenal of legal weapons to minorities who are willing and able to use them. Until the 1950s minorities were aggrieved but not aroused, victimized but not mobilized. Since then public interest groups have emerged to champion minority rights in the courts and in other forums. These groups—the NAACP, the ACLU, and NOW (National Organization for Women)—have fought successfully to extend the frontiers of the First, Fourth, Fifth, and Fourteenth amendments. As a result of their efforts, the Constitution became the functional equivalent of the Statue of Liberty—a beacon to the weak and the oppressed. Whatever the intentions of the Founding Fathers, the language of the Constitution, in its modern interpretation, offers considerable hope to the disadvantaged.

Administrative Law. The most common result of judicial review of administrative agency actions, either at the state or federal level, is for the court to sustain the agency.[33] This result confirms law professor Marc Galanter's argument that repeat players have the advantage in civil litigation.[34] The government is the quintessential repeat player. It has greater expertise, fewer start-up costs, greater bargaining credibility, and a greater stake in shaping rules of the game than other litigants, especially the one-shot litigant. It is not surprising that the government wins most of its cases.

Nevertheless, a substantial minority of administrative decisions reviewed by the courts are reversed or remanded, which means sent back to the agency for reconsideration. According to a study of state supreme court reviews of administrative agencies, nearly 44 percent of the court decisions did not fully support the agency.[35] Supreme courts are probably more likely than other courts to overrule agencies because they can decline to review "easy" cases in which the agency is certain to be sustained. However, it is clear that administrative agencies have lost some important cases in court, especially since the 1970s.

Who benefits when the courts reverse an administrative agency? The answer depends on who the plaintiff is and what issue is under consideration.[36] When the courts reverse a social welfare agency, the plaintiff is almost certain to be an individual claimant—a welfare recipient or a disabled worker, for example. Typically, the beneficiaries are members of a disadvantaged minority, and the losers are the citizens, in their role as taxpayers. When the courts reverse a regulatory agency, the plaintiff is almost certain to be a business such as an insurance company or a utility company. Normally, the beneficiaries here are members of an advantaged minority, while the losers are citizens, in their capacity as consumers.

If this pattern looks fairly symmetrical, it seems less so when one realizes that disappointed individuals are far less likely to challenge an adverse administrative action in court than are disappointed corporations. Only 8 percent of all final Social Security Administration decisions go to court, and only one-third of these result in the restoration of benefits for the claimant.[37] In contrast, about 40 percent of state public utility commission decisions in major rate cases are appealed to the courts.[38] The most frequent appellants are business groups, usually utilities, and the most frequent winners, when the public utility commission is overruled, are also business groups, again usually utilities.

These figures highlight an important difference between the "bias" of the judicial system and the "bias" of individual judges. There is no reason to believe that judges are biased in favor of business groups. If they were, one would expect the courts to be noticeably tougher on regulatory agencies, whose decisions are challenged by business groups, than on social welfare agencies, whose decisions are challenged by disadvantaged minorities. This does not appear to be the case.[39] However, the system *is* biased in that certain claims are more likely than others to be adjudicated. It is not absolutely clear that business groups use the courts more effectively than other groups, although that may be the case. However, it is clear that business groups use the courts more often than other groups. For this reason, tough judicial scrutiny of administrative agencies tends to benefit business groups.

The principal exception to these general rules is in environmental policy. Environmental statutes encourage citizen participation in administrative and judicial proceedings, and the courts generally have granted standing to these litigants. A wide variety of environmental groups have taken the government and industry to court. Indeed, the most frequent plaintiffs in federal district court cases involving environmental disputes are environmental groups.[40] Moreover, in many instances, environmental litigants are well funded, experienced, and persistent.

Who wins environmental cases in court? In one respect, the familiar pattern holds: the government is most likely to win. In another respect, however, a new pattern emerges: when the government loses a case, business groups are not necessarily winners. Rather, environmental groups are as likely to win these disputes as are industry groups.[41] These findings suggest that a well-organized majority can neutralize the advantages of the business community in court, if legislators adopt stringent statutes and if the courts are liberal in giving groups standing. Both conditions are met in environmental policy. As a result, environmental litigation differs from litigation in other regulatory policy arenas, where the regulated industries win most often.

Constitutional Law versus Administrative Law. If administrative law appears more fragmented and chaotic in its policies than constitutional law, appearances are not deceiving. Constitutions in the United States explicitly protect disadvantaged minorities. These minorities are identified with some precision in various constitutional amendments. Administrative procedure acts are more neutral. They seek to protect affected parties from arbitrary and capricious behavior by the bureaucracy, but they do not specify which parties are to receive protection. At the time of passage, the federal APA was expected to benefit business groups in particular, and it often has done precisely that. However, the emergence of broad-based public interest groups, which have secured standing, has transformed the APA into an instrument for protecting well-organized groups generally, whether they represent an advantaged minority or the majority of citizens.

Another important difference between constitutional law and administrative law is that the Supreme Court sets more precedents in the former than the latter. The Court, with limited time, has chosen to focus on constitutional law, which gives a certain coherence to constitutional law. In contrast, administrative law is largely the province of other courts, especially state supreme courts and federal circuit courts of appeals, and they frequently disagree. Moreover, administrative agencies sometimes announce that they will not follow administrative law precedents set by lower courts when they conflict with the directives of the agency head.[42] This remarkable doctrine, which has no legal basis, limits the ability of lower courts to set precedent and makes administrative law less coherent than constitutional law. This practice also illustrates another point: a court decision is only the beginning of a lengthy process with consequences that may be either narrower or broader than anticipated.

The Aftermath of Court Decisions

Confusion and Reluctance

Judges depend on other public officials to implement their policies. Implementers include bureaucrats such as regulators, police officers, and social workers; legislative bodies such as Congress, state legislatures, and city councils; quasi-legislative bodies such as school boards and zoning boards; and other judges—lower courts are expected to implement the policies of higher courts. The implementation of judicial policies, like the implementation of other policies, is not without problems, which may include unclear standards, poor communication, inadequate resources, and hostility.[43]

Unclear Standards. Judicial policies sometimes are vague, contradictory, or variable. This is particularly true of appellate court opinions, which must accommodate the views and sensibilities of more than one judge. As noted earlier, the judge assigned the task of writing an opinion for an appellate court often finds it necessary to yield to a colleague on an important point. A first draft that is crisp, blunt, and direct may end up a patchwork of compromises. The Supreme Court's decision in *Swann v. Charlotte-Mecklenburg Board of Education* (1971) illustrates this phenomenon. Divided but anxious to issue a unanimous opinion on school busing, the Court (1) endorsed busing as a permissible remedy but warned against busing small children; (2) established a presumption against one-race schools but declined to prohibit them; and (3) allowed lower courts to correct for residential segregation patterns but only if caused by school board decisions. Reflecting on *Swann*, a federal judge observed, "There is a lot of conflicting language here. . . . It's almost as if there were two sets of views laid side by side." [44]

An ambiguous opinion is only one of several sources of confusion. Even a clear opinion, decided by a close vote, sends conflicting signals. Astute court watchers know that a five-to-four decision against including evidence in a criminal case may yield to a five-to-four decision the other way in a subsequent case. A flurry of concurring and dissenting opinions attached to Supreme Court decisions also generates confusion. Although such opinions make it easier for judges to write their memoirs, they make it more difficult to implement judicial policies.

Poor Communication. People responsible for implementation sometimes are unfamiliar with the specifics of important court decisions, especially street-level bureaucrats, who do not make a habit of reading court opinions over their morning coffee. Following *Miranda v. Arizona* (1966), police officers did not clearly understand what was required of them.[45] After *Mapp v. Ohio* (1961), in which the Court ruled that evidence obtained in violation of the Fourth Amendment could not be used in state trials, police officers could not be absolutely certain under what circumstances evidence was inadmissible in court.[46] Following *Goss v. Lopez* (1975), in which the Court ruled that students who were suspended have the right to due process, school teachers had a "muddled" understanding of the procedures to be followed in school discipline cases.[47]

Some blame can be laid to the mass media, which are notoriously negligent in their coverage of court decisions, except for major U.S. Supreme Court decisions. When the Pennsylvania Supreme Court announced that public utilities are not constitutionally entitled to rates high enough to guarantee their financial viability—a decision hailed by one observer as an "extremely important" victory for ratepayers—the *Pittsburgh Press* covered the news in a brief notice on page fourteen. When a U.S. Circuit Court of Appeals overturned a lower court decision on comparable worth, the *Press* covered the story on page eight, despite the assertion that "the ruling could set standards for similar disputes across the country." Such limited coverage of important court decisions is quite common, and public ignorance of court rulings is, therefore, hardly surprising.

Inadequate Resources. Many court orders explicitly or implicitly require the expenditure of additional funds for public purposes. School boards may have to purchase buses, hire drivers, and obtain more insurance if the courts require school busing as an antidote to racial segregation. When the courts require back pay for victims of employment discrimination by the government, agencies must somehow obtain the funds to carry out the order. When the courts require state bureaucracies to upgrade the services to the mentally ill and the mentally retarded, the states need to spend more money on psychiatrists, custodians, and physical facilities.

Lacking the power of the purse, the courts depend on legislative bodies to allocate the funds to implement court orders. But politicians have their own priorities, and minority rights are seldom high on their agenda. When Judge Johnson ordered improvements in the quality of Alabama's prisons, Governor George Wallace accused him of trying to turn the state's prisons into Holiday Inns. Eventually, the Alabama legislature increased appropriations to the state's prisons but not by enough to comply with the judge's directives.

Hostile Attitudes. Judges are widely respected in U.S. society, but their views do not command automatic deference. People charged with implementation often question the wisdom of judicial decisions, especially on matters of social policy. Many school board members strongly disapprove of busing; many teachers fervently believe in school prayer. Many police officers object to court decisions that limit their ability to put criminals behind bars. Where such hostility is present, resistance may develop.

If hostility runs deep enough, the implementers may not comply. The Boston school committee, all of whom were white, refused to draw up a desegregation plan demanded by Judge Garrity, who then took over the school system. Outright noncompliance is rare, but evasion is not at all uncommon. For example, as a response to tough evidentiary requirements in *Mapp*, some police officers resorted to perjury.[48] The public sometimes refuses to comply by taking evasive action. Many whites responded to court-ordered busing by sending their children to private schools or by moving to the suburbs.

It is clear that the implementation of judicial policies cannot be taken for granted, but one should distinguish between short-term and long-term implementation problems. Short-term problems are often formidable, but they do not necessarily doom judicial policies to failure. Most court orders are eventually implemented, and there are several reasons why this is so.

First, a single case may be ambiguous, but several interrelated cases enable the courts to establish a pattern of decisions that can guide implementers. Blockbuster opinions, such as *Brown*, *Miranda*, or *Mapp*, usually are followed by a series of interpretive opinions that reduce confusion. This clarification is strongest when the courts are reasonably consistent, as they have been in libel cases. Even when the courts are less consistent, as they have been in criminal cases, additional decisions usually clarify more than they obscure. Precedents are often deflected but seldom overturned. The norm of *stare decisis*, meaning deference to precedent, encourages courts to render reasonably consistent opinions over time, especially in matters of constitutional law, where the brooding presence of the U.S. Supreme Court ensures a modicum of consistency.

Second, knowledge of court orders travels slowly at first but eventually trickles down to the bureaucrats responsible for day-to-day implementation. Indeed, the mass media deserve some of the credit for this. For example, anyone who has watched a police drama on television knows about Miranda rights and their importance. Ironically, the mass media may have done more to enlighten citizens and street-level bureaucrats about court decisions through the entertainment programming of television than through the news reports of newspapers.

Third, institutions can deal with resource shortfalls in various ways, if given sufficient time. The deinstitutionalization of mentally ill and retarded residents was a quick way of coping with court requirements for improved care. Administrative reorganization and the hiring of more skilled personnel is another strategy. The Army Corps of Engineers responded to court orders to prepare environmental impact statements by establishing environmental units in their district offices and by hiring personnel with the necessary training.[49]

Finally, attitudes change over time. Police officers may not be enthusiastic about Miranda requirements, but they have learned to live with them. School boards may not be happy about busing, but they also have adapted. Immediately following an important court ruling, the disappointed parties assume the end of civilization. But, when the world does not come to an end, acceptance often follows. Perhaps the most striking illustration of this is the sharp change in the attitudes of whites toward school desegregation. In the late 1950s, 83 percent of southern whites objected to sending their children to a school that was half black; by 1981, only 27 percent objected.[50] For years, scholars have debated whether "stateways" can change "folkways." Although there are limits to what courts can accomplish, it appears that they have influenced attitudes on some basic issues.

Real Solutions and Solutions as Problems

Many scholars are reluctant to ascribe so much influence to the courts, instead seeing the policy impact of the courts as rather limited.[51] Political science professor Lawrence Baum wrote, "In reality, the Court's impact on society is severely constrained by the context in which its policies operate."[52] At first glance, this conclusion appears reasonable, given the implementation problems mentioned earlier. But most studies of the policy impacts of court decisions focus exclusively on short-term effects. If one looks at long-term effects, one sees the power of the courts.

One of the most conspicuous successes of the courts is the effort to promote racial justice. In education, voting rights, employment, and housing, the courts have breathed life into constitutional requirements for due process of law and have helped to ensure equal opportunity for racial minorities, especially blacks. This has not happened overnight. For a full decade after *Brown*, southern schools remained separate and unequal. In the mid-1960s, however, the picture began to change. By the 1972-1973 school year, 91 percent of black students in the South were going to school with whites.[53] Progress in northern schools, although slower, has also been noticeable.[54]

Court decisions on voting rights have produced quicker results, partly because all three branches of government moved aggressively on this issue. The Voting Rights Act of 1965 was followed one year later by an 8-1 Supreme Court decision affirming the act in full (*South Carolina v. Katzenbach*, 1966). Over the next two years, the Justice Department sent federal examiners to some southern districts and appointed poll watchers in others. The effects were dramatic. From 1964 to 1968 black registration rates in the South jumped from 38 percent to 62 percent.[55] Increased registration led to higher black turnout and to the election of black local officials, which in turn generated increases in public employment and other public services for blacks.[56]

The courts have been less aggressive in promoting equal opportunity in housing, partly because of the tradition of judicial deference to local zoning boards and city councils.[57] However, several state supreme courts have invalidated exclusionary zoning practices as violations of state constitutions. The desegregation of housing, like the desegregation of the public schools, is likely to proceed slowly. Eventually, the elimination of exclusionary zoning practices should result in some affordable housing for racial minorities even in affluent white suburbs.

Court decisions in administrative law also have had significant impact, especially in communications and environmental policy and in standards for institutional care. For years, station WLBT-TV in Jackson, Mississippi, fanned the flames of racial discontent in its editorials against integration and its acceptance of ads paid for by a local racist group. When well-known blacks were featured on network newscasts, the general manager would sometimes show a "Sorry, Cable Trouble" sign until the segment ended. A church-related citizen group, the Office of Communication of the United Church of Christ, opposed in court the renewal of the station's license on the grounds that the station had violated the Federal Communications Commission's fairness doctrine.[58] In two important decisions, *United Church of Christ v. FCC*, 1966 and *United Church of Christ v. FCC*, 1969, the U.S. Court of Appeals, D.C. Circuit, agreed with the church and ordered the FCC to grant the license to someone else.

The immediate consequences for Jackson television viewers were that the license was awarded to another company, which promptly hired a black general manager, assigned a black anchor to read the evening news, and improved the quantity and quality of news and public affairs programming.[59] The long-term consequences were even more significant. Using these cases as precedents, citizen groups intervened in administrative and judicial proceedings on behalf of television consumers, and, in many cases, they secured important concessions. In addition, these cases helped to establish standing for aggrieved consumers in other issue areas.

Court decisions on environmental impact statements also have generated far-reaching changes. The National Environmental Policy Act of 1969 (NEPA) requires administrative agencies to file an environmental impact statement for "major federal projects with a significant environmental effect," and the federal courts interpret the words *major* and *significant* rather liberally. When in doubt, they require the agency to prepare an environmental impact statement. The repercussions have been widespread. The Army Corps of Engineers, long known for its "edifice complex," began to look at nonstructural alternatives to dams and dredging projects.[60] The courts' interpretations of NEPA also sensitized other agencies to environmental impacts.

The consequences of judicial efforts at institutional reform have been equally profound. In 1973 a federal district court ordered the closing of Willowbrook, a New York facility for the mentally retarded, where conditions were shown to be unsanitary, unsafe, and inhumane. The immediate effects of judicial intervention were disappointing. The state's department of mental health at first refused to yield client records and failed to submit progress reports on time, as required by the court. However, between 1976 and 1979, the state bureaucracy opened 100 group homes for 1,000 Willowbrook residents. Community placement was achieved without lowering property values or destroying neighborhoods. Audits revealed that group homes were properly administered, and more important, that the lives of the residents improved. At first, the group homes resembled "puppet shows." Choreographed to behave as more intelligent people would, residents played parts they did not understand. Eventually, the puppets became animated, as they learned how to make decisions concerning choices of food and clothing.[61] Such choices, which most people take for granted, marked a major breakthrough and signaled a significant improvement in their quality of life.

These examples demonstrate the capacity of the courts to effect changes in the public interest, especially over time. Many court decisions produce tangible results that benefit disadvantaged minorities or the public. A problem with court decisions, however, is that they are not easily contained. They have spillover effects never imagined by judicial decision makers. Many of these unintended consequences are undesirable. At best, they detract from judicial policies; at worst, they undermine them.

The *Mapp* decision, extending the exclusionary rule to local police departments, appears to have resulted in greater reliance on plea bargaining in cases where evidence may have been obtained through questionable methods.[62] The *Goss* decision, requiring a hearing before suspension from school, discouraged teachers from disciplining disruptive students.[63] *Gault*, which established formal procedures for juveniles accused of a crime, made it difficult for juvenile court judges to counsel and advise informally, as they had done, in cases where no crime had been committed.[64]

The unintended consequences of school desegregation and environmental policy decisions have been especially troublesome. In many cities court-ordered busing prompted whites to abandon inner-city public schools and to place their children in private schools or move to the suburbs. When Judge Garrity took over Boston's public schools in 1974, 61 percent of the pupils were white; when he terminated his involvement in 1985, only 27 percent were white.[65] In those eleven years, numerous white parents, feeling abandoned by the courts, decided to abandon Boston's public schools.

Court decisions on air pollution have also been a mixed blessing. The courts imposed tough standards for the design of new plants, for example, by requiring the "prevention of significant deterioration" in air quality in wilderness areas and polluted cities. In enforcement cases, however, the courts relaxed the standards for existing plants, such as utilities, steel mills, and smelters. In effect, the courts have frozen existing technologies and facilities and discouraged the building of modern plants. According to some observers, this unintended consequence has increased the costs of achieving clean air.[66]

In environmental policy, as in school desegregation, the courts have accomplished what they intended to accomplish. School segregation and air pollution have declined appreciably, and the courts deserve much of the credit for this. However, the country paid a high price for these gains, probably higher than necessary. Nor is this surprising. Judges are not very good at calculating costs, and they are not particularly inclined to do so. Judges think in terms of rights and duties rather than economic analysis. In contrast to politicians, judges have no need to hide the costs of their actions or to think much about them. There is, in short, an irony here. In courtroom politics, costs are often manifest, but irrelevant. The costs of judicial decisions, although unintended, are not always unforeseen, but judges maintain that they are not responsible for the adverse consequences of their actions.

The Paradoxical Decree

Although less sensitive to costs than other public officials, judges are more sensitive than is commonly supposed to the consequences of their actions. Judges recognize the limitations of a single court order and, because they see the potential for implementation problems, judges sometimes are unwilling to entrust the delicate tasks of implementation to the bureaucracy. In certain cases, judges have assumed responsibility for carrying out their own orders, becoming, in effect, managers and administrators.

Nowhere is this more evident than in the behavior of federal district court judges who have coped with school busing and institutional reform cases. These judges have not issued orders and hoped for the best. Rather, they have upgraded the court's capacity to receive feedback, to learn from it, and to correct errors. The principal mechanism for this judicial role is the court decree, which judges use to fashion relief in an ad hoc manner and on a continuous basis.[67] The modern decree is a paradox. It is at once extremely specific as to the affected parties and extremely fluid, giving the judge wide latitude. It contains detailed instructions and calls for a continuing dialogue, progress reports, and midcourse corrections. All of these characteristics reduce implementation problems and narrow the gap between intended and actual policy impacts.

One characteristic of the decree is its specificity. When Judge Garrity issued his first order concerning Boston's schools, he specified not only the racial balance to be achieved but also the geographic boundaries of new community school districts. From that moment, Garrity became, in effect, the superintendent of the Boston school system. He assigned pupils, hired staff and administrators, closed and upgraded schools, and acted on spending requests. He justified these tight controls on the grounds that it was necessary to prevent sabotage by the Boston School Committee, which had openly resisted the court's efforts to desegregate the public schools.

Judges have been equally specific in institutional reform cases. Judge Johnson took over Alabama's prisons and mental health facilities, issuing detailed requirements for nutrition, personal hygiene, recreational opportunities, educational programs, and staffing ratios.[68] Judge Orrin Judd took control of Willowbrook, ordering outdoor exercise for the residents five times a week, a ratio of one attendant for every nine residents, and the repair of all the home's toilets.[69]

A second characteristic of the decree is its continuity. In contrast to the standard pattern, a judge does not simply issue a single decision. The decree is the first step in a long, protracted, interactive process. The judge meets frequently with parties to the case and listens to their grievances. He or she receives progress reports, dispenses criticism and praise, and issues new orders. Judge Garrity issued 415 school desegregation orders from 1974 to 1985. While this probably qualifies him for the *Guinness Book of World Records*, other judges also have issued large numbers of court orders.

A third characteristic of the decree is its fluidity. In anticipation of unexpected developments, judges retain the option of modifying their initial order. To assist them, they often appoint special masters. The use of masters is not new, but it has grown, especially in school desegregation cases. Garrity appointed four masters and two experts; the masters held hearings and proposed a plan, which Garrity modified and incorporated into his second decree.[70]

Instead of masters, some judges appoint monitoring committees to serve as their eyes and ears. The committee's task is to inform the judge as implementation problems arise. Johnson established monitoring committees, called human rights committees, for each of Alabama's major mental institutions. Among other tasks, these committees were authorized to inspect institutional records, to interview patients and staff, and to consult with independent specialists.

Monitoring committees are seldom greeted with open arms by the bureaucrats whose performance they are to investigate. In Alabama the director of one mental health facility barred his staff from talking with the monitoring committee without his permission. Johnson intervened to overturn that policy, but problems persisted. The monitoring committee in the Willowbrook case also ruffled a few feathers through its relentless insistence on community placement. Eventually, the Willowbrook monitoring committee was abolished by the New York state legislature, which grew weary of its criticisms.

Judges are fallible, and their decrees are seldom perfect. Judge Garrity unnecessarily polarized the races by pairing Roxbury, the heart of the black ghetto, with South Boston, the citadel of white resistance to busing. A more judicious solution might have been to pair South Boston with nearby Dorchester or to intersperse South Boston and Roxbury students throughout the city. Judge Johnson undermined his credibility by insisting that all Alabama prison cells be sixty square feet. No Alabama prison cell met this specification, which lent credence to Governor Wallace's charge that Johnson was insensitive to the costs of prison reform. Johnson later modified his order on prison cell size, and other judges have done the same.

At its best, the modern decree is an error-correction device that works two ways. First, it enables the judge to identify and correct errors made by government officials, who may not share the court's commitment to a particular policy goal. Second, it enables the judge to correct errors made by the court when it goes too far. The judicial decree, therefore, represents a milestone in judicial policy making. It is the court's way of saying that judicial activism and judicial responsibility must go hand in hand. If judges are going to make public policy in highly controversial issue areas, they cannot simply render a decision and walk away. Although the decree does not guarantee that the courts will be alert to implementation problems, it does provide ample opportunities for judicial oversight.

Summary

The failures of other branches of government and the litigious character of U.S. society go a long way to explain the courts' prominence in making public policy. Although courts avoid macroeconomic policy and foreign policy disputes, they directly address other issues, which are characterized by high conflict and manifest costs. Issues addressed by the courts are also marked by high technical complexity, high moral complexity, or both. They are among the most vexing problems society faces.

In reaching decisions on these issues, judges are guided by factors that transcend politics—law, evidence, and judicial philosophy. But, judicial decision making is also political. Judges are usually affiliated with a political party, and their voting behavior reflects party affiliation. Internal politicking, especially on supreme courts where several judges must agree on the wording of an opinion, gives judges the opportunity for leadership. In the courts, as elsewhere, political leadership can make the difference between arriving at a tough policy and a weak one, between a clear policy and a vague one.

Many court decisions are at first diluted by unclear standards, poor communication, inadequate resources, and hostile attitudes. Over time, however, most are successfully implemented and have the impact they were intended to have. Unfortunately, they often have unintended consequences, some of which may be attributed to judicial insensitivity to consequences. But even if judges wished to take consequences into account, they cannot foresee every result.

Courts have changed in many ways. More women and blacks sit on the bench, lending more judicial support to minority rights in constitutional law disputes. More public interest groups litigate in court, which results in occasional triumphs for environmental and consumer interests. Finally, the choice between judicial activism and judicial restraint has been resolved largely in favor of judicial activism. The courts are more likely to overturn statutes, more likely to overturn administrative agency decisions, and more likely to prescribe specific ground rules and remedies.

Activism and liberalism are not one and the same. In constitutional law, activism runs in a liberal direction; in administrative law, activism runs in a conservative direction. Criminal justice and environmental protection are exceptions to these general rules. In criminal justice, judicial enthusiasm for defendant rights waxes and wanes; in environmental protection, the courts support environmentalists on standards, business groups on enforcement. Whatever the policy tilt of the courts, the fact remains that judges are making policy.

Notes

1. Martin Shapiro, *Courts: A Comparative and Political Analysis* (Chicago: University of Chicago Press, 1981), 105-124; Richard Posner, *The Federal Courts: Crisis and Reform* (Cambridge, Mass.: Harvard University Press, 1985).
2. Donald Horowitz, *The Courts and Social Policy* (Washington, D.C.: Brookings Institution, 1977), 9.
3. Richard Neely, *How Courts Govern America* (New Haven, Conn.: Yale University Press, 1981), 212.
4. J. Woodford Howard, Jr., *Courts of Appeals in the Federal Judicial System: A Study of the 2nd, 5th, and D.C. Circuits* (Princeton, N.J.: Princeton University Press, 1981), 25-33.

5. See *United States v. Richardson*, 418 U.S. 166 (1974); *Valley Forge Christian College v. Americans United for Separation of Church and State*, 454 U.S. 464 (1982).

6. *Amalgamated Meat Cutters v. Connally*, 337 F. Supp. 737 (1971).

7. *United States v. Curtiss-Wright Export Corp.*, 299 U.S. 304 (1936); *Dames & Moore v. Regan*, 453 U.S. 654 (1981).

8. Federal judges are not entirely powerless in these matters. District court judges can—and do—encourage parties to settle a case without going to trial. Also, judges may refuse to hear a case on the grounds that a party lacks standing, that the issue is not ripe, or for other reasons.

9. The U.S. Supreme Court is required to hear the following kinds of cases: (1) disputes between states; (2) cases in which a federal court has held an act of Congress unconstitutional, if the federal government is a party, and cases in which a state supreme court has held an act of Congress unconstitutional; (3) cases in which a state court has upheld a state law against a claim that it conflicts with the Constitution or federal law; (4) cases in which a federal court has overturned a state law on grounds that it conflicts with the Constitution or federal law; and (5) decisions of special three-judge federal district courts.

10. Hughes denounced Roosevelt's plan in a calm but forceful letter to Senator Burton Wheeler. The letter is credited with weakening congressional support for the court-packing plan.

11. Henry Glick, *Supreme Courts in State Politics* (New York: Basic Books, 1971).

12. Herbert Jacob, *Urban Justice: Law and Order in American Cities* (Englewood Cliffs, N.J.: Prentice-Hall, 1973).

13. Marc Galanter, "Why the 'Haves' Come Out Ahead: Speculations on the Limits of Legal Change," *Law and Society Review* 9 (Fall 1974): 95-160.

14. Glendon Schubert, *Quantitative Analysis of Judicial Behavior* (Glencoe, Ill.: Free Press, 1959); S. Sidney Ulmer, "The Political Party Variable in the Michigan Supreme Court," in *Judicial Behavior*, ed. Glendon Schubert (Chicago: Rand McNally, 1964), 279-286; Malcolm Feeley, "Another Look at the 'Party Variable' in Judicial Decision-Making: An Analysis of the Michigan Supreme Court," *Polity* 4 (Fall 1971): 91-104.

15. Philip Dubois, *From Ballot to Bench: Judicial Elections and the Quest for Accountability* (Austin: University of Texas Press, 1980), 231.

16. C. Neal Tate, "Personal Attribute Models of the Voting Behavior of U.S. Supreme Court Justices: Liberalism in Civil Liberties and Economics Decisions, 1946-1978," *American Political Science Review* 75 (June 1981): 355-367; Sheldon Goldman, "Voting Behavior on the U.S. Court of Appeals Revisited," *American Political Science Review* 69 (June 1975): 491-506; Robert Carp and C. K. Rowland, *Policymaking and Politics in the Federal District Courts* (Knoxville: University of Tennessee Press, 1983).

17. David Whitman, "Reagan's Conservative Judges Are Singing a Different Tune Now," *Washington Post National Weekly Edition*, Aug. 24, 1987, 23.

18. Bernard Schwartz, *Super Chief: Earl Warren and the Supreme Court* (New York: New York University Press, 1983), 40-44.

19. Lawrence Baum, *The Supreme Court* (Washington, D.C.: CQ Press, 1981), 156-162.

20. Martin Shapiro, "On Predicting the Future of Administrative Law," *Regulation* 6 (May/June 1982): 18-25; R. Shep Melnick, *Regulation and the Courts: The Case of the Clean Air Act* (Washington, D.C.: Brookings Institution, 1983).

21. Much of the credit for the unanimous decisions goes to Earl Warren, a remarkably adroit political leader. Warren's handling of the *Brown v. Board of Education* decision is a good case in point. When Warren took over as chief justice, the Brown case had already been argued, and the Court was prepared to vote five to four in favor of desegregation. In a clever ploy, Warren suggested that the justices postpone the vote. Instead, Warren led a free-wheeling discussion that ultimately revealed some common ground on which they could agree. The process was not easy. It took three separate conferences and numerous private conversations between Warren and individual justices before Warren's efforts were successful. In 1954 the Supreme Court issued a unanimous opinion in a case that was easily one of the most important in U.S. history. See Schwartz, *Super Chief*, 72-127.

22. Archibald Cox, *The Role of the Supreme Court in American Government* (New York: Oxford University Press, 1976), 38-39.

23. Vincent Blasi, "The Rootless Activism of the Burger Court," in *The Burger Court: The Counter-Revolution That Wasn't*, ed. Vincent Blasi (New Haven, Conn.: Yale University Press, 1983), 198-217.

24. A. E. (Dick) Howard, "State Courts and Constitutional Rights in the Day of the Burger Court," *Virginia Law Review* 62 (June 1976): 873-944; Mary Porter, "State Supreme Courts and the Legacy of the Warren Court: Some Old Inquiries for a New Situation," in *State Supreme Courts: Policymakers in the Federal System*, ed. Mary Porter and G. Alan Tarr (Westport, Conn.: Greenwood Press, 1982), 3-21; Robert Pear, "State Courts Surpass U.S. Bench in Cases on Rights of Individuals," *New York Times*, May 4, 1986, 1.

25. Ibid.

26. Charlotte Carter, *Media in the Courts* (Williamsburg, Va.: National Center for State Courts, 1981).

27. Norman Davis, "Television in our Courts: The Proven Advantages, the Unproven Dangers," *Judicature* 64 (August 1980): 85-92.

28. Jonathan Casper, "The Supreme Court and National Policy Making," *American Political Science Review* 70 (March 1976): 50-63; Baum, *The Supreme Court;* Harold Spaeth, "Burger Court Review of State Court Civil Liberties Decisions," *Judicature* 68 (February-March, 1985), 285-291.

29. Casper, "The Supreme Court and National Policy Making."

30. Robert Dahl, "Decision-Making in a Democracy: The Supreme Court as a National Policy-Maker," *Journal of Public Law* 6 (Fall 1957): 279-295.

31. Geoffrey Stone, "Individual Rights and Majoritarianism: The Supreme Court in Transition" (Washington, D.C.: The Cato Institute, 1985), monograph.

32. Michael Rebell and Arthur Block, *Educational Policy Making and the Courts: An Empirical Study of Judicial Activism* (Chicago: University of Chicago Press, 1982), 36.

33. Martin Shapiro, *The Supreme Court and Administrative Agencies* (New York: Free Press, 1968); Jerry Mashaw et al., *Social Security Hearings and Appeals* (Lexington, Mass.: D. C. Heath, 1978), 125-150; Craig Wanner, "The Public Ordering of Private Relations, Part Two: Winning Civil Court Cases," *Law and Society Review* 9 (Winter 1975): 293-306; Stephen Frank, "The Oversight of Administrative Agencies by State Supreme Courts: Some Macro Findings," *Administrative Law Review* 32 (Summer 1980): 477-499.

34. Galanter, "Why the 'Haves' Come Out Ahead."

35. Frank, "The Oversight of Administrative Agencies."

36. It also depends on the court. For example, the D.C. Circuit Court of Appeals, during the 1970s, was much more supportive of environmental protection than other circuit courts of appeals. See Lettie Wenner, *The Environmental Decade in Court* (Bloomington: Indiana University Press, 1982), 35-63.

37. Mashaw et al., *Social Security Hearings and Appeals*, 125-150.

38. William T. Gormley, Jr., *The Politics of Public Utility Regulation* (Pittsburgh: University of Pittsburgh Press, 1983), 94.

39. Frank, "The Oversight of Administrative Agencies."

40. The gap has narrowed as industry plaintiffs have become more common. Also, industry groups are more likely to file appeals in appeals courts than environmental groups. See Wenner, *The Environmental Decade in Court*, 35-63.

41. Ibid., 94.

42. According to Mashaw, this is the practice of the Social Security Administration (SSA), the National Labor Relations Board (NLRB), and the Internal Revenue Service (IRS), among other agencies. See Jerry Mashaw, *Bureaucratic Justice* (New Haven, Conn.: Yale University Press, 1983), 186. The SSA's refusal to follow precedents set by lower federal courts aroused considerable controversy during the Reagan years, when the SSA cut financial awards to disabled workers. However, there is no evidence that this policy of selective adherence to precedent (or nonacquiescence) is changing.

43. Donald Van Meter and Carl Van Horn, "The Policy Implementation Process: A Conceptual Framework," *Administration and Society* 6 (February 1975): 445-488; Carl Van Horn, *Policy Implementation in the Federal System* (Lexington, Mass.: D. C. Heath, 1979); George Edwards III, *Implementing Public Policy* (Washington, D.C.: CQ Press, 1980).

44. Bob Woodward and Scott Armstrong, *The Brethren: Inside the Supreme Court* (New York: Simon & Schuster, 1979), 112.

45. Neal Milner, *The Court and Local Law Enforcement: The Impact of Miranda* (Beverly Hills, Calif.: Sage Publications, 1971), 225.

46. Horowitz, *The Courts and Social Policy*, 226.

47. Henry Lufler, "The Supreme Court Goes to School: *Goss v. Lopez* and Student Suspensions," (Ph.D. diss., University of Wisconsin, 1982).

48. Horowitz, *The Courts and Social Policy*, 234.

49. Daniel Mazmanian and Jeane Nienaber, *Can Organizations Change?* (Washington, D.C.: Brookings Institution, 1979), 37-60.

50. Jennifer Hochschild, *The New American Dilemma: Liberal Democracy and School Desegregation* (New Haven, Conn.: Yale University Press, 1984), 180.

51. Kenneth Dolbeare and Phillip Hammond, *The School Prayer Decisions: From Court Policy to Local Practice* (Chicago: University of Chicago Press, 1971); Milner, *The Court and Local Law Enforcement;* Baum, *The Supreme Court;* Charles Johnson and Bradley Canon, *Judicial Policies: Implementation and Impact* (Washington, D.C.: CQ Press, 1984).

52. Baum, *The Supreme Court*, 211.

53. Ibid., 187.

54. Charles Bullock III, "Equal Education Opportunity," in *Implementation of Civil Rights Policy*, ed. Charles Bullock III and Charles Lamb (Monterey, Calif.: Brooks/Cole Publishing, 1984), 68-69.

55. Richard Scher and James Button, "Voting Rights Act: Implementation and Impact," in *Implementation of Civil Rights Policy*, 40.

56. Albert Karnig and Susan Welch, *Black Representation and Urban Policy* (Chicago: University of Chicago Press, 1980); Peter Eisinger, "Black Employment in Municipal Jobs: The Impact of Black Political Power," *American Political Science Review* 76 (June 1982): 380-392.

57. Michael Danielson, *The Politics of Exclusion* (New York: Columbia University Press, 1976).

58. The fairness doctrine, abolished by the Federal Communications Commission in 1987, required broadcasters to devote a reasonable amount of time to the discussion of issues of public importance. When covering such issues, broadcasters did not need to provide "equal time" to all points of view, but their coverage had to be balanced and fair.

59. Fred Friendly, *The Good Guys, the Bad Guys, and the First Amendment* (New York: Random House, 1975), 89-102.

60. Mazmanian and Nienaber, *Can Organizations Change?*

61. David Rothman and Sheila Rothman, *The Willowbrook Wars* (New York: Harper & Row, 1984).

62. Horowitz, *The Courts and Social Policy.*

63. Lufler, "The Supreme Court Goes to School."

64. Horowitz, *The Courts and Social Policy.*

65. Matthew Wald, "After Years of Turmoil, Judge Is Yielding Job of Integrating Boston Schools," *New York Times,* Aug. 22, 1985, 16.

66. Melnick, *Regulation and the Courts.*

67. Colin Diver, "The Judge as Political Powerbroker: Superintending Structural Change in Public Institutions," *Virginia Law Review* 65 (February 1979): 43-106; Abram Chayes, "Public Law Litigation and the Burger Court," *Harvard Law Review* 96 (November 1982): 4-60.

68. Tinsley Yarbrough, "The Judge as Manager: The Case of Judge Frank Johnson," *Journal of Policy Analysis and Management* 1 (Spring 1982): 386-400.

69. Rothman and Rothman, *The Willowbrook Wars.*

70. J. Anthony Lukas, *Common Ground* (New York: Alfred A. Knopf, 1985).

8   Living Room Politics

The United States is a representative democracy. Americans are taught as early as grade school that government and public policy are based on the consent of the governed. President Abraham Lincoln said that American government is "of the people, by the people, and for the people," and every national leader before and after him has cited the "will of the people" to justify particular courses of action.

Debates about the role of citizens in guiding public policy go back to the founding of the country. James Madison and other authors of the Constitution were strong advocates for democracy, but they did not believe that elected representatives should slavishly follow mass opinions in determining public policy. Many of the Founding Fathers feared that the public could be unstable, tyrannical, and even dangerous to liberal democracy.[1] They believed that periodic elections give citizens sufficient safeguards against elected representatives who served them poorly. In between elections, leaders should govern as they see fit. This concept of democracy was perhaps best summed up by the British political philosopher and statesmen, Edmund Burke. In a treatise on representative democracy, Burke said: "Your representative owes you, not his industry only, but his judgment; and he betrays instead of serving you if he sacrifices it to your opinion."[2]

The fact that thousands of elected officials must face the voters every so often keeps many citizens involved in government at the most basic level. But, for the most part, public policy is not made and implemented by the *public*. Instead, elected officials, bureaucrats, judges, and corporate leaders determine public policies. They are attentive to, not ruled by, the concerns of the public—a point underscored throughout this book. And yet, people's opinions influence the course of public affairs and occasionally, when aroused, play central roles in politics. This chapter on living room politics explores how public opinion, the mass media, and public officials interact over public policy choices between elections.

Public opinion is a potent weapon of democracy, but it is not something one can visit, like a building, or read, like a book. There are many publics, many opinions, and many voices in American society.

Public opinions are defined and channeled into the policy process by the media, public officials, and citizen activists.[3] Elected officials gauge public opinion by scrutinizing opinion polls and television and newspaper reports and by talking with interest group representatives, friends and coworkers, and perhaps the local gas station attendant.

The mass media—television, radio, and newspapers—are the principal vehicles through which public opinions are expressed and manipulated.[4] Policy makers, the press, and interest groups attempt to shape the view of reality that is presented to the people. Journalists influence the public's understanding of politics and public policy and then inform public officials about what the "public" thinks. Perhaps most important, the media frame political and policy discussions, telling people what issues are important and who favors each position. When the media or public officials succeed in defining the parameters of the policy debate they are exercising what E. E. Schattschneider called "the supreme instrument of political power." [5]

The public does not make policy directly, but citizens *can* be more than just an audience watching contests between political elites. Citizens can choose policy options that affect their states and communities. Through ballot initiatives and referenda—devices of direct democracy available to citizens in most states—voters can force state legislators to write new laws or to eliminate old ones. Citizens who are angered by government decisions or frustrated by inaction can go beyond passive forms of democratic participation and organize grass-roots political movements to achieve their objectives.

Bystanders and Activists

Public opinions are involved in virtually everything that government institutions do, yet most citizens are typically little more than bystanders.[6] The public policy enterprise occurs in the background of their lives: they hear noise, but seldom listen. A much smaller "attentive public," probably no more than one American in ten, closely follows public affairs. They read newspapers carefully, write letters, and call elected officials; they have opinions and they express them. On rare occasions, the bystanders are drawn into the fray. When large segments of the public become concerned about issues, their preferences can become a powerful force.

Top-Down Public Opinion

Contrary to the civics book notion that the public will drives elected officials to carry out the public's wishes, political elites usually decide what public opinion is, what it means, and whether to use it or ignore it.

This does not mean that public opinions are unimportant, only that they are defined by public officials. In this view, public opinions should be thought of as ammunition used by political elites to support their point of view and to advance policy positions.

The creation, interpretation, and use of public sentiment by public officials, the media, and interest groups in the policy process has been called "top-down public opinion." [7] Political elites "construct" a notion of what the "public" wants by listening to a variety of people and to reports on public sentiment.[8] According to political scientist V. O. Key, public opinion is "private opinions which government finds it prudent to heed." [9]

Policy formulation and implementation occur within the boundaries of political culture established by public opinion. The nation's political culture comprises "the enduring beliefs, values and behaviors that organize social communication and make common interpretations of life experience possible." [10] According to political scientist Robert Weissberg, "Virtually all the alternatives . . . considered [during policy debates] will be at least *tolerable* . . . by the vast majority. Thus although the precise preferences of 50 percent plus one may not be satisfied by the policy outcome, the losers would not regard the results as completely unacceptable." [11]

Under these circumstances, the public's greatest power is as a deterrent. Just as massive nuclear arsenals presumably deter the United States and the Soviet Union from starting a nuclear war, public opinions constrain what government institutions can accomplish or even propose. A "law of anticipated consequences" usually checks public officials from enacting policies that offend fundamental values in the political culture. Elected officials know that if the public is ignored or offended it can be mobilized by political opponents who urge voters to "throw the rascals out."

Political elites also wield interpretations of public sentiment in day-to-day struggles for power and policy advantage. Legislators and chief executives cite public support as the rationale for policy innovation, such as tough new laws against criminals. Governors and legislators also use public opinion as a shield against modifying existing policies, such as tax rates. Unless reliable and up-to-date public opinion polls are available—and they usually are not—each side in a policy debate can claim public support.

Chief executives are especially dependent on mobilizing public support for their positions; they must maintain the perception that the majority stands with them. Scholar Richard Neustadt argued that the principal power of the presidency is the "power to persuade." [12] Legislators try to read the tea leaves of public opinion to see how well the president or governor is doing before deciding whether to lend their support. If the public seems to favor the president's policies, members of Congress may be reluctant to criticize. Conversely, when a president's popularity dips, congressional support may erode quickly. The following excerpt from the *New York Times* is instructive:

Democratic senators and representatives used to cringe when President Reagan made one of his televised appeals for public support on a budget or tax issue before Congress. They knew that the telephone calls and letters would pour in and that they would have to explain over and over again why they were not giving a popular President their wholehearted support. But the Democratic cringing became gloating last week as Mr. Reagan's latest appeal . . . was met by widespread . . . and even startling indifference. The public indifference to President Reagan's entreaties emboldened Democrats to press ahead with their own policy initiatives and to treat the President as "a kindly old relative that you don't have to pay much attention to," according to Senator James Sasser of Tennessee.[13]

Bottom-Up Public Opinion

The public is not always passive. Large segments of the public, marginally interested or even disinterested in politics, may be awakened gradually.[14] Salient issues, such as war, civil rights, morality, public health, or economic hardship, can stir the passions of ordinary citizens. When this happens, public opinions may exert significant pressure on political institutions and public officials from the bottom up. Citizens' concerns are most commonly expressed through elections or indirect plebiscites—public opinion polls. But bottom-up public opinion is felt more directly. Some people may abandon their bystander status and vote on policy issues or even become active participants.

Referenda and Initiatives. Citizens can select policies and structure government institutions by voting on referenda and initiatives. There are no provisions in the U.S. Constitution for national referenda or initiatives, but thirty-seven state constitutions authorize referenda that give citizens a voice on measures approved by state legislatures. Typically, referenda allow citizens to vote yes or no on amendments to state constitutions, on state capital spending projects, such as highways or new prisons, or even on major state laws, such as environmental protection and health care programs.

Initiatives—provided for in twenty-one state constitutions—give citizens the right to petition public officials to place issues on the ballot for approval or disapproval, without waiting for the state legislature to act.[15] Before questions are put before the voters, a significant number of state residents must sign petitions, usually 5 percent to 10 percent of the number voting in the last statewide election. If the qualified initiative receives majority support, the legislature is expected to enact a law embodying the purpose of the initiative. Initiatives have been employed on a wide variety of policy questions, including tax and spending issues, public morality, business regulation, and U.S. foreign and defense policy.

Giving the public a vote on policies has a long tradition in American politics. Referenda were first used in 1778 when Massachusetts voters approved the state's first constitution. The initiative grew in importance during the late nineteenth and twentieth century as the Progressive political reform movement swept the country west of the Mississippi River. The influential Progressive reformer, Robert M. La Follette, summarized the rationale for referenda and initiatives:

For years the American people have been engaged in a terrific struggle with the allied forces of organized wealth and political corruption. . . . The people must have in reserve new weapons for every emergency if they are to regain and preserve control of their governments. Through the initiative and referenda, people in an emergency can absolutely control. The initiative and referenda make it possible for them to demand a direct vote and repeal bad laws which have been enacted or to enact by direct vote good measures which their representatives refuse to consider.[16]

Since 1976 these instruments of "direct democracy" have been used with increasing frequency. The number of state ballot initiatives doubled between then and 1986.[17] In the 1980, 1982, 1984, and 1986 elections more than 200 public propositions appeared on state ballots, and one in four was an initiative.[18] In 1986 voters weighed important, complex, and controversial issues such as:

—establishing a state sales tax in Oregon, which failed
—imposing stringent regulations on the production and disposal of toxic chemicals into California's water supply, which passed
—reducing acid rain in Massachusetts, which passed
—adopting an equal rights for women amendment to the state constitution in Vermont, which failed
—expanding worker's compensation in Wyoming, which passed
—prohibiting the use of state funds to fund abortions in Rhode Island, which failed
—allowing people to grow marijuana for their own use in Oregon, which failed

Grass-Roots Politics. Many citizens engage directly and vigorously in the political life of their communities, states, and nation. The New England town meeting, the governing body in hundreds of small communities, invites every citizen to have a say in the course of public policy. Grass-roots political movements have sprung up to demand reform—sometimes with striking success, and at other times with stunning failure. For decades prior to the Civil War, for example, abolitionists sought the end of slavery. In the middle of the nineteenth century suffragettes began to press for the right to vote for women, which was granted by ratification of the Nineteenth Amendment to the Constitution in 1920. Agrarian populists and labor unionists at the turn of the century demanded economic justice for low-income Americans.

Since World War II American politics has witnessed strong public movements to secure civil rights for blacks, to stop the war in Southeast Asia, to clean up the nation's air and water, to end the deployment of nuclear weapons, to crack down on drunk drivers, to curb utility rate hikes, and to stop abortions. Each of these political movements emerged outside of conventional political arenas, was sparked by unelected leaders, and characterized by large, vocal, and active participation from citizens who previously may have played little or no role in politics.[19]

What makes citizens stop relying on the voting booth and march in the streets? What makes people switch from watchers to central players? Grass-roots movements spring up when citizens become impatient with the pace of decision making, frustrated by the unwillingness of public officials to address their concerns, or angered by laws that infringe on basic rights or fundamental interests. When public opinion is "carried through from conversation to action [it] almost always carries with it a sense of outrage or injustice. At this point it is no longer opinion at all . . . but rather a state of emotional shock . . . a feeling of deprivation." [20]

Citizens frequently are drawn into political conflicts when they believe their health, safety, or property is threatened by government policies. The issue could be a proposed nuclear power plant, a school desegregation order, or a new condominium development that alarms people sufficiently to act. Under these conditions, a small group of citizens, who normally eschew politics, can be motivated to attend meetings, join protest marches, contribute money, and become political animals. Public opinion from the bottom up is expressed when communities mobilize to protect their vital interests.

Citizens, Politicians, and Journalists

Living room politics involves the interaction of political leaders, who want to control and manipulate public opinion; citizens, who want to bring about changes in government policy; and the media, which serve as conduits of important political information about the public. On rare occasions citizens join together to fight the White House, the capitol, or city hall, but even "spontaneous" outbursts of public concern are unlikely to occur or succeed without the drum beat of newspaper and television coverage and strong political leadership.

The instruments of mass communications—television, radio, newspapers, and magazines—are the most important weapons in the battle for public opinion. Whether public opinions influence policies from the top down or citizens agitate from the bottom up, the mass media are involved. The media not only keep the attentive public informed, but also prominently feature stories that may eventually stir the normally apathetic mass public.

Public officials and citizens can communicate face to face, but probably not on a regular basis. The media have become the principal intermediaries and therefore exercise enormous power.[21] The media influence people's perception of what is important, frame the terms of debate on many questions, and magnify the voice of a few political figures. From time to time, the media switch from an information "channel" to an information "source" to promote particular policy concerns. When a network news program depicts the problems of homeless Americans for five minutes a night for an entire week, it is not just a conduit of facts and opinions, but a source of information with potentially powerful consequences for public policy.

Living room politics, like all politics, is dominated by political elites, rather than by the public or even journalists. Journalists usually take their cues about policy issues from public officials. News organizations are not neutral, but the media seldom create policy debates on their own. Media criticism of U.S. policy in Central America, for example, evaporated when public officials on Capitol Hill muted their criticisms and was renewed when members of Congress started attacking again. Tom Brokaw of NBC News explained: "Congress is supposed to represent the people and when there is no opposition in Congress, there isn't much we can report." [22]

Policy makers use the press and television to build public support for their policy preferences. They depend upon the media for feedback about policy initiatives and programs. But what officials read in the press and see on television is not an independent measure of public concern. Media critic Leon Sigal observed: "Listening to the news for the sound of public opinion, officials hear echoes of their own voices. Looking for pictures of the world outside, they see reflections of their own images." [23] What elected officials regard as public opinion is often derived from what other political actors say, rather than from systematic evidence gathered through reliable public opinion polls.

Citizen activists are also adept at using the media to pursue living room politics. They have learned that when one is losing a political battle one "expands the scope of conflict," and tries to draw in members of the "audience who might support your cause." [24] The process goes something like this: a group is upset about an issue such as high state taxes. The group members collect signatures on petitions, hold press conferences, march to the state capitol building, release public opinion polls, make speeches, appear at editorial board meetings, give interviews to newspapers, and appear on public affairs programs. If they are skillful, diligent, and a little lucky, they can garner millions of dollars worth of publicity. The press and television give more exposure to their issue; the public becomes more aware and more interested; support builds; the media report that public support is building. Eventually, policy makers, sensing a groundswell of public concern, respond by cutting taxes.

Bringing Issues to the Living Room

The media magnify and promote issues to the top of the agenda by what they highlight in the limited space and time available. The media may not tell people what to think, but they tell people what to think about.[25] The nation's leading newspapers—the New York Times and the Washington Post—can present only about ten stories on their front pages; the network news shows have time for only fifteen to twenty stories in their half-hour shows.[26] Because most people have no personal contact with the political process, it is not surprising that citizens are dependent on the media for interpretations of the world around them.

Elected officials gravitate to issues that are salient to the public: reports in the media tell them and the public what is important.[27] Elected officials know that issues so identified by the media are likely to become priorities for the public.[28] In this way the media enhance issues they cover and diminish the political significance of problems they ignore.[29] The same is true for individuals; presidents and governors receive by far the greatest attention from television. This attention gives them considerably more power than other political actors to set agendas, frame policy debates, and influence public sentiment. Conversely, ordinary citizens, even if they represent a widely held view, have trouble gaining access to the public airwaves and to newspaper columns.

Media surveillance of the political process helps keep issues on the agenda, especially if a president or governor addresses a policy question.[30] Once Ronald Reagan raised the issue of tax reform, Congress found it difficult not to act on it because of the number of articles and television stories chronicling every twist and turn of the legislative process. Public opinion polls revealed that most people were indifferent to the tax reform bills moving through Congress. Given the conflict generated by tax legislation, many members would have been happier if the law had died a quiet death. But the media spotlight made it all but impossible to avoid. Speaker Thomas P. (Tip) O'Neill, Jr., said, "I have to have a bill, the Democratic party has to have a bill. . . . If we don't we'll be clobbered over the head by the President of the United States."[31]

The public's agenda is not set in a single stroke; rather, it is built through a cycle of activity that elevates issues initially of interest to a few into issues that concern a broader public. The process through which media, government, and the citizenry influence one another has been labeled "agenda building" by scholars Gladys Lang and Kurt Lang.[32] Intense media attention to issues such as tax reform, the Watergate break-in, or the Iran-contra affair often transforms intramural squabbles into public controversies. A press secretary to a member of Congress describes agenda building on Capitol Hill:

> If I leak a story ... in the *New York Times* on asbestos and the name Y is attached, what happens is an immediate phenomenal reaction. The calls come cascading in, and the name Y and asbestos in schools are intertwined. Suddenly, he's nationally known because of asbestos compensation and asbestos in schools. Then other members are calling Y asking about the report, asking for more information.... Then he can introduce a bill. He kicks the tail of the administration and gets lots of co-sponsors who go out and get [media] hits themselves.[33]

The conventions of newspaper reporting and television news influence the kinds of issues brought to the public's attention and the way they are dealt with by public officials.[34] Extreme viewpoints are often highlighted because provocative statements and actions make better television. Complicated issues—international debt, for example—that are hard to explain and impossible to depict with pictures frequently are eschewed in favor of events, such as a natural disaster or a public demonstration, that can be filmed. News reports often convey a heightened sense of alarm about policy problems. Issues are personalized, dramatized, and a crisis atmosphere is created. In many cases, however, the "crisis is a function of publicity."[35] Public officials then feel compelled to take some action in order to ward off more negative stories.

The media's power to create a mood of urgency and demands for action was reflected in the sudden emergence and disappearance of public concern about famine in Africa.[36] Despite urgent pleas from West African countries, U.S. aid to the region actually declined between 1981 and 1983. Then, for an entire week in October 1984, NBC news televised shocking and gruesome footage of starvation, suffering, and death on the parched deserts of Ethiopia. NBC reported that 6 million people were suffering from starvation and that 500,000 would die within a year. A torrent of mass media stories poured forth during the next month. The dramatic and sustained coverage provoked strong public reactions, millions of dollars in private contributions, and a huge increase in federal aid to the drought-stricken nations. All this attention, however, did not begin to solve the real problems, and, within two years, the issue had disappeared from the media, American living rooms, and Congress's agenda. Starvation and death in West Africa continued.

Framing the Issue

Newspapers and television producers simplify complex issues, place them into common frames of reference, and explain new policies with familiar terms.[37] When the media organizations report an event, a speech, or a policy proposal, they not only describe it but also give the public a context with which to interpret it. "The way the press frames an issue is as important as whether or not it is covered at all. If the press characterizes a policy option one way early on in the decision-making process, it is very difficult for officials to turn that image around to their preferred perspective," according to media analyst Martin Linsky.[38]

Because the media's descriptions of a problem often influence public perceptions, they may narrow the options available to public administrators. A policy debate can be labeled a "partisan squabble" or a matter of "urgent public concern." A governor's speech can be characterized as a "fight for his or her political life" or a routine report to the public. If dangerous polychlorinated biphenyls (PCBs) are discovered in a local warehouse, news stories suggesting that the public's health is gravely threatened can provoke panic, forcing public officials to react to an emergency that may not exist.

The destruction of a civilian Korean airliner by Soviet military planes in 1984 at first was portrayed as an act of cold-blooded murder. Subsequent reports suggested that the downing might have been a mistake and introduced the fact that the United States sometimes uses civilian aircraft for spying missions over Soviet airspace. Most news organizations, however, continued to portray the incident as a wanton act by a callous nation. Tax reform was framed as a contest between politicians who sought lower taxes, fairness, and simplicity and those who wanted to protect the so-called special interests of the privileged few. In the end, it was hard for politicians to vote against reform, no matter what their misgivings.

The Myth of the Neutral Media

Just as public officials claim they are not trying to manipulate the press, journalists perpetrate the myth that they are merely reporting what they see. Walter Cronkite, the former CBS news anchorman, closed his nightly broadcast by saying, "That's the way it is," implying that he was merely letting people know what had happened that day. In fact, the media are not neutral observers of the passing scene: there is a difference between the news and the truth.[39] Newspapers, television networks, and local stations shape the news and thus influence public officials and public opinion.

Bureaucratic routines, organizational politics, competition, and economics distort the view mass media organizations present to the public. What reporters think is probably less important than how they work. "News is thus less a sampling of what is happening in the world than a selection of what officials think—or want the press to report—is happening." [40] Reporters generally have little knowledge of what the mass audience thinks and pay much more attention to colleagues and superiors in their organization. Journalists and television crews position themselves where they decide news will be "made," and, in so doing, they make news.

Journalists and news organizations also can become active participants in the policy process. Newspaper investigations of problems in a local police department or fraud in defense contracting practically force public officials to address the problems. Media organizations commission public opinion polls, then report findings that may alter public policy. For example, when U.S. Embassy personnel were taken hostage in Iran in 1979, ABC News devoted an entire late night broadcast to discussing the situation every day. The ABC program contributed to the nation's anxiety and the pressure on President Jimmy Carter to take action.

Although less important than bureaucratic conditions that drive news reporting, the personal biases of journalists and media managers cannot be overlooked. Media watcher Herbert Gans pointed out that most journalists have a reformist/progressive attitude toward government. [41] They are deeply suspicious of government policy makers and the ability of political institutions to solve problems. These views lead to predictable, formulaic stories about incompetence, fraud, waste, and abuse. Stories about effective programs or the achievements of dedicated civil servants are scoffed at as "not newsworthy." In the shorthand of reporters, "Good news, bad story; bad news, good story."

Real Opinions, Soft Opinions, and Nonopinions

A sizable industry is devoted to surveying the public's thoughts on every subject from baseball players' salaries to the morality of public figures. All the major television networks, newspapers, and magazines regularly commission public opinion polls or report public attitudes toward political officials, government institutions, and policy issues. Are the concerns measured in public opinion polls what people are really thinking about or merely pale imitations of preferences expressed by public officials through the media? Are Americans like the hapless couple depicted in the cartoon who tell a poll taker, "We don't have any opinions today. Our TV is busted."

When people have little or no personal experience or stake in the outcome of a policy debate, public attitudes are likely to reflect views expressed by public officials and reported in the media. For people to hold real opinions, the issue must be important to them and they must have information upon which to base a conclusion. On many policy questions, people have either no opinion or what might be called "soft" opinions, which may change rapidly in response to events or new information. Where the public holds real opinions—the issues that touch basic values, strong preferences, or fears, news reporters and public officials are far less persuasive. The public is also less malleable when the policy remedies under debate are controversial.

Opinion polls suggest that many Americans are deeply troubled about abortion and drug abuse, but the polls show differences in their responses. The vast majority agree that drug abuse should be curtailed quickly and by whatever means necessary, even if certain constitutional protections for citizens must be bent to enforce the laws. The public is easily riled to righteous indignation about crack cocaine dealers and the devastating effects of drug abuse on people's lives. In short, although few people favor drug abuse, the intensity of feelings about the drug issue can be influenced through the efforts of public officials and news organizations.

Abortion is another matter. People believe that abortion is an important issue, but they are deeply divided about the proper course for public policy. Some believe that abortions constitute the taking of a human life and should be outlawed. Others believe that a woman has an absolute right to determine whether to complete a pregnancy and that government should not interfere in this intensely private decision. News organizations are not attempting to shape people's attitudes about outlawing or guaranteeing abortions, perhaps because taking either position will cost them public support.

When large segments of the public have direct personal experience with a problem, pollsters are more likely to measure genuine concerns rather than media-manipulated sentiment. Public anxiety about unemployment is a good example. During the early 1980s, millions of American workers were unemployed, and millions more had jobless relatives or friends.[42] Public frustration about the energy crisis of the 1970s was no media circus, either. Millions waited in line to buy gas and worried whether they would have enough fuel to heat their homes.

Pollsters tap genuine concerns when they quiz people about problems affecting their health and the well-being of their families. Public fears about the Acquired Immune Deficiency Syndrome (AIDS) are palpable. As early as 1985, only a few years after the disease was discovered, pollsters found that 97 percent of the American public knew of the

AIDS epidemic and 70 percent regarded AIDS as a direct threat to their health. More than half said the government was not doing enough to halt the disease; only 2 percent felt government spending was too high.[43] By way of comparison, in that same poll, only 44 percent knew that the U.S. House of Representatives was controlled by the Democratic party, which has been the case since 1955.

When pollsters and journalists venture into subjects that are unfamiliar to the public, they often discover, and then communicate, soft opinions or nonopinions to policy makers. Out of politeness or fear of appearing ignorant, people will answer questions about policy issues, even when they have no knowledge or opinions. When this happens, public officials and journalists are more likely to draw false conclusions about what the public really wants. Public opinion jells only when the issue becomes sufficiently important for people to pay attention to it. Until then, public moods can swing widely.

On many public issues Americans hold ambiguous and contradictory opinions, and on such issues public officials are free to interpret what the sentiment is. For example, one might suppose that on important perennial issues such as taxes, spending, and the budget deficit, the public would hold rational views. Yet most polls show that the public wants *lower* taxes, *more* spending, and a *balanced* budget, too! People are unwilling to accept the logic that all three cannot be done simultaneously. Elected officials and pollsters, therefore, are free to argue over what the polls mean, but they cannot ignore them. Even inconsistent and confusing public attitudes establish the options.

An exchange between Representative David Obey, D-Wis., and Louis Harris, a well-known public opinion pollster, during a hearing of the Joint Economic Committee reflects the problem of interpreting opinions about fiscal policy.[44] After reviewing the results of the poll, Obey challenged Harris to support his claim that the public was willing to raise taxes and *cut* spending to reduce the deficit:

Mr. Obey: So do you think that your data demonstrate that people are willing to accept tax increases that they have to pay rather than some other fellow, and are they willing to support any tax items which really raise some dollars as opposed to small change?

Mr. Harris: Well, Mr. Chairman, that's a judgment call. . . . The people are not going to rise up in this country and say "Please tax me." What they will say is "when the leaders have the guts to stand up and say as a last desperate measure we'd better raise taxes as well as cut the federal spending to the bone," you're going to get more people saying, "Amen, thank goodness we have leaders like that."

Mr. Obey: . . . the only response I would have to that is that we had a poll of sorts in November [1984] and I think a lot of people would say that there was a candidate [Walter Mondale] who did stand up and suggest that and he didn't seem to be universally accepted by the country.

Officials feel justified in ignoring polls when they contain confusing or even irresponsible expressions of public sentiment. Obey explained to Harris: "The job of national leaders is not to make decisions on the basis of a public opinion poll. We are supposed to both represent and lead public opinion and that means that we have to help shape as well as follow public opinion." [45]

Polls and pollsters affect the understanding and impact of public opinion simply by asking certain questions. When pollsters asked respondents whether President Reagan was "lying or not" during the Iran-contra affair, they were implying that he might be a liar. When pollsters ask for opinions on various "crises"—drugs, energy, crime, drunk driving, garbage—and report the results, they may be magnifying concerns that exist primarily in the minds of pollsters, journalists, and public officials. When people were asked during the 1988 campaign whether it is important to know if presidential candidates have committed adultery, pollsters and journalists were implying that personal moral conduct is an important criterion for judging potential presidents.

Despite their limitations, public opinion polls perform valuable functions in democracies. They are the only mechanism, outside of elections, through which the concerns of the ordinary citizen are expressed to political elites. The results of polls are often more representative of public sentiment than elections because voter turnout, even for presidential elections, is only slightly more than 50 percent. Polls can put issues on the public agenda that go beyond the wish lists of special interest groups. And finally, polls provide some feedback about public satisfaction with the direction and performance of government.

The Conduct of Direct Democracy

The most direct method by which citizens select policy options is through initiatives and referenda. Most initiative and referenda campaigns rely on volunteers, but some have become costly public relations efforts requiring millions of dollars for television advertising.[46] Supporters and opponents of ballot questions spent $32 million in 1984 on ballot qualification fights alone! [47] The campaign over California's gun control proposition cost more than $10 million.[48] Initiatives that would have required deposits on bottles in Montana, Arizona, and California were defeated by heavy spending from out-of-state beverage interests. Ninety-seven percent of the funds used to successfully oppose an antismoking initiative in California were contributed by out-of-state tobacco firms.[49]

Initiative and referenda campaigns have spawned an industry that collects signatures and mounts public awareness advertising campaigns.

These services are available for hire, but they are expensive, and only groups with money can afford them. The Florida Medical Association organized an initiative drive to impose ceilings on financial awards in negligence suits. The doctors dished out $3 million in fees for canvassers who went door to door in "friendly" neighborhoods seeking signatures to place the question on the ballot. The canvassers assured citizens that passing the initiative would reduce medical costs, but did not mention that their ability to sue for damages would be curtailed. The Florida Supreme Court refused to qualify the issue for the ballot because of the misleading campaign.[50] Reacting to tactics that undermine the democratic nature of the process, Colorado, Massachusetts, and Nebraska now prohibit paid solicitors in initiative and referenda campaigns.

Governors, state legislators, and others aspiring to elected office are using ballot questions to gain political visibility, public office, and policy objectives. In California, the nation's leading initiative state, gubernatorial candidates Thomas Bradley and George Deukmejian led initiative efforts on toxic waste and gun control, respectively. They hoped that by timing initiatives to coincide with their bids for office, sympathetic voters would turn out on election day. It is difficult to ascertain how initiatives affected the outcome of this close election. It is clear that the handgun registration initiative attracted considerable voter interest and an extraordinary 75 percent to 80 percent turnout in certain parts of the state.[51]

As David Magleby, a leading student of the initiative process, pointed out, elected officials see referenda and initiatives as another tool in their political arsenal. If they win, initiatives allow legislators and governors to bypass the lengthy, arduous, and chancy legislative process. Even if they lose, politicians can gain political visibility through free media time.[52]

Not all initiatives and referenda are fostered by big business and statewide political candidates. In fact, questions about civil rights and moral issues are often spurred by grass-roots organizations whose volunteers collect signatures and operate on shoestring budgets. Large corporations are not interested in spending their money or credibility on campaigns about the regulation of pornography, funding for abortions, or civil rights for disabled Americans.

Battles over the insertion of equal rights amendments (ERAs) into state constitutions—amendments that would guarantee equal rights or equal protection under the law to women—are an example of low-cost, door-to-door campaigns waged with intensity by citizen organizations. Since 1973 twelve states have voted on ERA referenda. Voters have approved five and rejected seven. No state ERA has passed since Massachusetts amended its constitution in 1976. Typically, the pro-ERA forces included state chapters of the National Organization for Women (NOW), the League of Women Voters, and labor organizations with large numbers of women. The anti-ERA coalition encompassed the Eagle Forum, founded by Phyllis Schlafly; the Daughters of the American Revolution (DAR); the Federation of Women's Clubs; and assorted conservative organizations. The costs of ERA ballot fights have been considerably less than the campaigns in which business and industry are involved. Pro- and anti-ERA groups spent a combined total of $60,000 in Florida and $68,000 in Massachusetts, for example.[53]

Popular Leaders

Elected officials, media elites, and large corporations play central roles in living room politics. Public officials and private leaders attempt to manipulate public opinion to suit their specific purposes. Journalists and pollsters shape public opinion in policy debates. The public, however, does not merely follow elected officials and media personalities. In fact, many leaders of initiative and referenda drives and grass-roots citizen campaigns come from the ranks of ordinary citizens. These individuals, who have the power to persuade, have transformed national, state, and local politics by mobilizing citizens into taking political action.

On state ballot questions, Howard Jarvis's name is associated with Proposition 13, one of the most influential citizen campaigns in recent times. This tax and spending initiative, which was approved overwhelmingly by California voters in 1978, launched a drive to cut taxes and spending in many other states. Jarvis became so identified with government tax reform and spending limitations that subsequent California initiative campaigns revolved around positive and negative campaign ads about Jarvis himself, rather than about the policy choices.[54]

Less well known, but more typical of the citizen activist, is Ray Phillips, an octogenarian who led Oregon Taxpayers United. He and his volunteers led a tax reduction movement. Phillips described his motivation:

I like being a rabble rouser. If the legislature did what it was supposed to do, we would not have to be out collecting signatures. The legislators spend too much time listening to lobbyists and not enough time listening to the people. Taxpayers don't control taxes anymore. That's what our measure would do—give power back to the people.[55]

Important grass-roots political movements have been led by individuals who emerged from nonpolitical roles into the limelight and became identified with their cause. Dr. Martin Luther King, Jr., a charismatic preacher, developed a large, loyal following as he organized demonstrations, marches, and other efforts to secure the full rights of citizenship to

black Americans. Ralph Nader, a shy, ascetic lawyer, raised the consciousness of the American consumer and helped bring about new
consumer protection laws. His nationwide network of state and local
organizations continues to monitor industry for dangerous products.
Phyllis Schlafly, a self-described housewife, energized a large conservative movement in dozens of states to stop the ERA.

The Power of Public Opinion

Living room politics has been the catalyst for significant and startling
changes in government policies. Public opinions—whether they origi-
nated at the top or the bottom, played a critical role in forcing a
president from office, ending the Vietnam War, bringing about stronger environmental laws, halting the growth of nuclear power, cracking
down on drunk drivers, and slowing the growth of government spending. Citizens exert a powerful policy influence in the voting booth, on
the streets of America, and perhaps most significantly, in the minds of
elected and appointed leaders.

Public Opinion and the Media

Shifts in public support for government policies, often stimulated by
media coverage, have brought about important changes. Extensive
television coverage of the civil rights marches in the South during the
1960s exposed racism and the use of excessive force against peaceful
individuals protesting racial discrimination.[56] Television scenes of the
Vietnam War, showing bloody battles and the destruction of a country,
crystallized public opposition to America's involvement.[57] Coverage of
the nuclear accidents at Three Mile Island and Chernobyl undermined
public support for nuclear power and halted the construction of nuclear
power plants.[58]

The power of public opinion—and the role media organizations and
political elites play in shaping it—was evident during the Watergate
scandal.[59] Despite the efforts of the Democratic presidential candidate,
George McGovern, to make an issue of the Republican-financed break-
in at Democratic party headquarters at the Watergate during the 1972
campaign, President Richard Nixon was reelected with one of the
largest votes in American history. A few months later, public support
for Nixon fell precipitously. The House Judiciary Committee approved
articles of impeachment, but the president resigned before the Senate
began hearing the case. How did this tidal change in public attention
and support occur?

The president lost the battle for public opinion because of incessant
media reports about his role in ordering the surveillance of his oppo-

nents and then covering it up. The Senate investigating committee hearings, the impeachment hearings, and the battles waged by the president, independent prosecutors, and the U.S. Supreme Court over access to tape recordings and documents kept the Watergate crisis, as the press dubbed it, before the public for more than two years. The gradual unfolding of the misdeeds and the drama of new revelations prolonged the story, giving Nixon's opponents ample time to convince the public that he was lying. Eventually, the Watergate issue was framed as a struggle between upholders of the Constitution and those who would subvert it for political gain.

Public opinion was a major force in Nixon's resignation. The president understood that the Republicans in the U.S. Senate would not support him, primarily because the public no longer supported him. The media's principal contribution to changing public opinion was their extensive coverage of critical events in ways that were essentially unfavorable to President Nixon. The Langs conclude that

there could have been no real public opinion on Watergate without the media. They alone could have called into being the mass audience of "bystanders." It was the media which, by reporting and even sponsoring polls, presented the cast of political actors in Watergate with a measure of public response to their every move. . . . The impression of public support made it easier to move against Nixon.[60]

Passionate public responses to issues are unusual, but they have far-reaching effects. Public policies may be changed quickly when large segments of the public rally around issues of high salience. Politicians feel compelled to act rather than face a disgruntled, even angry, citizenry. One reason the public seldom gets aroused is that public officials are adept at anticipating serious problems and responding to them before people get angry.

Problems that are widely recognized as serious by the public generate anxiety and often lead to demands for action. Government funding for research to find a cure for AIDS jumped by more than 200 percent after public opinion polls revealed widespread fear about the epidemic.[61] State lawmakers toughened laws against drunk driving in dozens of states in the wake of polls revealing public outrage at trivial penalties given to drunk drivers involved in vehicular homicides.

Given the weight assigned to public opinion in the myth and reality of American politics, it is perhaps surprising that strongly held public preferences sometimes are ignored. Politicians are known to use public opinion polls when they support their point of view and to ignore or denounce them as unreliable when they bring unfavorable, unwanted, or inconvenient news. Public officials often believe that poll results put them in an embarrassing position. If they follow public opinions as recorded in the surveys, cherished positions may have to be abandoned. If they ignore the polls, their opponents or journalists may chastise them for disregarding the will of the people.

Fortunately for politicians, journalists seldom call attention to public officials who fail to respond to sentiment expressed in public opinion polls. Public concern about aid to the contras, who were fighting a guerrilla war against the Communist government of Nicaragua, were not only ignored by elected officials, but also by the media. According to several polls, Americans were deeply suspicious of aid for the rebel fighters, even though President Reagan waged vigorous campaigns to change their minds. Despite the indications of wariness, Congress authorized $100 million in military and humanitarian aid for the contras in 1986. Only 1 percent of the news articles on aid mentioned the opinion polls, and, according to one analysis, most of those stories implied that the public did not understand the intricacies of the conflict.[62]

As intermediaries between the public and political leaders, the media influence policy choices and the evaluation of programs. Policy makers are preoccupied with managing the news because it commands public attention in a way that no elected officials or interest group possibly can. More than half of the senior federal government policy makers contacted in a recent survey reported that the press has *substantial* effects on federal policy. One in ten believes the press has *the* dominant influence on policy. To some extent, press influence has become a self-fulfilling prophecy: "If policy makers themselves believe the press is influential, then by definition it is." [63]

Managing the press and responding to it often becomes a surrogate for managing public opinion and responding to it. Interactions among the media, public opinion, and public officials affect public policies in subtle ways. According to Linsky, extensive press coverage oversimplifies and nationalizes stories, forces quick responses, pushes decisions up the bureaucratic chain of command, and creates supportive climates for some options and excludes others.[64] Two case studies illustrate the dynamic relationships involved in living room politics and their influence on government policies.

Love Canal. In the late 1970s state and local health officials discovered that between 1942 and 1952 Hooker Chemical Company had deposited 21,000 tons of hazardous chemicals in an abandoned canal in Love Canal, New York.[65] The Environmental Protection Agency (EPA) commissioned pilot studies to ascertain the possible health and environmental threats posed by chemicals that were leaching into the groundwater, yards, and basements of homes around the canal. President Carter declared the Hooker site at Love Canal a national emergency, and hundreds of residents were evacuated from the area. Media attention to the problems at Love Canal influenced these decisions.

After Love Canal became a national issue, a consultant was hired to examine the possible genetic effects of the leaking chemicals. The consultant examined individuals who had experienced serious health problems, such as cancer or birth defects. By first selecting people with known health problems, the consultant hoped to determine whether a more thorough investigation was warranted. Research uncovered chromosomal aberrations in twelve of the thirty-six people tested. Without more rigorous and comprehensive tests, however, it was not possible to establish a definite link between the chemicals dumped in the canal and the health problems experienced by people in the pilot study.

Fearing that the preliminary study would be leaked to the press, the White House staff decided it would release the report and promise further investigation. But before they could act, the report was published in the *New York Times*. Love Canal was hot news. In the ten days following the publication of the findings, the *Times* printed thirty-one articles on Love Canal, including eight front-page stories and three editorials. Other newspapers and the television networks ran dozens of related stories describing serious threats to health from the uncontrolled dumping of hazardous wastes.

To put an end to stories about government insensitivity to the problems of Love Canal's residents, the White House decided to relocate 710 individuals. The pressure to respond so as not to appear callous and indifferent had been intensified by media coverage. Ironically, the complete review of the EPA pilot study was finished the same day. It concluded that there was "inadequate basis for any scientific or medical inferences from the data (even of a tentative or preliminary nature) concerning exposure to mutagenic substances because of residence in Love Canal." If the Love Canal story had not been framed by the media as a dangerous health threat to hapless victims, the government might have undertaken a lengthier investigation and might not have spent millions to relocate the families.

Like many episodes of press and public involvement in the policy process, the Love Canal story had far-reaching effects. The spotlight was turned toward one example of a broader national problem—the cleanup of abandoned hazardous waste dumps. The publicity that resulted from the Love Canal incident helped focus public attention on this lingering problem. Soon after, new environmental legislation to clean up abandoned waste dumps was enacted by Congress.

Disability Reviews. An Office of Management and Budget (OMB) investigation of the Social Security disability insurance program launched during the Carter administration estimated that as many as 20 percent of the people receiving benefits were ineligible for the aid.[66] Disability payments are reserved for individuals who cannot work due to physical or mental problems. The preliminary review indicated that some able-bodied people were "ripping off" the program. Based on this information, the Social Security Administration (SSA) launched a comprehensive effort to rid the program of ineligibles who might be costing the government as much as $2 billion annually. When the Reagan administration came to office, the review process was accelerated, and some local news stories suggested that people were losing benefits despite legitimate claims. Public awareness of the issue expanded dramatically when CBS televised a story about a man who had committed suicide and left a note blaming the SSA for cutting off his payments and "playing God." Other network and newspaper stories quickly followed, emphasizing the theme that deserving people had been wronged by careless government bureaucrats.

Bolstered by negative media stories, members of Congress, editorial writers, and advocates for the disabled stepped up pressure on the Reagan administration to revise or drop the disability reviews. A television special, hosted by Bill Moyers of CBS, featured a cerebral palsy victim who had lost his disability assistance for what appeared to be inappropriate reasons. Other stories reported that people had died from disabilities deemed not serious enough by the government to keep them enrolled in the program. The television program "Real People" ran a story about a wounded Vietnam veteran—a recipient of the Congressional Medal of Honor—who was about to have his disability checks cut off.

Administration officials claimed that the stories of deserving people incorrectly dropped from the disability assistance rolls were exaggerated, unrepresentative, and even false. They noted that some of the people depicted in the stories were working full time, yet still claiming benefits. Eventually, senior White House staff concluded that the rising tide of negative stories left the impression that Reagan's budget cuts were inhumane and unfair and that such publicity undermined the president's efforts to achieve further spending reductions. The only way to mute the criticism was to suspend the reviews and that is exactly what they did. Later, legislation revising procedures for removing individuals from the program swept through Congress.

Choosing Policies in the Voting Booth

Referenda and initiatives give millions of Americans a direct say on policy issues, and liberals and conservative groups have been equally successful with the voters. A study of nearly 200 initiatives between 1977 and 1984 revealed that 44 percent of the seventy-nine proposals backed by liberals were approved, and 45 percent of the seventy-four conservative-sponsored initiatives were approved. (The remainder were classified as not having ideological content.) [67]

Tax and government spending limitations have been aggressively pursued through the statewide initiatives. "No other issue cluster ... has faced popular scrutiny more often. Win or lose, the tax cut movement has ... been deciding the bounds of political debate on tax and fiscal policy," wrote Patrick McGuigan, the author of an authoritative newsletter on referenda and initiatives. [68] The modern tax revolt began with California's Proposition 13, which reduced property tax revenues by 57 percent and limited future increases to no more than 2 percent annually.

Between 1978 and 1984, however, only three states of the nine that voted on Proposition 13-type initiatives approved them, as shown in Table 8-1. But voters in eleven states approved moderate tax and spending measures referred to them by state legislatures that were trying to head off more Draconian revenue cuts. Alaskans dropped the income tax; North Dakotans reduced the income tax bite; and Washingtonians eliminated the state inheritance tax. [69]

What followed passage of Proposition 13 shows that a state need not have a strong initiative process to be affected by initiatives passed in other states. [70] In fact, legislators in states without the initiative process interpreted the rash of tax and spending initiatives as a message they must heed. They thought voters wanted lower taxes and changes in the methods of taxation. In 1965 less than half of the electorate thought that taxes were too high. More recently, nearly 75 percent complained that taxes are excessive. And eight Americans in ten now think that government funds are often wasted. [71]

Even a defeated initiative may trigger a remedial or preemptive policy response. In South Dakota the Public Utilities Commission approved special rates for the elderly and the poor, following the defeat of a similar but more comprehensive rate initiative two years earlier. The California state legislature responded to an antinuclear initiative while the campaign was still under way. One week before the scheduled election, the legislature approved a weaker version of the antinuclear initiative, which was subsequently rejected by the voters. Even a defeated initiative may serve as a catalyst, prodding politicians or bureaucrats to act before the voters take matters into their own hands. [72]

This kind of direct democracy also has given voters a voice on issues of social policy. [73] Since 1982 voters have cut abortion funding in Colorado, but defeated similar proposals in Arkansas, Oregon, Washington, and Rhode Island. Citizens rejected stricter regulations on the sale of pornographic materials in Maine and Utah, endorsed prayer in the schools in West Virginia, and repealed the Massachusetts law requiring the use of seat belts. Laws restricting the disposal of radioactive waste

Table 8-1   Tax and Spending Cut Initiatives and Referenda,
           1976-1984

State	Proposition-13 tax cuts	Limited tax and spending cuts
Alaska		passed (1980, 1982)
Arizona	failed (1980)	passed (1978)
California	passed (1978)	failed (1980), passed (1982)
Colorado		failed (1978)
Hawaii		passed (1978)
Idaho	passed (1978)	
Maine		passed (1982)
Massachusetts	passed (1980)	
Michigan	failed (1980)	failed (1976, 1984)
Missouri		passed (1980)
Montana		passed (1980)
Nevada	passed (1978) failed (1980, 1984)	failed (1984)
North Dakota		passed (1978)
Ohio		failed (1983)
Oklahoma		failed (1979)
Oregon	failed (1978, 1980, 1982, 1984)	
South Carolina		passed (1984)
South Dakota	failed (1980)	
Texas		passed (1978)
Utah	failed (1980)	
Washington		passed (1979, 1981)

Source: Patrick B. McGuigan, The Politics of Direct Democracy in the 1980s (Washington, D.C.: Free Congress Research and Education Foundation, 1985), 52, 54, 55. Reprinted by permission.

were strengthened in Montana, Oregon, and Washington. Maine voters rejected a proposal to shut down a nuclear power plant. More stringent environmental protection laws were endorsed by voters in California, New Jersey, and Massachusetts. California voters declared English the state's official language and rejected a plan to quarantine victims of AIDS.

Citizens have used the ballot box to register dismay over U.S. foreign and defense policy. States and local governments have no control over foreign policy, and state initiatives and referenda are not binding on the federal government. Nevertheless, activists frustrated with U.S. foreign policy have used this tactic to goad the president and Congress into halting the production and deployment of nuclear weapons.[74] With nearly 20 million people voting, the so-called nuclear freeze referenda were the closest the nation has come to a national referendum on a policy issue. Similarly worded proposals calling for a halt to the arms race were approved by comfortable margins—averaging 60 percent— in ten of the eleven states and thirty-one of thirty-two communities where balloting occurred in 1982. Perhaps the measure won easily because freeze supporters encountered almost no organized opposition (except in Arizona where the measure failed) and outspent their opponents thirteen to one nationwide. Still, the vote can be considered a measure of the desire for reduced tensions in the arms race.

Policy from the Grass Roots

Grass-roots political movements grow out of the frustration citizens feel about the pace of reform or from their outrage at decisions that threaten their way of life. Seeking relief from the government, citizen groups have denounced U.S. foreign policy and pestered legislators, administrators, and judges to alter policies on a host of moral issues— from prayer in public schools to abortion.

The success of minority groups in quickening the pace of change is noteworthy. What began as an effort to secure basic rights gradually evolved into a broad-based effort to increase economic opportunities. The ability of leaders to mobilize minorities beyond protest and into the voting booth had positive effects on the appointment and election of minority officeholders, expanded employment opportunities for minorities in city governments, and enlarged programs for the minority community.[75]

Environmentalists also have translated widespread public support for environmental conservation and protection into political action and policy results. Beginning in the late 1960s, hundreds of national and local environmental groups achieved considerable success. Statutes have been passed governing air and water quality, control of toxic pollution, and the disposal of industrial, agricultural, and urban wastes. Regulatory agencies have been established at the state and national levels. Billions of dollars have been allocated to environmental protection and clean up. Environmental interest groups are represented in Washington and in state capitals. Obviously, these sweeping reforms were not stimulated entirely by citizens, but grass-roots environmental organizations were powerful agents for change.[76]

Environmental groups have effectively organized to stop nuclear power plants, dams, and toxic waste incinerators. When the New Jersey Department of Environmental Protection announced it would transfer 15,000 barrels of radium-contaminated dirt to a quarry near the rural town of Vernon, local residents rallied to thwart the plan. Thousands of people protested the decision, and hundreds followed Governor Thomas

Kean around the state, interrupted his speeches, and picketed his home. Locals prepared for civil disobedience and violent acts of sabotage. Fearing for the safety of citizens and state troopers alike, Kean reversed the department's decision and directed it to find another site for the dirt.[77]

Majority Rule and Minority Rights

Who benefits from living room politics? Who are the winners and the losers? Because living room politics concerns issues that arouse the public and galvanize ordinary citizens into action, one might glibly concluded that the public benefits. Unfortunately, figuring out who benefits from living room politics is considerably more complicated than that.

Living room politics can be the expression of majority sentiments, and public officials are inclined to heed the will of the people when public preferences are clear and reflect a broad-based consensus. However, when the majority supports a controversial course of action, policy makers may ignore it, especially if the public's wishes would infringe minority interests. Suppose that opinion polls show that most people favor isolating AIDS victims from the rest of the population. Political institutions, especially the courts, are unlikely to be guided by such opinions because the basic rights of a disadvantaged minority would be violated to allay the fears of the majority.

Well-organized and well-financed groups are more likely to have their views heeded than those who are economically disadvantaged. Those who are better off are generally more successful in directing media and public attention to their concerns. It is no accident that many ballot initiatives are of greater interest to white, middle-class voters, than to minorities and the poor. Disadvantaged Americans are more likely to go to the courts for help than to the ballot box (see chapter 7).

A central dilemma of democracy is the clash of majority rule and minority rights. Basic issues, such as war, civil rights, morality, public health and safety, are most likely to stimulate public concern and foster intense, divergent beliefs. Individuals with diametrically opposed positions on controversial issues, such as abortion, women's rights, or nuclear plant safety, usually do not find the alternative point of view acceptable.

When people are divided over an issue that arouses strong feelings, public officials search for Solomon-like compromises that might satisfy the losers as well as the winners. Finding such answers is often impossible. When accommodation fails, the policy process grinds to a halt because neither side is willing to budge. Elected officials and administrators either ignore the problem as long as possible or pass the buck to another institution—the judiciary or the president. They may even pass the buck to the voters, hoping to find an answer in the majority will expressed via referenda.

When majority preferences are honored, the losers may be angry, alienated, and resort to unconventional methods, including civil disobedience and violence. Indeed, many of the most violent or potentially violent episodes in American political history took place when the losers felt the political system no longer cared about them. Riots and violence over racial segregation and injustice in the 1950s and 1960s and demonstrations against the Vietnam War that ended in violent confrontations between marchers and police and national guardsmen are but two vivid examples. More recently, individuals opposed to the U.S. Supreme Court's legalization of abortions have bombed abortion clinics. Environmental activists have sabotaged chemical plants and physically blocked the construction of nuclear power plants and hazardous waste disposal facilities.

Well-organized, sophisticated segments of the citizenry benefit most from living room politics, but, when minority concerns are trampled upon, the potential for political instability rises. It is perhaps for this reason that politicians fear citizen participation. Once citizens are drawn into the conflict, they demand satisfaction, and once the genie is out of the bottle, it is hard to get it back in again.

A Potent Weapon of Democracy

Whether through the informal plebiscite of opinion polls or through active participation, citizens can have a powerful influence on the implementation and impact of public policies. Public pressure may be brought to bear on the tactics and pace of program administration. The public's evaluation of government policies, institutions, and political actors, which are shaped by the media, may influence financial support for a program or cause its cancellation. Public perceptions of a specific leader's popularity may embolden or intimidate other political leaders. Finally, angry citizens can force radical changes in policy.

Public and Media Evaluations of Government Policy

Americans are generally skeptical about government programs and institutions. Such perceptions are based partly on personal experience, such as frustration with the IRS, a state department of motor vehicles, or the local building code enforcement officer. For the most part, however, the public's understanding of politics and policy comes to them via newspapers and television, which not only reflect this skeptical attitude about government but also encourage it.

As messengers of public concern and guardians of the public interest, reporters often deserve high praise. Journalists criticize weak government policies and inform the public about crises and conflicts, fraud and corruption. Journalists root out corrupt public officials and call attention to the insensitivity and injustice of public institutions. Media scrutiny, followed by public anger, can spur an indifferent, cautious, or incompetent agency or legislature to positive action in the public interest.

However, the contributions of media organizations and journalists to policy implementation can be a mixed blessing. Media publicity can divert administrators from important tasks to relatively trivial matters. During the summer of 1987, for example, federal, state, and local officials were perplexed about how to deal with an ordinary garbage barge because news reports focused attention on it. The barge posed little or no threat to public health, but the wave of stories about it generated fear about what was on it. The barge *Mobro* picked up 3,186 tons of normal household refuse and waste from construction sites from Islip Township on Long Island. The tugboat *Break of Dawn* towed the barge to North Carolina where the crew expected to unload their cargo, but local officials refused to grant the necessary permits. Subsequent attempts to dock and unload were rebuffed in Mississippi, Alabama, Florida, Texas, Louisiana, New York, and three foreign countries. Meanwhile, environmental regulators and elected officials from all levels of government wrangled over where to unload it. Eventually, the contents of the barge were buried in a landfill near the original source of the refuse. Public anxiety, political grandstanding, and a crisis atmosphere had been created, mostly by the media.

On balance, the intense interest in the pariah garbage barge was probably a useful contribution to public education. The tale of the *Mobro* and the *Break of Dawn* highlighted a genuine problem—the disposal of solid waste in a country that is running out of landfill sites. Environmentalists and government officials had been trying, largely without success, to raise public awareness about the mounting problem of finding safe, efficient methods of recycling and disposing of trash. The barge provided an unexpected but welcome boost for their cause. "For anybody who works with waste, the barge has been like a religious experience," observed Gerald Boyd of New York's Legislative Commission on Solid Waste.[78]

According to some analysts, the media's influence on elected officials and the public is pernicious. Timothy Cook argued that members of Congress are less concerned with the public interest than with what will sell with the media.[79] Obsession with the way things appear in the press, he maintained, drives elected officials to search for overly simple answers to complicated questions. The need to explain one's position in a thirty-second spot on television encourages legislators to latch onto symbols and slogans, rather than carefully crafted solutions. As a case in point, Cook cited the Gramm-Rudman-Hollings Deficit Reduction Act, which mandated across-the-board spending cuts to reduce government spending. The measure was simple and straightforward, but it did not solve the budget deficit. Since the law was passed, Congress and the president have continued to struggle for a politically acceptable formula for achieving real spending reductions.

The attitudes news organizations have toward government institutions and programs color their reporting. According to Lewis Wolfson, a former reporter and editor, the press is "not inherently interested in what's involved in developing a policy or administering a program or what impacts these decisions may have at the grass roots." If a policy fails, journalists "rush to discover what went wrong, looking more for incompetence or corruption than for shortcomings of the policy-making process that may have compromised the approach from the start." [80] In consequence, the public may be led down the path to ignorance rather than understanding.

The pervasive role of the media in shaping the public's view of politics helps explain why it is difficult to galvanize the public around some issues. People trust and understand what they can see more than what they hear.[81] It is impossible to show in visual terms that deficit spending harms the nation's economy or that the depletion of the ozone layer can cause the earth's temperatures to rise dangerously. These limitations of mass communication circumscribe the issues that engender broad public participation.

Sensationalizing administrative shortcomings and the foibles of public officials may damage otherwise effective programs and erode their base of public and political support. Consider the media's role in the implementation of the Comprehensive Employment and Training Act (CETA).[82] The law called for CETA administrators to take on some nearly impossible tasks. Press accounts ridiculed the hiring of ineligible workers, blatant political patronage, and programs of doubtful value. Although such practices were the exception rather than the rule, the public and political officials believed the program to be riddled with fraud, waste, and abuse. In fact, CETA's problems were caused as much by congressional pressure to spend money too rapidly as they were by unscrupulous or incompetent administrators. Nevertheless, a negative image plagued CETA, and its public service jobs component ultimately was terminated.

By ridiculing the National Aeronautics and Space Administration (NASA) for failing to launch on schedule, the media may have contributed to the space shuttle disaster. Elected and appointed officials bristle at media criticism and try to avoid it. At times, their thin skins cause irresponsible behavior, such as the decision to launch the *Challenger* despite warnings about faulty O-rings and inclement weather.

On the evening of January 27, 1986, the television news networks announced that the launch had been delayed for a third time. Following are the remarks of Dan Rather of CBS on the decision to "scrub" the flight:

Yet another costly, red-faces-all-around-space-shuttle-launch delay. This time a bad bolt on a hatch and bad weather bolt from the blue are being blamed. What's more, a rescheduled launch for tomorrow doesn't look good either. Bruce Hall has the latest on today's hi-tech low comedy.[83]

The other networks were equally harsh. And the *New York Times* described the situation as a "comedy of errors."

The following morning, NASA launched the space shuttle and seven astronauts perished. Ultimately, NASA must accept responsibility for the disaster. Its flight schedule was unrealistic, and it should have resisted pressure for a premature launch. However, the reality of media pressure is undeniable. As one NASA official put it:

Every time there was a delay, the press would say, "Look, there's another delay.... Here's a bunch of idiots who can't even handle a launch schedule...." You think that doesn't have an impact? If you think it doesn't, you're stupid.[84]

The media's relentlessly unfavorable portrayal of political institutions, public officials, and government programs fosters negative public attitudes about the public sector.[85] Media analyst Michael Robinson calls these feelings about the political world "video-malaise."[86] Cynical views about government and political figures are conveyed not only by news and public affairs programs, but also by soap operas and drama series as well.

Contempt for the political world is pervasive on entertainment television. There is no television series in which political figures are cast in positive roles. Television regularly portrays "heroes" doing battle with evil politicians. An episode of "Miami Vice" captures the prevailing mood of prime time television. The main character, police officer Sonny Crockett, attempts to clear an individual who, in his judgment, has been wrongly accused of a murder. He meets resistance from a district attorney, who is mounting a campaign to be elected mayor of Miami. The district attorney and Crockett clash over whether to proceed with the prisoner's execution or wait for evidence that might clear him.

D.A.: Why are you trying to clear this scum?
S.C.: My conscience bothers me.
D.A.: My conscience is clear.
S.C.: I'm a cop; you're a politician. For you, a conscience is optional.

The Impacts of Initiatives and Referenda

Initiatives and referenda probably have been more successful in stopping or slowing down social, political, and economic change than in bringing it about. Voters have halted restrictions on the sale of pornographic literature, and rolled back state laws requiring that drivers wear seat belts. Initiatives and the political fallout generated by them have restrained public spending. Voters have mandated expenditure limitations and tax policies that have altered the political economy of more than a dozen states. Resources for public institutions, the poor, and minority groups have been cut, while property owners have retained a larger portion of their income.

Public officials often are unable to implement public ballot decisions because the decisions are not clear or call for significant policy adjustments.[87] California's Proposition 65 required state government to reduce substantially the flow of toxic chemicals into the state's water supply. Administrators found it extremely difficult to identify and classify all the chemicals that might harm the water supply, to determine safe standards, and finally to establish a system for monitoring thousands of chemical manufacturers and users.

Nuclear freeze referenda and initiatives clearly revealed the public's anxieties about a nuclear holocaust, but the measures had little practical impact. Most freeze propositions required state and local officials to communicate with the president and Congress about the deployment of nuclear weapons. The results were not binding on federal officials, and no freeze on deployment has been imposed. The initiatives constituted a symbolic victory.

Like any other method of decision making, initiatives and referenda have their strengths and weaknesses.[88] On the positive side, initiatives give citizens an opportunity to raise issues that elected leaders and interest groups might just as soon ignore. Initiatives also can help overcome stalemates in the legislative process. Taking policy choices to voters can be an effective method of legitimating controversial decisions. On the negative side, initiatives and referenda are blunt instruments. It is not possible to reduce complicated questions to one-line explanations. Ballot questions—with the choices restricted to yes or no—lack the deliberation and accommodation of legislative institutions and administrative agencies. And initiatives and referenda may not be as sensitive to minorities as the courts might be. Evidence suggests that interest groups and political officials are seizing the tools of direct democracy to seek victories that they were unable to gain through mainstream institutions. The practice of direct democracy is becoming professionalized and costly and, therefore, may be moving beyond the reach of volunteers. Finally, the opportunity to palm off difficult decisions may encourage irresponsible behavior by public officials. Rather than take actions they were elected to perform, they may wait for voters to send a clear signal. By then it may be too late.

Summary

Living room politics is a unique, important, but often misunderstood, part of democratic government. High school civics books and Independence Day speeches may exaggerate citizen control of the policy process, but many sophisticated observers also may underestimate the power the public wields in policy making.

For most citizens, politics and public policy are another form of entertainment. They find it interesting to tune in now and then, but not to stay tuned. From time to time, however, large segments of the public hold strong opinions on public issues, and an enraged, out-of-control public is a formidable threat to political stability. In full force, the power of public opinion and citizen participation has driven high officials from office, changed the course of American foreign and domestic policy, and stopped countless government proposals from ever getting off the ground.

The mass media are particularly important players in living room politics. Newspapers, television, and radio are the principal sources of information about politics and government for most Americans. The power of the media derives not from a conspiracy to lead American policy in a particular direction, but from the fact that most people have no way of conjuring up a different political reality.

Legislators, chief executives, bureaucrats, corporate leaders, and even judges are sensitive to the need for public understanding and support because without it government can lose its legitimacy—the very foundation of governance. Public officials must not only understand but also manage public opinion in order to build support for their cherished programs and to maintain control of the political process.

Notes

1. W. Lance Bennett, *Public Opinion in American Politics* (New York: Harcourt, Brace, Jovanovich, 1980).

2. As quoted in Leo Bogart, *Polls and the Awareness of Public Opinion*, 2d ed. (New Brunswick, N.J.: Transaction Books, 1985), 3.

3. See, for example, W. Russell Neuman, *The Paradox of Mass Politics* (Cambridge, Mass.: Harvard University Press, 1986); and Benjamin Ginsberg, *The Captive Public* (New York: Basic Books, 1986).

4. Martin Linsky, *Impact: How the Press Affects Federal Policymaking* (New York: W. W. Norton, 1986), 36-37.

5. E. E. Schattschneider, *The Semi-Sovereign People* (Hinsdale, Ill.: Dryden Press, 1960).

6. Neuman, *The Paradox of Mass Politics.*

7. The concepts of top-down and bottom-up public opinion are borrowed from Cliff Zukin of the Eagleton Institute of Politics at Rutgers University.

8. Bennett, *Public Opinion in American Politics.*

9. V. O. Key, Jr., *Public Opinion and American Democracy* (New York: Alfred A. Knopf, 1961), 14.

10. Bennett, *Public Opinion in American Politics*, 367.

11. Robert Weissberg, *Public Opinion and Popular Government* (Englewood Cliffs, N.J.: Prentice-Hall, 1976), 213.

12. Richard E. Neustadt, *Presidential Power: The Politics of Leadership from FDR to Carter* (New York: John Wiley & Sons, 1980). See also Samuel Kernell, *Going Public* (Washington, D.C.: CQ Press, 1986).

13. Linda Greenhouse, "Silence Is Heartening to Democrats," *New York Times*, June 19, 1987, A20.

14. Neuman, *The Paradox of Mass Politics.*

15. *The Book of the States, 1984-1985* (Lexington, Ky.: Council of State Governments, 1984), 167-169, 225.

16. Ellen Torelle, comp., *The Political Philosophy of Robert M. La Follette* (Westport, Conn.: Hyperion Press, 1975), 173-174.

17. Michael Nelson, "Power to the People: The Crusade for Direct Democracy," in *The Clash of Issues*, 7th ed., ed. James Burkhart et al. (Englewood Cliffs, N.J.: Prentice-Hall, 1981), 25-28.

18. Patrick B. McGuigan, *The Politics of Direct Democracy in the 1980s* (Washington, D.C.: Free Congress Research and Education Foundation, 1985); and Patrick B. McGuigan, ed., *Initiative and Referendum Report*, December 1986/January 1987.

19. Barry Commoner, "A Reporter at Large: The Environment," *New Yorker*, June 15, 1987, 46-71.

20. Bogart, *Polls and the Awareness of Public Opinion*, 198.

21. See, for example, Linsky, *Impact;* Stephen Hess, *The Ultimate Insiders: U.S. Senators and the National Media* (Washington, D.C.: Brookings Institution, 1986); and Austin Ranney, *Channels of Power: The Impact of Television on American Politics* (New York: Basic Books, 1983).

22. As quoted by W. Lance Bennett, "Marginalizing the Majority: Conditioning Public Opinion to accept Managerial Democracy" (Paper presented at the Annual Midwest Political Science Association Meeting, Chicago, Illinois, 1987), 16.

23. Leon V. Sigal, *Reporters and Officials: The Organization and Politics of Newsmaking* (Lexington, Mass.: D. C. Heath, 1973), 186.

24. Schattschneider, *The Semi-Sovereign People*, 2-3.

25. Donald L. Shaw and Maxwell E. McCombs, *The Emergence of American Political Issues: The Agenda-Setting Function of the Press* (St. Paul, Minn.: West Publishing, 1977).

26. Sigal, *Reporters and Officials*, 12.

27. See, for example, David E. Price, "Policymaking in Congressional Committees: The Impact of Environmental Factors," *American Political Science Review* 72 (June 1978): 548-574.

28. Linsky, *Impact*, 90.

29. Sigal, *Reporters and Officials;* and Shaw and McCombs, *The Emergence of Political Issues.*

30. Timothy E. Cook, "P.R. on the Hill: The Evolution of Congressional Press Operations," in *Legislative Politics*, ed. Chris Deering (Homewood, Ill.: Dorsey Press, forthcoming).

31. As quoted in Steven V. Roberts, "A Most Important Man on Capitol Hill, *New York Times Magazine*, Sept. 22, 1985, 48.

32. Gladys Engel Lang and Kurt Lang, *The Battle for Public Opinion: The President, the Press, and the Polls During Watergate* (New York: Columbia University Press, 1983), 58-61.

33. As quoted by Timothy E. Cook, "Marketing the Members: The Ascent of the Congressional Press Secretary" (Paper presented at the Annual Midwest Political Science Association Meeting, Chicago, Illinois, 1985), 15.

34. See for example, Edward Jay Epstein, *News From Nowhere: Television and the News* (New York: Vintage Books, 1983); W. Lance Bennett, *News: The Politics of Illusion* (New York: Longman, 1983); and Sigal, *Reporters and Officials.*

35. Sigal, *Reporters and Officials*, 186.

36. See Christopher J. Bosso, "Mass Media, Mass Politics: Making the Ethiopian Famine a Public Problem" (Paper presented at the Annual Midwest Political Science Association Meeting, Chicago, Illinois, 1987).

37. Linsky, *Impact;* and Sigal, *Reporters and Officials.*

38. Linsky, *Impact*, 94.

39. Edward Jay Epstein, *Between Fact and Fiction: The Problem of Journalism* (New York: Vintage Books, 1975).

40. Sigal, *Reporters and Officials*, 188.

41. Herbert J. Gans, *Deciding What's News* (New York: Pantheon Books, 1979).

42. Donald C. Baumer and Carl E. Van Horn, *The Politics of Unemployment* (Washington, D.C.: CQ Press, 1985).

43. Victor Cohn, "Fear of AIDS Is Spreading Faster than the Disease," *Washington Post National Weekly Edition*, Sept. 16, 1985, 37.

44. U.S. Congress, Joint Economic Committee, *Public Attitudes Toward the Deficit and Tax Reform*, 99th Cong. 1st sess., April 4, 1985, 76-77.

45. Ibid., 1.

46. Reported in "Liberals, Conservatives Share Initiative Success," *Public Administration Times*, Feb. 15, 1985, 1, 12.

47. McGuigan, *The Politics of Direct Democracy*, 42.

48. Joseph F. Zimmerman, "Initiative, Referendum, and Recall: Government by Plebiscite," *Intergovernmental Perspective* (Winter 1987): 32-38.

49. Ruth S. Jones, "Financing State Elections," in *Money and Politics in the United States*, ed. Michael J. Malbin (Chatham, N.J.: Chatham House, 1984), 2 '6-207.

50. Manning J. Dauer and Mark Sievers, "The Constitutional Initiative: Problems in Florida Politics," in *State Government: CQ's Guide to Current Issues and Activities, 1986-1987*, ed. Thad Beyle (Washington, D.C.: Congressional Quarterly, 1986), 29-32.

51. Richard Gable et al., "The 1982-83 Gubernatorial Transition in California," in *Gubernatorial Transitions: The 1982 Election*, ed. Thad Beyle (Durham, N.C.: Duke University Press, 1985), 123-158.

52. David B. Magleby, *Direct Legislation: Voting on Ballot Propositions in the United States* (Baltimore: Johns Hopkins University Press, 1984).

53. McGuigan, *The Politics of Direct Democracy*, 93-106.

54. Ibid., 58-59.

55. Ibid., 63.

56. Doris Graber, "Say it With Pictures: The Impact of Audio-Visual News on Public Opinion Formation" (Paper presented at the Annual Midwest Political Science Association Meeting, Chicago, Illinois, 1987).

57. David Halberstam, *The Powers That Be* (New York: Alfred A. Knopf, 1979); and Peter Braestrup, *Big Story* (New York: Doubleday Anchor, 1978).

58. Peter M. Sandman and Mary Paden, "At Three Mile Island," in *Media Power in Politics*, ed. Doris Graber (Washington, D.C.: CQ Press, 1984), 267; and Christopher Flavin, "Reassessing Nuclear Power," in *The State of the World 1987*, ed. Lester R. Brown et al. (New York: W. W. Norton, 1987), 57-80.

59. Lang and Lang, *The Battle for Public Opinion*.

60. Gladys Engel Lang and Kurt Lang, "The Media and Watergate," in *Media Power in Politics*, 209.

61. Cohn, "Fear of AIDS is Spreading."

62. Bennett, "Marginalizing the Majority," 33.

63. Linsky, *Impact*, 84.

64. Ibid., 86.

65. Adapted from Linsky, *Impact*, 71-78.

66. Adapted from Linsky, *Impact*, 49-60.

67. "Liberals, Conservatives Share Initiative Success."

68. McGuigan, *The Politics of Direct Democracy*, 46.

69. Ibid., 45-66.

70. David B. Magleby, "Legislatures and the Initiative: The Politics of Direct Democracy," *State Government* (Spring 1986): 31-39.

71. Susan Hansen, "Extraction: The Politics of State Taxation," in *Politics in the American States*, ed. Virginia Gray, Herbert Jacob, and Kenneth N. Vines (Boston: Little, Brown, 1983), 441-442.

72. William Gormley, Jr., *The Politics of Public Utility Regulation* (Pittsburgh: University of Pittsburgh Press, 1983), 208.

73. McGuigan, *The Politics of Direct Democracy*; and *Initiative and Referendum Report*, December 1986/January 1987.

74. McGuigan, *The Politics of Direct Democracy*, 67-92.

75. See, for example, Rufus P. Browning, Dale Rogers Marshall, and David H. Tabb, *Protest Is Not Enough: The Struggle of Blacks and Hispanics for Equality in Urban Politics* (Berkeley: University of California Press, 1984).

76. Commoner, "The Environment"; Daniel A. Mazmanian and Jeanne Nienaber, *Can Organizations Change? Environmental Protection, Citizen Participation, and the Corps of Engineers* (Washington, D.C.: Brookings Institution, 1979); and Lynton Caldwell et al., *Citizens and the Environment* (Bloomington: Indiana University Press, 1976).

77. Carl E. Van Horn et al., "It's Just Dirt: A Case Study of Radium-Contaminated Dirt in Montclair, New Jersey." (New Brunswick, N.J., Eagleton Institute of Politics, Rutgers University, May 1987), photocopy.

78. Neal R. Pierce, "Hats Off to the Pariah Barge Mobro," *Public Administration Times*, June 15, 1987, 2.

79. Cook, "P.R. On the Hill."

80. Lewis Wolfson, *The Untapped Power of the Press: Explaining Government to People* (New York: Praeger, 1986).

81. Graber, "Say It With Pictures."

82. See Baumer and Van Horn, *The Politics of Unemployment*, 198-199.

83. As quoted by David Ignatius, "Maybe the Media Did Push NASA to Launch the Challenger," *Washington Post National Weekly Edition*, April 14, 1986, 19.

84. Ibid.

85. Linsky, *Impact*, 146-147.

86. Michael J. Robinson, "Public Affairs Television and the Growth of Political Malaise: The Case of the 'Selling of the Pentagon,' " *American Political Science Review* 70 (June 1976): 409-432.

87. Magleby, "Legislatures and the Initiative."

88. Magleby, *Direct Legislation*.

THE POLICY PROCESS
AND ITS CONSEQUENCES

PART III

The six chapters of Part II examined policy making in a number of different institutional settings, which help define different kinds of politics. The various politics can be compared and contrasted in terms of their scope and the intensity of conflict involved, the complexity of the problems to be dealt with, and the public salience and visibility of the issues. Political institutions, with their characteristic political environments, have their own distinctive styles for approaching policy issues and for formulating and adopting policy responses. *Describing* and *analyzing* the politics and policies of these various institutional settings was the purpose of Part II.

In Part III the questions are more normative and evaluative. Having studied how the public policy process works, the reader should begin to ask how well it works. Explaining and evaluating the performance of political institutions, and the value of the policies themselves, are formidable tasks that require judgments about complex conditions and outcomes that are difficult to measure. How well do government institutions carry out national ideals? How much progress has the United States made in reducing racial discrimination? How much nuclear deterrence is enough? These questions have to be answered with considerable caution and care and some degree of uncertainty. The intention of the last two chapters is to stimulate constructive thinking about indisputably important matters.

Chapter 9 explores the functioning of American political institutions, their leaders, and those who actively seek to promote or thwart public action. Several questions are considered: How well do these individuals and institutions respond to society's problems? To what extent do public officials lead, as opposed to follow, in the resolution of public problems? Why are some problems either ignored or addressed in a haphazard manner? What kinds of results can be expected from different political and institutional arrangements? Will reforms in the structures and process of American politics make a difference? In short, the chapter raises broad questions about the relationships between governance and policy consequences and between the performance of American political institutions and the policy process.

Chapter 10 describes and evaluates the consequences of American public policies. Several critical questions are addressed, including: What is known about the actual effects of major public policies? How effective are public policies at achieving announced objectives? How are public benefits and costs distributed in American society? What conception or definition of fairness or justice can be applied to this distribution? Although these questions cannot be answered completely, evidence is provided for readers to consider in reaching their own judgments.

9 Institutional Performance

Politicians and citizens in the United States believe that having properly structured political institutions is essential to freedom, democracy, and prosperity. The Constitution reflects this view by prescribing certain relationships among these institutions and between them and citizens. Characteristic of the culture of the United States are unquestioning support for electing legislatures and executives, an independent judiciary, and federalism. Despite the symbolic reverence afforded to government institutions, they are continually examined and criticized by citizens and politicians alike. Explanations and evaluations of government's performance are another political tradition.

The principal observations and conclusions offered in Part II provide a useful starting point for an explanation of institutional performance.

—Corporations focus primarily on one goal, company profits, and board-room politics is highly centralized—dominated by top executive officers—although pressure is growing to expand the number of actors involved and to consider other goals. Corporate decisions, made privately, have far-reaching consequences for society.

—Bureaucracies like to define issues so that they are compatible with standard methods of operation. Policy decisions are made at various levels in the organization by administrative officials who are subject to a number of outside influences, including legislative committees, interest groups, chief executives, and courts. The standards for bureaucratic decisions are often explicit, but they can be quickly and dramatically changed by outsiders.

—Legislatures react to many issues, but are often slow to make decisions. Decision making is decentralized and subject to many influences, most notably well-organized, well-financed interests. Majorities rule when they are assembled, but the institutional structure of most American legislatures does not encourage the formation of decisive working majorities. Issue characteristics and contextual factors have a great impact on whether decisions are incremental, innovative, gridlocked, or symbolic, and on whether the decision-making process is slow or rapid, decentralized or centralized.

—Chief executives address highly visible issues and dominate public perceptions about government, but the policy significance of a chief executive's term may be quite different from its image. The essence of chief executive leadership is persuading other policy makers, especially legislators, to transform chief executive priorities into policy. This part of the policy process is always difficult, even for presidents making foreign policy.

—Courts consider a more restricted range of issues, but are capable of decisive policy actions, which sometimes have significant effects on society. The politics of judicial policy making are controlled by clear, specific procedures and criteria. The independence of the courts is rarely challenged.

—Public opinions are influential in American politics. When highly salient issues are involved, the public may directly change public policy through grass-roots organizations and initiatives or referenda. But, there are also instances in which public opinions are manipulated by media elites and government officials. The public, therefore, can be an active agent of democracy or a fairly weak, passive part of the policy process. Although it would be going too far to assert that media and governmental elites conspire to keep the public passive, political elites enjoy much more latitude in their policy actions when the public is passive.

Do these disparate observations form some larger picture? The answer is that American political institutions reflect rather faithfully their historical and philosophical roots. Their performance can be explained fairly well by reference to the free market/procedural democracy model of politics discussed in chapter 2. American political institutions perform different roles in striving to uphold the basic principles of the market paradigm and the ideals of procedural democracy. Understanding these differences is the key to explaining institutional behavior. Board-room politics and living room politics expand the system's repertoire of policy-making processes in interesting and important ways, some of which push the political process beyond the limits of free market/procedural democracy.

An Analysis of Conventional Political Institutions

Courts and Legislatures

This analysis begins with a comparison of two very different political institutions: the Supreme Court and Congress. The Court acts on the basis of a philosophical view of procedural democracy; Congress understands procedural democracy on a more personal level.

Why has the Court been the political institution most inclined to act decisively to secure the rights of disadvantaged minorities? The reason is that the Supreme Court justices, in their role as interpreters of the

Constitution, have been forced to define in legal terms what the main principles of this document mean in specific circumstances. The nature of the judicial process—using written opinions to establish precedents that guide future decisions—induces justices to take a philosophical look at constitutional principles. The logic of the Constitution is derived from a school of thought that places importance on certain procedural values. In the case of disadvantaged minorities, the guiding principle is equality of opportunity, and the specific means to achieve equality of opportunity are the equal protection clause and the due process clause of the Fourteenth Amendment. The context in which the Court makes decisions, and the process employed, encourage it to be decisive about the core principles of procedural democracy.

Supreme Court interpretations of constitutional principles have done a great deal for advantaged minorities as well as the disadvantaged. This outcome of Court decision making can be seen as another indication of the pervasiveness of the market paradigm, which discourages distinguishing between market participants. The protection given to property ownership is an obvious example of the Court's adherence to market principles, but a more interesting example is the freedom granted to the press. The press has continually invoked the Constitution on behalf of its right to publish or display all sorts of misleading and distasteful material. Anyone who has stood in a check-out line at a grocery store can testify to the alluring, but false, headlines used by some newspapers and magazines. By defining libel and slander restrictively, the Court has allowed the press to continue printing sensational material. The courts believe there should be a marketplace of ideas in a free society and that valid ideas persist and invalid ideas perish in such a setting. Therefore, the Court protects and promotes economic and information markets. However, the courtroom is not a marketplace of ideas; rather it is an exclusive setting in which a small group of people decide important questions using specialized discourse and arcane language.

The Court's strength depends upon its adherence to the central principles of the Constitution, and the Court is generally reluctant to expand the number or meaning of these principles. However, when the Court breaks new constitutional ground, as it did several times under Chief Justice Earl Warren, it is difficult for it to ignore subsequent cases pursuing related questions. Still, to venture too far into politics is to risk confrontation with Congress or the president, as has nearly occurred over issues such as busing and school prayer. The Court's role in the American system is to define and protect the rules of the game, but the game of politics and economics, for the most part, is played elsewhere—at least for the first few innings. Gridlock and indecisiveness on the part of elected officials have made the Court a more prominent political player.

As suggested in chapter 2, the market paradigm fits well with cloakroom politics. Citizens register their preferences for representatives who then try to give their constituents what they want at the lowest political cost. Those who are successful in retaining elected offices are, in most cases, efficient producers of political goods. Citizen preferences can be expressed individually or through political parties or interest groups. It is not surprising that citizens prefer interest groups over individual action or parties. Individual political action often is regarded as quixotic, and many Americans find parties constraining— they do not always like their allies within party coalitions. Interest groups are effective, aggressive, and self-interested; they operate as if politics were a market where each person's pursuit of self-interest is justified because it is part of a system that maximizes collective welfare. Indeed, the idea that interest group competition produces policies that serve the public interest is accepted by most politicians, and it is supported by an elaborate theoretical structure developed by political scientists under the name of pluralism.[1]

Why then does Congress specialize in policies that carry particularized benefits, created in decentralized settings where interest groups are accepted participants? Why is meaningful congressional policy action difficult to bring about on matters that do not carry clear benefits for constituents? The answer is that the legislative version of the market paradigm encourages such behavior. Like businesses in a market, legislators like to make a profit, and their profits are measured in votes. To secure comfortable electoral margins, they hand out benefits. Who gets the benefits? Those who can pay with money or votes. Should the legislators view this posture as improper or unethical? Not really. The existence of winners and losers is quite consistent with the dominant political philosophy of the country, with the culture, and with the institutional environment in which Congress operates. If one assumes that the political marketplace is open, it is fair and just to respond to articulated demands and to maximize voter satisfaction. Pork-barrel politics is a proven way of doing this.

It is alleged that one of the advantages of a free market economic system is its self-correcting character. If producers churn out too much of a product, its price falls; then new buyers are attracted, and eventually the price stabilizes. If only a little is produced of a product people want, its high price attracts the interest of potential producers. Periods of vigorous consumer spending generate rising prices and high levels of production, which eventually result in overstocked inventories and falling prices. These self-correcting factors are not automatic; rather, they are linked to government monetary and fiscal policy. But what about political markets? Are they self-correcting?

Recent history suggests that congressional self-correction mechanisms do not function very well. Congress practiced dispensing benefits in exchange for votes from the 1950s through the late 1970s. Federal spending and taxes grew to the point that they became highly salient issues. Deficit spending provided temporary refuge, but soon the deficits became an issue. Various reforms were tried, but none of them broke the pattern, and Congress now faces difficult, painful choices. The pluralist ethic is very much alive, but there is a widespread recognition that Congress must restrain its inclination to pass out benefits to every group that asks. This recognition could encourage more centralized, presumably party-based, decision making.

The failure of self-correcting mechanisms in markets and politics is a reminder to maintain the distinction between theory and reality. Just as markets do not always work as they are supposed to because entry is restricted, consumer knowledge is imperfect, large producers conspire, or various other distortions occur, political markets also have flaws. Voter knowledge of issues and candidates is not what it should be. Some groups such as the poor, are not represented in a way that reflects their numerical significance. Some politicians engage in deceptive advertising and get away with it. Because elected politicians establish the rules of politics, it is not surprising that they use the rules for their own advantage and distort political markets. Political reform is always needed in a system that depends on periodic corrections of destructive tendencies, but reformers should be clear about their goals. Are they trying to make procedural democracy live up to its ideals, or are they trying to institute a new kind of democracy?

Congress and the Supreme Court have characteristic strengths and weaknesses. Congress is especially good at receiving and responding to signals from political interests that are organized to send them in conventional ways such as voting, lobbying, and contributing. This relationship with Congress helps keep the populace reasonably happy, especially advantaged minorities, who get more than their share of benefits. Even groups that are not part of the president's coalition, such as business groups during a Democratic administration, can benefit under this system because committee decision making gives them a chance to shape policy despite presidential opposition. The style of many members of Congress—heavy reliance on casework and personal advertising—makes government accessible to many people. However, Congress's inability to act decisively, which is a byproduct of its accessibility, contributes to the public sense of distrust and disappointment in government.

Congress can be compared to network television in that people seem to like most of the programs on television and they usually admire their representatives, but there are widespread complaints about the overall product. Network executives and members of Congress agree that the quality of the product could be higher, but contend that they are simply responding to the signals they receive—ratings, polls, and letters—that tell them what people want. Once subsidies have been dispensed, all that Congress has left, other than symbolism, is redistribution and coercion, which are not the kinds of policy tools members like to use.

The Court can be decisive because its brand of procedural democracy is highly codified and, therefore, relatively easy to apply to specific cases. The Court must understand the rules because it is the principal guardian of procedural democracy. To perform this guardianship well it must be somewhat removed from popular passions. Citizens and politicians often fail to grasp some of the unpleasant nuances of procedural democracy, for example, that Communists and Nazis have the right of free speech. The Court is not a very good vehicle for popular participation, although class action suits and other advocacy efforts have made it a forum in which some popular causes have been advanced. The Court will never lead the way to radical social changes such as wealth redistribution, public ownership of industry, or income guarantees, but it sometimes forces the system to live up to its ideals, which can cause a good deal of distress in certain segments of society.

Chief Executives and the Bureaucracy

The bureaucracy resembles the courts in some ways and legislatures in others. It resembles the courts in having formal and specific decision criteria, though not so specific or complete as to eliminate discretion. The courts have laws, the Constitution, and legal precedents to guide their decisions, and bureaucratic agencies have written statutes and rules. The agencies resemble legislatures because they are highly vulnerable to politics. Agencies can be battered by citizen groups, legislators, chief executives, or judges, and their vulnerability has led them to assume a defensive posture toward the outside world. Standard procedures, public hearings, citizen advisory councils, bureaucratic hierarchy, and participation in subgovernments are all forms of defense. Even innovation, which bureaucracies are quite capable of, is usually a response to a threatening political environment.

American bureaucracies are highly political, not because they want to be, but because they are forced to be to defend themselves against stronger political institutions. The pluralist ethic also operates in the administrative state. Bureaucratic officials know they cannot succeed if they offend powerful interests, and they need to know who are their agencies' friends and enemies in the legislature and the office of the chief executive. Agencies are increasingly conscious of their public image, but administrative policy makers cannot depend upon voter satisfaction; they have to make sure their services and procedures are defensible. They wrap themselves in a mantle of lawlike formalities and try to maintain other forms of protection, so as to be prepared if political headhunters start looking in their direction.

Chief executives are the principal agents of majoritarian rule in pluralist politics. They are the main corrective force against the potentially harmful effects of fragmentation toward which legislatures drift if left to their own devices. Chief executives often try to define a public interest that is separate and distinguishable from the sum of parochial interests. They set certain goals—a cleaner environment, better schools, less poverty—and try to figure out ways to achieve them. The problem is that they have limited authority to act on their own, and convincing legislators to follow a clear and consistent policy path is extremely difficult.

The nature of this difficulty should be apparent by now. Legislators have their own relationships with voters and they do not like having them disrupted by chief executives. Legislators sometimes can be convinced that departing from their cherished mode of operation—giving subsidies to the organized—is necessary if a crisis is to be avoided, but they require a good deal of proof that conditions warrant such extraordinary action, as well as skillful coaxing and public pressure. Some chief executives are able to provide the proof and the coaxing and to apply pressure; others are not.

The strength of chief executives lies in their ability to command attention. Their efforts to assemble ruling coalitions and resolve crises provide most of the action and drama in politics, and the media find action and drama irresistible. People identify with chief executives and, for the most part, with *their* legislators, but not with the legislature as a whole. This interest and loyalty give chief executives a certain amount of leverage that can be used to pursue policy objectives. The greatest weakness of chief executives is their lack of power, influence, and authority over other political elites, which stems from the independence of government institutions and the weak party system.

The strength of bureaucracy lies in its staying power. Bureaucracies are essential to the operation of government, and elected officials recognize this when they stop to think about it. Bureaucracies can be decisive, even innovative, if the political environment is supportive; but most show a marked preference for stability and continuity. The weakness of bureaucratic agencies is their formal and informal subservience to political institutions and interests. They can usually defend themselves against abolition, but they have to be constantly on their guard. The bureaucracy is the punching bag of American politics; it takes many blows but somehow remains intact.

Alternatives to Conventional Politics

Politics and public policies are not captives of government institutions. Private institutions also shape public policy, as do individual citizens and grass-roots organizations. Board-room politics and living room politics reflect contrasting philosophical principles and cultural values.

For most corporate decision makers the market paradigm is the world view of utmost importance. They have no doubt about the value of the pursuit of private gain because it is accepted as an essential part of a system that maximizes social welfare by translating free competition into overall economic efficiency and productivity. This world view is part of what enables corporate decision makers to lay off thousands of reliable skilled workers in Michigan, Pennsylvania, and Texas while they commit funds to new automobile and steel plants in Mexico, Taiwan, and South Korea. They argue that market forces should dictate wages, plant locations, and, ultimately, living patterns. Many corporate leaders understand that markets can be cruel to human beings, and they sympathize with the plight of their workers.

Rhetoric and reality frequently are at odds in the board room. Government intervention is abhorred when it costs money, but eloquently defended when it protects or subsidizes. Herbert Simon's pioneering work on corporate decision making demonstrates that private sector decision making is neither simple nor automatic.[2] Economic theory holds that businesses attempt to maximize their profits. Simon showed that in practice large corporations with many decision makers normally choose options that satisfy as many interests as possible, rather than seek optimal profits in every circumstance. In this way, corporations resemble legislatures and public bureaucracies because bargaining and accommodation figure in their decision making. This kind of decision making is found particularly in publicly owned corporations, those that are subject to a great deal of government regulation, and those that are controlled by public officials. In such institutions decision makers sometimes are forced to confront the fact that the pursuit of private gain and the enhancement of society's well-being may not be equivalent. Private decision makers are not completely removed from, or ignorant of, concerns about the common good. Still, the market paradigm dominates this arena of politics in a form that is relatively pure and undiluted.

"We the people," the opening phrase of the Constitution conveys an unmistakable message: government should be controlled by the citizenry. Certain Americans throughout the country's existence have taken this message seriously. They have attempted to make the public an active instrument of policy making, to work out of a more participatory mode of democracy. Their successes—town meetings, initiatives, referenda, recall, grass-roots movements—add important elements to American politics. But participatory democratic practices often are in conflict with the market paradigm and procedural democracy. Clearly, many Americans believe there is an important difference between pursuing private gain and serving organized interests, and the achievement of collective well-being. Because of this belief, living room politics is very much alive.

Living room politics, in its ideal form, represents occasions when politicians take a back seat to citizens, when popular feelings are registered in a clear, unmistakable way. This activism is what Jean Jacques Rousseau saw as essential to democracy, and what contemporary advocates of participatory democracy would like to see strengthened in American politics. However, it would be naive to think that the dominant forces could be removed from any arena of politics. The mass media and communication technology have shown themselves to be both friend and foe of democratic reformers and activists. The media reach people, but they also bring their own priorities, procedures, and prejudices into the information they transmit. Grass-roots leaders and mainstream politicians sometimes find, to their mutual surprise, that they have much in common because they all have to deal with the media to succeed and they find this difficult and frustrating at times.

Direct democracy is easily perverted to demagoguery or captured by elite interests because symbolism and showmanship are so much a part of its practice in modern societies. Living room politics springs from the genuinely democratic impulse to allow people to determine the rules under which they will live. But one must be ever mindful of the gap between the ideal and reality in politics. Just as real markets often are woefully inadequate representations of the market paradigm, initiatives, referenda, and grass-roots movements can be a far cry from the ideals of unitary or strong democracy.[3]

Performance Appraisal

The preceding brief analysis of American political institutions shows that these institutions are driven by philosophical principles, constitutional prescriptions, cultural traditions, and economic forces. Here the focus shifts to evaluation. How well do American political institutions work? Should Americans be satisfied with their performance?

One way of approaching these questions is to take a broad look at society and examine how happy people are with it. American society has positive and negative characteristics:

—individual freedom of thought, movement, religion, life style, and consumption

—widespread prosperity, but a persistent underclass

—real and symbolic violence

—great cultural, educational, residential, and aesthetic diversity

—a materialistic, pragmatic value orientation

—a pervasive belief in the importance of individual and group competition

—a tradition that people have a recognized right to participate

American society is a fairly faithful reflection of the principles that have guided its development. American political institutions carry out their basic mandates to let markets allocate values and to provide representation for the interests of the organized.

Some positive aspects of institutional behavior were pointed out in Part II. Corporate boards are more representative and less incestuous than they used to be; some companies are innovative and public-spirited. Modern bureaucracies are seldom "captured" by narrow interests, and most listen to a wide variety of interests. Chief executives can be powerful agents of change and usually are given the leeway they need to be effective in crises. Even legislatures are capable of major breakthroughs when political and economic conditions are ripe. The courts address some of society's most troublesome controversies in a forthright and reasonable manner, and they can, over time, foster significant changes. Public opinion, once aroused, has played a constructive role in disputes like the Vietnam War, environmental protection, and others.

Those who want a society that is more cohesive, peaceful, humanistic, cooperative, competitive, and democratic would be inclined to give American political institutions a less favorable overall evaluation. However, such critics would acknowledge that dominant forces in society—legal, social, political, and economic—have been pushing in a direction that is quite different from what they advocate; that is, toward a strong private sector and a government that acts cautiously to correct the problems that private sector competition leaves behind. American political institutions were not designed to be strong enough to chart an independent course for national development because the Founders feared what unchecked political institutions might do.

Assessing institutional performance on the basis of broad societal outcomes—how happy, wealthy, and wise society is—leads to endless debates over questions that are difficult to answer with any precision. For this reason, it is necessary to introduce some guidelines and standards into an evaluative discussion. Six criteria—stability, representativeness, responsiveness, public awareness, efficiency, and competence—are identified as positive characteristics of political institutions in the sections that follow. Before considering standards for evaluation, however, it is important to look at society's expectations about the performance of government institutions.

Americans generally impose high standards of performance on their political institutions. They expect them to be open, efficient, effective, and caring. These expectations are significant because the design of political institutions limits their ability to solve problems. Consequently, the government's lack of effectiveness in treating visible problems engenders disappointment among the citizenry. Politicians are major culprits in this regard because they often make absurd claims about what they plan to accomplish and then blame everyone else in government when they end up accomplishing very little. This behavior adds further conviction to voter feelings of cynicism and distrust of government.

Americans are unrealistic in their expectations about government. They want government to solve their problems but to leave them alone. There is, too, something of a double standard in society. Government officials are subject to codes of conduct that are much stricter than in the private sector, but they are held in lower esteem than their private sector counterparts. During the Reagan administration an unprecedented number of unethical conduct cases, such as conflict of interest, patronage, and special favors, cropped up among presidential appointees; in most cases these officials were behaving just as they had done in the private sector from which they came. The media is highly attuned to matters of corruption in government, and their coverage of allegations, investigations, indictments, and convictions keeps the public aware of the problem. Corruption may be a *constant* problem in government, but it is not *pervasive;* and it is not a primary determinant of institutional performance.

In addition to facing a demanding audience, government institutions confront many difficult problems. There is a good deal of truth to the notion that these institutions clean up society's messes. Problems like poverty, unemployment, pollution, and crime may be unsolvable in a society with a dominant private sector and an ever-changing economy. But these are some of the matters with which government is expected to grapple. The number of intractable problems at the top of the agenda seems to be increasing rather than decreasing. The New Deal bit off some of the easier problems: providing a reasonable income for the elderly and the disabled, guaranteeing worker rights, and building a physical infrastructure for economic development. The New Deal provided reasonably effective solutions, such as Social Security, the National Labor Relations Act, the Works Progress Administration (WPA), and the Tennessee Valley Authority (TVA). Since the 1960s the government has directed attention and money to the more difficult problems, such as poverty, but the returns have been disappointing. With budget deficits looming, policy makers have less ammunition to attack these problems. It is not only the nature of the institutions but also the nature of the problems that make effective government action difficult.

Americans are fixers. If something is not working properly, the American instinct is to find a cure, usually through technology. This fix-it mentality is evident in almost every aspect of American life, including government and politics. The Constitution, for example, places great emphasis on staving off governmental pathologies—tyranny, excessive democracy—by certain institutional arrangements. Perceived malfunctions of government generate suggestions for reform that typically reflect a structural/mechanical approach to political problem solving. Americans, therefore, have established a civil service to correct the evils of the spoils system; created regulatory agencies to curb private sector abuses; reorganized the executive branch to make departments more responsive to chief executive preferences; and instituted initiative and referendum procedures to make government more responsive to citizens. There is an obvious and natural link between performance assessments and proposals for reform as shown in the discussions that follow.

Stability

Government stability may be the most important standard by which to judge the success or failure of political institutions, and the American system would get high marks on anyone's stability scale. From a world perspective, the peaceful transference of power from one regime, usually defined by its leader, to the next is still one of the most difficult problems for countries to solve. The U.S. constitutional prescriptions regarding presidential succession have passed all tests, including the Watergate crisis, with flying colors. Furthermore, when the institutions are unresponsive to strongly felt public desires, there are other mechanisms, such as living room politics, through which discontent can be expressed without threatening the stability of the system. The premise underlying American government was that allowing the market economy to work was the key to social and economic progress, and, therefore, to social contentment. Having a *stable* government was considered more important than having an *enlightened* one, and here American institutions have fulfilled their essential mission.

Economic markets are not expected to be stable in the same way that governments are. Indeed, the private sector is supposed to be dynamic, innovative, and ever-changing. But changing private sector markets can have profoundly painful human consequences, and liberal reformers have sought to smooth away the rough edges of business cycles through economic planning and joint public and private ventures. The idea is that planning and partnerships can make less wrenching the transitions caused by declining industries, changing raw material costs, or population migrations.

Pennsylvania, hard-hit by economic dislocations, developed an extensive network of economic planning and development groups and provided funds for encouraging entrepreneurship. It sponsored programs to put public employee pension funds to work in venture capital efforts, created seed venture funds for small new companies with innovative business plans, and established advanced technology centers. The centers administer grants that subsidize projects undertaken jointly by private companies and state universities in areas of developing technology. All of these economic development efforts are overseen by the Ben Franklin Partnership Board, made up of representatives from business, labor, and government. The board does not make investment decisions; these are left to private fund managers and venture capitalists. The state's role is catalytic, making information and money available and sponsoring institutions and programs that bring private and public sector groups together. In all these activities, a concerted effort has been made to minimize state-imposed administrative requirements, an effort considered crucial for maintaining private sector cooperation.[4]

At the national level some Democrats in Congress have proposed the creation of an industrial development bank to subsidize the modernization of declining industries and to provide venture capital for companies in promising new industries. Also proposed is the establishment of an economic cooperation council, composed of business, labor, and government representatives, that would look at the position of American industries from a world perspective and advise businesses how best to compete with foreign enterprises. These institutional innovations are part of what has been called an industrial policy (see chapter 10).[5]

Legislation to establish such a bank or council has failed repeatedly to go very far in Congress because Democrats and Republicans alike are wary of government involvement in capital investment decisions and because organized labor has been supporting these proposals.[6] An economic development plan featuring a tripartite council to direct strategic economic investments was defeated by Rhode Island voters in a 1984 referendum. The plan was defeated because many voters felt that it catered to elite interests and offered little or nothing for the average citizen.[7]

Interest in these new kinds of institutional arrangements is, to a large extent, an outgrowth of the widespread recognition during the late

1970s that wages could not go higher in core industries if American companies were to stay competitive in world markets. In fact, the wages of many industrial workers have declined steadily since 1970, and the question that is asked with increasing frequency is: Will management share profits and the power to make operational and investment decisions with labor? And, will profit sharing and cooperative management produce demonstrably better products and enhance worker productivity? This type of sharing would represent a major institutional change in board-room politics.

Representativeness

Another standard by which to judge the success or failure of political institutions is their representativeness. A simple way of approaching this matter is to ask: Who gets into policy-making circles and who does not? The answer to this question has been that well-educated white professional men, especially lawyers, tend to get in; women, blacks, the poor, and those with limited education do not. Despite years of effort to change the skewed demographic composition of policy makers, little progress has been made. Legislatures used to be biased in favor of rural areas, but much of this bias has been corrected by Supreme Court rulings upholding the principle of one person, one vote.[8] That public officials of all sorts are better educated than the average citizen is not surprising, and it is not a primary concern of most critics. But other aspects of the leadership profile are troubling, as is the fact that the demographic patterns are quite consistent across institutions.

In Congress women comprise less than 5 percent of the members. They make up 7 percent of top bureaucratic officials, but a much higher percentage of government employees overall. Seven percent of all federal judges are women. Women hold 6 percent of the governorships and 3 percent of the mayoralties. There are almost no women in top corporate management positions, although they have made substantial gains in middle management and more than half of the boards of directors of major companies include at least one woman.[9] Women have made their greatest gains in state legislatures and city councils, where their numbers rose from 5 percent in the early 1970s to 15 percent in 1986.[10]

For blacks and Hispanics the picture is much the same. The black share of top federal policy-making posts—Congress, courts, the bureaucracies—is about 5 percent; the Hispanic share is 2 percent to 3 percent. Blacks have 5 percent of state legislative seats and no governorships,[11] but there have been two Hispanic governors in the 1980s, Toney Anaya of New Mexico and Robert Martinez of Florida. Like women, blacks and Hispanics are still virtually absent from the top of corporate hierarchies, but they have made significant advances in middle management. The main bright spot in minority representation is the steady election of black and Hispanic mayors in major cities such as Atlanta, Chicago, Detroit, Los Angeles, Newark, New Orleans, Philadelphia, and San Antonio.

Women and minorities still face an uphill struggle in obtaining positions that will give them policy-making power. This problem is longstanding and will improve slowly at best. It is difficult to determine all the causes and assess the significance of the unrepresentativeness of policy makers, but clearly racial, gender, and ethnic discrimination are part of the answer. According to the traditional qualifications, such as advanced degrees, relevant work experience, and references, associated with top corporate, bureaucratic, and judicial positions, the pool of eligible women and minorities is relatively small. This situation is changing as more women and blacks are going to law schools and business schools and working their way up through corporate and bureaucratic hierarchies.[12] Still, the preferences and commitments of those making appointments also make a big difference. Jimmy Carter made a commitment to appoint more women and blacks to the federal court system, and 30 percent of his appointments went to these groups. Their share of judgeships before Carter was about 10 percent. Ronald Reagan did not make this commitment, and less than 15 percent of his court appointments went to women and blacks, although he did appoint the first woman to the Supreme Court.[13] In the private sector, a few historically male-dominated companies like International Harvester (now Navistar International), Nabisco, and R. J. Reynolds Tobacco have broken with their own traditions and appointed women vice-presidents.[14]

The selection processes are obviously different for elected officials. A critical problem for women is recruitment—getting women into state and local party organizations, getting some of them elected to state and local offices, and then supporting female candidacies for more visible, powerful offices. Racial prejudice seems to be the primary reason blacks are not selected. White voters have shown a clear, sustained disinclination to vote for black candidates at all levels of government. For the most part, black candidates win only where blacks are the majority or near majority of voters. This pattern was very evident in Jesse Jackson's bids for the presidency. In 1984 Jackson received nearly 80 percent of the black vote in Democratic primaries, but only 5 percent of the white vote.[15] By 1988 Jackson's share of the black vote was higher than 90 percent; his support among white Democratic voters was between 15 percent and 20 percent in most northern states, but remained below 10 percent in the South. Although it is possible for white males to represent the interests of women and minorities, no group with distinct interests would be well advised to rely to any great extent on the altruism or empathy of elected officials, particularly in a system in which factional competition is central to the governing process.

Responsiveness

For most reformers demographic representativeness is not an end in itself, but a means to an end. The true objective is a political system that is responsive to popular needs and preferences. Reformers cite as evidence of the government's lack of responsiveness problems such as the spread of AIDS, the nuclear arms race, ozone depletion, soaring medical costs, and homelessness, which receive much less attention than they deserve.

The government has a basic responsibility to take the lead in diagnosing and making plans to avert potential catastrophes because the private sector cannot be relied upon to do so. Chief executives and the courts sometimes take steps to head off potential crises, but legislatures find it especially difficult to respond to anything other than an immediate crisis. Judgments about which problems are the most important at any given time are difficult to make with certainty. Some problems turn out to be less serious than they first appeared, and government institutions are seen as justified in the scant attention they gave them. Moreover, small steps may eventually yield substantial returns. Nevertheless, analysis of major institutions suggests that they often ignore problems for which no popular and easy solution is apparent, and they do this to the detriment of society as a whole.

Campaign Finance Reform. One of the most called-for political reforms among citizens, scholars, and politicians concerns the ever-increasing amounts of money spent to get people elected and to influence officials once they are in office. Critics allege that politicians have to spend so much of their time attending to money matters—giving speeches to donor groups, attending fund-raisers, meeting with contributors, planning media promotions, and so forth—that they have little time for the public's business. This problem is prevalent at the national and state levels. For most politicians, just maintaining their positions in the highly competitive political world is almost a full-time job. In such an environment, politicians can be responsive to money, but little else.

Senator David Boren, D-Okla., has proposed campaign finance reform legislation that would extend to congressional elections the public financing system that currently governs presidential elections. Candidates would receive public funds to match their privately raised funds during the primaries; party nominees would receive full public financing for the general election. Spending ceilings would be imposed for all candidates who accept public funds. These ceilings would be fixed for House elections but would vary according to state populations in Senate races. Also proposed was a reduction to $3,000 from $5,000 in the amount political action committees (PACs) could contribute to candidates and a limit of $100,000 in PAC funds per candidate per election.[16]

Campaign finance reform creates sticky problems. First, the Supreme Court has ruled that candidates cannot be forced to limit their spending.[17] The limits, therefore, would have to be high enough to dissuade most candidates from turning down public financing; if they do not accept public funding, they could raise and spend unlimited amounts on their own and possibly sabotage the reform. Boren's proposal would allow House candidates about $650,000 and Senate candidates anywhere from $680,000 to $5.5 million. These figures represent roughly half of what is currently spent on competitive House and Senate races and would cost taxpayers $100 million. Even with generous funding, wealthy candidates might prefer to finance their own campaigns.

A second problem is that PACs devise ways around spending limits as quickly as they are imposed. Their latest tricks include subdividing to form many separate organizations, each one able to contribute up to the limit, and organizing drives to have members or sympathizers contribute to candidates or parties as individuals, as well as to the PAC. They continue exercising their right to spend as much money as they want in *independent* campaigns for and against candidates, a practice that would not be stopped by public financing. Moreover, PACs have many supporters among elected officials, some of whom will go to great lengths—filibuster, for example—to protect their current prerogatives.

Third, spending limitations almost certainly would favor incumbents, especially in the House of Representatives, where the incumbent reelection rate in 1986 was 98 percent. Incumbents enjoy mailing privileges, travel and staff allowances, and other advantages that are valued at about $1 million a year.[18] Serious challenges to House incumbents frequently cost more than $1 million, but it would defeat the purpose of reform to set the public spending ceiling that high, and high spending limits would no doubt raise the ire of taxpayers. Another problem is that incumbents are naturally reluctant to change the system that keeps them in office. With so many strikes against it, campaign finance reform may be a "dead duck"; however, the growing number of politicians who are disenchanted with the constant need to acquire money may some day bring about a change.

Corporate Responsibility. Since the late 1960s corporations have been the targets of a number of citizen protests and lobbying efforts by unions, churches, public interest groups, and grass-roots organizations. These protests have brought to the attention of corporate managers and boards, politicians, and the public such examples of corporate abuse and social irresponsibility as operations in South Africa, discrimination against blacks and women, and the exposure of workers and the public to dangerous chemicals. Many of these efforts have stimulated changes in corporate policy and, perhaps more important, have served to politicize corporations. The once sedate stockholder meetings have been turned into forums for discussions of a wide range of political and social issues and for shareholder or proxy resolutions.

This movement has spawned a number of corporate reform proposals, most of which aim to make managers more accountable to individual and institutional investors and to the public. These proposals include giving all shareholders, regardless of the size of their investment, one vote on proxy resolutions; taking the selection of directors out of the hands of management and putting it into the hands of shareholders; and requiring that corporate boards include government or other outside representatives.[19] Such reforms probably would have to be imposed on corporations through regulatory statutes, a development which is unlikely. Nevertheless, the accountability movement has made corporate decision makers more aware of their public responsibilities. Because they are sympathetic to genuine expressions of public sentiment, some corporate managers willingly make policy changes, as long as the changes do not threaten profitability. These citizen challenges to corporate decisions are another form of direct democracy, but corporations seem destined to remain largely autonomous for the foreseeable future.

Public Awareness

The picture presented so far of the public's role in the political process has not been entirely complimentary. Public opinion often is manipulated by political and media elites. Many expressions of public opinion suggest that Americans are concerned mainly about the economic well-being of their families and communities, that they are unreasonably impatient with government, and that they are ignorant of many aspects of national and international politics.

Proposals for greater public involvement in public policy decisions should be scrutinized carefully. The political education of citizens is not a high priority in the United States. Americans seem content to speak through elections and then to allow political elites representing various interests to hammer out the details of public policy. Some observers, however, believe that the ignorance, apathy, and parochialism of the American public is best viewed as a result, not a cause, of a political system that does not value democratic participation and does not encourage civic education.

Over the years many reforms aimed at increasing the quantity and quality of citizen participation in American government have been advanced. The question is whether these reforms can be effective if adopted in a piecemeal fashion, or whether a comprehensive system of citizen education and involvement is necessary for the reforms to have their desired effect. Political scientist Benjamin Barber believes the changes have to be comprehensive; he has proposed extensive reforms that begin with institutionalized neighborhood assemblies nationwide. The problem, according to Barber, is that Americans have no place to meet to learn about and discuss issues. Therefore, all neighborhood groups from 5,000 to 25,000 should have a facility that can be used for regular public meetings to discuss local or national issues. Once established, these assemblies could vote on local issues and choose local officials (in some cases by lot), be tied into a national electronic civic education network, and eventually vote on national issues through electronic referenda. Barber also would establish universal citizen service requirements, democratize the workplace, and generally reorient society around communal concerns and civic responsibilities.[20]

Such comprehensive changes seem highly improbable, but some of the specific proposals deserve consideration. Despite the fact that state initiative and referenda campaigns are now very much a part of media- and money-based politics, they often constitute authentic expressions of popular sentiment. Furthermore, they are popular: state polls show public support of 70 percent to 75 percent, and a majority of Americans favor the adoption of a national referendum procedure.[21] A national referendum, which could be established by constitutional amendment, could be used to discourage or break deadlocks within Congress or between Congress and the president. If national institutions were deadlocked, the voters could settle disputed issues with the next election. Most other Western democracies have national referenda, and their use, which is infrequent, has not disrupted the process of government. The requirement for a national youth service is also intriguing. It could provide a much-needed avenue for class integration in a society that is increasingly segregated on the basis of income.

Electronic plebiscites are less appealing. As Barber acknowledges, this innovation should be approached with caution because the potential for abuse is great.[22] However, as part of the electronic civic education network, the use of television cameras in the courtroom might be beneficial. The presence of television cameras in Congress is now accepted, and they have not disrupted or fundamentally altered the legislative process. The audience usually is small, but not insignificant. Court proceedings in Florida have been televised for more than ten years. The results have been generally positive—lawyers and judges do not play to the camera, and witnesses and jurors are not confused or intimidated by its presence. The response from citizens indicates a genuine fascination in seeing how the judicial process really works, a development that advocates of participatory democracy would no doubt applaud.[23]

Efficiency

American government is far from efficient in the way it makes and implements policies, and many of the inefficiencies stem from basic tenets of the Constitution such as the separation of powers, bicameralism, and federalism. The Framers believed that there was more to be feared from government action than there was to be gained from it, and many Americans share this sentiment. If stability is the strongest *virtue* of American government, inefficiency is probably its greatest *vice*.

The nature of this inefficiency has been amply demonstrated in Part II. Congress has difficulty making controversial policy decisions and, when it reaches decisions, the policies are often symbolic, vague, ridden with compromise, and internally inconsistent. When Congress cannot decide, problems are either left unresolved or settled by the courts or state governments. Bureaucratic implementation of ambiguous statutes frequently leads to new problems, and an ongoing cycle ensues of legislative patchwork, discretionary enforcement, public and/or interest group complaints, and more patchwork. Chief executives have trouble making government more efficient because legislatures often refuse to cooperate. Chief executives cannot force cooperation because legislators are virtually immune to sanctions that might lead to cohesive action. National or state policy is all too often a mish-mash of statutory actions taken by small groups of legislators whose principal aim in formulating the statutes was to serve organized groups or the localities they represent. Almost everyone gets something, but there is no clear policy direction, and a great deal of overlap, duplication, and lack of coordination occur.

The solution? Students of the problem suggest some combination of discipline and central control. They see strong political parties, such as those found in Europe, as the best source of discipline. Political scientist Leon Epstein, however, believes that disciplined parties are unlikely ever to take hold in the United States because candidate-centered elections are deeply rooted in the culture and supported by elected officials.[24]

Expectations about the potential strength of American political parties should be modest, but several reforms have been proposed to enhance their role in financing campaigns. For example, it might be possible to increase the limits on direct national party contributions from $5,000 per election for House candidates to $15,000, and from $17,500 to $30,000 for Senate candidates, and to increase or remove altogether the limits on party spending for other campaign services, such as polling and advertising. Epstein regards such proposals as reasonable and potentially effective because they acknowledge that election financing is the principal area in which contemporary American parties could exert significant influence over the political process.[25] Invigorated national parties might push the government to act more efficiently.

Another approach to discipline is what political scientist Theodore Lowi called "juridical democracy." [26] What Lowi had in mind was that Congress should be prevented from passing so many vague, ambiguous laws. The Supreme Court could take the first step by resurrecting the reasoning it used in declaring unconstitutional Franklin Roosevelt's National Industrial Recovery Act. The Court said that policies that delegate power to administrative agencies without defining the precise standards that should be used during implementation are invalid under the Constitution.[27] Lowi would like to see this logic applied to modern statutes that fail to specify the rules of implementation and therefore convey vast discretionary power to administrative agencies. Presidents could take another step in the right direction by refusing to sign vague laws. These types of actions, it is believed, would force Congress to discipline itself to enact statutes with clear standards. Lowi also would have Congress periodically review all its laws to prevent overlap, duplication, and other inefficiencies.[28]

Although many legislators claim to endorse the principles of juridical democracy, few have allowed them to affect the way they make policy. However, several conservative judges, including Chief Justice William Rehnquist, have shown an interest in trying to define the limits of legislative delegation. The Rehnquist Court may challenge some of Congress's most open-ended regulatory and service delivery statutes.

Another reform proposal that would complement stronger parties by enhancing the power of presidents is to increase the term of House members from two years to four and possibly to decrease Senate terms to four years. The idea is to tie congressional electoral fortunes more directly to those of presidents, who have an obvious stake in emphasizing party loyalty; and, perhaps more important, to do away with midterm elections, which almost invariably contribute to gridlock among policy makers, because the president's party tends to lose seats. Such a change would encourage a more national outlook among House members and should reduce their obsession with reelection, casework, and pork-barrel policies.

A different gridlock-breaking device is the line-item veto. Governors in forty-three states have this power, and President Ronald Reagan stated repeatedly that he wanted it so that he could eliminate wasteful spending and reduce federal deficits. In 1985 Senator Mack Mattingly, R-Ga., introduced legislation that would have given the president an item veto over appropriations bills on a two-year trial basis. The measure was derailed in the Senate by a filibuster organized by Appropriations Committee chairman Mark Hatfield, R-Ore., and it was never given serious consideration in the House. Another proposal would allow an item veto to be overridden by a majority, rather than a two-thirds, vote of Congress.[29]

State-level experience with the item veto is difficult to apply to the national government for two reasons. The specific nature of the item veto powers of governors varies from state to state, and most states are constitutionally bound to balance their budgets.[30] Nevertheless, the item veto would be a powerful addition to the presidential arsenal of policy-making weapons. It would give presidents the threat to veto pet projects of legislators and thereby enhance presidential bargaining power. Whether this change would result in greater government efficiency and spending reductions is less clear and would depend on the nature of presidential policy objectives. Governors have used the item veto most frequently when they faced majorities of the opposition party; such usage confirms the suspicion that a presidential item veto would be used mainly for partisan purposes.[31]

Competence

Another set of standards for evaluation involves the competence of institutional actors. Are American policy makers knowledgeable and skilled enough to accomplish their tasks? Most elected officials are lawyers or businessmen, which means that, on average, they are well educated. State and local politics traditionally serve as the first test of aspiring politicians' interest and ability, and the more successful move on to Congress or state executive positions. Those who make it that far tend to stay in politics a long time. They are career politicians and policy makers.

Legislatures. The U.S. Congress stands out among the national legislatures in the world for the low turnover of its members and its preponderance of lawyers—nearly 50 percent in recent Congresses, whereas in most West European countries lawyers comprise about 20 percent of the legislatures. Most European legislatures include more journalists, teachers, intellectuals, and blue-collar workers than the U.S. Congress.[32] Low turnover among legislators would seem to earn Congress low marks for representativeness and accountability, but high marks for competence, although much depends upon what kind of competence is sought. American legislators know a good deal about their specialized committee decisions, but tend to be weak when it comes to formulating long-term answers to major national or international questions.

Bureaucracies. The American bureaucracy is not generally regarded as one of the the most professional or competent in the world. The civil service system ensures a certain level of competence, but training for public service is not taken as seriously in the United States, nor are career civil service positions prized as highly as they are in Western Europe. In France, for example, top civil service jobs have been controlled for years by elite Parisian families who go to special schools and see themselves as guardians of the national interest.[33] Except for the Foreign Service, most American administrators see themselves as employees of a specific agency or department, rather than as members of a corps of public servants. The prevailing view is that the American civil service system encourages mediocrity rather than excellence; the alleged shortcomings make bureaucracies easy targets for politicians and journalists. The situation is neatly captured in a survey of people who had recently dealt with a bureaucratic agency. Seventy-one percent of those polled thought their particular problem had been handled well, but only 30 percent had a generally favorable impression of bureaucratic performance.[34]

Bureaucratic reforms at the national and state levels typically revolve around the same themes: providing incentives for better performance, making it easier for managers to fire unproductive employees, establishing clear lines of authority, and improving the image of public employees. In 1978, at President Jimmy Carter's behest, Congress passed a major civil service reform act. This legislation created the Senior Executive Service (SES), which is composed of career executives with outstanding records who were willing to trade tenure and job security with a particular agency for the chance to get large bonuses and faster promotions by filling in wherever they were needed most in the executive branch. The new law also required agencies to make performance assessments of all their employees and use these appraisals as the basis for firing incompetents and rewarding strong performers.

Those who have assessed the results of these changes agree that they have been minor. The SES has not been used consistently by presidents and department secretaries as a source of talented, neutral managers, mostly because top executive branch officials were not looking for neutral managers to help them run their agencies. A distressingly high percentage of senior executives have been successfully recruited by the private sector in what some regard as a serious government "brain drain."[35] The employee performance assessments have been difficult to develop, are viewed negatively by nearly all federal workers, and have not resulted in noticeably higher firing rates. Merit pay systems have been very difficult to implement, especially in agencies undergoing budget cuts, and merit pay does not appear to be a primary motivator for employees.[36]

The Civil Service Reform Act of 1978 was developed by a staff of more than 100, most of whom were career government employees. Not surprisingly, President Reagan decided to take a different approach when he set up his commission to study the federal bureaucracy. He brought in approximately 160 business people under the direction of J. Peter Grace and turned them loose on the bureaucracy to find ways to improve management and cut costs. They produced forty-seven separate reports packed with nearly 2,500 recommendations on more than 180 distinct issues.[37]

To achieve better management the commission recommended centralizing functions, such as research and development, information collection and transmission, employee training, and personnel and financial management. Central control would be exercised through a newly created Office of Federal Management, which would be part of the Executive Office of the President and would replace the Office of Management and Budget (OMB). These recommendations stemmed from the Grace Commission's inclination to view the federal government as one very large organization, rather than as a series of organizations.

The cost-cutting proposals included major reductions in employee benefits (retirement, health, and sick leave), cutbacks in the number of low- and mid-level employees and their salaries, more contracting out and privatization of government services, and better use of pay incentives to motivate performance, especially for top executives. The commission's diagnosis was basically that the bureaucracy was heavy with clerical employees and middle managers, who were overcompensated relative to their private sector counterparts, but it acknowledged that top managers were undercompensated. The commission estimated that if its recommendations were acted upon, $425 billion could be saved over a three-year period. A separate assessment by the General Accounting Office (GAO) and the Congressional Budget Office (CBO) estimated the potential savings at just under $100 billion.[38] The Grace Commission was criticized for being myopic and simplistic because it brought all sorts of business-oriented biases into its analysis of government operations. Congress largely ignored its recommendations. However, the Office of Personnel Management (OPM), which was created by the 1978 reform, tried to implement a number of Grace Commission recommendations, such as linking pay to productivity, during the Reagan administration.[39]

Judiciary. The power and prestige of American courts are unrivaled in the world. They do far more than merely apply laws to specific cases; the courts make policy. Although many people are made uneasy by the extent of judicial intervention, it is not clear that the courts' major policy-making role can be greatly diminished. Warren Burger and William Rehnquist have been outspoken critics of judicial activism, but under their leadership, and with conservative Republican presidents making the last eight appointments, the Supreme Court made many important policy decisions. There seem to be too many laws, too many precedents, and too many litigants with standing for the Court to make a dramatic reversal in its policy-making role.

One way to ensure judicial competence is to improve the quality of appointments to the bench. Chief executives can appoint advisory panels to make recommendations; groups of citizens and legal professionals then narrow the list of potential nominees to candidates with outstanding records and abilities. The use of advisory panels would not eliminate partisan considerations, but could ensure that only truly competent individuals are considered. President Carter created panels of this sort to assist him with circuit court appointments, a practice that was dropped by President Reagan.

The proper connection between the law and science is of increasing interest in modern society, and the competence of judges is tested as they confront highly technical questions. Agencies like the Environmental Protection Agency (EPA) make complex scientific assessments about what industries can and should do to comply with environmental statutes, and these assessments often are contested in court. These cases can be difficult for judges. Although they are inclined to defer to agency expertise on technical matters, they maintain a role for themselves in taking a "hard look" at the evidence and the procedures an agency employed in making its assessment.[40] However, reviewing the adequacy of evidence presented on whether automobile emission technology permits industry compliance with legislated emission standards can involve the judges in issues beyond their expertise.[41]

Appeals court judge Harold Leventhal, who had extensive experience with such matters, proposed that judges hire scientific experts to serve as aides in highly technical cases. The aides would not judge the adequacy of agency rulings, but assist judges "in understanding problems of scientific methodology and in assessing the reliability of tests conducted by the agency in light of specific criticisms."[42] Such individuals would operate like special consultants or law clerks, in that their advice to judges would not be a matter of legal record, and they would not normally be cross-examined.[43]

Judges must also be able to understand and evaluate social science evidence in deciding certain cases. As noted in chapter 7, judges, using this kind of evidence, issued decrees that prescribed specific changes in schools, mental health institutions, and prisons. When judges take over administrative functions, questions naturally arise as to the basis on which their decisions are made. How many prisoners in a given space are too many? What level of integration in a city's schools must be achieved to protect the constitutional rights of children? Some observers suggest that judges convene panels of social science experts to advise them on such questions, as Leventhal suggested in environmental policy.[44] But it is doubtful that social science knowledge is sufficiently reliable or predictive to serve as an institutionalized source of "facts" on which to base legal decisions.[45] However, as long as the panels of social scientists are confined to an advisory role, and their comments to judges are revealed to the attorneys in a case and subject to challenge, there is probably nothing harmful in this sort of change in judicial procedure.

Chief Executives. If national politics are the leading edge of American politics, then presidential experiences should shed some light on the future for governors and mayors. One problem is that the public relations aspects of the job have become so dominant in the media age that competence is now what good looks used to be—a desirable quality, but not necessary. Chief executives can be, and are, packaged and sold all over the country. The more visible and salient the politics, the more likely it is that public relations specialists will dominate. In the United States, chief executive politics is the most visible form of politics and, therefore, the most prone to deceptive appearances.

Successful chief executives must be able to perform their many difficult political and administrative tasks with many people watching and waiting to exploit every failing, public and private. Furthermore, in a nation of divided rule and undisciplined parties, chief executives lack the authority to do what they would like. Their leadership, as has long been evident to insiders, is more a matter of symbolism than substance. The ability to engage successfully in symbolic rhetoric in front of huge, but usually remote, audiences is rapidly becoming the primary qualification for chief executives. There are people with substantive knowledge of politics and policy who are also skilled in the use of symbolic rhetoric. But the likelihood is low of finding someone with extraordinary ability when their qualifications are defined mainly by public relations criteria. This note of caution should go out to states and localities. So far they have benefited, in terms of the competence and integrity of their chief executives, since their politics became more visible and competitive. But they may be reaching the top of the curve that plots the relationship between money spent during campaigns and the competence of officials elected.

At the national level the enormous gap between presidential rhetoric and presidential performance seems likely to remain a constant. Reforms aimed at strengthening political parties by reducing the number of primaries and increasing the power of party elites in the selection of candidates seem unlikely to reverse the basic trend, even if adopted. The irony is that the Founding Fathers went to great lengths to find an appropriate device, the electoral college, for selecting a president precisely because they wanted to have someone who was competent, but not necessarily popular.

It was not all that long ago—just prior to 1940—that state governments were weak and, in many cases, corrupt. Governors' powers were limited; their offices were poorly staffed; money and favor-trading pervaded legislatures; and the bureaucracy was filled with patronage appointees who did more political work than government work. A good deal of progress has been made since then. Governors have been granted broader powers, and they exercise them more vigorously. State legislatures sit longer, and legislators are better paid and less corrupt. Bureaucracies have been enlarged and revamped, with most appointees governed by merit systems. Innovative policies are coming from the states: education reform, far-reaching environmental statutes, welfare-for-work programs, requirements that businesses provide day care for their employees' children, joint public and private economic development efforts, and others. The states are also the source of trend-setting initiatives and referenda, and these forms of public expression are now an accepted part of state politics. As a result, respect for state governments is growing.

Most big city governments also have become much more professional in outlook and practice. In comparative terms, subnational governments in the United States continue to stand out in terms of the authority they have and the services they provide. Nevertheless, in polls taken during the 1970s and 1980s, citizens consistently have expressed more confidence in the federal government's effectiveness than they do in that of either state or local governments.[46]

Board Rooms. Private sector competence and effectiveness are difficult to characterize in general terms. The country has experienced a steady stream of economic difficulties since the 1960s, and at least some of these problems can be attributed to private sector decisions and practices. Still, in comparison to most of the rest of the world, Americans enjoy a very high standard of living, and there are consistent signs of innovation and vitality in the private sector.

American industry has depended for years on the high-volume manufacture of standardized products by workers who performed repetitive tasks for union-negotiated wages. Consensus is growing that this production style cannot compete effectively against European and Japanese systems that are more flexible and yield higher quality products, or against cheaper systems, organized along American lines, in developing countries. The slow death of the U.S. steel industry testifies to this fact. Most analysts attribute the demise of the one-time giant of American business to the failure of corporate leaders to modernize plants and change their product orientation soon enough to avert disaster.

Although it has been struggling, the domestic automobile industry looks as if it will survive. That struggle is reflected in numerous plant closings and layoffs, the increasing number of production facilities relocated in foreign countries, and the increasing number of foreign automobile companies with plants in the United States. As in the steel industry, management appears to have been rigid and backward-looking to the point of giving more innovative competitors a decided advantage. However, problems of this sort are to be expected in market economies, and they can even provide valuable lessons for the future.

The experience of the steel and automobile industries, for example, seems to have led to a new consensus about the importance of investment in infrastructure, research and development, and methods to improve worker productivity. Most Americans believe the future of U.S. industry rests with high technology products, telecommunications, and farming, in which the United States has what economists call "comparative advantage." The private sector has become much more attentive to international markets, a fitting development because that is where the fate of American industry will be determined.

Summary

The competence of American policy makers is not the main issue with regard to institutional performance. The more fundamental issue is political will or the lack thereof. Overall, one of the greatest failings of American public institutions is their indecisiveness. This failing is obvious to anyone who has studied Congress, where indecision in the form of stalling, ambiguous statutory language, symbolic responsiveness, and passing the buck has been raised to an art. Former Ohio State football coach Woody Hayes always explained his reluctance to use the forward pass by saying, "There are three things that can happen when you pass—completion, incompletion, and interception—and two of them are bad." This philosophy captures the essence of legislators' attitudes: faced with the choice between taking forceful action to resolve a problem, which could be ineffective or unpopular, or using one of their polished methods of delay, obfuscation, and pacification, they will invariably choose the latter.

Indecisiveness is not simply a product of the fear of making mistakes. It also stems from the fixation that elected officials have with public opinion and the extraordinary role played by interest groups in American politics. The socialization of conflict and increased public and group participation in decision making have produced, in a political system of fragmented power, more gridlock than direction, which is another way of saying that democratic decision making is cumbersome. Powerful groups in society often disagree about the steps that should be taken to resolve problems. The government apparatus is designed to reflect such disagreement, and it does, through inaction. This inaction then becomes the target of reformers and other critics because chief executives are almost always unsuccessful in charting a clear course of government policy, bureaucrats are paranoid because they never know when elected officials are going to turn on them, and the public is confused and disillusioned.

But overly harsh judgments about the performance of American political institutions smack of cynicism. In this postindustrial age, government institutions of all sorts face vastly expanded policy agendas. The rapidity of change in society denies policy-making institutions any opportunity to rest on their laurels. A steady stream of demands can be heard from groups who want more or less from government, as technological and social changes alter the environment within which they operate. As the government has taken on new tasks and sought to satisfy more demands, its old responsibilities have not withered away. Instead, the earlier commitments usually have become permanent. The inability to shed old baggage is another reason why government institutions are reluctant to take on new problems. This reluctance to act has a positive side: it reduces the chances of making big mistakes.

The reform impulse enjoys continuing popularity in the United States because it offers methods for overcoming governmental problems that will not cause a great deal of pain. Americans are always searching for a "quick fix." But the reality of change is that it is slow and that it is a cumulative process rather than a single decisive act. Some of the most significant reforms, such as equal rights for women and minorities, have followed a long painful course, with the courts pushing over an extended period of time and the elective institutions often resisting. Most important political changes or reforms involve a redistribution of political power or privilege, and such changes come slowly in a democratic society.

In many ways the question is whether private sector performance is rewarding enough to justify a government that is so timid that it rarely acts in a disruptive way. Everyone says they want "the people" to decide the answer, but are the people in any position to decide? Are alternatives stated in a way that people can understand and make reasoned judgments about what is in society's best interest? In general, the answer to these questions is no, primarily because a good deal of what the people know has been packaged for them by people who have a vested interest in keeping things much as they are. Nevertheless, history makes clear that when conditions get bad enough, decisive popular action is likely. In a free society widespread suffering can lead to strong expressions of citizen preference and significant changes in institutions and policies. Citizen inattentiveness to politics and government and policy gridlock is an indication of relative prosperity. Perhaps there is some wisdom in letting peoples' sense of economic well-being determine the government's policy.

Notes

1. For the classic statements of pluralist theory, see Robert A. Dahl, *Who Governs?* (New Haven, Conn.: Yale University Press, 1963); or Nelson W. Polsby, *Community Power and Political Theory* (New Haven, Conn.: Yale University Press, 1963). For the classic critiques of the pluralist position, see Peter Bachrach and Morton S. Baratz, "Two Faces of Power," *American Political Science Review* 56 (December 1962); or Theodore J. Lowi, *The End of Liberalism*, 2d ed. (New York: W. W. Norton, 1979).

2. See Herbert A. Simon, *Administrative Behavior: A Study of Decision-Making Processes in Administrative Organizations* (New York: Macmillan, 1957); or James G. March and Herbert A. Simon, *Organizations* (New York: John Wiley & Sons, 1964).

3. Jane Mansbridge, *Beyond Adversary Democracy* (Chicago: University of Chicago Press, 1983); Benjamin R. Barber, *Strong Democracy: Participatory Politics for a New Age* (Berkeley: University of California Press, 1984).

4. See Walter H. Plosila and David N. Allen, "State Sponsored Seed Venture Capital Programs: The Pennsylvania Experience," *Policy Studies Review* 6 (February 1987): 529-537; and Walter H. Plosila, "A Comprehensive and Integrated Model: Pennsylvania's Ben Franklin Program," in *Technological Innovation*, ed. D. O. Gray and W. Hetener (Amsterdam: New Holland, 1986), 261-272.

5. For the most widely recognized statement of the industrial policy position, see Ira C. Magaziner and Robert B. Reich, *Minding America's Business: The Decline and Rise of the American Economy* (New York: Harcourt Brace Jovanovich, 1982).

6. See Ross K. Baker, "The Bittersweet Courtship of Congressional Democrats and Industrial Policy" (Paper presented at the Annual Meeting of the Midwest Political Science Association, Chicago, Illinois, April 1986).

7. John Carroll et al., "Economic Development Policy: Why Rhode Islanders Rejected the Greenhouse Compact," in *State Government* 58 (Fall 1985): 110-112.

8. The most important case in this area was *Baker v. Carr*, 369 U.S. 186 (1962).

9. For figures on the bureaucracy, see Randall B. Ripley and Grace A. Franklin, *Congress, the Bureaucracy and Public Policy*, 3d ed. (Homewood, Ill.; Dorsey Press, 1984), 39; for Congress, see Robert L. Lineberry, *Government in America*, 3d ed. (Boston: Little, Brown, 1986), 364; on the courts, see Everett Carll Ladd, *The American Polity*, 2d ed. (New York: W. W. Norton, 1987), 290; and Sheldon Goldman and Thomas Jahnige, *The Federal Courts as a Political System*, 3d ed. (New York: Harper & Row, 1985), 55. Corporate figures were taken from *Business Week*, June 22, 1987, 72-78; and *Wall Street Journal*, July 17, 1987, 21.

10. Robin Toner, "Gains Predicted for Women in Races for Statewide Office," *New York Times*, May 19, 1986, A1, B7.

11. Figures were taken from Ripley and Franklin, *Congress, the Bureaucracy and Public Policy*, 39; Lineberry, *Government in America*, 364; Ladd, *American Polity*, 290; Goldman and Jahnige, *Federal Courts*, 55; and *The State of Black America* (New York: National Urban League), 1987.

12. See *Business Week*, June 22, 1987, 72-78.

13. See Goldman and Jahnige, *Federal Courts*, 55.

14. See *Business Week*, June 22, 1987, 72-78.

15. See Gerald Pomper, ed., *The Election of 1984* (Chatham, N.J.: Chatham House, 1985), 22.

16. See "Clashing Plans for Campaign Reform," *National Journal*, Feb. 21, 1987, 420; and Maxwell Glen, "On the Front Burner," *National Journal*, Oct. 25, 1986, 2560-2563.

17. *Buckley v. Valeo*, 424 U.S. 1 (1976).

18. Gary C. Jacobson, *The Politics of Congressional Elections*, 2d ed. (Boston: Little, Brown, 1987), 37.

19. See David Vogel, *Lobbying the Corporation* (New York: Basic Books, 1978), 219-220.

20. Benjamin R. Barber, *Strong Democracy* (Berkeley: University of California Press, 1984), chap. 10.

21. See David Magleby, "Legislatures and the Initiative: The Politics of Direct Democracy," in *State Government* 59 (Spring 1986): 34; and James L. Sundquist, *Constitutional Reform and Effective Democracy* (Washington, D.C.: Brookings Institution, 1986).

22. Barber, *Strong Democracy*, 289-290.

23. See Norman Davis, "Television in Our Courts: The Proven Advantages, the Unproven Disadvantages," in *Judicature* 64 (August 1980): 85-92.

24. Leon D. Epstein, *Political Parties in the American Mold* (Madison: University of Wisconsin Press, 1986).

25. Ibid., chap. 9.

26. Lowi, *The End of Liberalism*, 298.

27. *Schechter Poultry Co. v. United States*, 295 U.S. 495 (1935).

28. Lowi, *End of Liberalism*, chap. 11.

29. See Sundquist, *Constitutional Reform and Effective Government*, 209-215.

30. In some states governors can veto not only appropriations, but also statutory language included in appropriations bills; in other states they can only veto appropriations. In some of the cases where statutory language is covered by the item veto, the veto can be used only to strike language from the bill; in other

cases it can be used to change the language. Some states even allow governors to change appropriations figures, not just to veto them. Additional variations exist. See James J. Gosling, "Wisconsin Item-Veto Lessons," in *Public Administration Review* 46 (July/August 1986): 292-300.

31. See Ibid., 293; and Glen Abney and Thomas Lauth, "The Line Item-Veto in the States: An Instrument of Fiscal Restraint or an Instrument of Partisanship?" in *Public Administration Review* 45 (May/June 1985): 1110-1117.

32. Lawyers and businessmen usually make up a large percentage of European conservative party legislators, while the other parties have many educators, journalists, and political organizers as candidates. See J. Blondel, *Comparative Legislatures* (Englewood Cliffs, N.J.: Prentice-Hall, 1973), 76-91; and *Guardian*, London, England, May 29, 1987.

33. See Ezra Suleiman, *Politics, Power and Bureaucracy in France* (Princeton, N.J.: Princeton University Press, 1974).

34. See Daniel Katz et al., *Bureaucratic Encounters: A Pilot Study in the Evaluation of Government Services* (Ann Arbor, Mich.: Institute for Social Research, 1975), 120-121.

35. See Howard Rosen, *Servants of the People: The Uncertain Future of the Federal Civil Service* (Salt Lake City: Olympus Publishing, 1985), 76.

36. Ibid., 80-81.

37. See Charles T. Goodsell, "The Grace Commission: Seeking Efficiency for the Whole People?" in *Public Administration Review* 44 (May/June 1984): 196, 198.

38. Ibid., 199.

39. For discussions of the Grace Commission's findings, see Charles H. Levine, ed., *The Unfinished Agenda for Civil Service Reform* (Washington, D.C.: Brookings Institution, 1985).

40. Harold Leventhal, "Environmental Decisionmaking and the Role of the Courts," *University of Pennsylvania Law Review* 122 (January 1974): 514.

41. The example is based on *International Harvester Co. v. Ruckelshaus*, 478, F.2d 615 (D.C. Cir. 1973), which is discussed by Leventhal in "Environmental Decisionmaking," 531-543.

42. Ibid., 550.

43. See Ibid., 550-555.

44. See Peter W. Sperlich, "Social Science Evidence in the Courts: Reaching Beyond the Adversary Process," *Judicature* 63 (December/January 1980): 280-289.

45. See David M. O'Brien, "The Seduction of the Judiciary: Social Science and the Courts," *Judicature* 44 (June/July 1980): 8-21.

46. The question was: From which level of government do you feel you get the most for your money—federal, state, or local? In the 1980s the average response has been: federal, 33 percent; state, 23 percent; local, 29 percent. See David R. Berman, *State and Local Politics*, 4th ed. (Boston: Allyn & Bacon, 1984), 13-17.

10 Assessing American Public Policy

The political struggle that yields public policies is not just a game about the exercise and maintenance of power. Whether governments and private corporations produce effective policies and programs profoundly affects the nation and its citizens. At stake are national survival, the quality of life, and the nature of justice in society.

Public policies are developed and implemented by private corporations, courts, legislatures, chief executives, administrative agencies, and citizens. Chapter 9 examined the performance of American political institutions and processes. This chapter considers some fundamental questions. How well do public policies serve the needs and wants of the American people? Does the United States live up to the ideals set forth by elected leaders and the Constitution? Is the nation better off or worse off at the end of the 1980s than it was fifty, twenty-five, or ten years ago? What pressing problems has the nation failed to grapple with effectively? It is no understatement to say that these are difficult questions to answer. A selective report card on the nation's policy accomplishments and failures is offered here; the record is reviewed broadly, and many more questions are raised.

Choosing Yardsticks

What criteria should be applied to an assessment of public policy? What evidence is available to measure policy performance? Against what standards can progress and failure be judged? The question is not just whether the public policy "glass" is half full or half empty, but which glasses should be examined. There are many inherent difficulties in assessing public policy. Following is a discussion of a few of them and how they might be handled.

Principal Policy Goals

Before evaluating any public policy, one must decide what questions to ask, which is not as simple as it sounds. What is important to one observer may not be important to another. People in different circumstances have distinct views of the world, its problems, and public policies. When one asks different questions, one comes to different conclusions. As the old saying goes: where you *stand* depends on where you *sit*.

Consider the diverse experiences and expectations of an inner-city resident and the suburban homeowner whose dwellings may be less than an hour away from each other. The city dweller is more likely to be concerned about crime, public transportation, air quality, over-crowding, and housing. The suburban homeowner is more interested in the state highway system, the availability of safe drinking water, and recreational opportunities.[1]

Public policy concerns also are shaped by the nature of the times. Some goals, such as peace and prosperity, always command attention. Other issues, like drug abuse or education, may seem urgent one year, but less pressing the next. Circumstances change; policies change; new problems arise; or new aspects of old problems are recognized. During the late 1960s, for example, Americans were enmeshed in a harrowing struggle over the rights of black Americans to enjoy the same public facilities, schools, mass transportation, restaurants, and parks as white Americans. The importance of guaranteeing civil rights has not diminished, but the policy questions have changed. Once the question of public accommodations was more or less settled, policy makers and citizens could try to decide how far the government should go in promoting economic and social opportunities for minority groups.

Conceptions about the proper role of government provide the framework for evaluations of public policy. The question of how extensively government should be involved in American life is highly controversial, and the answer changeable. Should the government provide food, shelter, and clothing to homeless Americans? Should the government tell private corporations where they can build factories and office buildings, regardless of the impact on transportation and water quality? Should government officials tell employers what kinds of people they should hire, who should be promoted, and when? Because people disagree about what government ought to do, they often disagree about what governments actually accomplish.

Despite disagreement about whether government should increase its involvement, reform programs, or get out of the way, there is fundamental agreement on the nation's principal public policy aspirations.[2] They are (1) to defend the nation; (2) to achieve sustained economic growth; (3) to ensure equal opportunity; (4) to provide a "safety net" for the disadvantaged and senior citizens; and (5) to protect the environment. This assessment of American public policies is organized around these five broad goals.

The stability of these central policy goals throughout modern American history reflects a widespread consensus about government responsibilities in American political culture. In contrast to other nations, battles in American politics usually take place over means, not ends. Public officials fight fiercely about how basic values will be expressed and defined in practice, but almost always there is little conflict over the values.

Most political disputes occur at the margins, rather than over fundamental principles. What is at stake in these struggles is not whether public policies should help the poor, for example, but how much and in what way. Lawmakers often fight over subtle differences in the language of a statute or an appropriations bill because they know that their decisions may one day have profound consequences. Only in rare instances, such as the New Deal of President Franklin Roosevelt, do major changes occur quickly.

Weighing Evidence

How does one know whether government policies and programs are effective? Reliable, objective information is available for evaluating many policies. Government agencies and an army of public and private analysts monitor unemployment, inflation, trade balances, life expectancy, race relations, the quality of the environment, and so on. Knowledge about the efficiency and effectiveness of public policies has increased substantially since the 1960s. Policy makers can be better informed than ever before about conditions in society and the possible effects of their actions.[3]

In spite of these gains, policy makers still may not know enough about the effectiveness of public policies to reach sound conclusions. Too often they are unwilling to use information that is available. It is embarrassing to discover that a once-ballyhooed policy does not work; therefore many lawmakers do not ask probing questions, authorize careful evaluations, or listen to disconcerting evidence. Politicians often are fixated on who gets what, when, and how, instead of the real bottom line: does the policy work?

Establishing cause and effect relationships between a government action and a societal consequence is very difficult. If millions of Americans are illiterate, should the schools be blamed, or is the high rate of illiteracy due to the high numbers of immigrants pouring into the country? If minorities increase their membership in the professions, should credit accrue to civil rights laws or are there simply more minority applicants who are better prepared? Because a single government policy cannot be isolated from other events, trends, or policies, the specific impacts of government decisions may go undetected.

Making Judgments

After evidence is gathered about the impacts of a policy or program, standards must be applied to judge success or failure. For example, the unemployment rate among Americans is carefully calculated and reported each month, but the raw data do not speak for themselves. Is a 6 percent unemployment rate alarming or acceptable? Sound public policy conclusions should not be based upon the optimism or pessimism of the observer, but where do analysts turn for standards that yield reasonable judgments?

The determination of standards begins with an examination of the objectives of the policy. However, an analyst must be sensitive to distinguish between pronouncements and results. Public laws, regulations, and judicial decrees state objectives; they are not automatically translated into positive outcomes. Political leaders frequently engage in hyperbole, claiming that new laws and policies will solve longstanding problems. But the solution may not work in practice, or the problem may be much more difficult than originally envisioned. Therefore, careful observers ignore the rhetoric and examine the impacts of policies on people, institutions, and society.

A thorough evaluation of public policy also requires looking beyond contemporary policy debates. Policy makers should anticipate and address problems before they become unmanageable crises or potential catastrophes. Only governments have the broad powers to act on behalf of an entire state or nation. Scientists warn, for example, that the ozone layer that shields the earth from harmful ultraviolet rays is gradually diminishing, causing the earth's temperature to rise. Unless use is curtailed of pollutants that harm the ozone, the earth's fragile ecology could be severely damaged. Problems of this magnitude exceed the scope of individuals, corporations, or single nations.

Public perceptions should be considered in judging policy performance, but analysts must resist the temptation to conclude that public satisfaction is all that matters. Public opinions about government policies are often based on fragmentary or unreliable information. In addition, policies should not be judged according to whether an individual feels personally better off than before. The perspective of most citizens is narrow, limited to their families, jobs, and neighborhoods, but what is good for one family may not be good for another family. Majority preferences may be insensitive to minority rights and needs. Indeed, disadvantaged minorities often receive benefits they would probably be denied if public policies were based exclusively on majority sentiment.

Sound conclusions about the efficacy of public policy are possible when meaningful comparisons are found to put the naked evidence into perspective. Placing current policy performance in historical perspective is particularly valuable. Taken as a raw number, a 6 percent unemployment rate does not reveal much. Its significance is established only by comparison with peak levels of nearly 11 percent in 1982 and with the lower than 6 percent rate of the previous three decades. Based on the data, one could conclude that the unemployment rate is moving in the right direction, but that it remains troubling.

Comparing U.S. policy performance with experiences in other countries also may be useful, if handled with care. Public health officials need to know, for example, that infant mortality rates are higher in the United States than in seventeen other countries because these data may suggest that Americans have inadequate access to health care. Conversely, Americans find little comfort from the fact that U.S. toxic waste cleanup efforts lead the world; most still would judge U.S. efforts inadequate. Comparisons of different states, communities, and population subgroups also may yield insights. Ideally, analysts would like to know what conditions would have been like without a public policy or program. Because such knowledge is unattainable, analysts often compare states that have programs with those that do not or compare groups in the population that have received services with those that have not. In this way, it may be possible to understand what difference the program made.

The following review of five principal policy goals examines how the United States measures up by comparing current performance with announced objectives and by looking at historical and cross-national comparisons where appropriate. The impacts of public policies on different groups of Americans are highlighted. Each section recounts accomplishments, failures, and unanswered questions. The conclusion discusses the challenges facing the nation and its leaders in the years ahead.

Defend the Nation

The U.S. Constitution declares that a primary purpose of government is to "provide for the common defense." Nothing could be more fundamental than ensuring the survival of the nation, protecting its vital economic interests, and preserving the freedom of its citizens. U.S. territory has not been the scene of armed conflict since the Civil War, but Americans and their leaders have had grave concerns about the nation's security since World War II. These anxieties derive from the perception that in the age of nuclear weapons the Soviet Union and other foreign powers are potential adversaries capable of seriously threatening U.S. economic interests and national security.

Consequently, since the end of the war a bipartisan consensus has existed for maintaining sufficient military power to deter the Soviet Union and other nations from pursuing hostile intentions.[4] The American commitment extends beyond defending U.S. soil, citizens, and overseas investments. U.S. policy makers believe that military force and the threat of nuclear retaliation must be used to protect allies and to counter Soviet attempts to expand its influence. American lives and military resources were spent defending Korea and Vietnam from Communist regimes. In 1988 more than $13.6 billion in U.S. foreign and military aid was distributed throughout the world—to Israel, Egypt, Saudi Arabia, Afghanistan, Nicaragua, and dozens more.

Soldiers and Dollars

Disputes over national security policy often have been heated. They have centered around two broad concerns. First, when should U.S. military forces be involved in hostile actions? American involvement in Vietnam provoked one of the most damaging internal political conflicts in the nation's history and has had lasting effects. Second, how much conventional military and nuclear weapons does the country need? Critics argue that the military establishment and many U.S. politicians exaggerate the threats posed by the Soviet Union and other nations and that the defense budget is larger than necessary. Supporters of a large defense budget maintain that it is the price that must be paid to protect U.S. interests at home and abroad.

National security policy not only affects the nation's survival and prosperity, it also influences domestic priorities and is influenced by them. The funds that remain after defense spending requirements have been met determine whatever else the government can do, and defense spending consumes nearly one-third of the trillion-dollar federal budget. Strong national security requires the fostering of industries to design and manufacture ships, submarines, tanks, airplanes, and nuclear weapons.

The strength and self-reliance of a nation's economy shapes the strategies that must be taken to defend it. The United States is one of the most independent and self-sustaining nations in the world; it has abundant raw materials necessary for survival and adequate food supplies for the entire population. Yet, the United States depends on other nations for oil and other materials, and it sells its products and services around the world. Hence, U.S. policy makers must be concerned with the political and military situations in dozens of other nations.

Unlike inflation, air pollution, or crime, large segments of the public do not "experience" national security problems, except in times of war. The public must be convinced to support defense spending and military commitments, or the president and Congress may eventually feel compelled to reduce those commitments. A portion of the public also must serve in the military. Since the mid-1970s, U.S. armed forces personnel have been volunteers—a change that reshaped the composition of the military substantially. Soldiers in the modern volunteer army are more likely than in the past to come from low-income, poorly educated, and minority backgrounds.[5]

Since the end of World War II, political leaders have convinced the public that the Soviet Union poses a serious threat to the nation and its allies. The public favors arms control agreements and greater efforts to reduce tensions, but has been willing to pay for a large defense establishment in the meantime.[6] Americans have never been offered an alternative to the postwar defense strategy of nuclear containment and a large worldwide military presence. The candidate with the strongest views against the defense establishment this century was Senator George McGovern, the Democratic nominee for president in 1972. Although he lost in a landslide to Richard Nixon, most observers do not believe McGovern's proposals to slash military spending cost him the election.[7]

Given the prevailing political climate, presidents, members of Congress, and military professionals have a relatively free hand to determine defense policy and the size of the defense establishment. The debate is carried out within the boundaries of broad public support. Policy makers disagree over issues such as the amount of defense budget increases and how military commitments can be most effectively carried out, but few credible voices call for significant reductions in military spending or for a less ambitious U.S. foreign policy. However, policy makers operate under much heavier constraints when it comes to putting American men and women into dangerous military operations.

The size of the defense budget is based on perceptions of risk and assumptions about the strategies that will be most effective in minimizing those risks. Unlike government entitlement programs that can precisely define needy populations and spend accordingly, the task of constructing defense budgets is a deadly guessing game. If military power is inadequate to protect vital economic interests, the problem may not be apparent until it is too late to do anything about it. How serious is the military threat posed by the Soviet Union and other foreign powers? To what extent should the United States shield other nations against military attack? Should the United States respond to all situations in which potential adversaries wield military influence, even in small countries like Angola and Nicaragua? How many weapons are needed in the U.S. strategic defense arsenal to discourage an attack from the Soviet Union?

The decline and resurgence of U.S. military expenditures since the end of World War II reflect changing perceptions of the Soviet threat.

From 1945 through the 1960s, military spending constituted nearly 9 percent of the gross national product (GNP). By the 1970s the defense budget had dropped to 6 percent of the GNP, despite the expenses connected with the Vietnam War. By 1980, the end of Jimmy Carter's administration, defense had fallen to 5.3 percent of the GNP.[8] Defense spending accounted for more than 50 percent of the federal budget in 1960, 42 percent in 1970, and only 23 percent in 1980.[9]

The gradual drop in military spending was spurred by détente between the United States and the Soviet Union. Détente—a French word meaning a lessening of tensions between nations—was promoted by President Nixon during the 1970s and was reinforced by arms treaties, the normalization of relations with the People's Republic of China, and the end of the Vietnam War. The downward trend of defense spending reversed toward the end of the Carter administration. President Carter's final budget, for fiscal year 1981, proposed a 5 percent real increase in defense spending—enough to boost it 5 percent above inflation.[10]

Ronald Reagan campaigned for the presidency in 1980 by promising major increases in military spending. He scoffed at détente, saying such policies were based on false assumptions about Soviet intentions. He pointed to America's humiliation over the taking of hostages in Iran as proof that the United States had become a weaker nation. Once elected, he referred to the Soviet Union as the "evil empire."

During Reagan's presidency, the United States accomplished the largest sustained peacetime expansion of military spending in its history. By fiscal year 1988, the military budget had more than doubled over the fiscal 1980 outlays; its share of the federal budget had risen from 23 percent in 1980 to 32 percent, and its share of the GNP had jumped from 5.3 percent in 1980 to 6.4 percent.[11] Most of the increased spending went to purchase or modernize weapons systems and supplies.

How Much Is Enough?

Is the United States more capable of protecting itself and projecting its influence around the world than it was before the military expansion? Were the benefits worth the costs? The Reagan administration argued that the massive military buildup of the 1980s brought the Soviet Union to the bargaining table and brought about an arms control agreement—the first to result in the destruction of an entire class of nuclear weapons. Critics maintain, however, that the Soviet Union was willing to bargain because of its need to reduce defense spending and to improve relations with the rest of the industrialized world.

Despite the reductions in intermediate-range nuclear weapons, the strategic nuclear defense arsenal on the ground, in submarines, and in bombers remains larger than ever. The United States has embarked on the development of a defensive weapons system, popularly called "star wars," that could cost billions more. Star wars' boosters promise it would substantially undermine the current Soviet threat, but detractors maintain that it will launch another escalation in the arms race with the Soviet Union.

For all the additional spending, the United States does not seem to be substantially more capable of accomplishing its foreign policy objectives than it was before the buildup. Not all problems of national security can be solved by pouring billions of dollars into the military establishment. The Soviet Union, Iran, Libya, and other nations remain hostile to U.S. policy interests. Military might does little or nothing to deter suicidal terrorist attacks on U.S. citizens and military personnel. Despite the large show of force to protect civilian oil and gas tankers moving through the Persian Gulf, including aircraft carriers and other warships, dozens of tankers have been damaged or destroyed by small Iranian ships.

Finally, American politicians are always reluctant to engage U.S. forces in armed conflict, especially if a confrontation with the Soviet Union is risked. The Soviet Union continued its occupation of Afghanistan despite U.S. protests and refusal to sell the Russians grain. After terrorists killed more than 200 U.S. Marines in Lebanon, the remaining troops were withdrawn immediately. President Reagan was unable to convince the public and Congress that substantial military aid to the opponents of the government of Nicaragua was justified as a means to protect vital U.S. interests. Indeed, Americans are skeptical of involving American soldiers in conflicts that do not directly affect U.S. territory. Public opinion ran strongly against military involvement when World War II began in Europe; U.S. troops were not committed until after the Japanese attacked Pearl Harbor in late 1941. Large segments of the public opposed subsequent military actions involving American armed forces in Korea and Vietnam.[12] In fact, one lasting legacy of the war in Southeast Asia is the so-called Vietnam syndrome—a deep distrust of U.S. military involvement in other nations. Such concerns continue to shape public opposition to U.S. involvement in Lebanon, Nicaragua, and the Persian Gulf.[13]

Difficult challenges confront U.S. national security policy. Can the armed forces be made more effective in meeting new threats to U.S. interests? Specifically, how can the United States protect itself from terrorism and further hostage-taking incidents that endanger U.S. citizens and warp U.S. foreign policy? Can the spiraling cost of nuclear weapons be reduced through additional arms control agreements with the Soviet Union? Can the United States use its influence to promote freedom, human rights, and democracy throughout the world? A consensus has yet to emerge on how to answer these troublesome questions.

Achieve Sustained Economic Growth

Sustained economic growth is a central policy goal of all governments. This broad goal subsumes several specific economic objectives: rising standards of living and wealth, low levels of unemployment and inflation, increasing productivity of the work force, expanding exports, and so on. Policy makers of all stripes want to promote economic growth and vitality; this goal is as universal as that of defending the nation. Although defense and foreign policy stimulate debate, the sharpest partisan and ideological disputes take place over the extent to which the government can and should manage the economy.

The achievement of economic goals depends, perhaps more than for any other policy objectives, on the policies and financial resources of both the government and the private sector. Government involvement in fostering a healthy economy comes primarily in two forms: *macroeconomic policy* and *investments* in human capital and the nation's physical infrastructure. Macroeconomic policy encompasses matters such as the government's spending and tax policy, the supply and cost of money, and trading policies with other nations. When the economy is functioning at less than full employment, the government can increase public and private spending through fiscal and monetary stimulation, which in turn generates greater demand for goods and services and puts more people to work.[14] Federal Reserve Board decisions that establish interest rates profoundly influence the rate of inflation in the cost of goods and services and the ability of individuals and corporations to raise capital.

Government-sponsored education and research strategies also affect the ability of the nation to achieve its economic goals. Education and training programs translate directly into the quality and productivity of the workforce. America's colleges and universities have produced one of the world's most highly educated populations, but the supply of qualified individuals is not meeting the demand in some fields. The American Electronics Association estimated, for example, that between 1983 and 1987, only half of the 200,000 electrical engineers and computer scientists needed by business and industry would receive degrees.[15]

Government-sponsored research and development activities often generate new products and economic growth. More than half of the approximately $100 billion spent on research and development in the United States is supplied by the federal government. Since 1962 government research in the aerospace industry has yielded numerous products and productivity improvements. For example, the demand for light-weight, reliable circuitry helped spawn the development of microchips that eventually led to the development of the personal computer. Historically, countries with higher growth rates in research and development expenditures also have experienced greater gains in productivity and higher GNPs.[16]

Finally, the quality of the nation's publicly supported infrastructure is vital to a prosperous and expanding economy. But, the level of investment in infrastructure declined by 40 percent per capita between 1965 and 1984. Bridges, roads, and water systems are simply wearing out. A distinguished advisory panel estimated that planned government spending on infrastructure will have to increase by $450 billion before the end of the century to meet urgent needs. Most of the funds for this massive undertaking will be raised and spent by state governments.[17]

Private sector decisions have a direct influence on the size and health of the U.S. economy (chapter 3). Private businesses generate nearly two-thirds of the nation's gross domestic product (GDP) and control virtually all major manufacturing and industrial activities. The cumulative impact of corporate decisions is significant. If General Motors decides to manufacture automobiles for the U.S. market in Mexico rather than in Atlanta, the decision costs Americans thousands of high-paying jobs. Because IBM is the leading manufacturer of computers, its decision to develop faster computer processing equipment enhances the ability of the U.S.-based manufacturers to make faster, more reliable computers that can compete effectively in the world market.

Economic growth also depends on the behavior of investors, workers, and consumers. Workers' productivity and wage demands are important components in economic expansion. The preference of American consumers for imported products, such as Japanese automobiles and electronic equipment, means that billions of American dollars flow to other nations. Japanese consumers also prefer Japanese-manufactured products, even when U.S. products are superior.[18] And some argue that the Japanese government has erected barriers to U.S. goods. Effective government policies promote a prosperous, competitive economy, but many factors are beyond government control.

Mixed Success and an Uncertain Future

The United States has been the world's dominant economic power since the 1950s. American living standards have risen substantially during this period, with the per capita income of Americans doubling.[19] Americans are enjoying more leisure time, and they are retiring at a younger age than previous generations. By many standards the United

States remains an economic powerhouse. Nevertheless, it seems proper to conclude that the record is mixed and the future is uncertain.

Despite its strong showing, the U.S. economy has not always outperformed other nations. Since the mid-1960s, the economies of several countries, including Japan, France, West Germany, Italy, Austria, and Norway grew at faster rates than the U.S. economy.[20] Japan's economy expanded at roughly twice the U.S. growth rate. The spendable earnings of American working people have been declining since 1960.[21] By the mid-1980s, the wages of workers employed in the manufacturing sector in Sweden, West Germany, the Netherlands, and Belgium surpassed earnings of American workers in the same industries.[22]

Although the American standard of living remains high in absolute terms, it is gradually declining relative to other industrialized countries. Life expectancy is lower in the United States than in fourteen other nations. Infant mortality rates are higher than in seventeen other countries,[23] although they have improved since the early 1960s due to the introduction of medical assistance for the poor. The U.S. economy has been plagued with several recessions, periods of either no growth or decline. Severe recessions bringing high levels of unemployment occurred in 1954, 1958, 1975, 1979, and 1982. Since the late 1960s U.S. unemployment levels, on average, have exceeded those of several other nations, including West Germany and the United Kingdom.[24]

Since 1972 the economy has created more than 20 million new jobs to absorb the expanding workforce, but, despite that impressive record, not everyone who wanted to work could find a job.[25] During the 1950s and 1960s, unemployment averaged 4.6 percent; during the 1970s, it climbed to 6.2 percent; and the average for the 1980s has been nearly 8 percent. During the 1982 recession, unemployment reached 10.8 percent—the highest level since World War II. More than 12 million Americans were unable to find jobs. In the late 1980s the unemployment picture brightened, dropping to around 6 percent, but still above the 4 percent expected of a "full employment" economy.[26]

The aggregate figures mask some underlying problems. Several parts of the country have not fully recovered from the last recession. Unemployment levels in some states, including Texas, Louisiana, and Mississippi are twice the national average. And in some metropolitan areas, like Dallas, Flint, Youngstown, the unemployment rate is nearly three times the national level. Not counted in the official unemployment statistics are the more than 1 million "discouraged workers"—people who have given up looking for work because they do not believe any jobs are available—and 6 million part-time workers who would rather be working full time.[27] The reported unemployment figures understate the magnitude of the real demand for jobs by Americans.

Older workers who have lost long-term stable jobs due to changes in the structure of the U.S. economy present another vexing problem. While the service sector—telecommunications, insurance, banking, and restaurants—recovered rapidly from the 1982 recession, the manufacturing sector did not. As a result, many workers were displaced; that is, they lost their jobs permanently. These were usually experienced workers, but without the skills needed for new employment. It was not uncommon for displaced workers to take positions offering lower pay, longer hours, and reduced benefits. Steel, automobile, textile, and machinery workers account for more than half of the estimated 2 million displaced workers. Most of these people live in one of the eight states where the economy is dominated by heavy industry—Illinois, Indiana, Michigan, New Jersey, New York, Ohio, Pennsylvania, and Wisconsin.[28]

The United States also has struggled with inflation in the prices for goods and services for several decades. From 1950 to the mid-1960s prices increased, on average, no more than 2 percent or 3 percent. From 1968 to 1973 prices rose at a 4.6 percent average rate and from 1973 to 1980 at 8.9 percent.[29] Double-digit annual inflation rates were reached in 1974 and 1975 and in the 1980-1981 period.[30] A car that cost $2,000 in 1968 cost more than $12,000 in 1988.

Since reaching peak levels, inflation has fallen to levels no higher than 3 percent to 4 percent per year. Many of the same factors that contributed to the upward spiral of prices contributed to their decline: a surplus of fossil fuels and agricultural commodities, lower mortgage interest rates, and reduced wage demands from workers. If conditions change, upward pressure on inflation could return. The collapse of the oil cartel and the rapid decline in the price of crude oil accounted for nearly half of the decline in inflation from 1980 to 1985.[31] If Middle East oil exporters increase prices or become embroiled in a large-scale war, energy prices and inflation would shoot up again.

The New Economic Agenda

American policy makers are grappling with two relatively new economic difficulties, the burgeoning federal deficit and the decline of America's competitive posture in the world economy. Government policy makers and American citizens will be living with the consequences of these developments for many years, and neither will be easily resolved.

In less than a decade, the federal deficit, which used to be a relatively minor problem, grew to gargantuan proportions—a haunting symbol of ineffective government policy making. Between 1981 and 1988 the total national debt *doubled* to more than $2.3 trillion; it had taken nearly 200 years to accumulate the first trillion dollars of debt.[32] Annual budget deficits soared. In 1968 the federal government ran a deficit of $25 billion in a $178 billion budget.[33] In 1983 the deficit exceeded $200 billion in a $800 billion budget. In 1988, after concerted efforts to reduce spending, the deficit will still exceed $145 billion.[34]

The spectacular growth of federal debt during the 1980s produced an even more spectacular growth in the amount of interest the federal government must pay to service it. Paying interest to government creditors is the largest contributor to the growth of deficits and one of the fastest growing portions of the federal budget. In 1979 interest on the debt was $43 billion; by 1988 it had ballooned to $140 billion. Two-thirds of the money borrowed each year by the Treasury was used merely to meet interest payments. Because larger and larger portions of the annual budget must be set aside to pay investors, the funds available for productive federal spending have diminished.[35]

During the 1980s the federal government paid out about five dollars for every four it collected. In simple terms, Americans got more from government than they paid for. The government borrowed the rest from American and foreign investors. The long-term consequences of continued high deficits go beyond restricting federal spending. Brookings Institution scholars wrote:

If continued over the long run, large budget deficits would either reduce domestic investment [in plant, equipment and other forms of capital] or be financed by increasingly uncertain, and potentially reversible, capital inflow from abroad. In either case, living standards of U.S. citizens would fall.[36]

Although budget deficits have begun to move down from peak levels during the 1980s, serious problems remain. Future generations of policy makers and citizens have been saddled with the responsibility of paying these huge debts.

The struggle of the United States to remain competitive in the world economy may pose an even more difficult problem. America is facing some of the most serious economic challenges of its history. Its rate of technological advance has fallen behind many other industrial nations and even some Third World countries. Once the world's leading exporter, the United States regularly experiences trade deficits in excess of $150 billion. By the 1980s the United States was importing more than half of its televisions, radios, tape recorders, and phonographs. One automobile in four and one-fourth of the steel purchased in the United States were made abroad. During the 1960s foreign competitors held no more than 10 percent of the U.S. market for these products. During the 1970s the U.S. share of the world market for manufactured goods declined by nearly 25 percent, while every other industrialized nation either maintained or increased its share of the world market.[37]

The United States is plagued by declining productivity and skills shortages in its workforce. During the 1950s and early 1960s productivity increased at the healthy rate of more than 3 percent per year. During the 1970s the productivity rate plunged to just over 1 percent, and by 1979 productivity actually had declined. During the 1980s worker productivity rebounded slightly, increasing on average 1.2 percent. The rebound was due to the fact that fewer workers were employed.[38] At the same time, many of the skills demanded in a high-tech economy are apparently in short supply. "Clearly, the competitiveness of U.S. industry is threatened when many of its young workers lack the basic skills to be productive employees," the President's Commission on Industrial Competitiveness reported.[39]

In addition to its home-grown problems, the United States faces stiff competition in the world marketplace. Aggressive businesses from industrialized nations, such as Japan and West Germany, have been joined by efficient new companies from Korea, Hong Kong, Taiwan, and Brazil. Competition from abroad and ineffective public and private policies could lead to a U.S. economy that produces fewer jobs, lower quality jobs, and a reduced standard of living for Americans.

Critics charge that rather than adapting to the new world economy, U.S. policy makers have engaged in "historical preservation." [40] Rather than tackling the underlying problems, U.S. government policy makers and private sector managers have propped up weak industries with protectionist trade barriers that raise the costs of imported goods, loan guarantees that bail out bankrupt corporations, and other short-term expedients.

Although there is bipartisan agreement that the U.S. economy faces serious challenges, little consensus has been reached on the nature and scope of an appropriate government and private sector response.[41] Some argue that America's competitive weakness proves that government should restructure its policies to encourage corporate Darwinism—the survival of the fittest. Others contend that greater government planning and management of the economy is needed to match the coordinated efforts of overseas competitors. Some insist that U.S. industries will compete more effectively on the world scene when government subsidies and trade restrictions are removed entirely. Others maintain that government trade policies should either force foreign countries to open up their markets to U.S. products or shut them out of U.S. markets entirely.

The search for the correct approach to these problems may well dominate America's economic and political agenda for the next several decades. Finding a good solution will not be easy; it may require greater government involvement in the economy than Americans prefer.

Ensure Equal Opportunity

Since the founding of the nation, America's leaders have espoused a commitment to equality of opportunity. But, when the drafters of the Declaration of Independence wrote that "all men are created equal," they did not include blacks, women, and native Americans. Over time, government policies gradually extended political, social, and economic opportunities to groups originally denied them. The Constitution has been amended to ensure political rights for blacks and women. Statutes prohibiting discrimination on the basis of race, gender, ethnicity, and age have been applied to education, employment, housing, voting, and public accommodations.

The nation's moral credo rejects discrimination and advocates equal opportunity, but living up to this code and giving it practical meaning has been as difficult to accomplish as any aspect of American public policy. The battle over racial equality was marked by lynchings, bombings of black churches, and other ugly episodes. The uncomfortable chasm between American ideals and the actual distribution of opportunities and benefits was properly called an American dilemma.[42] Americans place a high value on individual initiative and self-reliance. But, there is a growing awareness that even in a democracy prosperity that is not shared is prosperity soon disdained. Working toward equity and giving people a sense of fairness is the glue that holds a democratic society together. Economist Arthur Okun commented that U.S. society awards

prizes that allow the big winners to feed their pets better than the losers can feed their children. Such is the double standard of a capitalist democracy, professing and pursuing an egalitarian political and social system and simultaneously generating gaping disparities in economic well-being.[43]

The fulfillment of the equal opportunity goal raises difficult questions about what equal opportunity means and how government should promote it.

—Should government guarantees of equal opportunities encompass both the political system *and* the economic system?

—Should government ensure access to opportunity for all *and* redress past discrimination?

—Should government ensure that individuals are able to take advantage of the opportunities available in the society *and* promote greater equality in the distribution of wealth and other social benefits?

Unfulfilled Promise

The United States has made significant strides, especially since the early 1960s. The United States no longer denies women the right to vote or hold office. Blacks and other minorities are no longer barred from voting or seeking office. The U.S. armed forces no longer segregates black and white Americans into separate fighting units. The Supreme Court has declared that school children should be educated in the same schools and classrooms. Congress has determined that Americans must not be discriminated against because of their race, gender, or ethnic origin when they apply to colleges and universities, seek employment or a house, and apply for insurance and bank loans. White Americans have become more racially tolerant.[44]

Despite these significant accomplishments, America remains a society in which millions do not fully enjoy the nation's political, social, and economic benefits.[45] Poverty, homelessness, and hunger remain serious problems in one of the world's most affluent nations. In 1986 more than 30 million people, or 13.6 percent of the population, could not afford the basic necessities of life according to government standards.[46] Poverty has grown more pervasive. After dropping to 11 percent in 1973 from 22 percent in 1960, poverty gradually increased to numbers that exceed the levels before the recession of 1982.[47]

Income and wealth also are unequally distributed. The bottom 20 percent of all U.S. families received only 3.8 percent of the total money income in 1986; the top 20 percent received more than ten times as much, or 46.1 percent of the total.[48] Inequities in the distribution of income have not improved since World War II.[49] Instead, "there has been an increase in income inequality in the United States during the last decade and a half," according to Census Bureau official Gordon Green.[50] The equity of income distribution in America ranks eighth among the eleven members of the Organization for Economic Co-operation and Development, which includes the United Kingdom, Japan, Canada, Australia, and Sweden, among others.[51] The ownership of wealth is even more maldistributed than income: more than three-quarters of all the privately owned wealth is in the hands of 20 percent of the population.[52]

Federal, state, and local tax systems do little to redistribute income, and in some ways they increase inequities. According to Benjamin Page:

The federal income tax is more egalitarian than other taxes. But the progressivity of the actual effective rates—as contrasted with the nominal schedule rates—is rather mild and has been eroded over time. Taxes on the rich are not very high. . . . [V]arious exclusions and exemptions and deductions from taxable income greatly benefit the rich.[53]

The tax code revision of 1986 eliminated millions of poor and near poor Americans from the tax rolls, but even after these major changes tax laws remain inequitable.

People earning the same income often pay very different amounts in federal taxes. High-income Americans may pay less in taxes than people who earn a great deal less. Inequities persist because the tax code contains a host of exclusions, preferences, and deductions. For example, homeowners are permitted to deduct *all* of the interest they pay on mortgages for their primary residence and for a vacation home. The owner of a $60,000 house and the owner of a $5 million mansion can deduct the entire amount of their interest payments from their tax liability. The home mortgage deduction amounts to a direct subsidy of more than $40 billion to high-income individuals. People who rent or have modest mortgage payments receive little or no tax benefits.[54]

If federal income taxes do little to redistribute income from the rich to the poor, payroll taxes and state and local income taxes accomplish the opposite: the more money a person is paid, the lower the percentage of income paid to the government. Social Security taxes, for example, are withheld at a flat rate and only on $45,000 in income. The $250,000-a-year investment banker on Wall Street pays the same amount in Social Security taxes as the $45,000-a-year civil engineer. State and local taxes, which rely heavily on the sales tax, are regressive. People with low incomes pay the same tax rate as those with high incomes. But a larger share of the poor person's income is used to purchase goods and services necessary for survival.[55]

These disparities are especially difficult to justify in a society where economic hardship is not random. Minorities are much more likely to be poor, unemployed, and otherwise disadvantaged than white Americans. In 1986 the poverty rate was 31 percent for blacks and 27 percent for Hispanics, but it was only 11 percent for whites. Approximately one child in five under the age of six lived in poverty during 1986, but 46 percent of black children and 41 percent of Hispanic children were poor.[56]

Unemployment rates follow a similar pattern. In September 1987, for example, the unemployment rate for white adults was around 5 percent, but it was 12 percent for blacks and 8 percent for Hispanics. The picture is even bleaker for young people. During the same month, 15 percent of white teens were unemployed, as opposed to 30 percent of black and Hispanic teenagers.[57]

Women head more than half of all poor families, continuing a trend that has been called the feminization of poverty.[58] Most poor women were widowed or divorced and left without economic support for themselves and their children, and many are unwed mothers. Eighty percent receive no financial support from the child's father. Teen pregnancy rates have jumped by 20 percent since 1970; two-thirds of those mothers will spend at least some time in poverty. Many poor women are poor even though they work full-time, year-round jobs. Because of inflation, the purchasing power of their minimum-wage jobs has eroded by one-quarter in five years.[59]

Progress for minorities has been slow because in many ways, the United States remains a racially segregated society. Minority groups are concentrated in metropolitan areas; they may be kept from living in suburban communities by discriminatory real estate sales practices or the lack of affordable housing for moderate- and low-income individuals. Efforts to desegregate the schools have had limited success. Although the number of black children attending predominantly black schools in the South dropped from 81 percent in 1968 to 57 percent in 1980, black children attending predominantly black schools in the North increased from 67 percent to 80 percent during the same period.[60] Minorities make up more than a fifth of the U.S. population, yet less than 10 percent of U.S. representatives are members of minority groups, and there are no black governors or U.S. senators.

Women have not achieved economic and political parity with men. Women have increased their participation in the workforce from 40 percent in 1970 to more than 50 percent,[61] and laws guaranteeing equal pay for equal work have been passed in many states.[62] But women earn on average sixty-three cents for every dollar earned by men.[63] Women are concentrated in several occupations—teaching, nursing, clerical positions—that pay less than jobs predominantly occupied by men—accountants, salespeople, and laborers—even though the female-dominated jobs require similar skills and training. Although women represent more than half the U.S. population, there are few women in leadership positions in business and industry or government. In 1988 women held only two U.S. Senate seats, two governorships, and twenty-three seats in the U.S. House of Representatives.

Prospects for Change

Strategies promoting social, political, and economic equity have been highly divisive and only moderately successful. The women's movement has failed to obtain ratification for the Equal Rights Amendment to the Constitution. Although the Supreme Court has endorsed the strategy of affirmative action, the practice still is subject to legal challenge and to resistance from many institutions. Inequities in the distribution of income and wealth were not addressed by the tax policy changes of the Reagan administration, and no major party candidate for the presidency in 1988 advanced any bold initiatives to redistribute income in America.

A major impetus for change may come from American business and industry's desire to remain competitive in the world economy. Business and political leaders are beginning to realize that the nation must fully utilize available human resources. For the foreseeable future, a significant portion of entry-level workers will be minorities, immigrants for whom English is a second language, and other low-income individuals.[64] This surge of disadvantaged workers may prompt unprecedented initiatives to bring these individuals into the mainstream of the American economy. Promoting greater equity may be a necessary step toward the realization of a more efficient economy.

Provide a Safety Net

The power of government has not been exercised in a radical redistribution of income and wealth, but American policy makers have erected a network of programs that provide financial support and health care to millions of citizens. Typically, these measures do not lift the poor out of poverty, but they may keep people from falling farther. Initiated by liberal Democratic president Roosevelt in the 1930s, these New Deal social insurance and welfare programs were considered an essential social "safety net" even by conservative Republican president Reagan.[65] The safety net, which supports elderly, poor, unemployed, and disabled Americans, is the largest segment of the federal budget, and it has grown so quickly since the 1950s that politicians are forced to ask some very tough questions. Can Americans afford these programs? Can the country afford to be without them? How can these programs be made more efficient, effective, and equitable?

Income Support Programs

Since the New Deal, the basic structure of the American welfare state has expanded to encompass new classes of beneficiaries and to authorize more generous benefits. Once a small fraction of the budget, income support programs account for nearly 40 percent of the federal outlays and a huge portion of state and local spending. Income support programs amounted to less than 3 percent of the GNP in 1960; by 1988 they accounted for nearly three times as much. Federal expenditures have increased tenfold in less than thirty years.[66] The Reagan administration and Congress slowed the trend of extending eligibility and expanding benefits, but safety net spending continued its upward trend.[67]

The number of Americans benefiting from the safety net has grown by leaps and bounds. Social Security—which aids retirees, the children of deceased workers, and disabled workers—is the largest federal program, with expenditures in excess of $225 billion in 1988.[68] In 1988, one American in six received Social Security retirement checks, and 90 percent of the working population contributed through payroll tax deductions to the program. An average of 2.3 million Americans received unemployment compensation each week during 1988 at an annual cost of $18 billion, and most of the nation's more than 100 million workers are employed by companies that contribute to the insurance system. Approximately 20 million people receive food stamps. Nearly 4 million American families receive public assistance.[69]

Income support programs come in two forms: programs dispensed *according to need* and programs distributed *without regard to need*. The latter are called "entitlement" programs because people receive benefits as a matter of statutory right. The largest income support programs, including Social Security and unemployment insurance, are available to eligible recipients no matter what their income or assets may be. Therefore, most income support programs are not subject to a means test: full benefits are extended to rich and poor alike with no questions asked. About 90 percent of the funds reserved for older Americans do not require applicants to demonstrate financial need.[70]

Social Security and unemployment insurance replace part of the income lost due to retirement, disability, or unemployment. The retiree who made $1,000 per month during his or her working years receives about a 60 percent replacement.[71] A typical unemployed worker is paid about $450 per month or about a 40 percent replacement of income. Unemployment insurance lasts only for a few months; during the deep recession of the early 1980s, less than half of the unemployed were receiving unemployment insurance checks.[72]

Social Security and unemployment insurance are based on the concept of social insurance. Beneficiaries contribute about 7 percent of their income into the Social Security trust fund to help cover the cost of benefits they eventually receive. Employers pay into an insurance trust fund from which workers receive benefits during periods of unemployment. There is not always a direct connection between contributions and benefits received. Generally, people who contribute more receive greater benefits, but individuals at the low end of the income scale actually receive a larger return on their contributions. The unemployed usually receive far more money than their employers actually contributed on their behalf. The difference is made up by other employers and by federal and state revenues.[73]

Intended as a partial supplement to private pension plans and family incomes, Social Security provides a financial base for those who could not adequately prepare for retirement. Social Security is the nation's strongest antipoverty program, and, along with medical insurance for senior citizens, it has contributed substantially to reducing the number of older Americans who are poor. Once the elderly were a disadvantaged group: in 1960 more than 25 percent of senior citizens lived in poverty. Twenty-five years later, just over 10 percent of the elderly were poor. Median family incomes of the elderly have more than doubled since 1960. In fact, their incomes have increased faster than the incomes of the rest of the population. The average Social Security check for a retired couple in the late 1980s was higher than $700 per month, which by itself provides sufficient income to live above government-defined poverty levels.[74]

The biggest challenges for Social Security have been controlling growth and keeping the system solvent. Some positive changes in the American population have had a dire effect on the Social Security trust fund. People are retiring earlier and living longer. Since the mid-1970s benefits have been riding automatically upward on the cost-of-living escalator. Payments increase at regular intervals due to legislated cost-of-living adjustments (COLAs), so that benefits roughly keep pace with inflation.

The Reagan administration offered several proposals for trimming Social Security benefits in the early 1980s, but these suggestions were met with a firestorm of criticism from Democrats and senior citizen groups who form a large, politically powerful constituency. A bipartisan reform commission made several short- and long-term changes in the program, but virtually all the modifications increased funds for distribution, rather than curtailing existing benefits.[75] Proposals calling for a Social Security means test, whereby older Americans with higher incomes might receive lower benefits, are unlikely to be supported by Congress. In the future, changing demography and the need to maintain a sound insurance system may force policy makers to tighten up eligibility criteria.

The other federal and state income support programs are reserved for the poor. Aid to Families with Dependent Children (AFDC) and food stamps are made available to individuals only after they prove they need assistance. A woman must have children and no other means of support in order to be considered for AFDC payments. She must not earn more than $3,000 in any given year and must have few personal assets.

AFDC is financed by states and the federal government and administered by states and localities, which determine eligibility. Benefit levels vary widely. The average benefit check for a welfare recipient is approximately $300 per month, but a Mississippi welfare mother with two children receives only $100, while a similar family in California is paid $500.[76] The typical welfare recipient is a white female; she remains on welfare for less than two years and works full time or part time.

Welfare and food stamps consume fewer federal dollars and represent much smaller portions of the federal budget—less than 5 percent—than the non-means-tested entitlement programs. Welfare and nutrition aid for the poor cost the federal government approximately $20 billion in fiscal year 1988, less than 10 percent of the cost of Social Security alone.[78] Food stamps are the fastest growing component of these programs. In less than two decades the cost of food stamps rose nearly twentyfold.[79] During the Reagan administration, programs for the working poor were cut by more than 10 percent.[80]

Unlike Social Security, which is widely regarded as a successful, but expensive program, AFDC is disliked by taxpayers and recipients alike. Even though only a small percentage of funds is spent on ineligible people, opinion polls consistently show that the public perceives the program as awash in corruption and abuse. Welfare recipients and others complain that AFDC payments are stingy and that the system encourages them to remain poor and discourages self-reliance. Policy makers have long agreed that the welfare system is "broken" and needs to be fixed.[81] One major problem is that the current approach penalizes those who want to work their way off welfare. Little effort is devoted to preventing people from slipping into poverty. Instead of leading to self-sufficiency, the system supports and encourages dependency at a marginal level of existence.

Reforms designed to overcome these widely recognized deficiencies have been advanced by several governors, but they have not been adopted nationwide.[82] Typically, these welfare reform strategies encourage or require recipients to seek full-time employment and get off welfare. Programs in California, Massachusetts, and Illinois fund education and training services to help welfare recipients become employable and provide day care for their young children. Reformers also argue that the government should try to prevent poverty by discouraging, through education and birth control, out-of-wedlock births and by insisting that absent fathers support their children.

Health Care

America's income support programs were spawned primarily by the New Deal, and the health care programs—Medicare for the elderly and Medicaid for the poor—were the off-spring of Lyndon Johnson's War on Poverty. When Medicare was adopted in 1965, the Social Security Administration (SSA) estimated that it would cost $8.2 billion in 1983. The estimate was terribly wrong. Medicare cost more than $78 billion in 1988; Medicaid cost another $31 billion. Government health insurance pays nearly half of the hospital costs and doctor bills for the entire nation.[83] Although government support for health care in the United States still trails that of other industrialized nations, the commitment has increased rapidly. When private contributions to health care spending are included, the United States leads the world in the amount of its GNP devoted to health care.[84]

Elderly and poor Americans are the principal beneficiaries of government health care programs. Medicare serves all Americans over the age of 65 regardless of need. Program participants pay for part of the cost of physician visits and hospital care, but most of the tab is picked up by the government. Medicaid is reserved for the poorest of the poor. Approximately one-third of America's poor population is not poor enough to qualify for Medicaid.[85] Millions of Americans who are not old or very poor have inadequate medical insurance.

Health care costs and government expenditures for health programs have skyrocketed, driven by three factors: demographics, "third-party" reimbursement, and the complexity of medical care. Increases in the aging and poor populations during the 1980s have resulted in greater outlays in these entitlement programs. Medical consumers and medical professionals are not motivated to keep costs down because three-fourths of all medical bills are borne by third parties, namely, the government or private insurance companies.[86] Consumer goods presently cost three times as much as they did in the late 1950s, but physicians' fees have jumped fourfold, and hospital costs have increased sevenfold.[87] The real costs of adequate care have risen because medicine has become more complex and specialized.[88] The enormous increase in government outlays for medical procedures and hospitalization has generated demands for a less costly health care system.

In many ways, Medicare and Medicaid meet their legislative objectives. Medicare provides financial assistance for a critical need of elderly citizens. Medicaid serves as an adjunct to food stamps and public assistance for the poor, the blind, and the disabled. According to the Council of Economic Advisers, "Access to medical care for these groups has markedly improved and with it have come improvements in the health of the poor." The council points out that reductions in infant mortality rates—a standard measure of access to quality medical care—are due to improved prenatal care practices of low-income mothers.[89]

Despite these accomplishments and burgeoning budgets, government health care programs have not substantially reduced many serious health care problems. Simply increasing health care expenditures does not necessarily lead to better health.[90] Infant mortality rates have declined, but they still exceed those in many other industrialized nations. For black Americans, the number of deaths per 1,000 births is higher than in Jamaica, Cuba, Brunei, and twenty-eight other countries.[91] Access to affordable, high-quality medical care remains a serious problem for millions of Americans, including many covered by Medicare and Medicaid. Medicare, for example, does not fund extended care in nursing homes—one of the most serious problems the elderly experience. Older persons must first exhaust their financial resources before they can turn to Medicaid for help.[92] The coverage and adequacy of benefits under Medicaid vary widely. Millions of Americans do not have adequate health insurance.

Most important, American health insurance programs do little to help prevent serious health problems.[93] Significant public health gains were realized in the first half of the twentieth century through government-sponsored measures to improve sanitation, water quality, and immunization against communicable diseases. Government-sponsored research contributes significantly toward the treatment of serious diseases, but many health policy analysts argue that government policy should be changed to encourage Americans to take more responsibility for their own health. Some of the leading causes of death—smoking, alcohol consumption, and diet—are influenced by personal choices. According to the surgeon general, smoking is "the chief, single avoidable cause of death in our society and the most important public health problem of our time." [94] Not only does the government do little to stop smoking, such as banning the product, it actually subsidizes the production of tobacco in several states.

Protect the Environment

Conserving the nation's resources and protecting its environment yield immediate, tangible benefits and long-term, intangible benefits. The primary purpose of environmental controls is improved public health—lower mortality and morbidity rates and reduced medical expenses. The long-term benefits derived from protecting the environment are less tangible and more diffuse, but critically important. President Carter's Commission on a National Agenda for the Eighties posed this question: "What value can be placed on public enjoyment of purer air, cleaner water, or protected wilderness, or more importantly, on preserving the long-term integrity of natural life support systems?" [95]

Compared with other goals, preserving and protecting the environment has been a central policy goal in the United States for a short period of time. Prior to the 1960s, concern for the environment centered on preserving the natural environment. Landmark policies adopted during the early decades of the twentieth century established national parks, forests, and wilderness refuges. The federal government is the nation's largest landholder: 700 million acres or a third of the entire country.[96] Environmental measures—such as the Refuse Act of 1899—were adopted to blunt the most egregious results of urbanization.

Although conservation goals have not been abandoned, environmental policies since the early 1960s constitute reactions to the consequences of an industrialized, chemically dependent society. For decades, American consumers and business took environmental quality for granted.

Vast quantities of hazardous and toxic wastes and chemicals were dumped into the land and water and released into the air. The publication of Rachel Carson's *Silent Spring* in 1962, perhaps more than any other single event, provoked an awareness of Earth's fragile environment. Her book documented that the use of the chemical DDT in farming destroyed wildlife and threatened humans. Ten years later the production of DDT was banned for use on American soil.

Concern over the deterioration of the environment generated widespread public support, marked by Earth Day 1970, for stronger environmental laws. Americans frequently are reminded of potentially harmful substances lurking in the air and the water. The poisoning of the food chain with cancer-causing PCBs (polychlorinated biphenyl), noxious fumes and smog in urban communities, and the contamination of water due to leaking toxic waste dumps are the price exacted for the casual attitudes of the past. According to environmental scholar Walter Rosenbaum, "We are practically the first generation in the world's history with the certain technical capacity to alter and even to destroy the fundamental biochemical and geophysical conditions for societies living centuries after ours." [97]

More than twenty major environmental protection laws were enacted at the federal level during the 1970s—the "environmental decade." Among the landmarks were the National Environmental Protection Act, which established a process of assessing the environmental impact of federal projects; the Water Pollution Control Act; the Clean Water Act; the Clean Air Act; the Insecticide, Fungicide, and Rodenticide Act; the Toxic Substances Control Act, which regulates the production and handling of toxic waste; the Resource Conservation and Recovery Act, which regulates the disposal of solid waste; and the Comprehensive Environmental Response, Compensation, and Liability Act, commonly called the Superfund, which established procedures for cleaning up toxic waste dumps. Hundreds of state and local laws also were adopted during this period. Standards for improving the quality of the air, water, and land were established along with government agencies to monitor and enforce compliance. Driving this surge of government regulation was the need to correct the harmful practices of private businesses and individuals.

A Legacy of Contempt

The laws and agencies created during America's environmental awakening set ambitious goals, but decades of contempt for the environment proved difficult and costly to fix. Citizens and policy makers began to realize that achieving better environmental quality will require years of sustained effort, billions of dollars, and profound changes in the way Americans do business and live. The national agenda commission offered this overall assessment:

Considering the scope of the task, notable progress has been made. The air is indeed cleaner, the water purer, and the total environment is therefore presumably healthier. . . . In very few federal initiatives of recent times . . . has so much been accomplished within such a brief span of time. . . . But this is not to say that pollution has been arrested, nor that the environmental objectives set forth in the 1970s will soon be reached. . . . [T]he nation will be facing more complex and intractable issues about the control of pollution while confronting new pressures on the domestic and global environment.[98]

The United States has stepped up its attack on environmental problems, but much remains to be done.

Water Quality. Water quality laws enacted during the 1960s and 1970s were supposed to ensure safe drinking water and to clean up polluted rivers, streams, and lakes. The National Technical Advisory Committee on Water Quality Controls reported, however, that there has been little improvement in water quality during the 1980s, according to measurements of five standard pollutants.[99] Pollution generated by individuals and industry continues to flow into surface and ground waters at alarming rates. The $100 billion spent on water pollution control measures have not significantly cut dangerous levels of toxic chemicals, bacteria, nitrates, and phosphorous in the water supply. A national survey of the nation's harbors and lakes revealed almost no improvement. Some important bodies of water, such as Lake Erie and the Chesapeake Bay, remain seriously polluted.[100]

Air Quality. Lawmakers hoped that the standards and enforcement mechanisms established by the Clean Air Act of 1970 would significantly ameliorate air pollution in five years. Despite progress, those hopes are yet to be fulfilled. On the positive side, dangerous lead emissions have dropped 86 percent, largely due to banning the use of high-lead gasoline. Particulate and dust pollution has declined by a third since the early 1960s. Overall, however, air quality improved by only 13 percent between 1975 and 1985. The air is still fouled with sulfur dioxide and carbon monoxide, which harm the respiratory system. Smog continues to generate unhealthy air in the nation's urban areas: in a recent four-year period, Los Angeles residents suffered through 250 days of unhealthy air.[101]

Toxic Waste. Notable success in protecting the public from the negative effects of toxic chemicals has been achieved by imposing sharp restrictions on the production and use of several cancer-causing products, including DDT, PCBs, and dioxin. Federal laws governing the handling of toxic wastes established procedures for assessing chemical hazards and disposing of them properly. Government agencies responsible for cleaning up abandoned toxic dumps have identified hundreds of dangerous situations and eliminated or curtailed many threats to the environment and public health.

Unfortunately, toxic waste problems are growing in complexity and scope. Many possibly toxic chemicals are being introduced so fast that government is unable to test them all for potential hazards. American industry generates 265 million metric tons of hazardous waste each year—more than 1 ton for each citizen. Up to a third of these wastes, most often in the form of "dirty water," are released untreated into the environment.[102] Little progress has been made in curtailing the flow of poisonous chemicals.

Progress on implementing the Superfund cleanup program has been slow and disappointing. According to the Office of Technology Assessment (OTA), there are 30,000 toxic waste dumps in the United States, thousands of which pose serious health threats. OTA estimates that cleanup measures could cost more than $50 billion.[103] The Environmental Protection Agency (EPA) identified more than 950 priority toxic dumps for remedial action, but in seven years less than 30 have been completely cleaned up. The $8 billion fund available under Superfund will not be adequate to the task. Often the health effects of toxic chemicals are impossible to detect accurately: the technology for defusing toxic bombs and neutralizing toxic soups is still in its infancy.

From React and Cure to Anticipate and Prevent

America's first two decades of serious environmental regulation were marked by uneven progress. Much effort and billions of dollars have yielded important but modest improvements. The problems that have been discovered and addressed await resolution, but the environmental threats in the immediate future may be even more intractable. An EPA task force reported that "newer" environmental problems, such as "indoor radon, global climatic change . . . acid precipitation and hazardous waste," will be difficult to evaluate and may "involve persistent contaminants that move from one environmental medium to another, causing further damage even after controls have been applied." [104]

Enormous expenditures and upheavals in industrial production practices will be needed to clean up and preserve the environment. These economic and social costs must be borne today, but most of the benefits will accrue to future generations. So far, private and public policy makers have been unwilling to take the necessary steps: the pressures for immediate economic growth have been too powerful to resist. The so-called "greenhouse effect" illustrates the trade-offs. Increased accumulation of carbon dioxide and other gases in the upper atmosphere has caused global temperatures to rise by three to four degrees in the last

100 years. Scientists project that similar temperature increases could occur by the year 2030, causing drastic changes in Earth's climate, severe flooding, drought, and famine on a scale unparalleled in human history. Reversing or slowing this trend will require reductions in the use of fossil fuels and unprecedented cooperation among nations.[105]

Compared with many parts of the world, the U.S. environmental protection record is admirable. The industrialized communist nations have relatively poor environmental records. Sulphur dioxide emissions from the Soviet Union are three times greater than the levels from the United States. Hundreds of thousands of people were exposed to dangerous radiation levels in the aftermath of the world's worst nuclear power plant disaster at Chernobyl in the Soviet Union.[106] Environmental degradation is widespread in the Third World, where the pressures for development to support exploding populations are intense. Twenty-eight million acres of ecologically valuable rain forests—an area roughly the size of Pennsylvania—are destroyed every year. If this destruction continues unchecked, the loss of the rain forests could become "an ecological disaster of major proportions."[107]

Clearly, public policy makers in this country and around the world must do better. The World Commission on Environment and Development concluded that "many present development trends leave increasing numbers of people poor and vulnerable while at the same time degrading the environment. How can such development serve next century's world of twice as many people relying on the same environment? . . . [T]he react and cure environmental policies that governments have pursued are bankrupt. . . . Anticipate and prevent is the only realistic approach."[108] Achieving a sustainable environment in the face of enormous worldwide development pressures will be extremely difficult, but the very survival of the planet depends on it.

Summary

Any fair assessment of American public policy would conclude that great progress has been made toward fulfilling the nation's goals and values. The United States is, in many ways, better off than it was fifty, twenty, or ten years ago. The nation is not engaged in open conflict with any nation. Significant arms control agreements have been signed, and the prospects for more far-reaching controls look better than they have in many years. After suffering through a particularly difficult recession in the early 1980s, the economy rebounded. Inflation ebbed and the economy posted consistent gains for several years running. The most egregious forms of racial and gender-based discrimination have been curtailed or at least identified. The social safety net of income support and health care for the elderly and disadvantaged survived attempted reductions. The first steps have been taken to preserve and protect the air, water, and land necessary for survival.

But U.S. public policies are not as effective as they should be. Massive increases in defense spending have not produced a country that is significantly less vulnerable to thermonuclear war or terrorist attacks. The rising tide of economic recovery has failed to lift all boats. In one of the world's most affluent nations millions are unemployed, homeless, and hungry. The gaps between rich and poor, black and white, have grown wider since 1980. Discrimination based on race, gender, age, and disability is still pervasive. The costs of income security and health care programs have risen so rapidly that their solvency is threatened, but benefits for poor people are barely adequate for survival, and the health of Americans has not improved significantly. The water and air remain dangerously polluted from automobile exhaust, industrial waste, and toxic chemicals.

Much, therefore, remains to be done. The problems facing policy makers and citizens are as intractable as any the nation has faced. Among the most pressing are

—reducing the budget deficit
—keeping America competitive in the world economy
—redressing discrimination against minorities and women
—bringing poor people into the mainstream of society
—improving the social safety net
—meeting unprecedented threats to the environment

If the past is prologue, there is reason to be deeply concerned about the willingness and ability of American political institutions to meet these challenges. Extraordinary skills, leadership, and cooperation will be required in the years ahead.

Notes

1. Center for Public Interest Polling, *Images III: The Quality of Life in New Jersey* (New Brunswick, N.J.: Eagleton Institute of Politics, Rutgers University, 1985).

2. See, for example, President's Commission for a National Agenda for the Eighties, *A National Agenda for the Eighties* (Englewood Cliffs, N.J.: Prentice-Hall, 1980).

3. See, for example, Carol Weiss, *Evaluation Research* (Englewood Cliffs, N.J.: Prentice-Hall, 1972); Peter Rossi and Howard E. Freeman, *Evaluation: A Systematic Approach*, 3d ed. (Beverly Hills, Calif.: Sage Publications, 1984);

and Arnold J. Meltsner, *Policy Analysts in the Bureaucracy* (Berkeley: University of California Press, 1976).

4. John D. Steinbruner, "Security Policy" in *The New Direction in American Politics*, ed. John E. Chubb and Paul E. Peterson (Washington, D.C.: Brookings Institution, 1985), 343-364.

5. B. Guy Peters, *American Public Policy: Promise and Performance* (Chatham, N.J.: Chatham House, 1986), 287-289.

6. Steinbruner, "Security Policy," 345.

7. Theodore H. White, *The Making of the President 1972* (New York: Atheneum, 1973).

8. Henry J. Aaron et al., *Economic Choices 1987* (Washington, D.C.: Brookings Institution, 1986), 75.

9. Council of Economic Advisers, *Economic Report of the President* (Washington, D.C.: U.S. Government Printing Office, 1985); and John L. Palmer and Isabel V. Sawhill, *The Reagan Record: An Assessment of Changing Domestic Priorities* (Washington, D.C.: Urban Institute, 1984), 8.

10. David A. Stockman, *The Triumph of Politics* (New York: Harper & Row, 1986), 107.

11. Steinbruner, "Security Policy," 349.

12. Leo Bogart, *Polls and the Awareness of Public Opinion*, 2d ed. (New Brunswick, N.J.: Transaction Books, 1985), 89-96.

13. W. Lance Bennett, "Marginalizing the Majority: Conditioning Public Opinion to Accept Managerial Democracy" (Paper presented at the Midwest Political Science Association Meeting, Chicago, Illinois, 1987), 16.

14. Joseph A. Pechman, *Federal Tax Policy*, 4th ed. (Washington, D.C.: Brookings Institution, 1983), 27-28.

15. U.S. Congress, Joint Economic Committee, *The 1985 Joint Economic Report* (Washington, D.C.: U.S. Government Printing Office, 1985), 67-68.

16. Ibid., 72.

17. Ibid., 70-71.

18. Bruce R. Scott, "U.S. Competitiveness: Concepts, Performance, and Implications," in *U.S. Competitiveness in the World Economy*, ed. Bruce R. Scott and George C. Lodge (Boston: Harvard Business School Press, 1985), 61.

19. Ibid., 38.

20. Ibid., 36-37; and Robert Kuttner, *The Economic Illusion: False Choices Between Prosperity and Social Justice* (Boston: Houghton Mifflin, 1984), 291.

21. Scott, "U.S. Competitiveness," 35-36.

22. Ibid., 39; and Robert B. Reich, *The Next American Frontier* (New York: Times Books, 1983), 118.

23. Reich, *Next American Frontier*, 118-119.

24. Kuttner, *Economic Illusion*, 291.

25. Reich, *Next American Frontier*, 207.

26. Donald C. Baumer and Carl E. Van Horn, *The Politics of Unemployment* (Washington, D.C.: CQ Press, 1985), 2-3.

27. Ibid., 3-4.

28. Joint Economic Committee, *Economic Report*, 36.

29. Kenneth M. Dolbeare, *Democracy at Risk: The Politics of Economic Renewal*, rev. ed. (Chatham, N.J.: Chatham House, 1986), 60.

30. Joint Economic Committee, *Economic Report*, 97.

31. Ibid., 25.

32. Ibid., 47.

33. Executive Office of the President, Office of Management and Budget, *Budget of the United States Government, Fiscal Year 1986* (Washington, D.C.: U.S. Government Printing Office, 1985).

34. Executive Office of the President, Office of Management and Budget, *Budget of the United States Government, Fiscal Year 1987* (Washington, D.C.: U.S. Government Printing Office, 1986).

35. Joint Economic Committee, *Economic Report*, 47-50.

36. Aaron et al., *Economic Choices 1987*, 4.

37. Reich, *Next American Frontier*, 121-122.

38. Scott, "U.S. Competitiveness," 30-31.

39. As quoted in Joint Economic Committee, *Economic Report*, 65.

40. Reich, *Next American Frontier*, 173-200.

41. See, for example, Scott and Lodge, *U.S. Competitiveness in the World Economy;* and Reich, *Next American Frontier;* and Sidney Blumenthal, "Drafting a Democratic Industrial Plan," *New York Times Magazine*, Aug. 28, 1983.

42. Gunnar Myrdal, *An American Dilemma* (New York: Harper & Row, 1944).

43. Arthur M. Okun, *Equality and Efficiency: The Big Tradeoff* (Washington, D.C.: Brookings Institution, 1975), 1.

44. William Schneider, "People Watching," *National Journal*, Jan. 12, 1985, 63.

45. See, for example, Okun, *Equality and Efficiency;* Dolbeare, *Democracy at Risk;* and, Kuttner, *Economic Illusion.*

46. Robert Pear, "Poverty Rate Dips as the Median Family Income Rises,' *New York Times*, July 31, 1987, A12.

47. Harrell R. Rodgers, Jr., *The Cost of Human Neglect: America's Welfare Failure* (Armonk, N.Y.: M. E. Sharpe, 1982), 31.

48. Pear, "Poverty Rate Dips."

49. Rodgers, *Cost of Human Neglect*, 29.

50. Pear, "Poverty Rate Dips."

51. Benjamin I. Page, *Who Gets What From Government* (Berkeley: University of California Press, 1983), 191.

52. Rodgers, *Cost of Human Neglect*, 28.

53. Page, *Who Gets What From Government*, 22-23.

54. Pechman, *Federal Tax Policy*, 60-128.

55. Page, *Who Gets What From Government*, 35-41.

56. Pear, "Poverty Rate Dips."

57. Joint Economic Committee, *Economic Report*, 29-31.

58. Pear, "Poverty Rate Dips."

59. Isabel V. Sawhill, "Anti-Poverty Strategies for the 1980s," Discussion paper (Washington, D.C.: Urban Institute, December 1986), photocopied.

60. Editorial Research Reports, *Education Report Card: Schools on the Line* (Washington, D.C.: Congressional Quarterly, 1985), 13.

61. Schneider, "People Watching," 59.

62. Renee Cherow-O'Leary, *The State-by-State Guide to Women's Legal Rights* (New York: McGraw-Hill, 1987).

63. Linda Tarr-Whelan and Lynne Crofton Isenee, eds., *The Women's Economic Justice Agenda: Ideas for the States* (Washington, D.C.: National Center for Policy Alternatives, 1987).

64. National Alliance of Business, "Employment Policy Issues for the End of the Century and the Year 2000" (Washington, D.C., Nov. 22, 1985), photocopy.

65. Stockman, *Triumph of Politics*, 8.

66. James R. Storey, "Income Security," in *The Reagan Experiment*, ed. John L. Palmer and Isabel V. Sawhill (Washington, D.C.: Urban Institute Press, 1982), 364-365.

67. R. Kent Weaver, "Controlling Entitlements," in *New Direction in American Politics*, 308.

68. Executive Office of the President, *Budget of the United States, Fiscal Year 1987*.

69. Baumer and Van Horn, *Politics of Unemployment*, 9; and Weaver, "Controlling Entitlements," 307.

70. Council of Economic Advisers, *Economic Report*, 167.

71. Peters, *American Public Policy*, 214.

72. Kuttner, *Economic Illusion*, 149; and Baumer and Van Horn, *Politics of Unemployment*, 14.

73. Baumer and Van Horn, *Politics of Unemployment*, 14.

74. Pear, "Poverty Rate Dips"; and Council of Economic Advisers, *Economic Report*, 166.

75. Weaver, "Controlling Entitlements," 320.

76. David Berman, *State and Local Politics* (Boston: Allyn & Bacon, 1984), 272.

77. Sawhill, "Anti-Poverty Strategies for the 1980."

78. Executive Office of the President, *Budget of the United States, Fiscal Year 1986*.

79. Ibid., part 5, 116.

80. Weaver, "Controlling Entitlements," 325.

81. Sawhill, "Anti-Poverty Strategies for the 1980s."

82. See, for example, Julie Kosterlitz, "Reforming Welfare," *National Journal*, Dec. 6, 1986, 2926-2931.

83. Council of Economic Advisers, *Economic Report*, 129, 132.

84. Peters, *American Public Policy*, 188.

85. Ibid., 186.

86. Weaver, "Controlling Entitlements," 323.

88. Council of Economic Advisers, *Economic Report*, 135.

89. Ibid., 137-154.

90. Ibid., 136.

91. Peters, *American Public Policy*, 185.

92. Ibid., 192.

93. Council of Economic Advisers, *Economic Report*, 130.

94. Ibid., 137-138.

95. President's Commission, *A National Agenda for the Eighties*, 49.

96. Congressional Quarterly, *The Battle for Natural Resources* (Washington, D.C.: Congressional Quarterly, 1983), 2.

97. Walter A. Rosenbaum, *Environmental Politics and Policy* (Washington, D.C.: CQ Press, 1985), 100.

98. President's Commission, *A National Agenda for the Eighties*, 47-48.

99. Barry Commoner, "A Reporter at Large: The Environment," *New Yorker*, June 15, 1987, 51.

100. Ibid., 51; and Victoria Churchville, "Clean Water Laws Didn't Save the Bay," *Washington Post National Weekly Edition,* July 7, 1986, 99-111.

101. Commoner, "The Environment," 47; and Philip Shabecoff, "As U.S. Air Quality Deadline Looms, Cities Are Giving Up Hope of Solution." *New York Times,* Aug. 10, 1987, A12.

102. Commoner, "The Environment," 52.

103. Office of Technology Assessment, *Technologies and Management Strategies for Hazardous Waste Control* (Washington, D.C.: U.S. Government Printing Office, 1983), 7ff.

104. Environmental Protection Agency, "Unfinished Business: A Comparative Assessment of Environmental Problems" (Washington, D.C., February 1987), photocopied, xiii.

105. Commoner, "The Environment," 54.

106. William U. Chandler, "Designing Sustainable Economies," in Lester R. Brown et al., *The State of the World 1987* (New York: W. W. Norton, 1987), 187-190.

107. Editorial Research Reports, *Earth's Threatened Resources* (Washington, D.C.: Congressional Quarterly, 1986), 163.

108. World Commission on Environment and Development, *Our Common Future: From One Earth to One World* (Oxford: Oxford University Press, 1987), 4.

Index